Echoes from The Chamber

From the Author —

In many ways this book presents a curved ball
It is really three books in one
The second part offers a total view on life -
the Universe and Everything; while the first part
shares my extraordinary journey leading to an
otherworldly event in Berlin, Germany which
led to the total insight.
The last part shares the consequential
events in Egypt as my own path unfolded.
Please don't be deterred by the handful
of pages which strip bare all that is quantum.

To you dear reader...
If my book helps you to discover even the
smallest profound insight towards the
meaning and direction of your life then I
will have done my job well.
Good Luck on your journey
Blessings — Richard Gabriel

AKA Rod Reynolds
        Ross-On-Wye
           October 2022.

www.richardgabriel.info   FaceBook — Richard Gabriel (White Tiger Logo)

Echoes from The Chamber

Richard Gabriel

authorHOUSE®

AuthorHouse™
1663 Liberty Drive
Bloomington, IN 47403
www.authorhouse.com
Phone: 1-800-839-8640

© 2012 Richard Gabriel. All rights reserved.

No part of this book may be reproduced, stored in a retrieval system, or transmitted by any means without the written permission of the author.

Published by AuthorHouse   06/06/2012

ISBN: 978-1-4685-8349-6 (sc)
ISBN: 978-1-4685-8350-2 (e)

Any people depicted in stock imagery provided by Thinkstock are models, and such images are being used for illustrative purposes only.
Certain stock imagery © Thinkstock.

This book is printed on acid-free paper.

Because of the dynamic nature of the Internet, any web addresses or links contained in this book may have changed since publication and may no longer be valid. The views expressed in this work are solely those of the author and do not necessarily reflect the views of the publisher, and the publisher hereby disclaims any responsibility for them.

Echoes from The Chamber

Sections

Part 1: The Journey Begins 1
Part 2: Questions and Answers 177
Part 3: The Calling from The Kings Chamber 251

Chapters

Pre~Ramble to the Event 1
Formations 2
Preparations 18
Matters of Quantum 22
Knowing the Atom 24
Plate 1: A Basic Atomic structure 28
The Rules of Vibration and Dark Matter 29
Hidden at the bottom of the Microscope 33
Gross Scenarios: With a simple Leaf on a Branch 41
      : With Echoes from the Past 41
      : With Jungle Beauty 43
      : With Dead Reckoning 46
      : With Planning to Heal 48
One to One 52
Learning by Curves 56
Perfectly Normal Afterlife 58
Meeting the Abyss in Real Time 61
A Challenge to Reality 67
Unwinding the Connections 70
How they could also Understand 79
A Look into the Higher Realms 81
The Man of Many Colours 85

Understanding Sexuality 88
What makes a Total Person: Genetic Pattern 100
                          : Stellar Influence 101
                          : Automatic Responses 101
                          : Traits of Conditioning 102
                          : Free Will 102
                          : Environment 103
The Engine that drives The Body 104
Astral Journeys 113
Awake when you go to Sleep 119
Waking Up 124
What about Karma? 126
Conscience 129
Plate 2 : The Living Map for any Person 131
The Living Map 132
The Law of Probability 136
The Birth Plan 139
Descent or Ascent? 148
Belief in God 151
Taking Stock 156
Chains of Conditioning 159
A Time to Die 161
The Future is Now 166
Reflections 171
Heading for the Chamber 172

Part 2: Key Questions and Answers 175

Part 1: The Journey Begins

Pre~Ramble to the Event

My story begins with an explanation of life, the universe and everything and ends in a story of exploration with my twin flame Judith, beneath the sands of The Giza Plateau Egypt. But how could this strange marriage work? As you will soon find, the latter story was only made possible following graduation from the classroom of my early experiences. It was the first story, and it will provide a context of understanding for you also to journey with me to its conclusion. And how could I possibly offer an understanding of these things if I did not also offer the quality of my journey to be tested along with it? The Probabilities of our lives are no accident ever; and mine has been extraordinary. I hope the details of my life may help you see how you also pre-planned for lessons in your life before it began. From *my* childhood strife, my youthful inhibitions and relationship tests, then to the sands and underground of Egypt; everything was inexorably linked and completely necessary, but I must dedicate the result, to you all for making it possible.

    I single out my twin flame Judith for making the choice to embark on this vital shared quest of re-discovery with me. I thank her for her unfailing guidance and connection to spiritual truth through all the trials we have faced. I dedicate it to my sons Jason and Dean, who yet unknowingly selected me and their mother to be providers of *their* Chains of Conditioning and the lessons *they* must still graduate from. I dedicate it the same to my sister and my departed parents, with thanks for all the illusions of pain I felt; but then was blessed with the lessons they provided. I thank and ask blessings for all those others with whom I have shared my heart; and hope the pain I produced by my own ignorance may have also been transmuted to understanding. All may judge me as they will, but hopefully after reading this work you will judge yourself with more understanding, and go with more freedom to the task that awaits *you*.

    Nothing is ever wasted.

Formations

What a roller coaster it has been! My memories reach back to my first few months and I have always been aware of it operating on two distinct levels, like two lifetimes rolled into one. My mundane life has been in constant competition with my compelling Supernormal journey. Of course they are intertwined, even during times of abject despair; or when burned by the heat of love and then frozen by the pain of its loss. I have known them all. But I also know that my route has been my own choice. The harder it has been, the stronger the lesson as I survived each distinct phase. My life raft and eventually my lifeline has been the understanding that came from the higher experiences. I am grateful of the pathway and the light it has given me. I regret the pain I may have caused others during my lesson, but enlightenment cannot be gained without scars; and nothing happens by accident.

My Supernormal experiences have happened randomly, frequently and in many different ways. They include most of the phenomena you might expect, such as precognition, clairvoyance, out of body experiences, manifestations, automatic writing and a multitude of other things. They are just aspects of the exploding gnosis in my life.

It is said that every effect is normal, and is only described as Supernormal because our scientific understanding has not yet caught up to it. It is said that in science, every effect can be described in terms that eventually lead to the cutting edge of quantum physics. The understanding I have been awakened to, passes through and beyond that barrier with precise attention to detail. It is said also that every effect to quantum and beyond, has a mathematical value. I leave mathematics to the mathematicians, but for me the recorded numbers of my birth were surely no accident. I was born 13th minute, 13th hour, of Friday 13th October 1950, and the number 13 has followed me with significance throughout my life.

My Supernormal experiences led me on an extraordinary journey to enlightenment. In 1981 I had a monumental *otherworldly* experience which changed my life forever. It opened my memory to the complete order of things in the universe. I call it my *Event*, and later you will read of it and share in the understandings I was blessed to know once again. I can look back and see the distinct phases of my personal development leading to the *Event*, and through the pages of this book I hope to be able to share their significance and crucial outcome in Egypt.

Despite the distraction of the experiences that spiced my pathway, the journey has been lonely. Even as a small child I felt singled out in some peculiar way. Strange things would happen to me that I could discuss with no one. Of course I experienced the normal things that kids do, but it was always spoiled by the crazy ideas filling my head.

I remember one occasion not long out of short trousers, instead of rushing off to play with pals, I invaded our front garden and built a faithful replica of Stonehenge in order to study it better. I wasn't savvy enough at the time to know my father had just beautifully prepared the ground for new grass seed. He caught up with me! It felt so unfair that my excavations and my big wonderful Stonehenge replica should be rewarded with slap marks and stinging legs for the rest of the day. I can look back and smile though because it sure gave a heck of an exhibition for neighbours to visit and gape over!

By the time I was old enough to think, I was already withdrawing into self for answers. The process was inevitable because my personality clashed with my father. He was working out *his* conditioning on me and this led to brutal incidents that were branded on my mind. The need to know why things were as they were became an obsession from these childhood roots.

I was drawn to mysteries. My mind pondered the Pyramids, the Planets, the nature of matter and other untouchable subjects. I saw things before they happened. I sensed and saw people in another misty world. As a baby-child my mother comforted me to sleep when the *faces* appeared in my bedroom to talk with me but only succeeded in scaring the hell out of me. I received inspired thoughts and ideas beyond my years. On another occasion as a young lad, I was sent to my bedroom for breaking the kitchen window. I was interested in physics, which led to pyrotechnics! I wanted to see what power could be generated from matchstick heads. So I built a homemade rocket from a cigar tube. I set it up on the bird table in the garden and lit the burner underneath. On its test-fire it zoomed across the garden, straight through the kitchen window. The punishment lasted a while, but the joy of the experiment is still with me now. Hehe!

Yet again I had been confined to my bedroom in punishment for another misdemeanour. My boredom was complete as I stared out the window at the passing cars. I was in my early teens and longed to be elsewhere. To relieve the boredom I started timing the cars at the end of our roadway, as they passed by one lamppost and the next. I figured the distance and found I could calculate the speed of the cars. It was good fun for a while, but boredom took over again. As my mind drifted, I had another of my strange daydreams. I got a picture in my mind of someone in a uniform standing by the roadside with a gadget like a gun. He was pointing it at the traffic. I knew the object was automatically calculating the speed of the passing cars.

Several years later I remembered my bedroom confinement as I made the connection to the Police radar speed-guns now in common use.

These were just a couple of tiny examples. My normal preoccupation was trying to understand why I functioned as I did. Who were the faces that came to me when I wanted to sleep at night? They were certainly people. They saw me and I saw them. It was like in a busy walkway, and when I cried in fright some spoke to comfort me and had the opposite effect. Why was my head filled with mysteries? What did they mean? Why did I have so many flashes of foresight? Why was it always of disaster? Why did I *always* have that euphoric feeling of invincibility, like if I jumped from a great height I couldn't die? I would just zoom out before reaching the ground! I must have been about four years old when I tried it from our garden shed roof. The fact that I almost broke my ankles and nose didn't deter me. The bravado that went with my feelings led to me probably being the most accident prone youngster for miles around. What was I supposed to do with all of this? What was the pull I always felt to the Orient, Tibet and to Egypt? I seemed to have been born with these obsessions and could have no inkling they would lead to adventures decades later underground at Giza and in the Great Pyramid itself.

I remained a loner through school and as I was growing I was more at home with gymnastics, field sports or martial arts than with football and other team activities. My aloof attitude got me into serious trouble many times with teachers and with other pupils. I think I was saved from many beatings because others were a bit wary of me. I could turn a person's head further down the bus on the way home from school as a party piece, just by boring into their mind. It freaked my friends when I did it.

Funny; I just remembered also one time when I was 11years old. There had been snow and ice overnight. At playtime, I watched from a distance as literally the whole school turned out to throw snowballs at a row of large icicles hanging from the high eaves of the school building. There was one giant icicle left. Dozens of the kids had thrown dozens of snowballs and no one could bring it down. I remember observing this for some time and I got bored watching; but as I was about to turn away I got one of those familiar strange feelings. It seemed as if my mind had gone telescopic and I felt a huge affinity with the giant icicle . . . like as if I understood it! I bent down and casually rolled a snowball. I threw it and turned away, knowing already that I would hit the object. I turned back as a huge groan was replaced with a huge cheer from the kids when the icicle smashed to pieces on the ground. That childhood event sticks in my mind as all significant events do.

Childhood was in the North of Scotland in a small countryside village called Kemnay, several miles outside Aberdeen. From our house the fields sloped to a gentle valley then rose steeply to a rocky hill a little over half a mile away. It concealed a rude granite quarry. Half burned gorse bushes and mica-laced rocks interrupted the short grass of the slopes. It was a forbidden dangerous playground but I often went there alone. At the edge of the fields when they had been furrowed for sowing, many large cobbles came to the surface. I liked to crack them open and sniff at the age-dust that puffed from the surfaces. I could dream of *how* they were made . . . and then I threw the halves, one this way and one that way. It did not matter because I just knew they could never be separated; but I puzzled over *why*? It would be decades later before I really understood.

I sometimes climbed right up to the edge of the quarry as it plummeted to either of the two lakes a few hundred feet below the sheer cliff sides of the excavation. There was a cable car then which pulled a descent cage to the centre of the quarry-drop and lowered the workers until they were ants at the bottom. I would have been punished if my parents knew I was there but it was too remote for anyone to know.

A few times I was urged to stand-up, right at the edge. The voice in my mind always told me if I jumped I would not, could not, die. I did it in my head loads of times with exhilaration—but settled for a pocket full of gathered mica-leafs and some firewood sticks to take back home.

My mother was the sensitive and my father was the brute. I was scared witless of him. *His* childhood had been dysfunctional and draconian and eventually led to my appearance—out of wedlock. So I was the undisguised Batard child which he was obliged to support through an expected marriage. He tried to live his trapped life again through me; but failed to realise I was here as an independent Presence to fulfil my own Birth Plan. In this life, he never did get it!

My sister arrived two years after me and was planned. Her life may have been easier but for the Birth-Plan handicaps she brought with her. My mother was a secret rape victim sometime after I was born. After twenty years of my family estrangement and shortly before her death we were within a week of family reconciliation, and she confided the facts to me.

I was as I was; but my sister was to become the protected pure swan which my mother could now never be, and the Stage was set for the pathways of Probability we would both face in life. By the time we reached teenage years I had already made peace with my *other* visitors. My sister however was being severely disturbed by the night-time ghostly appearances.

At eighteen years my conditioning was complete. Beyond my higher obsession I was driven by two imperatives. I yearned to get as far away as possible from the oppression of my father. Secondly I only wanted to do something that was so extreme it would prove *in my father's face*, that I was worthy of something after all. I therefore joined the military ranks of the Royal Marine Commandos. My conditioned inadequacy had begun its classroom cycle within me.

There is no doubt I was up to the task physically and quickly earned a recruit promotion. Unfortunately both mentally and emotionally I was still an undeveloped suppressed child. I could handle the rigours, but could not deal with emotional interaction. I retreated deeper and deeper into myself. The warning signs of my inner turmoil were missed even when they exploded into a punch which holed a glass door. In my stupidity I had taken no account of the fact that the glass was wire reinforced. As I withdrew my hand I snagged the glass and tore my wrist open. The instant payback almost cost me the use of my hand. Our choices and the reciprocal energy always determine the next turn of the path. The negative energy however had not finished its grounding, as at the eleventh hour I broke my leg on training exercise. Damage complications ensued with my knee which was not fully treatable. I watched with churned emotions as the rest of my training team departed on one of the last exotic commando postings of the time. Then suddenly I was handed an honourable medical discharge and found myself dumped into civvy-street, estranged from my family and wrecked. I was filled with the shame of what had happened and with a reinforced sense of failure.

I had one ace however. It was the same one which sustained me as a child when I had the crap beaten out of me by my father. It was an unshakable knowingness inside that no matter what happened, no one could really touch me. As I write this I am getting a flash-back of one really bad memory. I was only a few years old and spillages on the floor led to a severe leather—belt beating. I cowered but still defied him to,

'*Go on—Hit me. Kill me. I don't care. You can't touch me.*'

I knew that *he* knew what I meant as he stomped away screaming and shouting. My defiance of authority was part of my conditioned lesson and remains with me; and has enabled me to go without fear to the heart of my Birth-Plan tasks in Egypt in recent years.

Upon leaving the military I needed to recover. I was on the rebound from life. So was my wife to be. She was the runt of a large family. So she was the tomboy attention seeker yearning to be allowed to run and also to be the one in control. We were perfect as a mismatch in the moment; and a divorce about to embark on a painful nineteen year long journey until it happened. In the meantime I was to be the messed-up unprepared father to my two good sons and an increasing stranger to my wife. The lessons continued!

I slowly learned to keep the higher experiences to myself even though they always drove me crazy to understand. I knew about deaths before they happened. I was having plenty of involuntary Out of Body experiences and was experimenting with the induced Out of Body process. I pushed it too far on one occasion.

One night, my wife was elsewhere and I was doubly determined I was going to get it right. Tonight I *was* going to induce a Conscious Out of Body experience. I went through the text book preparation and felt the effect as it began to manifest. I was concentrating so hard I was wet with perspiration. Suddenly, I felt a pain and from a position on the bed I was launched in a sideways spin, landing in a heap on the floor. The pain was excruciating. It felt for a split second as if red-hot lightning had passed diagonally through my body from one shoulder to the opposite foot. I had actually lifted and spun sideways to the floor. I sat up in a terrible mess. I looked at my trembling hands and I swear I could see a glow. I had generated energy too great for my body to sustain and it had earthed out through me.

At other times I was only able to continue gentler practice in the early hours on my own downstairs. I had to be well away from my late spouse because the rise in energy always woke her from sleep in great confused discomfort. I decided to keep notes of my development. I remember thereafter on a few occasions jumping as if returning from an involuntary nap and found I had automatically written messages on my pad. Some of these are shared later in this work.

In the early years of marriage before we acquired our own home we lived with the family of my wife. Her extended family was large and included a nephew who was almost my age. One time he visited with some friends and we all somehow decided we would conduct an experiment with an Ouija board. In the bedroom our small group gathered around the board. We solemnly asked if there was anyone there. The upturned glass under our fingers began to move across the surface. We were unnerved but continued. I was deeply reluctant but the action came fast as the glass began moving to try and spell something against the letters around the edge. Suddenly one of the friends broke from the circle and dived for the window just in time to vomit out of it violently. We were all shocked and scared by now, and the session ended.

A short while later the voices in my head changed. I was being told to do destructive things. One morning I was driving my car and momentarily blacked out—like going in and out of a daydream. As I snapped out of it I realized I had my foot down hard on the car accelerator and I was speeding towards the fence on the other side of a road junction. Another time when it happened I realized I was being urged to pick up something to strike at the head of a companion. After a few of these incidents I was shocked to the core. I didn't know where to get help. I could only think of seeking out the Church Vicar where we were married. He received me immediately and listened well. He told me about the Rev. S. who lived some distance away and was charged by the Church with some expertise to deal with such things. I quickly arranged an appointment and a few days later set out to see him. On the way I got images of him with a dog and in a house with an unusual layout. His office was not on the ground floor and the dog was secured in another part of the house. Nevertheless the Reverend received me, and the ice was broken when I shared my images which proved to be completely accurate. He spoke at length with me explaining many things about Spiritual protection and malevolent or misguided souls. I received a blessing from him and departed, feeling freed again from the bad energy. My spiritual preparation continued otherwise in opposite proportion to the widening gap of understanding at home.

There was no lasting satisfaction in the continuing events of the next few years. Mundane life continued as it had through childhood and youth, as I wrestled with the far more important problems of higher understanding. In later marriage and as a father I was acutely aware of my inadequacy to provide a profitable, secure and happy environment for my family. I knew my higher restlessness drove everything I did, but I could not step away from it. It all seems so simple now that I can write with understanding. I bless the choice of pathway my loving sons and late wife entered into with me for their formative years—to give *them* their perfect Birth-Plan handicap for higher progression.

Every once in a while I would be satisfied briefly with a Eureka moment of understanding. But I was obsessional and any step forward led to another period of depression. I would get to a point where I could figure things no further. My frustration would increase until I felt I would go crazy if I couldn't come up with a better understanding on some aspect of the nature of things. I knew how to pray, and I sure did that. I didn't realise at the time how Synchronicities were arranged by Minders in spirit in answer to such prayers.

It was sometime later in my development. Out of Body experiences had already given me an acceptance of other dimensions of reality. I just couldn't fathom *how* such dimensions could exist. If there were these places they had to function within laws of Physics that were undiscovered. If there was such a place, there was no way all the people there would just be flying around with angel wings strapped to their backs! I had already decided any explanation of life would have to be explainable in normal terms.

I was aged 20 and already a year married and on one particular occasion the thoughts had been building again to drive me crazy. I prayed for help harder than I had ever done. Not far from where I lived, at the highest part of the town, the main road separated the housing estates from a long tract of disused ground rolling down into a shallow valley. Beyond the road, stood ruins of what was once the local brick works.

Old working sheds and tangled mechanical equipment lay everywhere. An old tall brick chimneystack dominated the skyline and cast a wide pencil shadow across the site. The nearby clay pit, filled with water, invited only passing ducks and foolhardy children. Away to one side of the clay pit there was an old abandoned orchard; a hangover from the time when the site was part of a farmer's land. Bramble thickets grew everywhere. These hazards, combined with the dangers in the ruined sheds kept all but the most familiar away from the place. If you knew the ground however, a beautiful secret walk was waiting. After dodging the thickets and finding the right trail, the old overgrown orchard could be found. Here was a haven for wildlife of all kinds, and in season the remaining gnarled fruit trees hung heavy with fruit.

I sometimes took my young nephew and his dogs through the site and down to the old orchard for a run around. On this occasion I was on a visit to my Nephew and was coerced into taking them for a walk. I didn't really feel like it at all so I was a bit grumpy when we set off. We waited at the roadside for a gap in the traffic and despite my warning advice, my Nephew and the dogs started running as soon as the way was clear. I called for the dogs to stop. I called for my Nephew to slow down. Both ignored me and I was forced to spring from my heels and give chase.

Our route through the brick works took us through the main loading shed. This shed was intact and reasonably well preserved. From memory, it stood approximately eighty yards long by perhaps twenty yards deep. One side was open to the air, where presumably loading vehicles once gained access. The ground was formed from compacted sand from the nearby estuary beach. It was flat, smooth and almost undisturbed. I ran as fast as I could to catch up with my disappearing charges. As I chased through the shed I tripped badly on something and nose-dived into the sand like a torpedo. I spit sand from my mouth and cursed as I jumped up to brush myself down. My Nephew and the dogs had disappeared somewhere up ahead. I cursed again and turned to aim a defiant kick at whatever had tripped me. I stopped dead, the dogs and nephew forgotten for a moment. Like a miniature monolith, an old book had been raised from the sand and was now standing vertical from the ground like a magician's trick. I glanced around and apart from the book, the ground was bare. I was incredulous, and even more so when I pulled the book from the sand.

I shook it clean and examined its title. It read, 'Life Beyond the Veil,' Book 5, 'The Outlands of Heaven,' by the Reverend Vale Owen. As I turned the pages, I felt a tremor of excitement and anticipation flow through me. I also felt the tingling across my shoulders and my head, like a static electrical wind. It was a familiar feeling and told me this was not just an ordinary coincidence. I feel it even now so many years later as I sit back from the keyboard and hold the book once again in my hands.

I later found the book was one of a series of 6 books written in the early 1900's by the Reverend G.Vale Owen, and was received as automatic texts from his Minders in spirit. (See the glossary for details.) The Reverend had resisted the interest his wife shared in the popular Spiritualism of the time. He also resisted for some years, the discarnate thoughts that seemed to fill his mind during his tranquil times of reflection. Eventually he was persuaded to sit and give a chance for these otherworldly thoughts to flow and be recorded by the pen in his hand. An amazing set of volumes were the result. The series describes everyday life in the levels of reality beyond the earth plane and gives details of all human activity beyond physical death. Readers are introduced to various helpers on a higher level who wished to add to the information. I discovered the series was still in print and I obtained copies. The original book is still a treasured possession. The experience left me in no doubt of the incredible power of the workings of Synchronicity. The book and its complete series gave me sufficient information to feed me for a while on my Gnostic journey. I urge anyone to seek-out these extraordinary volumes.

I am aware now, that the workings from divine levels down through the levels of creation to physical matter, operate universally and are not bound by the constraints of our known physics. They are not the exclusive property of any human religious faith or any one belief system. Omnipotent means what it means! I understand it is only by the sheer ignorance, stupidity, arrogance or greed of mankind, that we have tried to package universal truth to suit our own vested interests or exclusive belief systems.

The appearance of the Rev. Vale Owen's book was an answer to my prayers. I devoured the contents, and my mind was satisfied for a time as I tested the explanations. The Rev. Vale Owen was a Christian churchman and not surprisingly the information channelled through him was delivered with a Christian slant. This was forgivable, and didn't detract from the universal nature of the actual information.

Some good time later, the rumblings of discontent were building up within me again. I had read the books. I had digested their content. They had given me considerable possibilities of explanation for many of the strange events that had befallen me. The books vastly described aspects of life beyond physical life and presented new territory for me. My own experience now fell short and I knew I was approaching the next crossroads.

On weekends or in the evenings I occasionally took myself off for a long walk. This was just to blow the cobwebs from my mind and to get my thoughts straight. So it was one late Sunday afternoon. I was in town, walking the sleepy back streets and there was hardly anyone about. As I walked up a side road I noticed two pretty girls walking towards me on the same side of the pavement. They were a little older than me and my natural male instincts woke me up. It was so unusual for me to bump into two pretty girls in these unexpected circumstances on a deserted Sunday, and in this part of the old town. As they drew nearer I was surprised even more when they stopped to ask the whereabouts of the local Spiritualist Church. Like an idiot I spluttered with surprise. It was weird enough to encounter them; but on such a subject! I knew there was a Spiritualist church somewhere nearby, but I didn't know exactly where it was located. While I was discussing the possible location with them, an older man appeared from the very narrow road opposite. From the corner of my eye I noticed him catch to our conversation and move purposely in our direction. He apologised for interrupting but wished to introduce himself as the President of the local Christian Spiritualist Church. He indicated the location of the church not too far away, and the girls headed off to it. I was even more amazed!

Mr B. remained chatting to me for a few minutes. He said that most people who visited the church were regulars. On this particular evening however, he was awaiting the arrival of a new guest who didn't know the route very well. We agreed it was fortuitous that Mr B. had arrived at the right moment to direct the girls. As a parting shot he said to me that if I was on a loose-end I might like to join their Church service, soon to start. On pure impulse I agreed. The other new guest was nowhere to be seen so perhaps I was meant to take his place. We walked together to the converted house, which was now the Spiritualist Chapel. At the top of the stairs I caught my breath in groundless embarrassment. The place was full. I saw the two girls from earlier sitting comfortably in outside seats near the back. I humbly found my way past everyone to the only seat left in the middle and at the very back, then waited for the fun to start. I didn't know what to expect, but by halfway through the proceedings I was feeling somewhat cheated. This was just like a normal Christian church service. Where was all the mumbo-jumbo that was supposed to happen? After all, didn't Spiritualists have really strange meetings where dead people were called up!

Hymns were sung. A couple of Bible readings were given. The service seemed as if it was going to finish. The President took the stage and addressed the congregation. He thanked everyone for attending, especially the newcomers present. He spoke a few words of introduction for the visiting Medium, (to my shame, I have forgotten her name,) and yielded the stage to her. The evening then seemed to liven up.

The Medium spoke randomly to a large number of those present. She revealed personal details of friends and family who had died and linked successfully to one person after another. The impact was astonishing. More than one person broke down in tears of shock and joy at the messages of verification given to them. Their reaction was spontaneous and impressive. The information given was very specific. The Medium was not leading anyone with her commentary. I sat inconspicuously, wrapped in fascination as my first encounter with Mediumship unfolded. The Medium announced that the energy was retreating and she seemed to be concluding for the night. But she hesitated, fell silent for a few seconds, then held her hand to her forehead in concentration and spoke again.

'*Before I finish, there is someone else I want to come to.*' Without raising her eyes she pointed hard towards the back row and said, '*Yes you my friend. I wish to speak with you.*'

From where I was sitting I was able to trace the straight line from my seat down the length of her arm to her shoulder. I melted self-consciously into my seat. She looked up and began a session with me lasting at least twenty minutes. The impact of that reading remains with me to this day. She summarised the state of my life to date. She described all the main landmarks.

She introduced me to my Guide, or helper in spirit. Special reference was made to the higher pathway I had chosen and the task at the end of it. She referred me with very private details to family members who were no longer with us. Most significantly, she described the probability of several key directions that were likely in my life over the next ten years, culminating in a final gnosis. This event would arm me with the tools to carry out a task I was here to fulfil. The Medium was accurate in every respect, years ahead of events. These included working in Berlin, going back to College; close medical details, highly personal family details and much more; but importantly, she advised me on the Supernormal things, and spoke of a related book I would eventually produce as a part of my task. At the time, the probability of these events seemed too crazy to imagine.

I continued to visit the Church and in due course accepted an invitation from Mr and Mrs B . . . to join with their small development circle. This was also very new to me. I often meditated on my own though I thought nothing of its formal nature. That was just an ordinary and necessary part of my life. During meditation I would get powerful flashes of inspiration and ideas. The more I did it the more I found there were involuntary moments on a daily basis where information or didactic poems would jump into my mind. Now I was with others in a controlled environment to do the same thing. The weekly sessions helped me with my meditation technique and led to instances of deep inspiration and spontaneous clairvoyance.

On one occasion I saw a vivid picture in my mind of an old fireplace. I spotted a finger ring in the ash at the side of the fire grate. As was the routine, I shared my picture with the group. Another member of the group spoke up to say I had described the fireplace at his home and he had indeed lost a finger ring. He checked when he returned home and found the ring where I described it to be.

My time with the group lasted three years and was a huge benefit to me. However there came a time when the questions overwhelmed me again. It bothered me for example when good people came to the Church, or even to the development circle with such high aspirations, but so quickly fell back to gossip and judgement however mild, when the sessions ended. It was time for me to move forward.

Life continued within a less than perfect marriage and through the raising of my sons. I always struggled with my identity and began to notice how others were slaves to behaviour passed on to them also from their childhood conditioning. It was only after my Event in 1981 that I was able to return to my early life to fully understand its purpose and understand myself. My imaginative mind coupled with a hand for creativity and working with wood—steered me into construction. For some years I slipped into preoccupations of a more practical kind, trying to provide for mundane living. My writing and other thoughts now had to take a back-seat as daily affairs of home and work consumed me. During this period, other related interests were given an opportunity to develop as a pastime. I began involvement with Shotokan Karate and finally ran a Club with almost 600 members spread to include two other Clubs we initiated elsewhere. We followed the old traditional imperative to develop Spirit as our primary. On the physical side we were obliged by the controlling national body to undergo gradings where we surpassed ourselves. But we remained true to our purpose, and for a few, these disciplines allowed access to an extraordinary power within that we knew would remain with us throughout our lives. As a subsidiary to the Club activities—which were centred at the local YMCA building, I became involved also with *its* youth organisation and management. The management activities finally became a cross too heavy to bear, and I handed it all to others so I could return to my solo journey.

I recall also spending at least a couple of years studying the deeper meaning and effect of Astrology. I quickly dismissed the generalisation of popular astrology, but was fascinated by the accuracy of deeper one-to-one studies. My colleagues were willing subjects, and were equally amazed at the results. Yet again, a real understanding of the influences at work would have to wait until the time of my other-worldly *event*.

Lack of funds was always a problem and like many families in the town we supplemented our income by receiving young foreign language students—in our case by choice, from Germany. This was also a useful diversion from the inadequacies of our troubled married life. We played host to the older daughter and then the younger twins of a particular family from Berlin in Germany. Finally they travelled to stay with us privately for their holidays. We declined invitations from their parents to be their guests because we were simply too poor to pay for such a trip. They owned the equivalent of a market square public house. It comprised the ground floor and a three storey building above it, if the converted Mansard-roof was included.

We were host to the twins and their older sister for the second or third time while their parents were on holiday elsewhere. It was the last day before the girls returned home and we were stunned by the arrival at our doorstep of their parents seeking to greet us and give us a surprise. Before returning to Berlin with their children, they presented us with paid tickets for the whole family to travel to their home. We would only need a little spending money. We accepted with excitement and the trip was successful. It became instantly obvious to our hosts after we arrived however that we had practically no money to spend freely. Our fantastic friends made me an offer we could not refuse. For the first week my wife and children would be conducted about the city and its sights by our host's wife, while I worked to refit P's whole Pub kitchen—at the going cash rate for locals. This would be a fortune for me and I would have the last week to spend with my family unrestrained. It happened just as planned, but towards the end of my first week, there was another twist.

I was called to an interview with a local customer who owned a construction company. He reconstructed the whole roofs of buildings, often converting them to habitable accommodation in the process. He and other regulars had been following my working progress. We spoke through the interpretations of another regular customer who happened to be an English teacher in the local school. H. asked me many questions about my work and situation at home. I explained I was in a rut, earned little money and longed for an improvement which would help my family also.

He made me the offer! He explained he needed a Foreman for his timber construction crew. He had watched me working and inspected the result and was prepared to take me on if I was prepared to make the break and come to work for him. He explained also how my earnings would enable me to quickly set up a home for my family to join me soon. The deal would be for me to have the freedom every six weeks minimum to travel home on unpaid time to be with my family. This turned into casual UK work each trip to supplement my income while in the UK. My younger military involvement would enable me to get flights for rock-bottom prices with a special Military Flight Services operator.

The deal was enhanced with another offer from my host. In the roof level of the Pub building, only half of it had been converted to a dwelling for the occupying family. If I sorted my affairs at home and returned initially for two weeks to convert the other half into a self-contained bedsit, I would be allowed to use it rent-free for the whole of my eventual working time, or at least until I could set up our own family home.

The current situation was overwhelming. Prospects at home were at a dead end. The money situation was killing things further. Married life was a nightmare. Our sons were suffering the consequences. They had all enjoyed our brilliant holiday in Berlin and even the boys had picked up a few words in German language. They loved it there. My wife agreed and the deal was sealed. As I found later despite the huge benefit to our family, and despite preparing a family home for us in Berlin along with school places for my sons, my wife dashed the final part of the plan. She ultimately refused to leave the closeness of her family. I knew I had to return to the UK or lose my sons forever.

However in the time before making the decision to return to the UK it had been twelve years following the predictions of the Church Medium, and I had been working for nearly three years in Berlin Germany. I lived adequately in my rooftop bedsit except when I travelled home to the UK. My intense two long weeks of construction before my final move to work in Berlin had been enough for me to complete the dwelling. After work, my small bedsit offered considerable solitude. I was able to read study and write a lot in the late evening. On a spiritual level I had reached the barrier again. I was mindful of my session with the Medium so many years before because she had also predicted for something spiritual and very special to happen to me while there. By then, I had experienced so many Supernormal things and of such variety that my passive mind was consumed with the process of fitting them all together. My head ached with partial understandings. The brain-strain had been going on for a very long time, but I could get no further. I sent out prayers for guidance until it hurt. I meditated. I browsed the bookshops for inspiration, but nothing worked; until one very, very special night. I cannot understate the otherworldly experiences that I take for granted as a part of my life. precognition, premonition, automatic writing, inspired didactic poetry, flashes of deep awareness, out of body experiences, spontaneous clairvoyance, sight of people on another level, and much more. These occurrences were normal to me. However, the events of that one evening in my Bedsit surpassed them all—and ultimately led to this book, and a brand new adventure. That night became known to me as, *My Event*.

My work that day had been physically demanding and I was exhausted. I finished work late and couldn't be bothered to cook a proper meal for myself. I bathed and made a light snack. My bed was an army camp bed. With the duvet draped over the side, it made a good floor sofa to lean against. I usually sat there comfortably to read or write. Very occasionally I heard a sound from the neighbouring family, but generally I was insulated from all but the most violent thunderstorms that flashed and crashed above my high living space. While fitting the Bedsit out, no restriction had been placed on me for the choice of lighting and wall decoration. One large wall opposite the bed wall was very rough and undulating. I had plastered it freely to follow its flowing shape. I finished it with the side of a tiling trowel to produce faint vertical and horizontal lines. In the daytime the white painted wall looked almost completely flat and untextured.

For lighting I had fitted concealed floodlights along the wall, but for atmosphere I had fitted a spotlight stalk with various coloured spotlights. These were directed at the textured wall and depending upon the colour selected, a range of completely different moods could be created in the room. Using the spotlight colours, the textured wall came to life. Every visitor swore they could imagine different pictures emerging from it. On this particular evening I selected the red spotlight, grabbed my pen and pad and flopped down against the duvet. Even though I was tired I had a very strong feeling of something preparing itself to inspire me at last. Whenever something inspirational was about to visit me, I always had a sense of its presence as if it was something discarnate waiting in the wings for the best moment to put in an appearance. For example, whenever I receive didactic poetry I have the similar sensation that some people feel before a violent storm—when everything goes quiet and still. Even the air smells different. Or like when others have that tingling feeling of premonition before something big happens in their life. On this occasion the feeling of impending arrival was overpowering. I sat there droopy eyed, writing pad in hand with no idea of anything to write, but filled with increasing anticipation. I just waited, while staring into the far distance of the wall; but nothing came to me despite the huge build-up of power. Eventually, drowsiness overtook me and I must have dozed off to sleep.

My next recollection was of jolting wide-awake as if struck by lightning. My head was pounding and I was on my feet in a split second. For a short time there were flashes of light behind my eyes. I have tried several times to find an adequate description for the impressions in my mind in that moment. The closest I can manage is to remind everyone of the movie called *Total Recall*, starring Arnold Schwarzenegger. His active memory was falsely programmed into his mind. Eventually he has a total memory recall of his true lifetime. In my case, as I awoke, Gnosis was complete. It was just as if my mind had joined with another; but the other mind was *also* me; and the other mind had the complete memory of the process of life beyond life. There wasn't enough room in my head to contain them both instantly. The other memory was also my memory but I had to dive into it slowly to absorb everything. My God, I thought to myself, the actual structure of life and the universe was in my head!

I remember falling to my knees weeping and feeling as if I was going to drown in this sea of new information. I could see its complexity and its simplicity. Animated shapes evolved in my brain showing the nature of matter at its smallest. It all mingled and tried to burst out. Every emotion surged through me. I was seeing scenarios, I was seeing across vast distance. I was seeing how it all worked. I was overwhelmed with joy and fear and awe and humility; and questions, questions, questions.

'This was huge, why me? If this is true, what about that?' The answers flashed even before I fully formed the questions.

'If that is true, what about this? What about it all? What If, what if? A thousand times, what if?'

It was there. It was real. It explained everything. I rolled my own unanswered experiences through the knowledge again and again and again. My mundane mind was screaming, 'I have to test it. Is it real? There must be a flaw.'

On and on through the whole night I threw my every normal and Supernormal experience at it, and then I started with wider questions. Every time, without effort, without faltering, without fail, the bright light of an explanation lit up and spit right back to me. The knowledge begged to be challenged. I challenged it with everything I could consider, and then I tried again from another angle. I had to know if there was a flaw. I tried and tried to break it down, but it was unshakeable. I remained bolt awake trying to make sense of this new gift, if it was a gift. By morning I still had not wholly accepted it. Daybreak came. I needed more time. I telephoned my work boss and pretended to be ill. I stayed ill for the next day and then for the whole week. I *was* ill but in no way I could explain to anyone. I needed space to consider the implications of what had happened. Hour after hour and into the next night and throughout the week I kept looking for a flaw. I went for long walks around the leafy paths of the district like in a dream or a daze. I had to satisfy myself to the final degree. My mind had been awakened to remember the universal process and that it is a truth available to all but lies hidden to most for good reason. I racked my brain to think of every conceivable question on the nature of things and hurled it at the understanding until finally at the end of the week exhaustion overtook elation, and I rested deeply.

I recognised a distinction in the knowledge. It presented the strategy for life, but also revealed how our divine choices create infinite pathways of probability. I could see therefore that knowing the strategy did not automatically fill my head with all the infinite Probabilities for living it. These are ours to unravel within our own chosen pathways back to the end and the beginning.

Many years have passed, but I am as certain now as I was then, I am charged with the duty of passing this understanding to others for their inspection and validation and to test against their own lifeline. Maybe my experience will act as one of the catalysts to reverse the negative spiral in our world today. Maybe, maybe, maybe? The Gnosis is something that everyone is a part of and which everyone will remember eventually. It returned to me externally, allowing me to test it fully against myself. It would have been totally wrong to have accepted it at face value. Truth withstands any test; and each day I still find questions to test it. I ask you to do the same. If you are not interested, or not ready, or do not care, then fine! But if you are motivated to progress spiritually, then test the understanding against *your* experience and see where it takes you.

Whenever any new big life drama manifests itself to me, I offer it against the knowledge. I don't have to search for an answer. The process is like typing a question on to the computer and pressing search on the World Wide Web. The answer is automatically illuminated. So it is nearly three decades later. I continue to play my role on a mundane journey, dealing with the unknown tactics of living within the known strategy of life, trying to get rid of my remaining negativity. I long for the day when everyone has overcome the gross level of physical vibration. If we as a world ever make it that far, human life will be able to work across the dimensions freely with fantastic creative force just as we were able to do once before. So now it is not my aim to win any great literary prize. It is to find a way somehow of conveying the same message of understanding for you to test. Let us begin

Preparations

We had a new English teacher. Over the course of just a few lessons he had already grabbed the attention of our unruly class. He was an American and taught things differently. He used innovative teaching methods to give us new perspectives on language and communication. We could use first names in class, which was revolutionary at the time. But we always had to be respectful to each other. He had such a presence however that when the class became unruly, he just stood there with his arms folded, without a word, without a sound, and with a pitying look on his face. His energy alone was enough for the noise to subside. Consciously or otherwise we expected a reaction from him. First one, then more of us would notice him standing there like a sentinel saying nothing. A creeping calm would break out in the class until you could hear a pin drop in the final silence.

He impressed all of us. Our time with him was always surprising and fresh. He would lead every class into hot discussion without us noticing or realising his point had been driven home. For example, on one occasion the instruction was simple. Our teacher was now a Martian and he had just landed at our school in his spaceship. He knew nothing about our world. We would be allocated everyday objects and at the next lesson we would each be given a few minutes to describe our object for the Martian to understand. It seemed easy and it was something different to do, so we were excited about it.

Our Teacher took a worn exercise book from his briefcase. This was the one we recognised as his homework book. We all looked on attentively to hear his instruction. He had prepared for this; probably smiling to himself to think what we would do with our specially chosen examples. He opened the cover and ran his finger down the page. He called our names one by one.

'Jones for you, an egg. Liffin, a pencil. Baker you will describe rain; Myers you try a handkerchief. Gabriel, a lighter match,' and so on until we all had something to think about.

I thought about my object a lot before the next lesson. I felt very smug because I believed I had worked out my perfect answer in the first few minutes. Next day came and we were already halfway through our presentation lesson. My confidence was ebbing in direct proportion to the verbal contortions of the pupils before me. Our Martian teacher kept challenging them. As a result, each person was taking ages. He called our names at random and my heart missed a beat when I was summoned. I swallowed hard and walked forward to take my place at the front of the class. Now I had my chance to show everybody how clever I was!

'A lighter match is a small piece of wood with a blob of red.'

'Stop, stop, stop,' The Martian replied. *'But what is wood?'* he asked.

'A lighter match is a small piece of wood which was once part of a tree. The trees are chopped down and . . .'

'Stop, stop, stop,' The Martian interrupted again. *'But explain to me, what is a tree?'*

I stammered, *'Well, trees are living things growing from the ground and they are made from fibres of material called wood.'* Again I heard, *'Stop, stop, please stop.'*

By the time I tried to explain the idea of Ground, Branches, Leaves, Alive and so on, I'd had enough; and this was before I had even started on the good bit. The bit where the head of the lighter match goes pssssit when you strike it, and it bursts into flame. By then for all I cared, I would have quite happily given the Martian a box of matches to play with, plus a first aid kit for when he burned his fingers as a result. We were all humbled with a lesson in the art of communication. We learned well that we should never again take for granted, that which we take for granted. Years have passed but I still ponder the question. How do you best describe the lighter match to a Martian?

In using my own example, three possibilities spring to mind. One, give a box of lighter matches to the Martian and wait several years to see if he survives and figures them out for himself. Two, take as long as it takes to explain Life, the Universe and a box of matches, in the hope he will finally understand and agree with you. Or three, take time to get to know the world of the Martian. Find common ground for understanding and gradually develop mutual awareness of each other's knowledge. Regardless of the method used for communicating with the Martian, there would still be great frustration; because for those of us who know what a lighter match is, a lighter match, is a lighter match, is a lighter match, isn't it?

It just so happens at this very moment I am saying the very same thing to myself about my knowledge of life-continuation and how I am going to put it all into simple terms for others to consider. If *you* play the role of Martian for me, my task will not be to describe the finer qualities of a lighter match. It will be to give you a unified description for Life, the Universe and everything. On the face of it this seems a mind-boggling task, but for some, such a thing is as simple as a lighter match being struck. As a starting point, if we presuppose there *are* other levels of valid reality, then the place to focus our attention would surely be where these levels come together and interact with us in the physical. I am talking here about how the continuum operates between physical life and other levels. So let's begin to think how this can be tackled. When I was standing in front of the class in judgement from my teacher, I found each time he challenged me I had to think really hard to find the next step backward from each fumbled explanation. Each question posed another pre-question. In truth, explaining the lighter match could have taken a hundred associated topics to explain its nature. But for us and questions of existence the process will be shortened. We stand on the common ground of understanding on so many things already. We share language. We share the same time in history and have access to knowledge of our whole global development to date. But just as it was with the extensive list of topics leading to the understanding of a lighter match I must still wade through many topics before we get to the meaty stuff. However just as it is in the process of baking a cake, if you want to see a decent result—the ingredients and baking method have to be followed properly. Bear in mind also, even if you like the recipe it is up to you if you finally want a slice of the finished article!

People talk about having had mystical experiences which have changed their lives forever. Such people have been labelled fools or Saints, or have been advised they should get outside more often for some fresh air! I have some sympathy for visionaries because I went through my own life altering experience. I carry the understanding of an existence beyond our physical world and of its mechanics and interchange with our physical world.

When the understandings unfolded from my Event, it was still not enough for me. It is one thing to have knowledge of the rules but it is quite another thing to realise you are also in the game—and there are infinite tactics to be learned within the rules. If this applies to me then it also applies to you. If there is a structure and purpose to everything it is not enough to be asked, simply to have blind faith in its inevitability—even when it is backed by a good explanation. It is a first person reality to me, but it will be for you to test it against your personal experience before making up your own mind. During my Event, picture forms were played out to me. In my mind's eye, these were like holographic depictions, or geometrical objects, animating through a sequence to compliment my fresh thoughts and to bring the knowledge to life. I saw the pictures. I understood them completely. But much later when I tried to find ways to externalise them, I was once again standing in front of the disapproving Martian teacher.

I did not have the scientific vocabulary for the job. Therefore I had to go back to school. Over a long time I scoured bookshops and libraries, filling my head with the concepts and language of Quantum science. I knew there would be a harder task sometime in the future when I would have to simplify the language somehow for anyone else to understand. You will be able to judge my efforts in the next chapter; and I know there will be groans from some at the prospect of considering science and mathematics again, but if you can wade through the next chapter, the rest will be much easier. It is fundamentally necessary to understand the world of the smallest particle in order to understand everything else. My thought circuit probably started when I used to split the cobbles in the field as a child and discard them in different directions, still knowing they could not be separated. Over the years I spent hours with my head to the night sky trying to understand the universe. I progressed as I grew; now trying to understand the differences in people. I moved to puzzling over countries and beliefs, but reversing again to focus on individual people and their emotions. Ultimately I wanted to understand the makeup of everything. My Event demonstrated to me that first I really needed to understand the nature of substance and all the rest would fit into place.

It is a daunting task for me, a Layman, to lead you into the world of the smallest particle. If you are hungry to know, you will stick with my best efforts. Then hopefully at the end you will be as ready as I was to apply it out into the world of emotions, people, beliefs, countries, differences, and the nature of things in the cosmos as a whole. I hope it will be so.

Matters of Quantum

How can any greater understanding be complete without a complete understanding of the world we now inhabit? We function in a physical world. All around us there is gross matter. We are a part of it. Scientists seek to explain the workings of it all. They constantly examine the nature of the smallest known physical matter—the world of the molecule and the atom. The great dream is to find a unified theory which explains the interaction of all the energies and forces at work in the world. By examining the smallest particles, gross matter can also be understood. The Scientists who work in this field take their name from the description of the smallest discrete physical quantity. They are the Quantum Scientists.

Look around you. What do you see? You see, feel, smell, hear, and touch, all of the physical things available to our normal senses. What about the things that cannot be detected directly? There are many, and they are generally accepted as an invisible reality. The air for instance is filled with radiation from many sources. Radio transmissions compete with satellite and television signals. Microwave communications overlap telephone messages. We accept that all of these things are there because we have the modern technological instruments that put them to use and confirm their presence. Science explains to us how things work while technology allows us the practical application and confirmation of their reality. Experimental Physics at Atomic level coincidentally gave us the Laser in our C.D. players and the microwave oven. We all accept the benefits while rarely bothering to fully understand the processes involved.

At the cutting edge of Physics, many recent discoveries have a fundamental bearing on the understanding of the world we live in. We take the invisible force of gravity for granted. It will be impossible for us however to explore properly beyond our solar system without understanding the true nature of gravity. Gravity binds physical matter to the planet. We expend colossal amounts of energy trying to defy its effects but gravity still defies our attempts to understand it. Progress *has* been made. Single atoms are smashed together. These interactions yield clues to their nature. Many thousands of experiments are repeated. By measurement and interpretation of the results, the lesser universe is giving up its secrets to allow a clearer picture of the greater universe.

We know there is radiation everywhere. We are bombarded by light radiation from the sun for example. We take it for granted, but pass light through a prism and we see it separated into a spectrum of colours. In fact all forms of known radiation are identified as a part of the electromagnetic spectrum. This is a scale of measurement used to categorise all known electrical and magnetic frequencies of radiating energy. Microwaves have a lower frequency than Ultra Violet light or x-rays. The frequency range of visible light falls between them. Some forms of radiation can apparently pass through solid matter. If this were not so, how do you think radio waves produce music from your radio in a seemingly enclosed space?

Science is in general agreement that the universe began with the Big Bang. This was a rather big explosion. The makings of the whole Universe happened from nothing in a split second it is said. Radiation still reaches us from that event and penetrates deeply below the surface of the ground. All very intriguing, but what is radiation? Through what form does it exist and perform? These are not new questions. Around 400BC the Greek philosophers and mathematicians, Democretus and Leucippius proposed that all things were formed from tiny invisible particles, which they named *Atoma*. This Greek word means indivisible particle. It is only now, over 2000 years later that we are beginning to really understand the workings of the Atom. Let us put on our scientific hat and take a simple look at the atom as it currently understood.

Knowing the Atom

Look down the eyepiece of a microscope. Gross matter reduces to molecules which themselves are collections of atoms. Gross matter is made of minute moving clusters of molecules acting together as cohesive units; and all those molecules together form unique *apparently* solid objects.

Let us take one atom. It appears solid. But as we travel deeper into the microscope we see it is not solid. It is formed from even smaller dynamic parts. It has a tiny nucleus comprising specs (or particles) of motion called Protons and Neutrons. Around these there are other varied levels of activity governed by more specs called Electrons. The Protons and Neutrons of the atom nucleus are made up of even smaller specs called Quarks. These Quarks are regulated in some way by even smaller particles called Gluons. About five levels and that is it as far as everybody knows for sure at the moment!

A little more can be said about the Electrons. Each Electron operates within its own zone. This orbital zone is known as an Electron Shell, and the excitement level (vibrational quality) of an Electron, determines the Zone known as the Electron Shell. Changes to the energy (vibrational quality) of an Electron can obviously result in changes to the Electron Shell-geography for the entire atom.

So far so good! The brief description above sets the framework that is used by the Quantum Scientist to understand much more. The increasingly smaller particles cannot be picked up in the hand to be examined. They are too small for that. But scientists can try to understand more about them and even smaller parts, by examining the effect they have on their surroundings. So, they force them to smash together at high speed, and then they examine the outcome. The effects can be measured but are so faint that the experiments have to be repeated for multiple thousands of times. But even now, there are still more questions than answers. In Switzerland for example, there is a 27 kilometre circular underground tunnel. Atoms are magnetically controlled to race around this circuit, colliding with each other head on. Many new sub-atomic particles have been discovered as a result of these collisions. For anyone who wishes to study this topic specifically, there is an abundance of books dealing with the subject. They will do the job better than I can here.

If you try to imagine what the world would look like at atomic level, it would be a mistake to think of these sub-atomic particles like bits of microscopic grit whizzing around. They have very strange properties. If a single Electron is fired at a screen with a single tiny target hole, the strike can be detected on the other side of the hole. But if the same single Electron is fired at a screen with two separate target holes, the Electron strike can be recorded at both holes. Hmmm! Somehow, the single Electron is apparently able to pass through both holes at the same time. In fact all sub-atomic particles are capable of the same effect.

The name given to describe this atomic property is *Wave/Particle Duality.*

We are thus presented with; *The First Unanswered Question:*

How does Particle Duality work? We will return later to answer the question.

Let us take a look at the second enigma. Think how hard it would be to stand outside to grab a handful of wind. You close your fist on it and it is gone. But it is not gone. It continues blowing all around. It is here, there and everywhere. Open your hand and you can feel it. Close it slowly. You can still feel it. By the time your fingers have tightened it has gone from your grasp. Imagine if we could freeze-frame a section of wind as it passes. Can we now examine it? The answer is no, because the wind is dynamic. It implies movement and when it is frozen, its original movement ceases. It is no longer wind. The trouble with this whole scenario is that our point of observation is outside the quality of the wind its self. From our viewing point we can only measure the effect of the wind. The analogy of the wind serves to illustrate our second atomic effect. The motion of any sub-atomic particle means that it can't be measured without destroying its quality, and vice versa.

In summary, *The Second Unanswered Question* is: How can we measure and understand something that defies measurement?

The effect is known scientifically as *The Uncertainty Principle.*

We move on to the third question with another analogy. We start with two identical drinking glasses. One glass is filled with water. We pour water from the first glass into the empty second glass until it is filled to the brim. We look with amazement because the first glass is still filled with water. How could this be? Perhaps the first glass has some magical property. Perhaps it has a hidden energy source that makes more water appear from a hidden place? When atomic particles are collided, the collision produces a big shower of new smaller particles. More than 15 years ago, one of these test results showed evidence of the sub-atomic Z particle. The puzzling thing was that the Z particle had a mass over 200 times greater than an Electron and over 100 times greater than a Proton. The obvious question: How can a sub-atomic particle with such greater mass be produced from something with less or no mass at all? As with the cup of water, something was being produced apparently from nothing. Well at least for this third effect the scientists have come up with an explanation, which in answering the question, replaces it with another greater third question.

I'll try to clarify by asking the Photon to take centre stage. The Photon is a particle of light with properties both as a point and as a wave of force. It can be produced through electro-magnetic force; collision; chemical reaction, and as a natural phenomenon. When we switch on an electrical light, electromagnetic force is conducted to the filament as an electrical charge. The atoms of the filament are stimulated sufficiently so that high-energy photons are emitted as visible light. Photons can be produced naturally as in the case of a magnet. Energies lower than electrical energy operates within the magnet so we are unable to see visible light around it. However the magnet is indeed discharging Photons. The energy producing them is so low that they exist for only an instant. There is no visible light but there is sufficient energy to produce the properties we associate with a magnet. If like-poles of two magnets are brought together they push away from each other with invisible force. Likewise if opposite poles of two magnets are brought together they pull together. These effects are produced from the directional flow of the Photons being emitted by the magnet and then existing long enough to attract or oppose. We will learn later of the process that produces the attraction or repulsion. The Photons produced by a magnet are therefore acting as *virtual* light particles. Their energies are so low that they decay before becoming visible. These facts can be tied together to understand how the Z particle gained mass from a source with no mass. Quantum Scientists do propose the existence of an *unmeasured* virtual-energy form from which visible matter emerges. The scientists know it is there making up the greater part of all the universe, but it cannot be observed, and it cannot be directly examined. They call it Dark Matter. This produces our *Third Unanswered Question:*

Can Virtual Matter be properly understood and explained?

We can summarise the three main Quantum questions, which if answered and tied to an understanding of gravity, would explain how Matter and the Universe operates. These answers would give us the basis for understanding dimensions of afterlife and other multiverse dimensions of reality.

Question (1) How can we visualise the forces within an atom which account for its Particle / Wave duality?

Question (2) How can we understand the movement of forces within an atom which explains its ability to avoid measurement and proper scrutiny?

Question (3) How can the movement of forces within an atom cause matter to appear from an un measurable Virtual-energy source?

First we must plod a little way forward with the best explanations offered by the scientists. Superstring theory proposes that the sub atomic particles act like resonating strings or threads of energy. Any point of observation along the thread or string will give a representation of the whole energy thread. The idea seems plausible but does not answer questions one and two.

The same is true for the more complex Loop Quantum Theory. Quantum research still seeks the breakthrough that will provide a unified answer to all the questions. But before we try another approach, let us briefly summarise the known composition of: The Atom

Speculated Virtual Dark Matter leads to Gluons; then Quarks; which form the Proton and Neutron nucleus; (having mass, from particles with no mass!) surrounded by Electrons in their own vast zones of activity. The harmonic chord of their collective frequencies acts as the atomic glue to bind them uniquely together.

So now we have a standard picture of the Atom in our mind. But to really examine its workings, we have to provide a backdrop

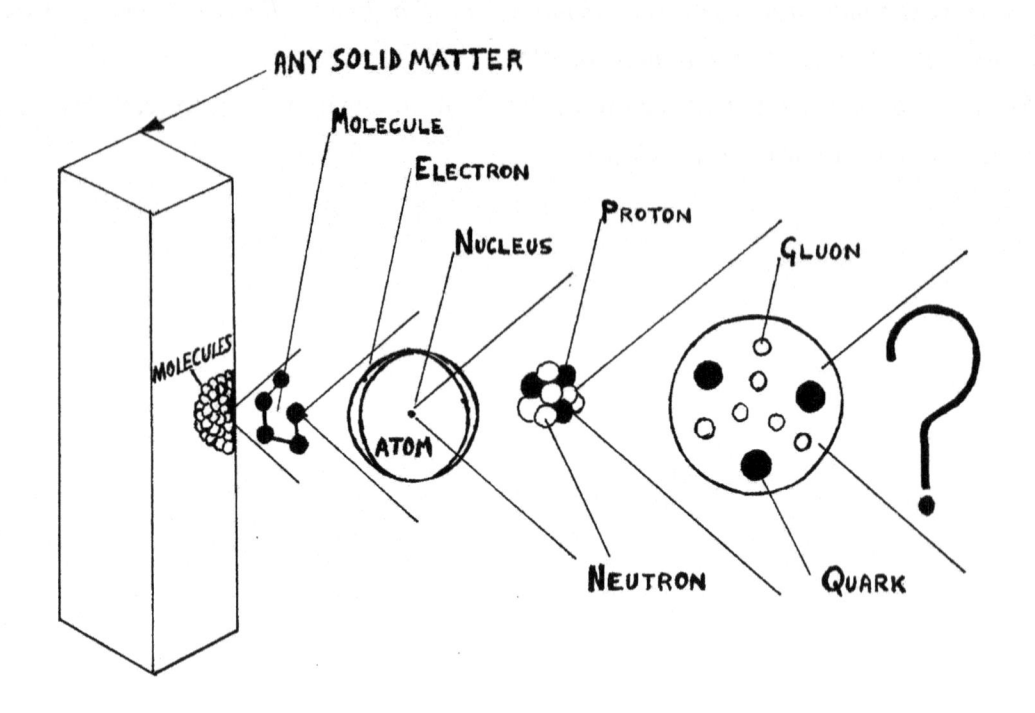

Plate 1: A Basic Atomic structure

The Rules of Vibration and Dark Matter

Think for a moment what it would be like, if you were able to visualise all of the invisible radio, television and all other transmissions present in the atmosphere. Have you ever seen on television the depiction of a shock wave from a really large explosion? The best example is from film footage of an atomic bomb blast. Within seconds, doughnut shaped shock waves spread many miles from the explosion. The same effect can be seen on footage of bomb blasts on the ground from warplanes.

If we viewed a radio transmission initiating from an antenna we would be able to see the disturbance in the atmosphere travelling out in all directions instantly just like the bomb-blast shock wave, but in all directions. A continuing transmission would produce sustained dynamic waves. If we could see the same effects from all other radioactive sources interacting with each other as they met, we would begin to appreciate the rhythmic chaos in the traffic.

The signals and radiations would be penetrating and overlapping each other through the whole depth of the atmosphere. The crescendo of explosive movement would distort the air around us, and would appear as a throbbing, dynamic sparkling mist. I am asking you really to imagine something that is almost impossible to imagine. But try hard. Just turn away from the page for a moment and try to think of as many sources of hidden radiation around you and their interacting patterns. X-rays in a hospital, Heat radiation from the sun, Individual Emergency services communications, Citizens Band radios, cosmic radiation, Telephone signals, Internet and Television transmissions. Colour frequencies; etc. etc. Every part of the electro-magnetic spectrum is represented at all times. These invisible signals fill the air around us, saturating the atmosphere and yet they remain totally invisible to our natural physical senses. Even beyond our atmosphere, movement is there. We accept the reality of the forms of radiation I have highlighted because we don't have to rely on our natural senses to verify their existence. All of them have a direct tangible impact on our physical lives and so it is easy to take their hidden presence for granted. Visible, and invisible, are an accepted part of our reality. The invisible radiation in our world functions at a refined level. The refinement of substance on any higher plane must therefore easily transcend our everyday senses. We need to play a Mind Game with ourselves if we wish to understand it fully.

Begin to form another mind-picture that will place us *beyond* our known reality—in order to try and understand it more. So for this trial exercise, imagine the refined world as having substance that is denser than air! Think of it as water, or perhaps plasma; or cold custard if it suits you! I will stick with plasma.

So, surrounding us entirely is a vast sea of plasma. It stretches in all directions; above, below and around us forever. We are picturing it as denser than air but in reality it is far more refined than the air we breathe; but ultimately condenses to form the air we breathe and everything we can or cannot physically perceive. It is finer than any matter, but condenses to form all physical matter.

We wish to observe its inherent properties so we will continue with our Mind Game and begin by observing its general characteristic from a position way out in deep space. As we become accustomed to our surroundings, we initially see only void around us. Gradually our senses detect movement. Think of a heat haze rising from the road up ahead and dancing in the air as we drive toward it. The sun is beating down and the air shimmers from the tarmac road. Our special vision allows us to see similar movement taking place everywhere around us. Infinite rhythmic distortions of the plasma are appearing and disappearing. Even when we try to focus on one specific area not far away, the shimmering seems to ebb and flow continuously. Densities appear, only to dissipate again, or ripple away from us with purpose. Our concentration deepens and we can see that there is a complete saturation of dynamic movement.

Consider a shock wave travelling through the deep ocean. A diver would barely feel the brush of pressure as the wave impulse passed by in an instant. Some hours later and hundreds of miles away, the same shock wave releases its energy in a large tsunami rising against the land. In our Mind Game scene, waves of movement transfer their energy throughout every space. There is no seabed here, so there is no landmass to concentrate the energy. Energy concentrations, or condensations, only take place at their points of interaction. Neither the roar of water from a huge waterfall, nor the surge of swirling, boiling waters from the pool below it, do justice to the complexity of vibrational movement around us. The impulses overlap each other and interact. Some are cancelled out by the exchange. Some movements are enhanced as their ripples collide, while others continue unaffected. The interaction could be described as infinite turbulence, producing infinite highs and lows of concentration. Consider in the bathtub when the water is sloshed about. As the surge of water from both ends of the tub meet in the middle it erupts in a crest and boils for a few seconds; or consider the multitudes of spreading ripples on the surface of a still pond when a thousand small pebbles are throw into it. Now translate that image in every dimension of our Mind Image.

Change the focus of this mind-picture and look out over millions of miles into the greater distance. The plasma conducts an infinite order of energetic impulses, interacting in an infinite variety of ways, continuing into the infinite reaches of space. Each and every space at this level of our awareness is filled with the greater or lesser potential for anything. The interactions of energy are sometimes as gentle as a feather on the breeze; or as ferocious as a grounded tsunami; or as vast and awesome as a supernova.

A sharp mind at this point would pose an obvious question:

'O.K. Buddy, we've got the mind-picture now. Something makes up all of what we know as empty space—filling all of the empty spaces between solid matter at atomic level! But what is this assumed plasma made of? It has to be made of something for the impulses to be carried along, hasn't it?'

This is a fundamental question to be answered shortly, but first I need to clarify why we have to use Mind Game viewing points to understand it all anyway!

Consider this: If you had a widget on the table, you can prod it, tip it over, examine it in detail, break it or dissect it. It can be fully scrutinised and tested through our normal senses. We could take our examination of the widget to extremes and look at it through an electron microscope. We could view its atomic structure. However, suppose it was possible for us to shrink ourselves down to the size of a molecule, while retaining or full natural senses. We would be able to examine the very fabric of the widget directly with the full application of our natural senses. In our normal world, our natural senses and instruments have their limits. As we delve deeper and deeper to understand the dynamics and forces that are smaller and smaller, we lose definition. It becomes harder to make any exact determinations. The dynamic effects may have a gross representation, but their quality can only ever be understood at quantum and beyond. You may say,

'Fine, but aren't we still going to be up against the second great quantum question anyway; IE. The effect is destroyed when you disturb its quality?'

I say the opposite is true, because if the quality of an effect is observed in the physical, then its quality/motivation must originate at a level beyond physical, and that is where we are heading, through quantum, via the super perception of our Mind Game!

I know I am stating the obvious, but the point I make is: If there are valid regions of reality beyond the point where our physical science stops, then there is only one route which will allow the full examination and understanding of them. We must adopt the perspective of someone actually occupying these other proposed regions and change our range of our perspective according to the situation.

To put it bluntly, I want to take you on a journey of examination by shrinking down to whatever size is necessary, and take our normal senses with us. I have kept the next few pages as simple as I can, even though they could be elaborated into a book on their own for the scientist. That is not what I am meant to do here. I will have done enough if I can convey the real workings of a single atom, and you will then also understand how its dynamics can be translated into the workings of everything. Back now to the dark atmosphere! Our mind picture continues. Appearing before us, large and bold, there is a functioning physical atom!

Hidden at the bottom of the Microscope

So, just like in a science fiction movie, we are viewing an atom big and large in front of us like a surreal dynamic architectural structure. We want to see how the Atom acts, reacts and shares affinity with its surroundings. We can scan through the different parts of the Atom, and the most obvious thing to notice is that the substance of the parts that form the Atom is not a lot different from the surrounding greater plasma of space. The components of the Atom appear like hotspots of differing density interacting together to form the atomic unit.

We already know from basic science, the Electrons orbit the Atomic nucleus within defined zones, or shells of activity. We know also that the boundaries of this region depend upon the energy of the Electron inhabiting it. Our viewing point takes us into the activity zone of the first Electron shell.

We can observe, there is no Electron particle whizzing around like a piece of grit. Instead we notice how this region seems like a denser area of plasma. There is an *order* of movement within this zone. We can observe however that the movement of the other components of the atomic unit are modulating the frequencies within this electron shell. Thereby, a hotspot of plasma has been created which is in regular orbit. A picture springs to mind here of the so called Mexican Wave seen at sport stadium gatherings. As a section of the crowd raises and lowers its hands the movement is continued around the stadium to produce the impression of a wave. The motivated energy of the whole crowd produces the effect. The wave is two dimensional, but the interacting frequencies in an electron shell produce a three dimensional hotspot in apparent orbit that does not stop. The plasma hotspot is in fact what science identifies as the Electron.

Moving closer to where the zone of the second electron shell begins, we see the first zone and the second zone are stable together even though their frequencies are not exactly the same. But there is an harmonic resonance between them. Think of a Basketball player bouncing a ball. His skills allow him to keep the ball in a regular bounce, even though he may do a pirouette between each bounce. His movements do not follow the same path as the ball, but he is able to synchronise his movements to the bounce of the ball and keep it bouncing. The adjoining electron shells are stable together in the same way. The dynamic resonance between them binds the zone of the first Electron to the second Electron like glue. The

Electron hotspot within each zone is a product of each zone frequency and the modulating interference from other zones. Here we need to understand another vital property . . .

We are building up a picture of our atom, separated as a functioning unit within the backdrop of the surrounding plasma. The atom as a whole has an identity. This is represented as a collective frequency of vibration. The collective vibration of the atom is not confined to the actual area of the atom. Its identity is dissipated out in ripples of vibrational influence in every direction into the surrounding plasma. These ripples of identity travel instantaneously, and then form part of the seemingly chaotic interaction we spoke of earlier. Science says that nothing can travel faster than light. But we are examining beyond the properties of so called particles that appear to us as light, and it allows us to see now how all things are in a state of natural instantaneous communication.

Let me state clearly here, the resonating signature of every particle is signalled instantaneously everywhere beyond it. Quantum Scientist Alain Aspect, settled previous scientific argument by experiment and proved this to be true for particles of physical matter; and if it is true for the smallest particle—it is also true for the gross matter that particles condense together to form. How do you think it is possible for the mother at home to know instantaneously that her soldier son has just died on the other side of the world? How do you think an animal can sense an event before it has reached them? How do you think that someone can see *any* event in their mind as it happens elsewhere? How do you think that any form of instant information sharing occurs over vast distance with no apparent tools? It is just a natural principle at work! However don't confuse this property at work with the higher effects of Precognition, or higher inspirations, because although they use the same basic principle, their operation depends on more complex motivations which we will explore later.

We can though now solve our first unanswered question, ie. Wave Particle Duality: When a free Electron is fired at a single aperture on a screen, obviously it will be detected on the other side of the screen. But remember when a single Electron is fired at a screen with two apertures, its presence is recorded exactly in the surrounding plasma as a specific vibrational signature. As the Electron reaches the apertures, the surrounding plasma on both sides of both apertures registers the motivated presence/frequency of the Electron. Thus it is recorded passing through both apertures at the same time. Simple!

Back now to our examination of the Atom. We probe deeper into the nucleus to study the Neutrons and Protons. Once again we must get away from the idea of the Protons and Neutrons acting like pieces of grit. We know from science the Protons and Neutrons are made up of smaller particles; the Quarks. The Protons and Neutrons are collectives of these particles, each of them with a unique identity (or vibrational signature). Their surfaces are dynamic like the Electron shell boundaries that are captive around them. Together they form the harmonically resonating atomic unit. We zero in on either the Proton, or the Neutron, viewing them from within *their* immediate field of influence. We find that both are formed from a collection of Quarks; and surprise, surprise! The Quarks yet again function together as coherent hot spots of Plasma with a unique vibrational identity. Can you see how each Particle in turn is formed from a grouping of smaller Particles (hotspots with individual harmonic vibrational signatures). The qualities of the ever smaller particles determine the properties of the larger groupings they form. Their quality helps determine the quality of the whole unit they are a part of. Attributes include their level of excitement (frequency,) the directional spin of their movement, and the combined complex interaction between all of the plasma Hot Spot components. Finally even the Quarks yield to smaller particles called Gluons, all acting according to the same vibrational principles as other Particles.

Particles resonate with a frequency and direction of movement which gives them individual identity, but does not prevent them functioning collectively as a chord of resonance. Consider this experiment: A few dozen balloons are filled with water and placed together into an even bigger rubber bag. A motion detector is fixed at one side of the bag. The opposite side of the bag is struck sharply. The motion detector immediately registers the transferred shock. The shockwave has travelled through the flexible contact surfaces of the smaller balloons without destroying their integrity. It is not necessary for them to be burst and mingle for the shock wave to travel through them. Benign forces acting on the atomic unit are transferred in a similar way. A simple example of this would be where external conditions cause the vibrational movement of molecules and the atoms of water to slow down. They condense closer together to form ice. When water is heated, the external forces excite the vibration of the molecules and atoms to the point where their fields of vibration can no longer maintain their cohesion. They separate into freed vapour, but do not lose their identity and their ability to condense together again. In an Atom, the Gluons, Quarks, Protons, Neutrons, and Electrons resonate together as a beautiful harmonising unit. The dynamic planes of contact between each component are held stable in an harmonic resonance, and this produces a singular identity for the atom within its surroundings. We can make a simple leap here and grasp that all other atoms and at higher levels, first the molecules—then gross matter, are all bonded together by the same method of infinitely harmonising resonance. An Atom will act in harmony or discord when brought together with another atom depending upon the second atom's resonating identity. Interaction or reaction is guaranteed in every case.

I have already described how the resonance of every Particle and therefore every Atom and then Molecule, creates ripples of disturbance in the greater surrounding plasma of space. These identity ripples are not restricted by physical matter. They are conveyed through Dark

Matter, or Virtual Matter, and are only impeded by their interaction with ripples from other identities. Ok, think of the Aura. This is an exact example of the effect I describe. An Aura is the projected ripple of identity from anything animate or inanimate. However when ripples of identity are conveyed into greater space, they also penetrate to multiple higher levels of refinement beyond our physical world—where equally valid levels of reality exist.

In order for us to further understand the workings of vibration, we need to see what happens when there is a Reaction from our Atom to an incoming free Photon. Just to remember, the Photon as a minute concentration of plasma moving with singular purpose from a reciprocal reaction event elsewhere. Its impetus came from its previous atomic interaction, and this provided its motivation for the journey. It too has a vibrational signature and a field of influence. Its resonance precedes it and is projected from it. Plasma is focused at its head, and its immediate field of influence acts like a slightly elongated sphere. The Photon reaches the Atom and smashes into the field of the outer Electron shell. The movement of energy of the Photon joins and mingles with the resonance of movement within the Electron shell. The added energy of the new Photon excites the movement within the Electron shell creating a higher resonance and causing the spatial area of the Electron to increase. As the Electron domain becomes more excited and increases in size, the chord of resonance it has shared with the other components of the Atom becomes disrupted. A tug of war develops where the resonance of the other atomic components is thrown out of vibrational balance by the unsustainable higher and more excited resonance of the outer shell. Within the outer shell the confusion of forces begins to create an eddy that develops into a second Plasma Hotspot. The conflicting Hotspots cannot be sustained and one Hotspot is instantly thrown away from the Electron shell as another free Photon—just as it had been for the arriving photon in the first place. Then the Electron shell may return to its normal state as a part of the atomic unit.

To an observer in the gross world, the breakaway Photon could be detected as a tiny flash of light. In the case of a Magnet, the atomic interactions are internal to the Magnet but create shells of influence that extend beyond the Magnet's surface. They are aligned at either end according to the directional spin from the energy of the whole Magnet's atomic structure. If same magnetic poles of two magnets are brought together with fields of similar directional spin, they crash against each other in opposition. At similar poles, the magnets would feel as if they were pushing against each other, which via the surrounding free plasma is exactly what does happen. Opposite poles brought together would welcome each other into an harmonious flow. Two such Magnets would act with attraction as a single enlarged Magnet.

Interactions between all things on the physical level are variations of these simple explanations. Particle accelerators make particles collide until the very fabric of the Atom is smashed asunder. However there is no difference in the process. Zones of atomic cohesion or discord are played out against each other to form new elemental freed Particles; or to bind together in the collective harmony of a new atomic identity. The same process happens as a natural progression in the process of physical birth and decay in all things. This would be better named the process of transmutation. Similarly the effect plays itself out through Chemical interaction. Larger bodies in the cosmos interact to an infinite scale with ever smaller bodies; until we are left with the seeming conundrum of gravitational force at our level. It is all the same! The vibrational harmonics between distinct physical matter, or matter at more refined levels, are all subject to degrees of harmonic attraction or repulsion. This coincidentally determines the *degree* of gravitational attraction.

I could go on forever giving examples atomic interchanges but I hope for now I have been able to covey the basic concept. All matter operates within a surround of finer substance, which I have called the greater plasma atmosphere, but described elsewhere as Dark Matter. But Dark Matter is in fact pure potential, and registers the impulses of everything in endless orderly chaos. We are unable to study it from our physical world because it exists beyond the limits of our physical tools of inspection. The space it occupies forms the lubrication to all matter at atomic level and reaches far beyond our imagination, infinitely into the cosmos. Within it there are zones or dimensions of higher but equally valid reality, and our temporary material physical world is a guest in this greater reality.

We began this technical section with three unanswered Quantum questions. The questions and their answers are so fundamental to the understanding of Life, the Universe and everything that I am just going to give a few more paragraphs to highlight them again.

Duality: How can Matter be in two or more places at once? Remember the Electron being fired at a screen, first with one aperture then with two apertures. For Electron, substitute the name Plasma Hotspot. As it travels toward the two apertures it creates a ripple of distortion in the surrounding plasma in all directions. The vibrational signature of the Electron hotspot is duplicated through these ripples. Although the Hotspot has a leading point of impetus, the *whole* field of influence of the Electron is representative of its core identity. The ripples of identity easily pass through both apertures simultaneously and inevitably combine to reform the signature of the photon *from* each aperture. Can you just imagine the difficulty faced by Earth science, trying to measure and quantify an Electron or other sub particle in free motion? When atomic particles are smashed together, the effect of their collision can be examined, but the results tell us very little about the particles in free flight. The moment they are freeze-framed, their free nature is destroyed. The Hotspot, which *is* the Electron for example, can only be itself when in free motion. The particle can never exist as an independent entity. Whether as a component of an atomic unit or as a free particle travelling through dark matter, its identity is reproduced in all directions instantaneously. There is a state where a pair of Electrons can exist with conjoined influence. Scientists have determined that one particle has an *up* spin and the other a *down* spin. Thereby their combined field of influence has a zero spin where both spins cancel each other out. In fact *all* manner of vibrational relationships exist at atomic level, and science has not even begun to scratch the surface of understanding.

However, the very existence of these pairs of Electrons provided the basis for a battle of the masters of Quantum Science; Scientists Niels Bohr and Albert Einstein. The Einstein camp declared: If the Electrons were separated, measurement could be applied to each of them without affecting the other. Bohr however, reminded Einstein: If an Atomic system is separated for measurement, the task becomes impossible because the system has been destroyed. It took another brilliant Quantum Scientist, Alain Aspect, some years later, to produce an experiment that clarified the answer. He measured the simultaneous effect of paired Photons from the same source instead of Electrons. The passage of Photons was more easily detectable. Simultaneous measurement at different viewing points produced identical results that vindicated the proposal from Bohr and Aspect. The scientists quantified the atomic process by effect rather than quality. Ie deducing the immeasurable by what it did instead of what it was.

We still have to deal with Virtuality and with matter appearing from nothing! At C.E.R.N. in Switzerland, thousands and thousands of Atomic collision tests are carried out. The results of the collisions are detected and examined. The main interest of the scientists however is not with the matter that can be seen. Their main interest is centred upon the matter that cannot be seen. In the experiments, powerful electromagnetic fields are used to contain and direct the particles. The particle collisions produce a shower of secondary sub particles. The mass of the sub particles produced has been found to exceed the mass of the original colliding particles.

It is very simple really. When the atomic collisions take place, there is such an explosion of primeval force, that particles freed from a stable atomic unit in the explosion create huge eddies. These provide sufficient motivation within the surrounding greater plasma for fresh matter to be actualised to stabilise them. New matter only *appears* to come from nothing. It comes in fact from the Potential of Dark Matter; which is the greatest volume of Virtual substance in the Universe. Gravity is now not so hard to comprehend. If you transfer the understanding of the forces of resonance at work within the unity of an Atom into the unity of forces working in harmony at human, Planetary and Cosmic scale, you will find no difference. Gravity is simply the binding force of harmonising or opposing resonance that acts between all things, even back to the Big Bang. But for us it acts according to the greatest atomic influences in our planetary system, and especially according to the resonating glue provided by our own planet.

I wonder if you noticed however one vital omission in my explanations so far? How does physical matter become actualised from Virtual/Dark Matter? I have said it can be motivated to occur, as freed Particles seek natural balance by drawing substance from the surrounding greater plasma, but I still need to describe the actual process. One again I will describe it as I was reminded; in the following life sized transmuting geometric shapes.

Imagine first a Mobius Loop. For those not familiar with this shape, the best way to describe it is to imagine for example a strip of paper about an inch wide and eight inches long. Take the strip of paper; make a half twist in one end and then join the ends together. If you place your finger on the surface anywhere and mark a cross on the spot, you can trace your finger around the surface and you will find yourself back at the beginning again. It is an infinite loop!

So ok, in your mind's eye, imagine the loop has a flow of energy moving around it just like your finger. Next imagine the loop is expanding just like wide flexible flattened water hose filling up again with water. Maintain the idea of the energy flow around it. As the loop turns into a Taurus (doughnut) shape, the energy flow can be seen to travel in a spiral direction around it.

Maintain the idea of the spiral energy flow but imagine the Taurus (doughnut) continuing to expand. Eventually it becomes a sphere, coincidentally just like our planet with its magnetic energy flow patterns. The energies continue in a spiral but the wavelength shortens and condenses at the core. The condensation is sufficient to produce new ejected fresh physical atomic matter. This is where we can detect it *at* Quantum. The process is not confined to singular events. It goes on all the time everywhere around us, within us and beyond us. It is motivated from the interaction of all substance, or from the wilful motivation of humankind at every level. The white noise of the universe is the echo of this infinite process. It is motivated from the interaction of all things to produce the fabric of the cosmos. It is motivated from an atomic explosion to produce destructive uncontrolled raw radiation. It is motivated by the splitting of single atoms, to produce multiple new particles. It is motivated by Pulsars, to produce radio signals that cross the universe. It is motivated by Black Holes, to produce the gross matter of new universes. It is motivated by the ambient vibrational signature of the universe, through an infinite hierarchy of realities, to produce the fabric of everything in an infinite living Mobius loop. It is motivated by mundane thought, to produce the conscious and subconscious realms that reflect our blindness. It is motivated by thought, to produce the temporary but valid realms of our dream state. It is motivated by the conscious inspiration of the sentient beings that inhabit the refined realms of reality far beyond our gross physical level. And every single example is inexorably linked!

From the basic workings of an atom can you begin to see the implications at last? The split cobbles thrown in opposing directions from my hand as a child, may seem to have been separated physically, but their vibrational bond truly could never be broken.

The collective vibration of thick oil has a vibration that opposes the vibration of water and prevents it from mixing. In the same way, if I, by my thoughts and deeds project a high vibration, then the lower vibrational thoughts of someone wishing harm on me will have no effect. Their thoughts will have lower energy. My higher thoughts will have provided a natural protection. But their motivations will have conversely condensed their host's Presence to a lower frequency.

Here is an important lesson to remember. In all of the process of creation, balance exists constantly in the chaos because the influence of everything transmutes everything. However the balance depends upon the conflict of vibration and the reciprocal reaction between all things. This comes from the resistance between one vibration and another. At a gross physical level, the differences in vibration are more volatile because of the dense nature of the medium. At higher refined levels the conflict becomes less and less as the balance relies more and more on harmonic resonance. The Godhead referred to without real understanding by so many religions, is the infinite perfection of balance between both. But the whole process is inevitable. God and religion is a human invention and *Contains*; while in truth—Matter at its Infinite Source is also the Virtual *omnipresent* fuel for our entire finite world. Religious definition is an illusionary system of control, while the whole process of existence is simply an order of infinite vibrational interaction and balance which can be universally understood. Our original off-world ancestors understood this. Beyond the DNA manipulations which created our human strain from Darwinian creatures, we retained the understanding. The battles between even our higher evolved ancestors ensured the start of the control systems which continue to strangle our freedom of universal understanding today.

Thought is tangible. Thought creates. It acts upon dark matter through the torus process—with the motivation to actualise a ballet of creation. We have forgotten our responsibility to use it wisely. Our sentient Presence belongs to a more refined level. We clothe ourselves in the flesh of the physical level and labour under the illusion that the lower vibration of sensation is our home. Let us move forward therefore and try to enact a few human scenarios. Maybe then we will be able to see how the understanding of the lesser universe can give a new insight to the world we live in.

Gross Matter Scenarios

With a simple Leaf on a Branch.

We can appreciate now how the atoms and molecules of the leaf are interacting in harmony. I have described how the stages of resonance act as individual signatures, combining to give an ever-greater collective signature. In this case, we call the final collective signature, a leaf. We know that sub particles reproduce their signature with radiating effect in the greater surrounding plasma. The same is true of combined molecular structures. The same is true of the final article; the leaf. Radiation is obviously stronger and denser near its source. Hence an *Aura* exists around the leaf as a projection of the life force of the leaf.

Let us expand our example by introducing the Gardener. He lifts his hand to cradle the leaf. He whispers a few words of appreciation at its beauty. The Gardener himself has a far more powerful Aura which mingles harmoniously with the Aura of the leaf. His positive thoughts enhance the vibrancy and the life force of the leaf, by directing virtual energy to it.

Conversely someone approaching the leaf or the tree with destructive ideas would actualise negative energy; or more accurately, the discordant energy would force the energy of the leaf to condense/contract. Experiments have shown conclusively that if someone directs kind thoughts and words to a plant, it helps the plant to flourish. If someone directs destructive thoughts to a plant, it withers. In fact, experiments have demonstrated that if someone simply voices their intention to destroy a plant or tree, the cellular activity of the tree will slow down or stop as if in anticipation of the act.

Let's try another example: Echoes from the Past

If only the land could speak to us, we could learn the history of ages! We shall reflect upon a lump of rock! The rock does indeed have an aura surrounding it. If we had fully evolved higher vision we could identify and interpret the thousands of frequencies in its makeup. All of them harmonise in further thousands of inner cycles, representing stages of its evolvement.

Consider the action in a television set. Electrons are directed by an electromagnetic field to be displayed as a picture on the face of the cathode ray tube. Minute differences in the signal frequency produce fluctuations in the Electron flow. The effect on the phosphorescent screen produces a picture which we accept. Using vibrational vision we could work directly with the signals that form the rock. We would be able to interpret the recurring data from the rock. Within the millions of interacting impulses, all information relating to the history of the rock are registered in its vibrational signature/its aura, in a state of Virtuality. We only have to play the part of a television receiver to access them. This viewing principle is true for all things, however complex.

People work with crystals, using to some extent the higher properties of their atomic structures. On a mundane level we already know how the vibrational qualities of mica crystals were once used to produce working radio devices. Natural Rock Crystal can be identified in a multitude of natural forms, from Diamond to Ruby, or from Moldavite to Quartz. There are thousands of examples, but in crystal there is a difference. The atomic structure of crystal has an ordered matrix. This projects a refined aura that can be manipulated. There is little difference between the principle of the frequencies of magnetic tape being modified to record sound and the aura of rock crystal being used to transmute and direct energy. A perfectly attuned sphere, or skull shaped rock of quartz crystal, can be more functional than a physical radio. Indeed it is understood by the author and many others, that older civilisations developed the properties of crystal to such high degree as to allow the transmission of vast refined energies around the planet. Yet again it is our ignorant invention that many feel the need to imbue crystal with personality and even with the greater containment of a pet name! To do so is to miss the whole understanding of their nature and potential.

A crystal skull or orb shape was developed to provide for a human icon of identity, possession and material power; *but serves no further real understanding of their nature.*

Armed with an understanding of how vibrational energy works we can easily relate to other situations. Some people have a sufficiently high vibration themselves that they can sense the power in a building. It is so easy to step inside a grand Cathedral or ancient Church and be lifted by the vibrations. Over centuries, visitors may have been ignorant of the process at work, but their higher exultations would have been sufficient to raise the vibration of the fabric of the building. A sensitive person would be able to detect and read this energy. Similarly, on the site where great cruelty or tragedy had taken place such as a battlefield or a gallows, the gross negative energy of previous activity would have condensed the vibrational quality of the surroundings, so that many would later feel the negative difference. People with a lower vibrational signature would feel the energy of negative surroundings, because more people at a lower vibrational level are attuned to gross physical vibration. People of course have the unique quality of being able to raise or lower our vibration by the motivated power of our own thought. In any situation we pick up whatever we are attuned to pick up. The quality of our Presence is entirely our own responsibility. If only we could all accept that we all have only ourselves to blame for ourselves!

A radio receiver needs to be tuned correctly to receive the selected station. We are no different. When you next visit a place of any significance, take a moment to *feel* the surrounding vibration. You will be tuning-in with your own vibration. Just maybe you will have developed to the stage where you can feel and see the memory of what took place there before you. The same is true for a humble rock, or a leaf, a place, or even another person.

We shall move on now with Jungle Beauty

A native tour guide is taking us to where Nature has developed to its full potential. The scene unfolds: Our sense of smell is overwhelmed with the scent of lush vegetation. We are being guided along a jungle path. To our right and left the foliage rises in a wall of dense green and gold. Above us, shafts of shimmering light penetrate the tree canopy to give occasional torchlight shafts of vision through the living screen in front of us.

We push our way along the trail, the parted leaves and grasses straining to embrace us again from behind as we brush slowly forward. Suddenly our senses are shocked as we approach the sound of rushing water. We emerge from the pathway into blinding sunlight and as our eyes adjust we find ourselves on a rocky platform jutting out from the valley side.

Around us the valley walls rise steeply in an almost continuous sea of lush green. Monet splashes of yellow and red tree-fruit, hang like coloured teardrops from the branches. In the near distance, the cascade of a high waterfall cuts the head of the valley. It emerges from the skyline as a huge roll of liquid blue. It is breaking into a million falling fountains, embracing the smooth rocky face and splashing down to the deep pool below us. Spray mist fills the air to mingle with the smell of the jungle. It produces a sweet narcotic aroma that fills the lungs and head.

As we move forward, the escarpment gives way on our left to an ample grassy clearing. We take positions on this high vantage point and rest. Under the warmth of the sun's rays we can relax and enjoy the scene before us. Looking up, the undulating waves of fine mist from the waterfall diffuse and refract the sunlight, creating a spectral rainbow dome above us.

Around our feet butterflies silently flit about, alighting frequently on the rocks beside us. We attune our ears to the intermingling symphony of background sound. Occasionally a single sound bursts forth as a distant monkey hoots its territory. Our native guide addresses us to explain how this is a Sacred site. Only elder members of the tribe or initiates are allowed to visit the site and are always accompanied by the Shaman. It is accepted by the tribe there is great power here. Energy can be gathered to the Presence, making it possible to form close contact with the world of Spirit.

So far we have been privileged only to witness the beauty of our surroundings through physical senses. We shall now step to our higher level so that once again we can interpret the things around us with vibrational sight. We are suddenly overwhelmed as we perceive the absolute kaleidoscope of powerful harmonious refined impulses permeating everything we see.

Our auras are infused and expanded by the surrounding refined vibrations to give us a heightened sense of awareness and well-being. We become accustomed and gradually see deeper and deeper levels of harmonic movement in all directions. We are able to focus in and out, enabling us to recognise individual signature ripples for all things living or non-living. In this special place, the conditions are just right for the cooperation of all things to merge in harmony. Within the local *greater* plasma, this huge movement of harmonious vibration is creating a colossal excitation, so that potential is being developed into harmonious new Plasma hotspots everywhere. The Shaman or the initiate is thereby enabled to absorb surplus higher potential from the cacophony of surrounding influence. They are able to harvest the potential for their own use. Their vibrations are so raised that they resonate directly with the new energy and their aura expands accordingly.

For the ordinary person a wish is often made: If only I could see with higher vision too. For the ordinary person, such premature vision would be so overwhelming it would be damaging to the more base vibration of the person. It would be like suddenly standing in the glare of the hottest sun without protection. The extra power gained by the developed Shaman can only be put to positive use. Lower vibrations **condense** to lower vibration, but higher vibrations **gravitate** to higher vibration. For a base person it would be like trying to harvest air with a shovel. The Shaman however is able to raise his vibration to the quality of air, and through the control of spiritual-will direct the excess potential to wherever it may have positive effect. If a base person were in any case to visit our special place they would experience either indifference or discomfort at the clash of their lower vibration and the more refined vibrations of everything around them.

I have used this elaborate example to illustrate the inevitable interaction of all things at a vibrational level. All things living or otherwise are the product of their own total experience. All inescapably react or interact at a vibrational level. *All past, present and future events exist forever in a genuine state of virtual reality, potential or strength of probability, and can be claimed by all those who have developed sufficiently to access and make use of them.* Our own personal vibrational field or Aura is entirely our own responsibility. Its collective vibrational level is a reflection of our stage of spiritual development. It represents our evolving vibrational signature. Every thought passing through our mind affects it.

Remember Cause, Effect and Consequence! *Cause* is not the hand reaching out to move something on the table. Thought originates the action. *Effect* is the hand reaching to carry out the action. *Consequence* is the impacting result of the action. In any environment we have the power of free will to follow positive or negative thoughts. Their energy will constantly modify our Aura. We can link ourselves to positive or negative environments and situations. Whichever they may be, they will have an inevitable positive or negative effect on our development. Think back to the waterfall scene. I manufactured the place from my own imagination. I wanted to create something approaching an idyllic scene in your mind. If you were sensitively tuned to the vision I will have succeeded in creating reality in print, originating out of virtual thoughts. Do you see; the very act of just thinking of such a glorious place is enough to create beneficial vibrations. Our thoughts will have turned passive potential into real energy, which can be a force for good or bad on anyone or anything making contact with our field of influence. I cannot emphasise this point strongly enough. Thought is not discarnate. Thought is tangible and can construct negative or positive energy. It is worth taking this opportunity to explain more fully how different energies affect us personally.

As stated, our Aura is a mirror image of our own collective state. It is a complete record of our progress in all of our doings. Our sensual impressions and our thoughts modify the existing myriad of vibrations making up our Aura. An evil or negative thought in our minds (negative potential,) creates a negative vibrational disturbance which can be malevolent to its creator. The effect is amplified in both directions as similar energies resound together. Like attracts like, and where the sum total of our Presence at any time reflects a malevolent disposition, we will unconsciously attract other people and situations to ourselves. This will open us to similar forces of greater strength as a reward. Once again, it is our own choice to invite such potential harm to ourselves. Thoughts must be guarded at all times in order to seek only the harmonious alliances and positive sources of inspiration. Consider the situation, where shock and horror are felt at the news of someone murdered in the so-called name of religion or politics. Ten years later and another few deaths are added to the hundreds of deaths since the first report. The stories are carried in the media and the items catch fleeting interest from most people. The news of a first murder induces a negative vibrational reaction of shock, but the news of more murders creates a familiarity—which conditions people to accept the news eventually with no outrage. It would be well to dwell on how easily we become conditioned to the negative things that happen in our world. Remember, we become conditioned more easily to negative, because we are of the negative. We have to put effort into raising ourselves to something higher, despite our weight of physical sensation. Constant negative input develops an aspect of permanent negative frequency in our Presence to handle similar news *without commitment.* For some people where the Aura is already saturated with negative impulses, one more event can be sufficient to cause a negative chain reaction. Like attracts like, and the conscious build-up of negative energy in an Aura, can create a force which is powerful enough to form negative vibrational hotspots that cannot be contained. A build-up of *Cause* or *Potential* has to be discharged, whether the energy is positive or negative. In one case where the saturation of negative energy comes from the obsessive watching of violent films for example, the person could discharge the energy by enactment of the violence seen. This has happened as we all can remember from the news stories of violent murders in recent times.

When we encounter the effects of deep negative vibrational influence it is entirely possible for us to remain pure and sound, but this may only be possible after years or lifetimes of development. When we reach that stage, we will find it possible to consider deeply the workings and effects of negative influence without being harmed. It is possible, but only from a position of enlightenment. Considerations can be compassionate while remaining objective and detached. This describes the higher quality of Dispassionate Compassion. In an enlightened state our natural positive vibrations would be far too powerful to allow the incursion of negative energy, even when it has to be faced Now, as a complete contrast to scenes of harmony we can consider the influence of negative vibrations with the next scenario.

Dead Reckoning

Upon entering a new picture we find we are walking along a dirt track bounded by dusty windblown flatlands. Scrub grass clings to the ground in untidy patches everywhere. There is a dust haze in the air preventing clean sunlight from breaking through. The heavy air smothers the light and diffuses it into an irritating dull fluorescent glare. Our walking is tiresome. The oppressive surroundings sap our energy. Wearily we approach a small group of ramshackle native huts that seem deserted. Their framing poles are rotted and tilting and the thatch fronds on the roofs are shrivelled and askew. As we draw closer we find with surprise, there really are occupants. The few blackened natives seem to be sitting about lethargically, peering through soulless eyes. Many stare to the inner distance of a more riveting scene, while the piles of scattered debris seem only to dress their despair.

We turn our heads to look at the villagers and notice their hair. At first glance we saw nothing unusual because everything here seems to fit. But the dirty grey strands of what was once hair, hangs now like straw chaff from every head the same. There is an unmistakable feeling of sickliness everywhere. As we walk on, we can trace the faint outline of previously cultivated plots of land at the sides of the pathway. The remains of long parched and dead plants cling to the ground like surreal lapel badges. Ahead of us we can hear the subdued rush of the seashore—and the sense of foreboding increases. Several fishing boats lie strewn like toys cast aside by a child. We reach the sea to retch from the smell of decomposition. For as far as the eye can see, the tide-line is marked by a ribbon of dead fish. The sea reeks with suspicion. There is something seriously wrong here.

We switch to our vibrational vision and immediately detect the powerful dense vibrations subduing everything. The reverberations of energy are disruptive and chaotic. Their frequencies are intense and draw close to the frequency of physical matter. This ocean of negative energy and its resulting negative potential is having a direct effect upon the substance of all physical matter here. Any potential harmony is being drowned and thrown out of balance by the continuing radioactive reactions. At sub-atomic level the negative force is acting like a tidal wave of destruction. Any living tissue is being forced to mutate. The villagers were the first to be affected. Many are already developing cancers. Their hair and sight have been affected. They are slowing down as their immune systems break down. The natural vegetation and plant life has been destroyed and the seashore is littered with death. The background impulses of destruction have contaminated everything.

Our perceptions sharpen. We analyse and trace back through the vibrational signatures to their origin. Our sight clears and we are able to inspect the vision of an idyllic tropical village. The sun beams its heat to the ground. The palm trees sway in the breeze. The sea laps gently to the golden sandy beach. The shore is lined with villagers. Young and old, men and women, all stand in hushed excitement as they stare to the horizon. Apprehensive glances pass between them. Suddenly from the entire line of the sky there is a blinding flash which penetrates like exploding neon into their faces. A short time later the hurricane shock waves reach them, carried along with a roar of sound. The island is torn about as if in the grip of a typhoon, and in the distance a huge mushroom cloud boils up into the sky. In the space of a few seconds the village has been ravaged. Somewhere in a distant place, men congratulate themselves on yet another successful nuclear test. A mistake is noted. The weather patterns have been wrongly diagnosed. The cloud of radioactive dust is spreading away in an unplanned direction. It doesn't matter however because there are only a few sparsely inhabited islands in its path and the inhabitants are unlikely to make a lot of fuss. Beyond the test explosion the villagers had tried to recover but were unable to escape the radiation. The unimaginably discordant force released by the explosion created awesome turbulence within the greater plasma field. The negative energy produced a holocaust of condensed lower energy. It would take many generations for the weight of negative potential to condense sufficiently for their world to gravitate back to harmony.

We may find it difficult to compare this scenario with the general effects of civilisation and peoples. However the combined influence of an ignorant world population, produces similar environmental and social damage to our whole Planet in every degree. Each happening has its own level of vibrational signature. Together they represent a collective vibrational signature. This may be positive or negative, but such world influences may only need one more incident of positive or negative vibrational influence to tip the scale. The planet lives as a vibrational body also and reacts to the potential we impose upon it. We determine the strength of good or bad probabilities for its future, and thereby our own future.

Perhaps now it may be useful to explore a scenario which tests the combined elements of the previous stories. Also as it gets harder to explain these alien concepts with you still as the Martian, it will be useful to pre-suppose a little more strongly that there are indeed powerful *Minders* working for us on a higher level.

As scenarios become more complex, they draw closer to the greater complexity of real life. This story examines the potential workings for events that may have seemed stranger than fiction, but were not really strange at all. The spiritual potential of a plan conceived in higher levels can take many generations to evolve and we should look at an imagined scenario

Planning to Heal

In our new vision we swoop down towards a large Cathedral type building. In the grounds a multitude of people mill about with the excitement of common purpose. From amongst them a queue gradually forms and snakes its way to the large entrance. The excitement of those in the queue joins the excitement of those who trickle from the exits at the other end of the building. We move on past the waiting people and notice how many of them are afflicted by some ailment or physical disability. Helpers accompany them to guide and assist where needed. The leaves of two huge oak doors flank the doorway like guarding sentinels to the inner lobby. Giant worn flagstones give firm comfort to the feet, and the presence of a wide stone-arched ceiling conveys solid protection to all who enter.

A wondrous sight awaits the visitors. The interior of the building is huge. Great stone vaulted sections seem to reach to the sky. The walls are lined with stained-glass windows which are impressive from outside; but their stupendous effect is only visible to those who now stand in front of them. Thousands of multi-coloured shafts of light pierce the air like a flickering rainbow. As eyes become accustomed to the display we begin to recognise the outline of deeper high ceilings from alcoves leading into the walls between the windows. People shuffle about everywhere chatting in muted tones and creating a respectful background hubbub. At the far end of the building the flow directs us to a huge draped altar, guarded at either end by delicately carved stone angels. Moving closer, we can see how the centre of the altar is laid bare and gentle flowing water is trickling down its frontage. At its base there is a huge blue-marble slab which has been hewn to form a shallow polished collection pool for the water. The sparkling liquid fills the pool and flows evenly over its rim to create a living gloss over its entire surface. It drains away silently into a discrete channel. The people file slowly past the pool and altar; mumbled prayers spilling from their lips. Hands reach to the water and return dripping for anointment to themselves and their charges. Some are clutching small containers, ready with awkward reverence to gather some of the flowing water. Faces are bright with expectation. At the far side of the altar, there is a distracting group who seem to be paying particular attention to someone. A better vantage point reveals a rich and regally clothed man confidently addressing the gathering in front of him. His lecture concerns the building we now occupy. He proceeds to give meaning and purpose to all we have seen. It seems that long, long ago, before the present building appeared, the site was even then regarded as a sacred place. A crystal spring had always flowed from near the top of the hill. The gentle slopes leading to the meadows below supported all manner of grasses, wild flowers and healing herbs. The water from the spring was seen as magical and visitors claimed cures from the drinking of it.

Megan lived in a nearby village and was regarded affectionately by everyone.

She had lived a dutiful life raising a large family. All eventually grew and departed. Her husband had been dead for some years and she spent her time helping others in her small community. In her life she had endured and survived all the hardships of her time. She had also survived the disability of a withered leg from a childhood accident. Megan sometimes escaped life by journeying to the magic hill. She enjoyed the tranquillity of the flowing spring and the lush surroundings, and felt a powerful affinity with the Spirit of the place. On one visit her world and life were changed forever. The shining light of a bright Presence appeared before her. The spectral form spoke to Megan and reminded her how she had once made the choice to live her life of sacrifice; and how this would pave the way for her to fulfil a special task. She would begin a cycle of Probability that would lead to the physical and spiritual healing of the many thousands who would follow.

She was shown how countless workers on a higher level had been motivating the energy of creation, to raise and enhance the conditions of harmony on the hill for years. She was shown how this was in preparation for the task of bringing healing and enlightenment to those who would visit. Her inner eye was opened to the understanding of many things beyond her experience. She was instructed to bathe regularly in the spring water. Her village friends soon began to notice how Molly was gaining strength in her injured limb and wanted to know the secret of her miracle cure. Molly proclaimed her thanks to her God and spirit, and to the power vested in the magical waters of the spring. Word spread fast. Soon others came to visit. They too were cured of their afflictions and before long travellers came from many miles away in pilgrimage to receive healing. Molly became custodian of the spring, passing the knowledge she gained to all who would listen. Over decades, a protective shrine was built. Additions over the years finally led to the vast beautiful building dominating the hill where we now stand.

Let us stand a little further back from this scenario and try to comprehend some of the vibrational interactions at work. Key elements in the story were the woman, Megan, who had been selected as a catalyst to bring the plans for the site to a conclusion. There was the site itself, which was vested with special healing power. Finally, there was a discarnate guiding Presence. In my explanations for the workings of vibrational forces through gross matter, I have so far deliberately kept away from the full idea of another living human dimension. That will come soon. In the scenario however, the appearance of a discarnate being was necessary. The story examined a naturally occurring power site. Visitors recognised this without understanding how it worked. Then, through one special person the course of local history changed forever.

With our special vision, we previously saw how gross matter is infused at every vibrational level with attracting frequencies. Under particular circumstance a surplus of energy is manifest. The frequencies of energy at the site were already powerful and positive. These were added to with every prayer-thought over the years, just like the gardener with the leaf.

The higher motivations built upon each other in a crescendo of power, infusing the very fabric of the building and the surrounding scenery. All those who could attune themselves to the prevailing frequencies felt a great boost of spiritual/vibrational energy. Visitors came with afflictions—revealed as imperfections of the body, or with sickness, disease or deformity. In a perfect healthy body, all the bodily systems would be working in perfect vibrational harmony. In an unhealthy body, the imperfections would centre upon a vibrational resistance where the natural frequencies were not fully synchronised. An infusion of surplus positive energy need be all that was required to align the frequencies again. Indeed any visitors to such a place arriving with high expectation would excite their own vibration naturally. This would make them doubly receptive to the positive power available.

I manufactured the healing hill scenario, but it is no different for those who visit real holy sites such as Lourdes or Majagoria; but the irony is that any place of natural balance can exist anywhere in the world and have the same result. I can speak from personal experience of this in the apparent wilderness of the deep Western desert. The same can occur naturally anywhere. However here is the double irony as I let you all into a little secret. The reason that every part of the rest of the world is not so, right now, is that in every other place there is a resistance of disharmony. In nature everything strains to evolve to a point of perfect harmony but it is our interference that causes the disruption. We too, are unable to achieve the physical form of perfect harmony because of the resistance of disharmony within us. This comes from our disharmonious thought processes as we offer negative resistance throughout our interactions. We covet, we complain, we try to possess; and worst of all we deny our own imperfection. We judge the darkness of others before ever judging the shadows in ourselves. The power to improve is within us. If we try always to adopt a naturally higher awareness we will attune to the prevailing higher positive vibrations around us. Likewise, in our higher state we are able more easily to detect any vibrations that are less positive and overcome them with harmonious motivated vibrations of light. This plus or minus process happens all the time, but we would take more notice if we understood how it worked.

I spoke earlier of the modified vibrations in structures and other places. Have you ever felt uneasy upon entering a strange building, when a shiver runs down your spine? Have you ever been in a social situation where instinct tells you that things are not as they seem? Conversely have you visited somewhere where you are elated by the surroundings? You may not realise it, but in these situations you are displaying your natural ability to *read* vibration. In the place we call home we unconsciously gather together all the things which are harmonious to us, so that our natural signature is enhanced by possessions of harmony. This is true for those of a higher or of a lower vibration. In our own environment we feel comfortable and secure as a result. But, we could be a whole lot more aware of differences in vibration and the story they can tell. The process is automatic until we understand how it works, when at last we can take full control of it and develop it a hundredfold.

As another example of the unconscious process at work, think of when we choose a holiday destination. Our choice depends upon a whole host of subliminal factors, but the bottom line is that we naturally seek out places which will harmonise with us at a far deeper level than anyone imagines. This leads upon arrival sometimes, to the feeling that it is somewhere you have always known. In all of these examples we are communicating at a vibrational level with everything around us. We experience vibrational affinity or resistance depending upon our vibrational compatibility. This examination of vibrational interchange neatly rounds us to the circumstance of close encounters

One to One

There is always a mutual vibrational response when two people meet for the first time, and it passes almost unnoticed for a lot of people. We each are responsible for our own level of awareness upon meeting someone. The vibrational response dictates the level of mutual compatibility between the two people. At its most extreme we immediately feel either very uneasy or completely at ease with someone. I have heard people say, *I can't stand her or him*, even though they don't even know the person! Unknown to them, a handshake of vibration has taken place that has determined the strength of resistance or harmony between the vibrations of both people. The person with the negative opinion has translated this silent recognition into an emotive negative response.

This can be taken a stage further. It is possible to walk into a crowded room and notice a stranger at the other side of the room, usually of the opposite gender, to meet eyes for a fleeting moment and immediately feel a oneness with them. An undeniable empathy has been felt between both people. The two people may never encounter each other again, or perhaps the harmonies at work will draw them into a further encounter and lead to a lasting relationship. The effect is real even when there is no conscious awareness of the process that is taking place. It is simply that there has been recognition of the strong vibrational harmony between them. A strong bond like this is essential for any partnership to be genuine and long lasting. Fast physical liaisons stem from primal urges, but they are determined to endure by the interaction of vibration at levels higher than the physical.

Higher vibrations eventually modify the physical form, but they affect interactions in many more subtle ways, as with music for example. Music can be inspirational or depressing. Music creates a mood and we take the effect for granted. We play music to suit our mood because its vibration sustains our mood at the time. It can be rightly stated that our choice of music gives a strong clue to our personal vibration. To put it bluntly, a spiritually, highly elevated person, would seek out mainly inspirational music while a blockhead would seek out musical confusion commensurate with their mind-set.

Music, or collective sound, exists not as physical matter, but as a physically detectable collection of higher frequencies. Music exists nearer to the nature of higher matter than to physical matter. As such it also has great power. The strength gained from inspirational music is healing. Powerful musical harmonies *actualise* refined energy which can be strong enough to realign negative vibrational frequencies. When feeling depressed, the inclination is to play music which fits the mood, and incidentally maintains it, instead of playing inspirational music to lift the depression.

The study of vibrational effect upon animals is another very special case. They too operate within the laws of the universe alongside us. Their worldly level is not below ours; it simply functions at a *different* level. Mutual benefit can be derived from our interaction with animals if we can follow their natural ability to read vibration. Animals are not encumbered with higher intellect and act according to instinct. They act according to *their* natural conditioning and have a full awareness of vibrational forces; depending upon the species for strength of ability. A dog which is harmoniously bonded with its owner, and is able to read situations way ahead of its owner's suppressed powers, can be a life saver. This is a simple example, and the stories are legendary of dogs being able to read the probability of situations way ahead of the event. It would be against common sense for me to seek examples of the higher awareness of animals to illustrate the point. Everyone has heard such stories. Suffice to say that when we refer to any animal and their remarkable powers of intuition, we can now see that their ability is the result of their closer affinity to higher levels of vibration. In the animal kingdom there are differences of higher awareness within their groupings. We know of the remarkable powers of the higher animals such as dolphins, or the apes, or in dogs and even pigs. This is just as it is in human society. Our directions from the beginning have led to groupings of population where a faster esoteric evolvement has taken place. More individuals in such a society are advanced in their vibrational development and have a greater gnosis to match.

We have taken a hard look at the source, the workings and some of the practical effects of vibrational forces. We have examined how a reaction or interaction is created between them. We have leapt from Quantum theory to everyday events in human terms. We have seen how the actions of vibrational forces, which operate and interchange close to our physical world—form only a tiny part of the whole picture. A glimmer of understanding now opens the door to explanation for so many everyday effects in our physical world. We shall return to many more of these later, but for now I would ask you to ponder these summations . . .

We have all heard of having a sixth sense or having an instinct for something. Well up until now you may only have thought of communication in physical terms; like telephone, speech, the written word etc. Can you now see that communication at the physical level is actually only as sophisticated as two tin cans and a tight string compared to the vast instantaneous communication that takes place at a higher level. Having sixth sense, or an instinct, or inspiration, or spontaneous empathy or revulsion etc, occurs out of higher science *beyond* quantum.

Vibrational movement does not respect distance or time as we know it. Everything, everywhere is in a state of constant universal communication. Recall our Quantum discussions. Do you remember how I described the difference of opinion which centred on the effect of Electron pairs? Einstein reminded Bohr that nothing travels faster than light and sought to emphasise the impossibility of communication between separated sub-atomic Electron particles. Bohr retaliated to remind Einstein of another rule. Separateness cannot exist for sub-atomic systems, otherwise the system is destroyed. So although it is possible to separate the natural pair of particles which form a sub-atomic system, their continued affinity and communication are assured, even if earth science cannot yet show how this works. Einstein's problem was that he had not freed his viewing point from the physical. Bohr and others; as the experiments of Alain Aspect demonstrated, they were able to reveal the possibility of faster than light instantaneous communication between particles. By implication, where all solid matter is composed of sub-particle matter, the same must be true at all levels of reality. In practical terms, if we could attune ourselves sufficiently, we need only touch the leaf of a tree to feel the sap rising from the ground and drawing up through the branches. We could feel the effect upon a leaf at the other side of the world from a tree destroyed at our feet. For now, we are lucky to be developed sufficiently for example, to merely sense personal danger ahead of an event; or to sense the distress to a close family member, many miles away. The greater potential atmosphere encompasses everything. It is comprised of infinite parts which are themselves the whole, just as with the inseparable, separated particles of the scientists. Physical matter is simply a condensation of vibrating matter forming a miniscule temporary reality within the whole picture. The world of vibration itself just *is*. No part of it can be affected but that every other part is capable of instant awareness. The vibrational world is flux. It is Potential. It is Virtuality, and all parts are accessible.

Hopefully I have provided you with a sufficient basis to start putting the rules of vibrational interchange to the test yourself. Think of situations. Switch to vibrational sight and try to work out exactly what is going on. The rules are universal so just seek out the interpretations appropriate to the situation. Test it and try it yourself before we move into deeper waters.

At this point, a proof reader friend said, *I'd like to test it but I don't know where to begin*! He was stuck. He didn't know how to enter the grey area between known-science and higher-science and was unable to relate it to mundane situations. Unfortunately, for so long we have been satisfied to stereotype the area beyond known science using familiar words and ideas like *The Paranormal* or the *Spiritual*. It is almost as if when we discuss things beyond known science we have become programmed only to accept intangibles. I am presented something old in a new way which is tangible and challenges all stereotypes of faith and spirit. Effectively by laying bare the workings of vibrational effect, the comfort blanket of conditioning is removed and this will naturally cause resistance. Any paradigm shift in thinking is a traumatic process, but the potential gain should outweigh any reluctance to test it yourself. The fact that you may have not yet discovered and understood the workings of a higher reality does not invalidate its existence. Ignorance is a self-inflicted condition.

I asked you to begin testing things for yourself, but I guess it is for me to start the ball rolling with an answer my friend's question. So I will expand the theme with a few more thoughts. All Religions herald a greater place beyond this world. Where do you imagine this universal understanding comes from? Why have none of them been able to give a tangible description of what it is like there? Is it not reasonable to presume if we have an inbuilt distant memory of this place and that some actual laws of physics must govern it? Could we stretch things more and say, if there is such a level of reality and we have lost our ability to discern it, there must be good reason. Something lost can usually be retrieved provided we have the tools. I hope I have started the process. Think of all of the Esoteric or paranormal mysteries you have ever heard about. Begin to consider them in the terms we have examined so far. Struggle to fully understand my explanations so far and apply them to these unanswered questions. See how the intangibility gives way to valid reality. I know I am asking you at an early stage to reconsider ingrained ideas, but I am tackling a barrier that has been formed over eons of time and which has almost blocked out the light. I have barely removed a few bricks from the wall. I seek to stir everyone out of their complacency right now to begin to examine the most neglected but most important thing in the life of everyone. It needs a fundamental shift in the way we look at things and perhaps this next chapter will better demonstrate what I mean.

Learning by Curves

I remember reading a particular science fiction story as a youngster. It was written by one of the famous science fiction authors but I cannot recall his name. In the story several of the top scientists in the world were suddenly uprooted from their jobs and families. With great secrecy, they were brought together at a covert research facility. Their expertise covered many disciplines from a background of space engineering and atomic research. It was explained to them that a film had been smuggled to them from a top-secret enemy establishment at great cost to life and resource.

A sombre mood filled the room as it was explained how the enemy had achieved the impossible, and in doing so now posed a most serious threat to the free world. The lights were dimmed and the film was shown to the expectant scientists. Despite its poor quality the content was unmistakable. They stared open mouthed at the military demonstration of an amazing new aircraft. It was several meters long, shaped like two saucers stuck together in a classic UFO shape. It was being controlled by a group of uniformed men who were positioned some distance away behind an impressive panel of switches, lights and buttons. There was no apparent means of power or propulsion. The craft managed to hover several feet above the ground, moving around on a small circular course to return to its starting point. As it landed, the upper part of the dome released and swung to one side. Despite the obscure angle of the film it was still possible to see the array of instruments inside. The film ended and the stunned silence was finally broken as the Director stood to address them all.

'Gentlemen,' he said, *'Our enemies have indeed created the first anti-gravity propulsion system for a flying craft. They have achieved the impossible! We have brought you together for obvious reasons. You represent the best minds in science we have to offer. You will be given every resource so that you can duplicate this achievement.'*

A sense of common purpose gripped the members of the new team. Their collective enthusiasm carried them through many difficult barriers. Days passed into weeks as they worked away at the problem. Finally, after some months, the science was solved and a prototype craft was ready for its first test flight. This craft was larger than the one shown in the original film. There was another difference. This craft was to be flown by a pilot from within the craft. The day of the test flight arrived and to the amazement of onlookers, the craft slowly lifted from the ground without a sound. It rose above the walls of the compound, flew around the perimeter walls and returned to gently land again at its starting point. There was an uproarious cheer. A short while later the entire team gathered together for the Director to give his personal thanks. His comments aroused shock, amazement and then feelings of great satisfaction—as a realisation hit them. The Director had said,

'Ladies and Gentlemen; Impossibility exists only for those who believe in it. We deceived you all when we brought you here. The film you saw was a fake. There was no such thing as anti-gravity before you came here, but now there is!'

The moral of the story is appropriate. The impossible exists only for the ones who believe it to be so; or to put it another way, those who say they can't, are usually right!

So far our pathway has taken its direction from established physics and physical matter. We are ready to embrace *after-life*, but only if we have learned something from the short story. But, the understanding so far isn't quite adequate to provide the link needed for further progress. We have walked right up to and beyond the cutting edge of earth science, but the science fiction story shows us how we can use lateral thinking to move forward again. So, even if your mind is still closed to the possibility of life beyond life; or if you half believe but need more evidence; then humour me for a while. Just like the scientists in the story, please accept the following assumption. Presuppose again that there most certainly *is* another dimensional world from whence we came, and to which we return. Do this with an open mind, and I will present an explanation of its nature, character and purpose—sufficient that you will concede a perfect fit with everything I have dealt with so far.

Perfectly Normal Afterlife

An Afterlife World! O.K. So where is it? This is a fundamental question that must be answered. Back we must go, and make use our extraordinary vibrational sight. Our next viewing point is from some distance in space away from the Earth surface. Hitherto we would have only seen the clear classical view of Earth as if from a Space Station. With vibrational sight we are bathed in an ambient sea of movement reaching far beyond us from the planet's surface. The Earth itself can be seen as a colossal amalgamation of vibrating plasma filled with rippling impulses of movement everywhere and in every direction. Every part of space is in a state of flux just like Aurora Borealis, but constant, everywhere, and way beyond our known limits of the electromagnetic spectrum. We can discern the interference patterns of the magnetic field, which seem like a living gossamer—web of fluctuating energy.

Hold this thought because I want to say something before we go much deeper into the scene. It is important for us to have a recap and consider some other important implications. Sorry about this but it really is necessary. Very soon we will have reinforced all the process involved, and then it will be plain sailing.

Briefly we have to go back to earth physics again. I have explained how beyond the smallest known particles; the neutrons, photons and gluons etc., the greater volume of space exists as a dynamic plasma which is more refined than any known atomic particle. This refined medium reacts not only at sub-atomic level but also throughout all physical matter. This refined Virtual substance is the greater medium within which gross matter coagulates. Sub-atomic particles are a coagulation of this vibrational substance. By simple deduction we and everything else physical, are also a coagulation of the same substance. The vibrational signature of all physical matter is projected out into the cosmos. This reflects all interactions, motivations, and events originating from the host. The signature field is in a state of flux as it absorbs the modifications of all interactions. Here is an extreme example that will surely hammer the point home.

Someone indulges in an act of gross deviance. From the moment the person forms the thought to carry out the act, they are providing the motivation that will draw substance from Virtuality. The process begins and immediately the energy of the drawn substance will register according to its vibration within the energy field (the vibrational signature) of the host. There will be an instant expansion or in this case, compression of the negative host frequency. If the person continues to feed this activity the effect will be more permanent. Think of it like water dripping on to sand. Eventually the water finds a pathway, which erodes into a rut, which erodes into a stream etc. Habitual or addictive behaviour reinforces the negative signature of the person. The negative impulse gains strength from the sensational indulgence of its originator. The empowered negative character-impulse will be strong enough to strengthen any other similar frequencies in the aura. As negative hotspots develop within the energies of the person, they must find a way to be discharged. The host becomes filled with the urge to pursue the deviation, and at best a habit is formed. At its worst if the person seeks continuing negative affinity, their behaviour may escalate to unacceptable deviance. The aura records it all as a constantly modifying vibrational signature, as it does for all things.

We have looked at the passage of a freed Photon, which describes the conditions for a single particle. I would like to clarify the means by which larger packets of knowledge or information maintain their impulse through matter and space. Supposing someone raises a strong desire-thought for help. Well ok if you wish, we'll say they are either consciously or subconsciously sending out a prayer for help. Once again at the start of the process, thoughts motivate! Fresh energy is actualised from Virtuality, and within the sender's aura a vibrational hotspot is created. The hotspot has an identity that corresponds to the frequencies created by the prayer. The hotspot has been given the impetus to transmit its encoded information in an identity burst, out into surrounding space and matter. It would be easy to say it shoots off in some direction like a bullet seeking a destination. However, it doesn't quite work that way.

We are back again to Wave/Particle Duality. The existence of the hotspot immediately causes the surrounding substance to register its Presence as an instantaneous ripple. I previously used the poor analogy of balloons in a bag to indicate how shock waves transfer through them without the loss of their individual integrity. Try another idea. Think of the hotspot as the first coin in a long line of coins end to end, flat on a frictionless surface. We tap the Hotspot coin at one end of the line and at the other end, the reaction is felt instantly when the last coin shoots away. It has become a vibrational/energy clone of the first coin. The hot spot was created and its signature was transmitted to be recorded at any point as a clone of its originator. Over its entire surface area the flux of movement represents the collective frequency of the hotspot itself. Its natural impetus discharges its identity in all directions into the infinite space. So, given suitable powers of detection, it would be possible at a destination point anywhere to capture and decipher the original prayer thought. With those updates, let us return to the story . . .

We look deeper to the surface of the Earth and the curtains are drawn from our eyes. We penetrate closer to the surface through infinite colours and rippling intensities. The movement of energy around us reacts in immediate response to the changing condition of their sources and to the feedback of a million other colliding vibrations. Deeper and deeper we go until finally we can see the effect of people going about their business.

Every person is surrounded by a field of light which is swirling with colour and changing intensity; each a unique vibrational signature. All churn with the virtual information of the complete human Presence who owns it. From some of them we occasionally see a flash of movement as a thought signal transmits itself outward as a hot-spot of energy. In fact as we widen our awareness we find the entire surrounding plasma is infused with overlapping impulses of deafening intensity. The area closest to the surface of the planet is almost like a buffer zone or clearing station for impulses as they instantly register everywhere, reaching out far beyond our present position.

The greater space continues to infinity and contains infinite levels of density. Beyond the level of our viewing point there are greater regions of finer and finer matter. We have been viewing from a point where movement is closest in vibration to physical matter. In our scenario we have been viewing from a level of reality just beyond physical. If we were viewing from the next level, the same could be said of the distance between there and our present viewing point. I use the word distance figuratively. As we have already seen, the vibrational substance of refined matter beyond quantum occupies the same space as physical matter. In the same way, other regions of greater refinement can occupy the very same apparent space as regions of lower refinement. When an impulse of any kind advances beyond our position, it is simply saturating out into greater space to reach its naturally occurring compatible vibrational level.

We will now select one of the impulses flashing before us to see where it leads. The sender of the impulse may not even know of its destination. From what we have learned so far we know that the ultimate destination point may be anywhere. We wish to follow it to its conclusion without having to dash about in space in a mad search for the recipient. The transmission of the impulse is instantaneous. When an appropriate recipient (at a higher level of reality) picks up the impulse, the impact of the pickup is *also* transmitted instantaneously as an impulse. We do not have to dash about in a search, because when we link to an impulse we are also instantly aware of its intended recipient. So let us use a specific example and see where it takes us.

Meeting the Abyss in Real Time

We focus, and in a split second we become one with the reality of a specific impulse. In a further split second we have travelled to the source of the impulse. We share the sensation of reckless movement in a vehicle. We have become attuned to the vibration of the man at the wheel. Gan is driving along a country road at great speed and with complete disregard. Our view is objective, but we can read his senses. His aura is filled with furious movement. Few bright colours can be seen. Dark crimson and muddy grey flashes swirl around him creating a halo of confusion. His perceptions become our perceptions. Gan's Business is struggling to survive. He has been working excessively for many months to save it. His first marriage failed some time ago and flashback memories disturb his mind. He is filled with anguish from the severe difficulties in his current relationship and he can barely make ends meet. He has not seen his own adult sons for many months. His divorced wife, who recently died of heart failure, was closer to their sons; but she is no longer here to help them emotionally. In his current relationship he is dealing with new stepchildren and all the conflicts of emotion that go with the situation. The problems have been affecting them too. He cannot see anyway forward. He is mentally and physically exhausted and feels as if he is staring into the abyss. His aura is dark and murky but extends a great distance from his physical form. This shows how he has undergone considerable spiritual development. Unfortunately, the input from his dire material world has created an overload of negative energy. The negative hot-spot within his aura threatens to smother his spirit.

He has driven to a remote, heavily wooded area. We are impressed by his feelings as he steps from the parked vehicle and gulps clumsily from a large whisky bottle. He wanders away, stumbling half senseless through the undergrowth. He pauses to stuff the fist-full of pills from his pocket into his mouth. He crunches them manically and pours the remaining alcohol into his mouth. He is tripping and falling; mumbling and screaming to himself incoherently. His mind and voice follow the newsreel in his mind which reinforce all the negative events in his life.

His has allowed the negativity in his life to take over, and this destructive force has compressed every positive aspect he has. His brain registers the smell of damp bracken and woody soil. He stumbles and falls, stumbles and falls. Finally he rolls from a last fall on to his side, propped clumsily against a tree stump. Dark emotions envelop him. His spiritual triumphs are denied and replaced with despair and hopelessness. His senses become dulled. His self-pity is complete. His aura is shrinking and becoming denser. The energies are feeding upon themselves. We are able to discern individual impulses. We are able to see how one very small but brightest part of his aura strains to escape the grip of his dark compressed vibrational field. These are the brightest energies, constrained and pressured now to a small area centred on his heart. As he slumps to unconsciousness, his mouth opens to issue a silent scream of '*God Help Me.*'

The last motivation is all that was needed. The hotspot of super compressed positive energy blasts free and radiates its identity and message into the greater space of virtuality, like an explosion of compressed air from the depths of the ocean. Out of abject despair he has sent out his distress signal. We link our perceptions to the speeding impulses and find our awareness passing through regions of finer and finer material. The brightness of this more refined matter is dazzling. We quickly adjust and shapes take form around us. The substance surrounding us is as far removed from the physical as air is to water. Our vision becomes more comfortable and an amazing scene confronts us stretching further and further into the distance. Our first impression is of vivid, glowing, florescent, living colour.

Visualise a flower; a Violet for example. Visualise the deep velvet violet colour of the petals. Stretch your imagination and think of the petals producing their own colour as if to be liquid light. The living colour seems as if when you touch it, your fingers would penetrate into the surface like fingers into water. Try to imagine the flower as if caught in the process of emerging from the air around it. From such a picture you may visualise a fraction of how everything actually appears. Absolutely everything we perceive at this heightened level of refinement has a similar vibrancy.

We find ourselves standing on a gentle grassy bank by the side of a rising trackway. The track meanders downhill for some distance, veering to the right as it follows the hillside. Gleaming outcrops of mountain stone are exposed occasionally from the verdant grass. The glowing grey of the stone blends with beautiful contrast to the vivid green of the grass. Fine powdered shale forms the track. The side verges are lush with wild flowers coloured blue and snowy white. The track disappears from view in the foreground and appears again some lower distance away, snaking down through the cleft of the far valley. We are able to make out a small stream as it spills lazily from the hillside to join the track. Millions of glittering shafts of light pierce our eyes from the moving surface of the distant water. In the far distance the track and stream merge into movement. Together, they have become a fine silver thread on the landscape and blend to the background as they disappear out of sight.

We turn our backs to the valley and look upward to the skyline where we lose sight of the track once again. It rises gently before us and seems to begin levelling some half a mile away.

The road rises with the ground and sweeps slowly to the left. Very close to us on our right there are magnificent Birch trees marking the start of a sentinel line which flanks the road. There is no breeze, but the leaves shimmer as if touched by a silent wind. Their colours are the colours of Autumn. Orange, amber and gold blaze their light together, as if it is a living flame that is decorating the air. The track fades from view as a large building rises from it. Its style would blend as well in the Austrian Tyrol as in the Scottish highlands. Majestic towers and battlements compete with the comical eccentricity of elaborate cantilevered balconies along the lower walls. Elevated walkways span sections of the ramparts to complete the effect of a deliberate fantasia. Even from this distance it is possible to pick out the elaborate woodcarvings everywhere. From our position the building is obscured by the hillside but gives the impression of great extent, and its warm countenance beckons us to draw closer.

We are distracted however by movement nearby in such way that is hard to describe here. A section of the air or atmosphere is becoming brighter and brighter. Imagine a camera photoflash in slow motion. We must avert our eyes as it peaks in brightness and slowly diminishes, and a human form slowly takes shape from within it. A man now stands before us, less concerned by our presence than we are of his. His look is preoccupied as he gazes with concentration into the distance. His apparel is light in colour and hangs loose about his body, like a baggy Chinese jacket and pantaloons. A red braided chord is brought together in a complex knot at his waist and simple slippers cover his feet. He is clean-shaven with youthful looks, though his frame and bearing suggest older years. His head is bare and his straight sandy hair falls loosely beyond his ears to his neckline.

Did you notice how we now stand in this account together, you as reader and I who have manufactured the story line? I stand with you as observers in the story and supply the description for us to continue. But now we must rise by another level. We must become interactive! Presently the stranger breaks his thoughts and turns to meet our gaze. He wishes to speak to us directly.

'You are visitors to this region. Hitherto it has served a purpose that you act as detached observers. Such detachment still serves its purpose, but if you came here to study the conditions and way of things, it is necessary for your understanding that you now become subject also to the laws of physics which prevail here. You read from the page, yet this reality from within the page, is becoming your reality. Thought is reality and is as valid as the effect derived from it. Our desire is to fully understand the possibilities of vibrational interaction. The Author of these words and the medium of the book remove you twice distant from the environment we describe, but by the laws governing vibrational field connections we stand side by side right now as you read on. There is much still to learn.'

'In my natural state, my home is a realm existing at higher refinement than the place we now find ourselves. Its beauty surpasses all things described to you thus—far but itself is only a shadow of yet greater lands. A short while ago you would have been dazzled by my appearance. It took a few moments for me to adjust my vibration to the lower frequencies prevailing. Yonder is my house. When travellers are ready they pass from this region through its doors and are helped to become acclimatised there, before rising to a permanently higher state. Other communities await the arrival of each wayfarer to welcome him or her with new delights and options. For anyone not yet prepared, an approach would only bring the discomfort of not belonging. If you were to be suddenly thrust beyond the doors, your experience of all things around you would be as my first appearance was to you here. There would however, be no adjustment of awareness unless you were ready. My home serves as a way—station, or academy for those who must progress to other levels. It is one among many, each dealing with specialities of life—science, but all working in unison towards a common goal. For now we must turn our attention and prepare to follow a far more urgent purpose. My colleagues and I detected an urgent signal from someone who holds special interest for me. You must appreciate and understand that for everyone who journeys in the physical world there are those of us here who are charged with the duty of keeping an eye on them constantly. We act to help and guide them when needed. We attend to any requests for assistance, provided the request does not contravene the natural laws of physics as they operate from this side of the material world. We could be understood in your terms as Social workers on a different level. I must attend to many clients and Gan is but one of them. Many of us consider with amusement, how vast the belief is in American Indian Guides. Much of the activity here is in the nature of teaching and in the administration of creative forces. A vast array of helpers across the globe is intensely involved with this. They may also be termed Minders, Guides, Watchers or Social workers. I am sorry to inform you, there would not be enough people from the noble Native American Indian race to provide sufficient cover for everybody. We work warmly across the world with native peoples in our midst. They form part of an army of guiding helpers for those passing through their physical life.'

'We gather now to deal with Gan. You picked up his despairing cry for help. My colleagues and I were attuned and so became instantly aware of his plea. You were focussed on his life and find yourselves in my company to see the workings of an answer. Now we must journey awhile.'

Moving down the track it is hard to disguise a feeling of surprise at our movement. We are not now actually walking in the physical sense. We travel forward perfectly naturally at walking pace but some slight distance above the ground. If we wished we could indeed walk in the normal sense. We need only attune ourselves to the refinement level of the matter around us. Thought is action here too and with a simple shift of frequency and motivation we appear to defy the laws of physical gravity. We continue forwards while below us the valley is becoming misty. The duller light closes toward us and we begin to enter the haze. The light is now suppressed and seems more like twilight. We move forward for what seems to be a considerable time, but in distance only seems to have been a few hundred yards. Shadowy forms appear ahead of us. It is possible to trace the outline of roughly built dwellings nearby. A row of houses border the roadway, separated by narrow garden strips. The gardens are unkempt. Amateur attempts have been made here and there to cultivate plants and grasses, but little care has been taken with any detail. Further ahead a group of people gather in the gloom. They have noticed us and hold back in suspicion. As we draw closer they slowly retreat in alarm. We are able to hear their excited tones as they point in our direction and scurry together to the opposite side of the road. They have turned into a side road, now shielding and averting their eyes from us. As we pass them, their conversation becomes more alarming. Suddenly, as if by collective decision, they have broken into a panic and scatter in several directions away from us. Tiredness overcomes us. In adherence with conditions we are forced to rest awhile in order to acclimatise. It is a chance for us also to catch up with a few more facts. Our guide addresses us again.

'For the people we encountered; we appeared to them as a painfully bright collective Presence. We must have seemed quite other worldly, just as I did to you when we first met. Their understanding of their condition and their grasp of the situation was insufficient for them to overcome their fear in order to accept us. So it is as we draw closer to the physical world, or Earth Plane. At each graduation of lower frequency we must acclimatise to become natural or acceptable to the level we wish to visit. The actual process involves us gathering by power of mind, the substance from the potential of the atmosphere surrounding and infusing us, in order to condense our vibration to surrounding levels.'

'I hear your thoughts! You wonder that you are not consciously motivating substance from the surround. It is so. By virtue of us motivating on a cause that takes us to lower vibration it is enough for new substance to gather to us. There is a stark difference between the states of substance on the physical plane and the states of substance existing beyond. An observer may conclude that the laws of physics operate from either side of a dividing line. This is an illusion. Knowledge of atomics at vibrational level and of the glorious interchange is sufficient for us to see how everything is intrinsically linked. Residents of other regions much like those we encountered, live beyond the physical plane, but now perceive an illusionary divide between themselves and yet higher realms. There are no dividing lines except in the mind.'

As we look around us, a change has been taking place that we hardly noticed. As if emerging from the twilight to dawn and an awakening day, it has become light. In fact it is we who have changed state and are now normalised once again to our lower surroundings. The light reveals a large stone courtyard. We have negotiated the arched entrance held aloft by rough-hewn stone blocks. Stone walls form an enclosure on three sides, rising above head height. On one of the sides, a second arched entrance gives way to an ample grassy meadow. All sorts of people come and go about their business quite unconcerned. The fourth walled side to the courtyard is broken with a flight of several wide and well-worn steps leading to an adjoining building. This house is more conventionally built, standing three floors high and decked with a pitched tile roof. There are few windows to interfere with the lines of rough-cut stones and nothing is remarkable but the considerable feeling of antiquity emanating from the entire place. Decoration or adornment is confined to the prolific lichen growth covering many surfaces. Abutting the walls we can see stone benches lined out for our convenience. We select a bench next to the water pool in one corner of the yard. The pool is fed by a steady trickle running from a water spout in the wall and extensive moss growth covers the stonework around it. An overflow gully can be seen to carry the water further along the wall and into the meadow. The water sparkles like a stream of liquid diamond. As we rest, our guide wishes to speak with us again. He ponders for a moment, fixes his gaze upon us and continues . . .

A Challenge to Reality

'Do you realise what is happening to you as you read the descriptions in this book. Your perceptions and parameters of reality are being challenged. My reality is here and now as I prepare with other helpers to tackle the problems presented by Gan. You accompany me as real-time observers to witness the processes involved, and as such you have joined with and accepted my reality. Can these words be considered invalid because they have also been channelled through the author? What is more important; the medium or the message? If thought is first cause, then the reality reaching to you from this page is as valid as the actual book bringing the explanations. Vibrational energies cannot be prevented from discharging their power and message, regardless of the medium. An earth scientist may disagree. His reality has a fixed parameter. His accepted reality must withstand physical tests and calculations. His instruments are bound by physical limitation. The scientist sets a parameter which is constantly moving and expanding. He nibbles at the edges of physical knowledge, making small advances but restrained by the limits of his own viewing point.'

'Think of a small dog sniffing along the ground. It is intent on sniffing all the wonderful smells to be found at every blade of grass. Its recognition is so focussed to the task that it fails to see the obstacle ahead and bumps straight into it. If it had been possible for the small dog to have had a wider viewing point which included the potential for other things along the way, it would have caught the smells and would have anticipated beyond its previous experience. If Earth knowledge has relied upon a ponderous nibbling forward from the edge of understanding, then by such meticulous method why have so many unsolved mysteries of life been left behind? It would seem that an overwhelming number of mysterious issues have been neatly sidestepped along the way. People have always wanted to know the secrets of the universe. Why are we here? Where did we come from? What is the purpose to everything? Science may have produced an advance in technology, but very little understanding has emerged about the more fundamental questions. Furthermore, where something cannot be quantified nor qualified; or where something defies examination; then at best the issue is side stepped. At worst, the issue and anyone who speculates upon it, have been reviled, denied, ridiculed or suppressed. Whole nations have been horrifically subdued in this way. There are many instances in Earth's history, where limited science and ignorance lead to unspeakable horrors. More recent discoveries of earth science often defy and totally contradict implacable

earlier ideas; but we still applaud ignorance. It is a contradiction in terms when the earth scientist promotes the furtherance of his craft by objective examination, while clinging to subjective expectation. To do so simply narrows the viewing point to a small dot when precisely the opposite is desirable. The things of which I speak are most important when the greater issues of life, the universe and everything, are being debated or examined. Any true enlightenment in this direction would open our understanding to the glorious purpose and interaction of everything.'

'Let us speculate the result, if freedom of expression were given for ideas and beliefs to be given space in the laboratory. Would chaos ensue? Would the world become overwhelmed with fools ruining the progress of science? Many foolish notions on the nature of things have roots in superstition for example. The vibrational frequencies are increasing at every level. As people try to find reason in it all—supposition and conjecture come before reason. More are seeking answers as they awaken to their higher mind. It will take time before truth and reality are understood for what they are. I will tell you of the process that takes place in the development of a Presence in physical form. Ignorance challenged by change creates unrest, and unrest seeks rebalance through familiarity. Familiarity demands understanding, but understanding begs questions. Questions bring answers, and answers lead to realization. Realization generates Awareness and kindles faith. Faith seeks corroboration and corroboration requires development. Development follows experience and experience provides conviction. Conviction needs strength, but strength builds through introspection. Introspection raises Scars and they are the food of compassion. Compassion is the banner of humility, while humility is the heart of Love. Love is the Soul of Spirit. We achieve it through tested experience. We wait here to see you stumble forward and to help when asked, or where we can, knowing that every stumble you make, is a leap towards enlightenment.'

'In the process, how then can such an expected mixture of ideas be examined seriously without discrediting the pathway to discovery? The answer to this conundrum is fairly simple. It seems that many ideas seeking to explain the nature of things only operate within set parameters. Such ideas require other ideas to conform to manufactured rules, or risk becoming discredited and condemned. This can exclude the nature of whole sections of society.'

'Any valid belief therefore, must be capable of embracing everyone and everything. Universal understanding can only come from universal explanation. It is a simple test of belief. If an idea or belief excludes one group or way of thinking, for the benefit of another, it is not universal and fails at the start. Most religions of the world have a basis in love and harmony to embrace all things. Over the years, the administrators of these religions have invariably added their own interpretations, which then exclude others who disagree. In this

way they have created exclusive groups which in turn give them power over their disciples. Their religions may have been founded in a Law of One, but become corrupt to the possibility of one truth. Eons ago everyone understood. The understanding was lost and then stolen, but the awakening has begun again.'

'In discussing the nature of all things an explanation must be free of all bias and bigotry. An understanding is valid if it is capable of embracing every awkward question, even though it may extend beyond current accepted science. If the idea or understanding passes this basic test, then it is worthy to be examined seriously by the scientists. A tenet or belief system does not exist without physical effects that challenge scientific thinking. It is these effects then that the scientist may look at to see where the gap can be closed between them and current scientific understanding. A little lateral acceptance is needed first, just like the scientists in the author's previous UFO story. Then, instead of just nibbling at the edge of understanding, the scientists could make reasonable assumptions based upon the idea and see if the physics will fit. In the same way through these pages, we endeavour to take you beyond your own limits, with a universal understanding that has no limits. By reverse explanation we hope you will join all the points together and make your own progress to understanding. I am going to give an example of the power in the test I describe'

'To a greater or lesser degree, very many of the world religions say, Our God is the true God. If you do not follow the doctrine of our God you will be damned. If you do not yield to our teachings you are a heathen or infidel. You will be banished or punished. Our God is omnipotent. Our God is omnipresent and we are the one voice of his word, his laws and his teachings. Well, consider this thought: If someone's God is omnipotent, and therefore encompasses everything; their God must also surely encompass the unbeliever. After all, omnipotent is final. The proponents of any one version of God slander their own belief if they simultaneously exclude non-believers. I must reiterate; a worldly understanding must fail if it is exclusive or seeks to contain in any way. When no flaws can be found, then earth physics and mathematics will surely catch up to give full explanation for the resulting effects.

Unwinding the Connections

Aaron our guide, continues,

'Now someone approaches and we still have an urgent task in hand. Fiona is an old friend of mine who can help us with our problem. She would be regarded both ancient and wise by earth standards, having lived many earth lives. She dwells permanently beyond the physical plane and comes to us from a Region far away.'

Her long yellow robe of gossamer fineness and quality seems to flow noiselessly with her movements. A narrow braided belt of interwoven colours gathers at the waist with a clasp, set with a sparkling sapphire stone. Her hair is long and dark with a hint of redness in the light. She arrives before us, standing dignified and tall. Her Presence radiates power and tranquillity. Her first words set the mood as she addresses Aaron.

'Once again my friend there is work we must attend.

She turns in our direction and with deliberation begins to explain.

'In another Realm far away from here there are those of us who have been closely following the events in the life of Gan even as they are at this moment unfolding. As you must now understand, our viewing point is wide indeed and the good souls who work on this side have been able to examine the multitude of circumstances having a bearing on the situation. From there, helpers, such that are needed, have already been directed to action on our behalf. You have undoubtedly felt the urgency in my Presence to move ahead speedily with the task. The urgency I convey is simply an urgency of purpose and not urgency of time; for time as you understand it is a physical measure. In the physical world, the urgency of time is real, for all things there are measured to the cycle of birth and decay. The physical state is a transitory experience measured on the earth plane against the parameter of time. This parameter is another false constraint which disallows the validity of physics beyond the Earth limits of time. When the senses evolve to see beyond the barrier of physical time, all things will be accepted as transitory to higher evolvement. Time could be regarded as a separate dimension, allowing events in space to be measured by their interval, thus proving useful to understandings at the physical level. The difficulty for the earthbound viewer is that nothing can apparently exceed the speed of light—which is transient between measurable points, so then arguably how can matter exist at less than the atomic level and escape beyond the speed of light? This is a seemingly impossible barrier to the understanding of

higher processes. If the evolution of state begins and continues beyond the birth and decay process; then adherence to the boundaries of earth science must inevitably deny complete understanding. Beyond physical matter, refined vibration and matter exists by the rule of higher physics. Higher rules are entirely compatible with known rules on the earth plane. They simply operate to be examined from different viewing points. Quite simply therefore, the transmission of information here is instantaneous. The fact that nothing physical can exceed the speed of light is also irrelevant here.'

'The author has kept a sense of timed urgency for purposes of delivery in the unfolding story of Gan. We shall continue to appreciate the physical urgency of Gan's situation but behind the scenes we shall continue to mull the understandings necessary to resolve things.'

As Fiona pauses, Aaron adds to our lesson.

'While we ponder these important issues, you may wish to consider something else. You may now understand how Fiona has come to us from another Realm. As we arrived at this place together we also appeared to the residents here as visitors from a higher Realm—and you all saw how we affected them. The effects of the vibrational world are truly wondrous. From beyond the physical, the virtual atmosphere encompasses everything to infinity. In the physical it is only possible to liken the living movement within it by imagining a complex mirage on the skyline for example; or by feeling the varying densities and quality of the air as we pass from ground to sky. Vibrational substance evolves from its peak at unimaginably sublime levels, reaching down through infinite variations of refinement until finally emerging at the point of physical matter to continue the cycle yet again.'

'On Earth, the populations of the world are organised according to a multitude of factors. Some of the more obvious include, Genetic Disposition; Local and National Environment; Historical Separations; Language; Technological Progress; Existential Beliefs, and so on. If we were to randomly select from all communities across the world, we would always find a mixture of what we would call, the good and bad of character. What do you think is meant therefore by good and bad?'

'You will have already grasped that all things from Virtual to Atomic to gross matter, exist as part of a cyclical process. In the physical, a cycle operates from Atomic to gross matter and back through decay to Atomic Matter. This however is not sufficient to explain the divine seniority of mankind or how it relates to bad and good.'

'The physical world is a temporary reality but is an intrinsic part of the greater reality. A vast interchange of communication takes place at all times throughout. Thereby, the conscious and unconscious thoughts of people in every Realm are reflected in the living environment they create for themselves. At every higher level there are those who are charged with the welcome task of overseeing everything at a lower vibrational level. Mankind carries a

divinity, motivated from the most sublime level. Mankind's life and development are modified by the quality of choice in everything it motivates. Whether Man realises it or accepts it, their situation at any moment is as a result of the greater and lesser choices along the way.'

'Our needs, our desires, our aspirations, translate into Vibrational impulses to form a cumulative vibrational record of everything we do. Impulses of a higher nature reach to the levels harmonising with their frequency to summon help or inspiration where needed. Selfish, destructive or generally negative thoughts create negative impulses. Negative impulses attract those who dwell close to the level of gross matter. In this way there is the constant danger of earthbound souls interfering with the clearheaded thinking of a depressed, ignorant, wicked or selfish individual. The evidence of that speaks for itself. When people cling to gross vibration they reap the reward of its continued reinforcement and disruption in their lives. If we wish therefore to define good and bad, we have to be honest with ourselves and understand the process taking place. Understanding comes only when we adopt a very wide viewing point. Generally bad can be defined as the creation, or implementation of lower vibration from any negative reciprocal reaction. However all lower energy must eventually gravitate to higher levels; so we must also accept that bad is good which has not yet evolved! On the earth-plane the lower vibration guarantees that every process is constrained. Human Earth inhabitants represent all levels of development and by the natural laws of science must endure a mixed co-existence. It could be said that in physical life, all types exist in happy discord. The gravitation process to refinement is however, inevitable. The process of life can be likened to rough-cut gemstones in a polishing machine. When the machine is finally opened, all have been polished to a high degree, as in the life process for all eventually. In Realms beyond the physical where this story is being played out, the laws of higher physics operate differently. By analogy a cork tethered beneath the surface of water remains for what it is. If the cork is released it will float upwards until it finds its own level of gravitation. It may float to the surface or be trapped at an intermediary level if it contains impurities or if it has become waterlogged. So it is for inhabitants of regions beyond the physical where people occupy many levels of reality; each refined to their own natural level. Beyond physical death, there are guides, (or spirit Social Workers,) along with friends, family or other interested parties who may be there to greet a new arrival.'

'Consider this: If you were to step indoors from a rainstorm, it would take you a while to become warm and dry again and for you to balance with the new environment. When you pass beyond physical death, your helpers ensure that the vibrational influences are manipulated for you to get your bearings again. Despite all help, some souls cannot be awakened to the reality of their new circumstances. If their attachment to gross matter is so great, then by their own choice they will dwell and interact with others of similar disposition

until awakening occurs for them to move on. Beyond death there is no reason for physical matter to form a constraint and to continue to bind the person to a common level with all other types. In due course, full awakening to their new circumstances would follow their gravitation like the cork—to the realm or region compatible with their own vibration. Each person at whatever level of vibration would find themselves in territory and amongst people as real to them as was the physical. These Regions are vast to accommodate all versions from the earth-plane. Within higher Regions of greater evolvement, the differences between residents are less marked. Variations within the region would be harder to recognise. At lower levels it would be possible to see how inhabitants ranged in similar frequency from the lower level new arrivals, to those who had progressed sufficiently to move to the state of a yet higher Region as a new arrival there. The descriptions so far, conjure up a picture of these Regions or levels being stacked one upon another like boxes on a shelf. Not so. You must imagine space, and ever-greater space being simultaneously occupied at differing levels of vibrational refinement.'

'It would be impossible for someone from a lower Realm to suddenly appear in a higher Realm. The visitor would encounter a vibration so bright and powerful that it would cause them serious harm. Stand next to a five-bar electric fire when only one bar is lit and the heat would comfort you. Light up all five bars and you would soon jump back in pain. There is a circumstance where a lower level inhabitant can visit higher regions. This usually happens to special purpose and under the strict protection of higher guides who can manipulate the vibrations around them. Conversely, the occupants of higher regions very frequently work at denser levels. They are able to make use of their natural power to help resolve situations, while appearing natural to the lower level by borrowing from the denser vibrational substance around them. It would be within their power to appear as solid as the locals, or as a spectral entity just like a ghost to someone on the physical plane. In summary, a person displaced from their own level would immediately appear as a blinding presence in lower regions or as dark as night to higher regions. From the mists of earth time and the corrupt memory that has survived, there has been much confusion from the records. In an age long gone when peoples knew of the hierarchy of Presence, they were able to interact freely between the levels beyond physical. As a descent to sensation took place, the peoples retained their advanced knowledge but then perished as it was abused. The lower world looks back with confusion and ignorance having lost the ability to discern where the records refer to simply advanced physical people as gods—ascending or descending in advanced craft or actually physical people ascending and interacting with vibrationally higher spiritual realms.'

'It would be reasonable for you to speculate what happens when a low vibration person awakens from the death and rebirth to spirit process. As I have already described, they

eventually find themselves conveyed to a region among others of a much closer vibrational signature than the variations on the Earth plane. Where possible they will still be helped to attend the last rites of their memory in the ceremonies on the Earth plane. There may even be a time of assisted recuperation where helpers can neutralise the vibrations created from circumstances beyond the person's control. However, eventually the person's senses awaken to the new situation. For such a person, the memory of their Earth life will be suppressed within them, to the same degree that the living reality of the higher realms was suppressed to them in their Earth life. Paradoxically, the new life of closer affinity with others of a similar vibration actually helps to accelerate the vibrational development of the individual. It works like this: If you filled a house with liars and deceivers and forced them to live together, it would be hard for the individuals to act according to character without being challenged. Each person would be able to easily spot the liar and deceiver in the behaviour of others there. All would be constantly challenged or be the challenger when such bad behaviour occurred. Living in such an environment would defeat the negative power of each person. They would be no longer able to discharge their destructive energy because everyone would be carrying a similar vibration. In a similar analogy, a room full of alcoholics would soon spot another alcoholic in their midst despite any protestation to the opposite. Every worst effort would be frustrated until discomfort and dissatisfaction set in. The constant failure of their negative powers would generate restlessness. The individual would begin to examine their own motives and reasoning to discover the cause of their impotency. Sooner or later they would yearn for something better. They would begin to search for an alternative while rejecting all they had hitherto considered acceptable. An evolvement of spirit would be taking place as the vibrational field of the individual became more refined. The cycle would feed upon itself as it gathered momentum toward an inevitable higher gravitation. Just as on the Earth plane, the person's memory would slowly return in proportion to their capacity to accept the understanding of it. Helpers would have anticipated the timing of these important changes and would be ready to help the person move-house to a region of higher refinement. Once installed there, the process continues once again.'

Aaron has paused to give a short sigh of resolve,

'But now we really must return to deal with Gan. Fiona and I both have a special interest in him, because Amy, his current partner, has been under the care of Fiona for many years. Furthermore, we know both our charges personally. Both of them are personal friends from the realms beyond physical. Later I will deal more with the actual mechanics of the birth–death–birth cycle. Suffice to say at this stage that Amy and Gan have interacted together in previous life cycles, sometimes as members of the same family that we have also *been a part of. On this occasion, by their own choice and the action of synchronicity they have been drawn together again on a combined learning curve. Their dates of birth are separated by some years, but are otherwise identical. To this point, their lives have run their separate courses according personal circumstance; but have nevertheless developed on almost parallel tracks of vibrational experience. From the first time of meeting again together in this life, vibrational recognition took place and the bond was re-established for their lives to be interwoven again.*

Consider this: A person who has performed the same task for many years is not necessarily better at it than the person who is less experienced. Conversely, the person with less experience is not necessarily the lesser person for it. The only unyielding difference is that one person may have walked the pathway of experience longer than the other. It is by their own choice that their levels of vibrational refinement are greater or lesser; according to their own understandings. The frequency of two people may be almost identical but their vibrational difference could be described as very loud and less loud. So it is with Amy and Gan. Amy is less awakened to the presence and reality of the greater world and as such, is less receptive to the inspirational impulses from her helpers here. Ironically it is her partner Gan who has placed himself in dire trouble. The connection between them has ensured that Amy has already felt or sensed a great unease for the wellbeing of her partner. Her higher senses would have gone to red alert as she detected the discordant signals coming from Gan. It is with this knowledge we go now to Amy. The conditions are such that Amy's vibration will have been raised in response to the alert she has detected from Gan. With her raised vibration she will be receptive to our presence.

As Aaron concentrates, our state begins to change again. Our surroundings are darkening and there is a feeling of being dragged through space. Fiona is our leader for this last journey down through the levels of refinement to be with Amy. Fiona has been able to use her natural link with Amy to focus on her vibrational field. We have been drawn to her like an aircraft on an instantaneous homing beacon. The sensation of motion slows and as we again adjust to our surroundings, physical earth comes into view.

Amy, on the Earth plane, has just completed a call to her work client and is sitting in her car. Her unease is revealed by the worried look on her face. Anxiety is rising within her and she just knows something is terribly wrong with Gan. Her rational mind tells her the feeling is totally irrational; but she still cannot ignore it. The impulses of distress from Gan have reached out across Space to link to her. The task for Fiona and Aaron is clear. They concentrate and focus their power to Gan and Amy. The effect is immediate as the full intensity of Gan's signal for help is now felt by Amy.

She argues with herself no longer. She starts her car and begins to drive without knowing exactly why and with no planned destination. Fiona and Aaron are impressing route changes to her and she responds by driving far outside her normal route. The further Amy drives, the more her stomach churns with anxiety. She finds herself near woodland. The car is parked and she is drawn to walk amongst the trees. No other person is nearby, and the woods seem to close around her, but she carries forward. She halts abruptly as she spies Gan's vehicle parked untidily amongst the trees. Fiona and Aaron hold the connection to Amy as her heart begins to race and she hurries forward through the branches while calling loudly for Gan. She stumbles forward and stops once again as her calls are returned by a muted sound to the right. Her head turns sharply and there lies Gan slumped against a tree in the undergrowth. Miraculously she has found him!

Gan is in a stupor and is a heavy weight to Amy; but much power is being directed to them from us. Gan is retrieved and brought back to the home of Amy. She has smelled the alcohol and assumes he is just intoxicated. She is unaware of the large cocktail of drugs also taken. Her own state of mental exhaustion weakens the link to Fiona and Aaron and further warnings no longer have the same impact. Several other helpers appear at our sides. These powerful souls are those whom Fiona previously prepared for this possible outcome. Together their motivation directs a stream of harmonious energy towards Gan which acts upon his physiological systems. The pills would fatally damage his bodily systems but their destructive vibrational energy is being neutralised by the more powerful higher energies sent from our gathered band of helpers. The power permeates his entire system to restore order and Gan slips into a deep sleep, and finally, freed from his physical senses we are able to reach him more easily on a higher level. Fiona has interrupted our concentration to say something very important.

'A physical person has a Higher Self; but the term is much misunderstood. From Earth descriptions we could believe that the Higher Self is a detached consciousness that some can tap into. In fact if we go back to the basic descriptions given here already for the workings of matter in vibrational terms, we can reconstruct the true meaning. Firstly, the life force of a physical person is motivated by an inhabiting divine Presence. We already understand that the Presence is a coagulation of refined vibrational matter that functions as a group of several harmoniously circulating higher energies within the Presence of the person—which are the controlling counterparts for specific biological zones of the physical body. One of those circulations is of vastly more refined material which acts as an anchor to all others. It is tiny but powerful and is often referred to as The Divine Spark. It follows therefore that this circulation holds the vibrational connection to highest levels. The quality of that circulation does not vary between us, but each person's vibrational level determines how powerfully they

can tap into it. In waking life, the conscious mind is bombarded with sensational input from the physical senses and masks the route to Higher Self. However when the physical body is at complete rest, or in sleep, the physical senses stop distracting; except if the person's unconscious mind has to deal with a backlog of noise from the day. This depends upon the person's vibrational refinement, and hence their ability to deal well with things. In sleep therefore it is possible for us more easily to make contact with our higher self and return to a waking state with wisdom. The understanding does not stop there, because it is also possible for a higher part of the Presence to separate from the physical form. An almost unbreakable link remains between this higher (but more aware) part of us—and the quiet physical body. People describe this as an Astral body, and the link as a silver umbilical cord. In this state, travellers can communicate objectively with helpers from higher levels or gather all sorts of experience both good and bad, and return with it to conscious state. The process is sometimes referred to having An Involuntary Out of Body experience. A Voluntary experience can be achieved through deep meditation.'

Fiona allows our concentration to return to Gan. He appears to us in his Astral form. His expression is crestfallen and miserable. In recent times he has become totally bogged down with material and physical issues. His natural state is expansive and enlightened. This has changed as the lower vibrations of gross matter and their material considerations have condensed his aura and frequency. His vibrational field has been contracting to become denser in direct proportion to these things. His higher vision was obscured as he descended into danger and as the higher purpose of his Birth Plan was set aside. But at last he can be called to conference, with his friends and helpers! He is reminded of the Birth Plan he helped to choose and is shown how the denial of this higher purpose lead to this current situation. He is starkly reminded of how by reaching for refinement, the currents of positive force carry the soul to ecstatic heights, but when reaching to the depths, negative force drags the soul to darkness. In Astral form, Gan has been separated from the deadweight chains of his physical life, enabling his helpers to bring him down to earth again. As Gan re-joins his physical body, his reawakening will make the final difference in motivating the positive energy being given to him. Throughout the whole night, healing work will continue with him as he sleeps.

Morning has arrived and Gan awakes. His conscious mind gradually fills with surreal memories of the previous night. For a second or two he catches a shadow in his mind of the activities that took place on a higher level. Before he can dwell upon them Amy has appeared. She is weary and distressed. Gan sits up. He is incredulous and stunned. He shouldn't have survived the night. He should not have survived the deeds of his last few hours. Now however he is feeling physically well. Our efforts brought success in more ways than one. Later more will be said of this story. Suffice to say for now that for both characters, powerful lessons shall be learned from this experience. If Gan had ended his physical life his pathway would have been reversed many years. Furthermore, his early physical death would have prevented the completion of his chosen Birth Plan and many people would have been denied the benefit.

Does the story sound contrived? I changed the character names in the story and it has been dramatised a little for this book, but generally it is a true account. If it were not so, then several years later I would not have been able to sit here now and personally *recount* the detail of it for you to consider. I used my own past experience to give you some real life action with the hindsight now of a much higher viewing point!

How they could also Understand

Let's have a last attempt to understand why so many Earth mysteries remain, despite the best efforts of the scientists. Let us investigate further with a little lateral thinking. An understanding beyond quantum will accelerate our understanding of life the universe and everything. But Quantum Scientists are stuck at quantum. They try hard with their physical experiments to find the missing link that would unify all forces, but so far, the search has been in vain.

So let us talk about my dog again! He was a Cocker Spaniel and was as daft as they come. Everyone loved him and his strange habits. When he was a puppy he would make everyone laugh when we took him for a walk. His sense of smell was acute and he would literally see with his nose. It seemed almost as if he was vacuuming the smells in front of him. As mentioned in previous text his sniffing concentration was so great that he constantly bumped his head as he walked into things. He looked around at other things only after he had spent minutes on a particular smell. If he had been born with the sense to look around as he walked, his general awareness would have doubled. Quantum scientists follow their scientific instincts in much the same way. If only a way could be found for them to work from wider tested assumptions. If only they could find a bridge between the implications of their research and the worldwide belief in a higher structure to everything.

The world is full of so called esoteric mysteries which centuries of science have failed to understand. Quiet experimentation has taken place behind university or government doors to harness the effect of telekinesis, or remote viewing and many other higher abilities. But science cannot explain exactly how they work. So, their effect and uses are quietly explored, while officially the traditional esoteric explanations are sidestepped or ridiculed. The scientists know that a hidden property of science must explain them all, but because such unfathomable things have been left behind by mainstream science, they can now only covertly explore them.

In simple terms, here are just a few examples: Worldwide there are documented cases where people have become instantly aware of events at a remote distant location, at the exact time the events take place. Or in another example where someone spontaneously becomes aware of events in another family member's life, even though they are separated by distance. Then there is the circumstance where a person receives irrefutable predictive information from an apparent discarnate source. Finally for now, there is the example where someone knows all about a place without ever visiting it, nor with any previous knowledge of it.

I could go on and on with more examples and I know you will think of many more yourself. In all of these we can find verifiable, documented evidence to defy all explanation. If there was just *one* solid undeniable example, it would scream to anyone with the sense to listen, that an undiscovered higher effect of physics must be taking place. But in fact there are countless such examples. In these, there is a way for the earthbound scientists to accelerate their understanding.

It is a bit like the earlier story of the UFO scientists who were tricked into believing that an anti-gravity craft already existed. It gave them permission in their minds to copy what had already been done. Here, we are talking about the realms beyond physical and how they seamlessly interact through quantum. To me they are a first person reality. To the scientist they are not. So let's try a recipe that would bring the opposing viewing points together. I will show you a Wish-News Headline Newspaper story, set some time in the future

Afterlife—Now a Reality? A few months ago under the initiative of the new Advanced Science faculty in Pittsburgh University, Professor Brad Sherman announced a major breakthrough to help understand the world around us. The University have been working closely with quantum scientists since their exhaustive research had identified startling corroborative evidence for remote out of body consciousness projection. Furthermore, they isolated from ancient and modern texts a clue that persuaded scientists to try some new quantum experiments. Professor Sherman announced in his worldwide telecast today that they have not only been able to prove and duplicate the conditions where consciousness can be projected out of body, but also that their scientific colleagues are beginning to understand the laws that govern it. He reported,

'*This is the biggest scientific breakthrough of modern time. Scientists have theorised for decades about the Multiverse universe we live in. Now we can prove a part of it. Science is now one step closer to understanding the dimension for Afterlife.*'

I hope this Wish-News is not just wishful thinking. I just feel that instead of acting like the sightless puppy, a more lateral approach by science would allow the scientists to search as the wind blows, and not by ignoring, denying or ridiculing its presence! Oh and by the way, I firmly believe that in closed government and research facilities they are already way ahead of my Future News-Headline anyway!

A Look into the Higher Realms

Before we move into a new area, a quick review will be our signpost forward. We have considered gross matter in the form of material substance. We have considered refined matter in the form of vibrational substance. Throughout the whole cosmos there are coherent levels, or planes of existence. There are no absolute barriers between these dimensions, but special conditions must be satisfied for movement or interchange between them. In our material world alone there are numerous levels of existence. Inanimate material is host to microscopic life, plant life, insect life, lower animal life, higher animal life and finally human life. Within each of these levels there are degrees of progress which aspire to higher levels. In humankind all manner of character levels are represented—from the most bestial and base, to the most saintly and enlightened. While bound to the material world, everyone is compelled to co-exist in a disharmonious unity. On a human level conflict ensues to produce a worldwide battle of ego, because self is mistakenly regarded as an infinite form. Self-fulfilment is sought through the acquisition of power and material things which are transient; or through dependence to sensation. The worlds of material substance are all worlds of lower order. They are temporary. They have their controlling origin in the more refined planes beyond physical matter. To feel at home or comfortable in the material world is a constraint in itself. Only by an awareness and aspiration to the levels of more refined vibration, can a person start to become one with everything which lies beyond self. The interchange of life at gross material level creates an average vibrational environment befitting its hosts. This material environment is a catch-all to its inhabitants, straining to build upon itself, reinforcing its own constraints. Cling to it and any attempt to elevate the spirit out of it, would be like struggling for firm ground in quicksand.

Beyond gross matter there is a vast domain, stretching to infinity. Its substance is pure potential where all things are represented at all times in a virtual state of flux. This substance is infinitely finer than the smallest atomic Gluons and itself exists in an infinite variation of densities. The density variations prescribe the coherent levels of reality, closer or farther away from the physical sphere. Likewise these higher levels of reality by degree are home to their vibrationally compatible residents. In the spheres removed from the physical, by natural placement of like-vibration, inhabitants live in environments that perfectly reflect their disposition amongst peers who share harmonious vibration. Just as our species is represented in lower and more highly developed forms elsewhere in the Cosmos; so it is that our species is represented in the valid dimensions of reality beyond physical—thinly separated in each case from other more fantastic sentient forms.

Within the higher spheres but still closest to the physical level, the average refinement will still be of low enough vibration for people with a large cross section of differing vibration to dwell there. Lower regions may be as vast as we understand Countries to be. They may be as small as Villages within a greater region. Certainly at the lower levels they will still reflect differences in race, religion and language. It is in fact the case that residents of regions closest to the earth plane very often cannot accept they have changed state, and so cling to friends, family or anyone in physical life whom they would still impress. Fix once again in your mind when we talk about levels, we are describing altered states not locations. In relation to environment, consider for a moment: If as residents of the physical world, our whole environment is a reflection of how we apply ourselves to it—how much more specific do you think the environment would be if people of polarised vibration inhabited a vast region. So, next question: If there are all of these planes, or dimensions of higher existence, what do all the people there do?

Many religious followers would be satisfied to learn they will all flap around in the sky with wings and a bright light around their heads, singing glories all day. Well sorry! That is not good enough. Others would be satisfied to know that they will all receive a feather to decorate their hair and become Native guides to those left behind. . . .Sorry again! Every faith has its own fantastic and mythical picture of what happens to the Spirit Presence when released from the physical body. Reality is much simpler than the myth. If I could generalise; the main concern of those in authority on other levels is in the management of people and creative forces. In the lower regions where there is only coarse refinement, people go about their business in communities much as they would on a pre-mechanical physical level. Mechanical development and industry serve a purpose on physical earth but are not required on higher levels. Higher laws of physics provide far more direct tools in the control of processes in loftier regions.

Those who are elevated high enough and who are also trained to it, can manipulate matter from the mind alone. A universal formula exists to describe the unshakable process. An understanding of this one principle should be taught in schools alongside all notable subjects.

Cause which is *Thought* is the creation of an *Action* in *Virtual* form

Effect is the event now *Actualised*

Consequence is the *Reciprocal Reaction* to the *Effect,*

Which gives rise to greater Negative or Positive *Cause* in the next escalation.

At the lowest vibration, when **_Cause_** is dressed as **_Effect_** it allows **_Consequence_**, (*Responsibility*) to be avoided. We see the results of this in the quality of the generations around us which we have failed. Vibrational refinement determines perfection, precision, and wisdom.

In the physical world there is always talk of the adverse effect we are all having on the environment. To be honest though, collectively, we are so poorly advanced spiritually that we only have a remote understanding of how interlinked we are to the very smallest changes in our environment. It is only when we dwell in higher regions, having become one with ourselves that we properly begin to understand the Cause, Effect and Consequence formula of creation. A greater appreciation of this will present itself later. Residents of lower regions may be aware of their beyond death continuation but resign themselves to the fend-for-yourself limitations of the environment they find themselves in. Others in their midst, sharing their disposition, also share their weaknesses. In the higher regions, harmony feeds upon itself to create sublime beauty. In the lower regions disharmony feeds upon itself to create ugliness. At either level the Consequence *cannot* be ignored. A person lost in themselves, will be eventually woken-up by the raw reality they have to deal with. Shaken from their complacency, they will arrive at self-realisation. The painful road to progress will continue for so long as the person takes to actually face and feel for themselves, the effect of their past actions upon others. When this hurdle is overcome, humility will have replaced their arrogance. Awareness and self-responsibility lead to remorse and a yearning for something better. This process may be fast, or may endure for the equivalent of many years; but when the time arrives, helpers will be there to guide them through the transition to a new home in another region that better reflects their progressed state; and so the journey continues.

Those whom they leave behind will have to continue to deal with an environment that produces from-the-hand, along with others who will be conducting themselves with similar temperament. In the lowest regions very close to material substance, the occupants may be of base spirit, but their bestial nature will be reflected in an environment that would seem closest to the stereotypical image of hell.

In order to appreciate the lowest regions of spirit, the imagination must be stretched to its very limits. Only then could we begin to picture the depravity and darkness of their world. To those who live there in unholy depravation, and for whom humanity is a foul and dirty word, their dark miserable ignorance is complete. These people play out their wickedness together in a bleak cruel, feudal society. But even for the poor wretches inhabiting these places there are watchers and helpers. Much power is needed to operate at these remote low levels and only highly evolved individuals could carry out the task. At all times the helpers are on alert to the slightest hint of contrition. Where inspiration can penetrate the wall of ego and prejudice, help is always waiting in good measure. Help is always given when needed or asked for, but never in a way that would prevent the free choice of the individual. Helpers always operate from the wider viewing point. They may occasionally intervene personally in a situation, but still never to compromise free choice. A stretched analogy in the form of another fun Scenario will perhaps better explain how the process works.

The Man of Many Colours

We shall follow the hypothetical path of someone by focussing again on his frequency (or vibration). This man is an inhabitant of one of the higher vibrational regions of Spirit. The difference is that instead of seeing his vibration for this exercise, we shall see him as a particular colour shade. He shall be called, The Green Man.

The Green man lived in a community for many years amongst others who had green skin. Many shades of green were represented there. The Green man noticed something very strange. He found he was arguing with people he met. He began to feel more and more out of place. His skin also began to change colour in direct proportion to his changing attitude. Others began to notice this and he was shunned. Finally he had to admit to himself that his skin colour had completely changed. He was now the Blue man! He was grossly unhappy and didn't know what to do. He became a loner preferring the despair of his own company. A Helper, whose skin was colourless, stepped forward to intervene. He laid a trail of blue arrows on the ground, indicating the way out. The Blue man often walked over the arrows in his wanderings but eventually he recognised the trail and chose to follow the arrows. He took a very long time to reach the border because he was distracted along the way and often lost sight of the arrows; plus no one dictated how fast he must travel. Eventually the Blue man found sufficient courage to climb the last hill at the border of his old world. He came to a clearing at the edge of a great forest. He sighed with apprehension and took advantage of some nearby seats to rest and gather strength. He could see there were several pathways leading into the forest. As the Blue man sat there, his eyes focussed on some coloured markings on the ground. His perceptions had opened a little. They were more arrow trails. Each was a different colour and each led in a different direction. The arrows all began at his feet. He sat a while longer and finally realised that one of the arrow trails was the same colour as his skin. He felt the affinity and sprang to his feet to hurry off along the blue arrow trail. He had walked only a short distance when the trail began to branch in more directions. He reflected for a long time. His eyes followed the line of his leg to the ground and the solution leapt back at him. Each arrow trail was now a different shade of blue his skin colour matched one of the shades perfectly.

Confidence returned and he set off again along his own arrow trail. He marched on for a long time, feeling more and more at home as he went on his way. Presently as he rounded a bend he caught first sight of other people again. They appeared as dots to him across the valley on the hill, but they were unmistakable. He could see the pattern of buildings and houses. Excitement filled his heart for he felt he was almost at the end of his journey. Up ahead he just knew he would belong. The trail led down into the valley and meandered considerably along the way. The Blue man made good speed and was now in the bowl of the valley. As he marched along his attention was suddenly drawn to another pathway that seemed to be running almost parallel to his own. The other pathway also had blue arrows to mark the way—though not his exact shade of blue. He began to hear the sound of voices and laughter. These were sounds he had not heard for a long time. The trees gave way to more open pasture and also revealed a small village. The other trail led directly to the village. He found that the sounds emanated from a happy band of people who were cultivating crops in a nearby field. They hailed him with a warm greeting. The Blue man was again confused. His own trail led into the distance toward the other community first seen. Unmistakably though, these friendly people also had blue skin. He was comforted by their presence and finally decided to meet and stay a while with them. The Blue man felt more content than for a long time. He would explore this new place and accept the friendship offered there.

Nearby the Helper was watching. As the Blue man walked off with his new friends the Helper gave an understanding sigh; knowing how he would have to start the arrow trail as the Blue man changed hue and became restless again. The perfect pathway was always ready for him. He would only join with it when *he* was ready. The Helper would be ready for every chance to show the best options, but the man could and would make his own choice. In the meantime the man's adventures and tribulations would build strength to his character and spirit whichever way he chose to go. He may have chosen his perfect pathway of strongest Probability, but in the deviations to it, he opened up other pathways of Probability which eventually would always lead back to his central pathway.

My little story was very basic but I hope it conveyed how free will is sacred. The Blue man could have opted to divert from the highlighted path at any time; the more extreme the deviation—leading always to the more extreme lesson. Helpers or Guides intervene by touching the mind of their Subject with inspiration. The Subject may or may not be ready to recognise these higher thoughts, and even if the inspired thought is recognised, the Subject can choose to accept or ignore it. In Gan's tale we saw how Helpers can perform complex vibrational manipulations to influence circumstances, but only to produce positive choices. No choice made by someone on the earth plane or above, is wasted. Indeed it is rare for someone to follow his or her perfect Birth Plan. Each direction taken evolves more character—building experiences.

As I move forward in my narrative I am conscious of the fact that my descriptions are emerging as pictures of real time physical events, even though we are viewing across different spheres of reality. I must remind you that from the start we have been adopting the most appropriate viewing point to the level of reality under observation. For an observer or resident on any one of these levels, reality is as solid as our physical one is to us because the inhabitants are of the quality *of* the level they occupy. More accurately, the inhabitants each have a vibrational signature which is of a plus or minus tolerance which harmonises with the tolerance levels of the region they have awakened or evolved into. Vibrational form is entirely relative in its appearance to the viewing point of the observer. I hope by now you would have something of a mind-map of our travelling progress through the reality levels from the physical to beyond. So, I think we are now ready to discuss gender.

Understanding Sexuality

This is a huge crucial subject that will not only provide us with the understanding of base energies at work, but will show how it is the lesser part of a much greater understanding. During this section we will also learn the exact nature of the circulating vibrational energies within each of us.

We have examined many aspects of the vibrational experience for a single person. But even Gan's story for example fell short of the intimate interchanges you could expect between bonded partners. These closer interactions need to be fully understood, and so we need to take an even closer look at the circulating (chakra) energies within us all.

Almost everyone would understand what a musical tuning-fork looks like. It is of course a two-pronged piece of metal that produces a resonating sound when struck. The tone of the sound is proportional to the balance of metal in the tuning fork.

When the tuning fork is given a sharp knock and its base earthed to something solid, the fork vibrates to produce a powerful pure note. The tuning fork can resonate without even receiving a sharp knock. If it is brought into close proximity with something producing a similar sound, the vibrations are sufficient to make the tuning fork resonate. OK. Now substitute the tuning fork for a person. Think of the note produced by the tuning fork as being like the vibrational signature of a person. As we have already seen, everything in the makeup of a person is represented by the complexity of vibrating circulations in their Presence. Every single experience past and present is captured in virtual reality and like the mass of data stored on a computer it can all be accessed. The vibrating tuning fork is my analogy for the collective consequence of the person's life. As the person goes through life, the pitch of the tuning fork is subject to subtle changes according to the experience of the person. The internal tuning fork does not need to be struck. It is sounding all the time, sometimes loudly, sometimes softly as the person interacts throughout their life. Let us take it a stage further to represent all the different (chakra) energies within someone. Imagine now, not just one tuning fork but a collection of tuning forks. They are all sounding off to produce a chord of sound, and the cord is the signature vibration of the person. It is never fixed, and fluctuates according to the dynamic modifications taking place within the individual. The energy field of a person is in fact made up of several circulations that are directly linked to key areas of the human body. Incidentally, the physical body survives as a result of food being digested to sustain it, while the Presence receives *its* food as fresh substance from the greater virtual matter of Space. Each circulation can be identified individually but cannot exist individually. The aura is the outer fluctuating boundary of the occupying Presence. The individual circulations are intrinsically linked to a body area controlling particular organs of the body. These centres of energy-circulation have been recognised across the world as the Chakra circulations. When the physical body is out of balance then the vibration of one or more of their Chakras are out of balance—or more accurately, out of perfect resonance.

The human body is a complex energy system circulating its energy like the magnetic energy of the earth. The lesser circulations within it are like the circulating energies within a single atom. These energies produce a polarity corresponding to the general flow. Circulation does not have a start and a stop point, but movement is linked between circulations from the groin through the lower middle and chest areas to the neck, brow and head. Once again it is worth reminding ourselves, the physical body exists as a collaboration of physical substance. The life force of the body exists as a collaboration of higher substance inhabiting it and not the other way round. It is also entirely possible as we have discussed, for a person to have an objective experience in astral form away from their physical body and be able to return with the full experience. The mechanics of this require the manipulation of the chakra energy-circulations I have spoken of, and now we will examine this in detail.

The word Chakra is a Sanskrit word which appropriately means wheel or circle. It identifies our individual circulations of refined energy which give motivation to the major organs and glands in our body. Try to imagine it this way by analogy. Visualise a section of river. The river course has shape and there are obstructions in it. Over the section that we are examining, there are multitudes of repetitive eddies and sub-currents and these combine as a part of the overall flow of the river. The eddies and currents may be repetitive but from one second to the next, their atomic content and movement is varied. So it is within us. We have individual energy circulations that are a part of an overall circulation, and all of it is in a state of flux.

Our inhabiting Presence takes up freshly created energy from the lowest point of our overall circulation at our Root Chakra. This centres at the base of our spine and is the negative (incoming) pole of our total circulation. Its general frequency harmonises with the frequency of Red and the note C, and if out of balance reveals disharmony through guilt or fears in particular to do with our sexuality. When we raise our vibration in any significant way, our thought provides the motivation for refined matter to be Actualised from Virtuality and enter our energy system through the circulating energy of our Root Chakra.

Our second circulation centres over the spleen and governs the reproductive organs. It harmonises Orange and the note D. Imbalance reveals problems with emotional and sexual guilt and creativity, and can identify problems with mood.

The third circulation governs the Pancreas plus the outer Adrenal Glands and the area of the Solar Plexus. It harmonises Yellow and the note E. Imbalance reveals problems with digestion and general physical energy. This can also reveal a problem with anger through feelings of victimisation or persecution.

The fourth circulation governs the Thymus gland and centres on the Heart. It harmonises Green and the note E. It reflects our feelings of affinity, love and wellbeing. Out of balance and it shows problems in our Endocrine system, our immune system, and can also reveal the presence of low compassion.

The fifth circulation governs our Thyroid gland and our Throat area. It harmonises Blue and the note G. It reflects our general growth, expression and communication, but imbalance reveals stress levels.

The sixth circulation governs the Pineal gland and centres on the brow (or third eye area.) The gland is appropriately light sensitive, and its vibratory state actually reflects our ability to see into higher refined levels. It harmonises Indigo and the note A.

The seventh circulation governs the Pituitary gland and the area of the crown of the head. It harmonises Violet and note B. It governs our general Endocrine system and therefore our general metabolism. It is our governing level of consciousness and reveals our ability to receive higher input.

Although the Crown Chakra is often regarded as the positive pole of our circulation there is another main Chakra that exists above our Crown Chakra. This chakra is the true polar circulation that links us directly from our own circulation to levels beyond us. It has been described as the circulation of our higher self, because it is our inbuilt bridge to the highest levels beyond us. Its colour can often be identified in varied strengths of silver, gold or white light.

For all of the major areas of circulation, any physical problem will be represented as an imbalance of the circulation governing that area. All methods of energy-healing deal with the input of surplus high energy from someone or an external source that works to re-harmonise the disrupted fields of a sick person. This is true of hands-on healing, or remote healing, or even prayer healing. In every case, the thought behind them motivates new high energy to Actualise from Virtual state to infuse the troubled circulation with harmony again. It is entirely possible for the physical sickness or affliction to be cured instantly if the conduit for incoming higher energy is very powerful. Keep sight of the fact that these energies are a product of the Presence, or higher form. They inhabit and motivate the successful functioning of the physical form. Without them there would just be an inert physical body, but beyond the decaying body, the Presence continues in a more enduring reality. Now that we have the picture of our main individual energy circulations we can step out to the larger picture again and proceed.

Part of our process in this life is to strive toward the perfect balance and as such no one at this level is ever is in perfect balance. On a minute by minute basis, or day by day, or event by event basis, the pitch of our inner tuning forks is tweaked this way and that. The reciprocal reaction and interaction with our environment and others we meet, directly affects the frequency of our inner and outer frequencies. An adverse effect from any of the former can show itself outwardly in physical sickness. By simple example a highly neurotic person who sees only the negative side of everyone and everything will carry frequencies within them that are discordant and disharmonious. They will feel at ease therefore, only when they relate to negative stimulus. Their condition will become self-fulfilling. Very simply, it works this way . . . When the person is a Grouch and everyone else is a target of their criticism. Their attitude creates a negative reciprocal effect from most others. The person registers the bad consequence in the reaction of others which their Cause and Effect created—as a validation to justify their own original criticism and bad attitude. This inbuilt conditioning allows them to avoid self-examination and thereby avoid Responsibility for their own vibrational state and resulting attitude. It is a control drama. Conversely, where a person seeks inspiration in everything, they are aspiring to the higher more refined vibrations that produce harmony. Their condition will also be self-fulfilling but this time in a positive way. If the person who is a Grouch acts negative to a positive person, their bad attitude has no effect, and it will simply bounce right back at them with greater negative strength. These descriptions are necessary to lay the foundation for how things work between opposite genders.

Throughout every one of these descriptions I would like for you to hang on to an anchor point in your mind. *Fix for all time* a picture of the representative process taking place within the atom between one electron shell and another. See the energies meeting. Think of the picture on a computer screen that visually shows you the frequencies of a piece of music for example, as the peaks of sound dance up and down a thousand times to create a pattern. Imagine the same pattern of movement taking place in three dimensions, over the surface area of a field of energy (electron shell.) Imagine this happening between two electron shells, and the two different fields harmonising together upon contact. Forever anchor back to this process taking place at every level in everything discussed in this book, and in particular where we are now discussing the harmonious or discordant meeting of energies between the circulating energies of partners. There are a multitude of factors which draw people together in a match. Here are two example Case Studies of opposite extremes in a coupled partnership.

Example 1: The male of the couple was a person who lacked the confidence to take the lead in anything. His nature was quite sensitive, but he was brought up under domineering preoccupied parents. The result was that he had a very low self-esteem and lacked any self-confidence. He thought he was a serious under achiever. In fact his supreme efforts to show everyone that he was good for *something*, resulted in him performing better than average in all that he did.

The female of the couple was a person who was the last in line of several siblings and grew up with the cast-off clothes and other things given first to her brothers and sisters. She compensated by developing into a tomboy in a subconscious attempt to be recognised. They became a couple at an early age. He wished only for someone who would compensate his feelings of inadequacy by sympathetically taking charge of daily routine; and she wanted to be assertively in charge of her situation. They were a perfect match but also a perfect mismatch. They would resonate together in comfort and apparent harmony for a time, but they would remain a perfect couple only for so long as their own unbalanced frequencies needed to readjust through experience and maturity. Their relationship would bring procreation, and the opportunity for both to walk a difficult pathway to understanding within themselves.

Example 2: Both subjects followed intelligent formative lives where they endured, faced and overcame adversity. Their outlook was expansive, and both had a natural tendency toward esoteric subjects. Their lives took them through relationships which were temporary, for they never felt the need to seek a long term partnership. They came together as a couple later in their lives through interest in similar subjects. There was a natural empathy of mind and spirit. Their vibrations harmonised, but this time at a much higher level than the first example. They were able to form a partnership which allowed them to be self-assured; and later their combined force produced advances in knowledge. Their partnership endured because their energies complimented, while in the first example the energies were dependent upon each other for harmony.

In life there are an infinite number of variations for relationships based on degrees of similar motivation. However there are many other factors that are influential before we even consider the workings of energy through intimacy. If we widen our viewing point again into the *assumption* of existential realities beyond physical, it is much easier to see how the process works. Couples can have been friends before birth, and as with the first example, what better way to improve personal refinement than by returning by consent into such a relationship that will give the opportunity of experience for this to happen. Similarly, the consequence could be foreseen of a relationship between enlightened individuals, to bring good to others through a conjoined task—as in our second example. Mitigating influences in the process would include all the differences of location, racial type, social background, timing, and language, etc.

Having formed a relationship, the development of the couple would depend on the close interaction and reaction between them, and this means the interaction and reaction of their energies together. After consideration of the type of compatibilities from a higher level that bonded them together, there is the interplay on a daily basis as their individual energy circulations become modified through experience. The consequence plays out from this through their modifying Presence and the resulting conflicts of vibration that will follow.

We have mentioned the chakra energy circulations already, and we need to consider more closely how these are affected between two people. The strength of individual body circulations depend entirely on the response of the individual to internal and external stimulus, (or motivation.) In the first place, since our descent to the physical level, humankind has been driven by low energy patterns to ensure our survival in this physical state through physical procreation. For so long as there are humans in physical form, the imperative will remain a part of us. Those more carnal in their nature will be drawn to the sensation of sexual pleasure to a greater degree than others whose vibration is closer to detachment from the physical. I know this is stating the obvious, but allowing for the basic imperative to procreate, it is possible to measure the inner degree of our attachment to low vibration, by the strength we give to pursuing sexual sensation even in our imagination!

The energy circulation responsible for sexuality is centred on the Root Chakra, but is linked to every other circulation, and relies on *their* feedback. Remember every Chakra circulation is affected by our sensational cognitive process. They do not function automatically. They need our motivation of thought. We are therefore responsible for them. When we are awake, we provide the feedback of attraction by subjective judgements in our choice of partner and our base energetic drive. We decide when we are most fertile for the process to take place. Choice is affected by the harmony of a person's character, or more specifically their ability in the moment to bond with the vibrational signature of the other potential partner.

I have already said, the Presence is sustained by new matter entering the circulations at the root Chakra. Partners of lower vibration, who feed more from the vibrational signature of sensation, use that incoming energy to enhance their personal sensational dependence. When someone *motivates* their thoughts toward sexual activity, their general vibration automatically condenses to a lower vibration in readiness. All sexual acts need the stimulation of the energy circulations that will excite the base energies. In those with a lower vibrational signature this is easier, especially when incoming fresh energy is converted to the compatible low energy needed for the process. Prior to the act taking place, the two-way feedback of sensation between partners prepares the energy circulations. When the energy centres harmonise together for sexual union, biological processes are activated and procreation would normally result. However, in just about every case, couples together are bonded as a result of frequencies in one partner compensating to harmonise with inadequate frequencies in the other, and vice versa. The coming together in the first place is almost never as a result of soul-mates harmonising. The energy therefore in a sexual encounter rises through the other energy centres while exciting them on the way, but is drawn to return to the lowest circulation before the power reaches the higher chakras. The liaison commences where initial physical contact excites the base chakra energies. Hot-spots of excess energy are created within each partner. The surge of movement through the other chakras is diverted back to the root in a climax of rebalancing. The hot-spots of energy created through most sexual liaison are not sufficiently refined to rise through the highest chakra circulations. The discharge of energy through purely physical orgasm therefore coincides with the effect—that it was originally motivated by natural process for the intention of procreation. The same process of energy circulation can occur by self-stimulation alone, aided by the virtual reality created in the minds of the couple. As humans, we have developed to where pleasure has become almost wholly centred on sensation, even through the use of self-stimulation. When the act is done, the whole body circulations have to be rebalanced again. The higher chakra circulations during the act were contracted and condensed. At its climax the excess hot-spots of excess energy were discharged into the whole system and shared between the couple. But the downside is that in the rebalancing of the whole system the vibrational signature of both couples would be depleted to a slightly lower level. This is the source of the indifference experienced following a completed act of base sexual union.

Physical ecstasy is totally different from a Higher ecstasy, even though they can be achieved simultaneously. The absolute rapture of the higher realms cannot happen while we are still attached to physical form. However sometimes for special prearranged reasons, Soul-mates find each other on the physical level. In the event of Soul-mates joining physically, their naturally raised vibrations would ensure even greater input of fresh vibrational energy at the root chakra. The rising hotspot of extra energy would also rise with a higher vibration. It would raise the other circulations accordingly and would not necessarily return to circulate completely at the root chakra. To say romantically, the couple would already have one-foot-in-spirit, and as such, the balancing of energy would have the possibility of also breaking free through the crown chakra. If this is achieved, a conjoined astral out-of-body event would take place between the couple in a union of spiritual ecstasy, but with their perception rising to a level beyond physical. I believe this greater process is the goal of so called Tantric sexual union, but I have misgivings that practitioners may have a lack of understanding for the true processes involved.

I selected extremes for example, and trust you will be able to see how every conceivable degree of this process occurs according to the inner and outer progress of individuals who come together for intimacy. The coming together of Souls is reserved on a much higher level. The coming together of people on the earth plane is primarily for purposes of procreation and for the survival of the physical species. We take it much further in order to feed the temporary sensation of physical pleasure. Couples who come together to compensate for the inadequacies in each other are seeking harmony by default. Couples, who come together as complete persons in themselves, are complimenting each other's harmonies to double their power.

All of this brings us right back to our Cause—Effect—Consequence formula. Work it out for yourselves. If the Cause/Motivation, is to exploit the other person physically or mentally for personal gratification; then negative energy produced will feed upon itself to condense the aura. If however the encounter is conducted through pure altruistic love, then beyond the physical sensation the aura will be enhanced for both to a higher level.

Our search for empathy with a partner takes us through a vast complication of choices. Our subliminal vibrations always drive these factors. We appear to others as the culmination of our past choices. We read each other at a higher vibrational level long before a material or physical judgement. When we meet someone new, a natural process takes place for us to recognise any sympathetic harmonies in the other person. We may become friends, enemies or lovers as a result of natural reciprocal reaction. The perfect relationship occurs when potential partners have already found *themselves*. When each already has a balanced Presence, they are able then to be one with each other.

It is worth mentioning the response of the physical body when someone *induces* an Out of Body experience. In the initial stages, the body shows signs of sexual stimulation without apparent reason. Briefly to recap this phenomena: Astral Projection or Out of Body (O.B.E.) experience is the effect when someone, while still in physical life, is able to raise their energy level sufficiently to project their consciousness beyond their body and return with subjective information or experience.

It starts when the subject meditates to raise their general vibration. All connection or response to physical sensation has to be severed. It is likened to a state close to physical death The Presence is gathered from the body, and with the help of new substance actualised through the root chakra, it is projected from the body to assume an objective detached position beyond the physical body. The technique requires the chakras to be perfectly harmonised and for the new energy to rise up through the circulation centres before acting as a carrier to the projection of the Astral body. The chakras of the body become enriched as the energy is channelled up to and beyond the head. Prior to full projection the person can experience a whole host of physical distractions like itches and twitches, particularly around the face. The hairs in the nose and ears are most sensitive and it takes a lot of will to ignore the tickling sensations. Immediately before projection the body feels as if it is floating or swaying. However before this, while the gathering of energy is taking place; and while not a single thought of sexual activity is in the mind, the sexual organs become aroused for a short time. This is from the increased vibration of new energy rising through the Root Chakra and is a validation of the processes I have been describing. As the energy rises beyond the Root Chakra the response disappears. The signs of physical arousal in this case are nothing to do with motivation towards sensation and pass quickly. However for those who have been practising techniques for OBE breakout, it can be quite disconcerting at first.

In some people, spontaneous sexual arousal can take place for exactly the same reason. The person may be simply excited, or inspired by something unconnected. But it happens because the rising energy is being held at the Root Chakra. If the person's vibration is developed, the energy can be controlled and directed to rise through all the Chakras in total exhilaration. It can be controlled by consciously seeing and motivating internal circulations to make the energy rise in a full cycle from Root to Crown and beyond. Many people who have abnormal sexual fixations could rectify the imbalance easily if they understood the process and applied the knowledge of its workings.

Since the decent of mankind to experience the nature of sensation, we have separated from the perfect hermaphrodite form into the differences of male and female. As we became entrenched to our lower vibrational environment a whole hierarchy of traits became embedded to our species on this level and back into higher levels. We met the unique requirements for our physical survival, with the males being the strategic hunters and gatherers and the women being the tactical emotional nurturers. Each in their own ideal state represents a collection of highly individual qualities which are necessary to the other to form a perfect chord in a material world. The merging of all traits through the union of gender, seeks to draw us closer to our original perfect form. We are so well defined at this stage in our development for the biological reproduction, that we pursue the means for gratification *beyond* procreation as a false validation of completeness!

There are some positive differences that can only be fulfilled when couples merge. For enlightened individuals, the combined cord of refined energy enables inspiration from within and from helpers beyond them; and this unity can lead to great positive achievement.

On much higher realms of reality, the whole consciousness of individuals or groups can be merged. Individuality however is never lost because gathered experience is a product of each part and can always be traced back . . . Or to put it another way. The final blend does not rely upon the destruction of the individual or its components, but only upon their change of state. This merging of Presence at such a high level has been referred to elsewhere as *The gathering of Souls.* In between and along the way, Soul groupings form. These are vibrational sub-groupings of people who are bonded harmoniously with each other. You belong to one such group! They do not go about their business (in earth terms,) like large cooperatives. They exist as separate personalities co-operating together in complete harmony across the spheres in their work, and are able to draw directly from the experience of each other through lifetimes. Please do not lose the perspective here. When I say they go about their business, I mean in pursuit of their development pathway. One grouping may comprise individuals who are in differing stages of an earth life, while others may be working at differing levels beyond physical. Such is the link that a member on the earth plane may be helped by another on a higher plane who would act as their Minder. It is sometimes the case that personalities who have developed to be a part of a grouping in this way, may opt to return to physical life as a part of the same family. Your anguish or your joy is always shared by others who are closer to you in a way you could not imagine in your wildest physical dreams. Bear this in mind when you next feel yourself to be in turmoil. Open your higher awareness and you will feel the presence of your partners from higher realms. Do this constantly and you will begin to recognise the distinct signals they are able to give us as a verification of their Presence. For example when I am working in higher thought or purpose, I get a single noise each time like the tap of a hammer from somewhere above my head at the level of the ceiling. I got one a moment ago as I was about to type these words. For me this is always accompanied by what I call a static electrical wind. My helpers are able to create sufficient vibrational disturbance to act like a wind around my body. I feel this like a static discharge around my back, neck and head.

If two personalities from the same group met as strangers in new earth lives, they would experience an unspoken unity stronger than steel, even if they did not understand why at the time. This would be the true coming together of Soul Mates. It is amusing and sad to see how we cling to sexual union and physical climax as the height of pleasure between people. Imagine for a moment that you had just met with your perfect partner; your Soul Mate on a higher level. Imagine you could alter your state of vibration so that you were absorbed into each other to feel every sense of the other; where you are able to absorb every experience of the other; where you are able to merge with the opposite gender qualities of the other. Imagine you could do this with no expense to your own individuality. Imagine the ecstasy of such a union. You can't? Of course you can't, because such heights of experience are reserved for the higher spheres, or rarely for those Soul-Mates who are able to unite from physical into astral form simultaneously. But, you can form an understanding and appreciation of the process involved. This will offer a wider perspective to the utterly mundane levels we allow our minds to follow as the sexes chase each other on the earth plane for yet another temporary sexual fix. Apart from procreation, in almost every case, a union on the earth plane reflects the coming together of unbalanced vibrations seeking strength from their opposite; until they hopefully find it within themselves through continued experience.

In our physical world we follow the conditioning from past generations. We have progressed to the dizzy stage where domestic partners become rivals, competing to gain dominance by reason of ignorance, or selfishness. The perspective is physical, and is crippled. It reflects to every aspect of our lives. The parenting of children is too often seen as an inconvenient barrier to our material pursuits, or our material gain, or our possessions, and our pursuit of more sensation. The task of parenthood is too often regarded as an encumbrance instead of a joyful test of our ability to teach them right. In a material world, children get in the way of these things. Our attitude contaminates their minds and they perpetuate the problem as they become conditioned to demand the same. Our real responsibility to children lies in their moral and spiritual development; not in satisfying their ever-increasing demands for all things transient, temporary and material. Different qualities in gender are meant to compliment and fulfil, not to act as a support or as a means of control. If the process of birth, death, birth were understood, we could all progress to co-exist in vastly greater harmony.

At much higher levels, differences of sexuality become less and less important. At our material level, sexuality should be viewed with more proportion and certainly understanding, or at least as a part of an even higher union. We live in a world where we no longer have to worry about the unwanted production of babies, and physical gratification rules! We have forgotten there is an infinitely greater pleasure to be achieved; but we have to go through the process of identifying and balancing our own inadequacies first.

Consider this little picture analogy: We begin a relationship as an incomplete person. We rarely, if ever, team up with a Soul Mate unless for a special task or purpose. We are inadequate, but qualities in our partner compensate for these as we gather experience to finally balance them within ourselves. It is as if we come to our partnerships as people without wings. As we develop and progress together wings should begin to grow. The maturity we acquire determines the shape, size and colour of our wings. Both partners evolve wings, but are not necessarily ready for first flight at the same time. The urge to fly is inevitable and clashes take place as one seeks flight while the other is not yet ready to leave the ground.

Eventually each partner has their own unique pair of wings. They bang and crash together constantly as they try to take flight within each other's space; and what of flight itself? Most often, partners wish to follow their own flight plan. First flight usually involves mistakes and crash landings. In their eagerness to fly they lose sight of each other. Instead of agreeing for each to take turns while the other stands ready to help in the event of a crash, they compete for take-off and follow flight plans where each is unable to rescue or help the other.

Partners have an unshakeable right to their own individuality and to their own pathway of progress. This need never be at the expense of someone else. Co-operation and recognition for the individuality of a partner would compensate for even major differences in character and enable a harmony of purpose. The result would always be better if the single motivation of a partnership was rooted as a desire for each person to bring out the very best in their opposite partner. The higher goal of each individual would be realised if paramount respect were given to individuality. Intimacy would be more fulfilling if each recognised their own purpose, but gave respect to the purpose of the other. Space should be given where needed; help when called for and selfless support at all times. This is love without a price-tag!

Meaningful relationships so often break down with truly awful consequences outweighing the effort that could have saved them. We are all inadequate. Accept it! Things are not perfect here. Accept it! Things can never be perfect here. Accept it! We have the power to change things in ourselves first and help our partners to do the same. Accept it! Partners grow their wings, then they take flight to view the very same scene as ourselves; perhaps only from a different height or aspect. If they are awakened to understand exactly where they and their partner are coming from, there is no reason on earth why partners cannot land to roost together to share and grow *together* from their experiences.

What makes a Total Person?

We have discussed many of the higher and lower features that affect individuals in terms of relationships, but now we shall examine the specific factors that form the makeup of an individual. At the start of my narrative I had to justify the existence of higher dimensions by going back to basics with Physics. The link between physical and beyond had to be demonstrated. We have dabbled around since then to understand some of the workings of our greater world. We now need to answer the question: What really makes a person? . . . *Any Person to be*. What are the universal forces which converge to produce the basic inert human creature? We will examine these now and you will see what baggage you decided to carry when you came into this, your life!

Genetic Pattern

The obvious physical starting point is in the genetic makeup. This constitutes the biological blueprint for the general characteristics of the person. Evolved traits are passed down through the generations, endowing gender, corporal features and automatic responses. Let's not forget that genetics also produce a social environment through the shared genetic traits of the surrounding family.

Our person therefore, may be represented as a flat nosed hunter, with a predisposition to folk lore from generations of ice hunters. Or maybe a brown eyed, olive skinned doctor in another country who comes from a generational line of healers. All physical traits have a basis in the genetic code. On the one hand Scientists are studying genetics to gain a better understanding of how we function. On the other hand they manipulate genetics for profit behind the banner of medical cures and improved food production. Their viewing point reaches only to the end of their noses. Wider understandings are being achieved despite their motives. We now know that genetic coding can be held partially responsible for specifically good or bad character traits. For example, scientists have found a gene that identifies an individual towards anti-social behaviour. We also know that congenital disease passes through the genes. There are so many examples known where genetic traits have been identified.

Stellar Influence

The genetic blueprint at birth is modified by stellar influence. In 1984, Geneticists in the USA found that genetic mutations were caused to test tube babies at their moment of conception by the power of altered magnetic fields. The scientists had touched upon another link. Cyclical magnetic stellar influences result in various effects being imprinted to every human being at the time of conception. Radiating energy from the sun and elsewhere in the cosmos, or magnetic fields generally, are known to affect the bio-rhythmic cycles and hormone levels in a female. Years ago, when women were brought to Machu Picchu in Peru for fertility rites, the Peruvians already understood far more than we do now about stellar energy and its affect upon new life. The Peruvians guaranteed best reproductive influences in their women through their ancient knowledge of the effects of stellar radiation. The women were brought to Machu Picchu at specific astronomical times of the year for procreation. This knowledge has been developed through millennia by observation and we know it today as the much maligned study of Astrology. In its most exacting form, it can be used to identify general and specific characteristics from the birth date, time, and place; and has been developed into a science of probability in many other areas. So, our *Person to be* has identifiable traits that come from stellar influences at the time and location of conception. Our *Person to be* is subject to monthly and seasonal cycles of magnetic influence reaching them from far beyond this planet. The responses of our *Person to be* are affected in this way throughout their life.

Automatic Responses

Any *Person to be* will have free choice in all they do. The choices made through life are as a result of many complications. However, the explanations above indicate why people born to similar times and locations have a predominance to appear and act in similar ways. Think back to the tuning forks again and think vibration. At conception, the fertilised biological egg is host to a new life. The genetic blueprint for the person will have been fixed according to vibrational and magnetic influences at that moment. The resonance of the tuning fork is beginning to sound, but is not yet free to resonate alone. There will be strong vibrational bonds to the mother. The new person will be forming its attachments to its new body. At birth, the person is now independent. Previously, home was a place on one of the higher planes where there was the comfort of compatible vibration. Now the person has to come to terms with an alien environment and cannot escape the restrictive influences of its new body. The tuning fork finally resonates alone, but with imperfect internal circulations of energy. Our

Person to be will spend his or her lifetime seeking to refine those energies back to perfect harmony.

Traits of Conditioning.

We must still deal with three other major unavoidable influences upon the life of our *Person to be*. These include National, Racial and Domestic conditioning. Under any one of these three areas, our *Person to be* would be expected to conform to the rules of law and life prescribed by their peers. Nationality is usually very recognisable but language and appearance are the obvious first signs. Since we all descended to the earth level, we lost the ability to communicate by power of the mind alone, and to freely manipulate the vibration of matter. Verbal communication evolved into a myriad of languages tied to nationality and region. In the same way, the physical appearance of a person is usually derived from the evolved genetic blueprint of a race, which in turn is tied to a Country or region. Nationality confers an inborn genetic conditioning and whether we like it or not, we all conform to a National or Racial expectation, regardless of whether Nationality ties with Race. Reasons can be simply attributed to the social evolvement in different places, each place modifying the conditioning. Differences in personal outlook, socio-domestic outlook and national outlook all produce their own prejudice. This results in lack of understanding, tolerance and wisdom, and all lead inevitably to conflict.

We have to keep pulling back to vibrational sight, because our evolvement over millennia has produced everything described so far—and every single influence has a vibrational signature or frequency that can be read and traced back with understanding.

All of these greater pressures are synthesised into the daily domestic scene of our *Person to be*, where free-will decides the outcome of every interaction.

Free Will

If we shifted our viewing point away for some distance we could see another good reason for the action of free-will. We are covering many areas of influence that have a bearing upon our *Person to be*. Finally within the package of conditioning, our subject is bestowed with free-will to find a rough or smooth passage through their life. If the free-will did not exist, all of the influences would become polarised as attitudes became reinforced through the generations. Free will provides the next spiritual evolutionary step forward from instinctive response. If we were armed only with instinctive response, we could only ever evolve to the levels of higher animals. We could have only risen to dominance on the planet as predators. Our saturation of the planet through population increase would have only led to self-destruction. The divine spark within us ensures our motivation from the most refined levels of matter, and this gives us our higher order of intelligence coupled with the free will to apply it and evolve back again to its source.

Environment

There is a final main influence, and that is *Environment*. This is the external reflection of all of us. But for a new-born, the environment is something he or she will only have a chance to add to or subtract from as they become older. During formative years, our *Person to be* will suffer the good or bad effects of their environment with little power to change things. But as our person grows and evolves, they will have a direct bearing on the entire environment. Choices made with wisdom or the lack of it, will have the most obvious impact, which can be determined in the vast differences of character in Society. But more importantly again at a vibrational level, the motivation of thought that our *Person to be* develops, will add or subtract to the vibrational signature of the whole planet. The harmony of the planet depends upon every individual.

These then in brief are some of the main factors that form the standard package of external influences for our *Person to be*, before even considering the internal influences that the incoming Presence will bring with them. All of these factors could have been expanded tenfold, but the purpose of our explanation has been served by a brief description of each. You will be able to refer to the pictorial summary of the whole process later in the book when we breathe the life of an incoming Presence, into our hypothetical *Person to be*.

The Engine that drives The Body

We have given our *Person to be* a suit of clothes, but he or she still has no life-force. A bit like a fine car without an engine! Our human vehicle also needs an engine. Well, the reality is that the Presence of a real person will be preparing to inhabit the new physical body for its temporary physical lifetime. The Presence of the incoming person will have an evolved vibration that represents every modification of experience they ever had. This will include all that they have ever been in previous physical lifetimes. We have to understand how this can be.

Question : Why on earth would a Person/Presence from a higher sphere of reality wish to assume physical form on a much lower, uninviting level. In very simple terms, you do not get the Manager's job until you have worked your way up from the basement. You do not end up as the best Manager possible until you have excelled in an apprenticeship. Each promotion requires a level of expertise. If you do not come up to standard, you just have to go back to the previous level to try again another way until you master it. So, the incarnation of a vibrational soul through a physical life span, in nearly every case happens because the person is deficient. Nearly all of us live this life because we are inadequate in some way.

We arrive to our physical body armed immediately with the ability to verbalise our vibrational condition emotionally. Emotion is a self-defence mechanism. It is signalled by a large flapping banner which proclaims; I am an incomplete person; I am not yet one with the world and myself. I mask this from the world by displaying it to the world through my emotions. Think back once again to the balanced atom being penetrated by the extra energy of an incoming Photon. The atom settles back down into a modified harmonious state, with the excess hotspot of energy being ejected as a new particle. We do the same! When our circulations are out of harmony, we try to discharge the hotspots of negative energy by projecting them in emotion. We do this with the unconscious desire to elicit positive responses that will feedback energy to balance us back to our level of harmony. At such a stage we have not yet learned we do not have to seek our balancing energy through the induced reciprocal reaction in others—and that it should be sought through an internal balancing process which we always have the power and choice to motivate. When a baby screams for attention and there is no physical problem, it is just the same as adult anger between opposing views. Someone who is *one* with themselves has a serenity that reflects their inner balance.

As we mature, we should begin to grasp the Cause/Effect/Consequence formula at work in everything that happens. *Most people however rely on emotion to disguise Cause as Effect and Effect as Consequence. Thereby they seek to avoid the Responsibility of their own actions, even though their actions emerged from their own uncontrolled motivating thought.*

You may say, well that's all fine and dandy, but how do we function in a world that is driven by emotive response. Well, we are here because we are inadequate in some way, and an understanding of the process does not exclude us from taking part in it to learn. So there must be a way of understanding how we can find the most tranquil passage. We need a sure way to decide before we respond if our reaction is going to have a good, bad, positive or negative consequence. The problem really provides its own answer. If we think back to the workings of vibrational substance, we can recall how all matter condenses to gross matter or gravitates to refined matter. We are inhabitants of gross matter. Our final destiny is to meld with the most sublime levels again. We will find there is still purpose when we get there, and we will discuss that later. Right now we are inadequate and have emotive responses. We must look to the motivation behind our responses. So, here it is, spelled out loud and clear once again: Our motivated thoughts form the *Cause*. Our emotive responses are the *Effect*. The *Consequence* can be good or bad in both directions, depending on our Reciprocal reaction. Are the resulting vibrations positive or negative? Remember, by reciprocal action, negative or positive impulses seek each other out to be amplified and fed back to the sender. Negative emotional vibrations prevent harmony. If by way of our inadequacy we cannot avoid an emotive response; by what yardstick do we judge ourselves? The test is simple. In any given situation, we must ask ourselves this question. Do we intend for our motivations to produce a good or bad response in others? Good motivations will produce a good vibration which will return to us. I know this is stating the obvious, but if so, why is it that we get carried away with our own emotions and forget their negative effect on ourselves and others? The answer is, we are still inadequate!

The recipient also has a choice to respond with pure or misguided motivation. However if the sender has produced fine vibrations, then a negative response will not be there disturb the sender. They will only feed back to fulfil themselves within the vibration of a recipient. The very best we can achieve is by always aspiring to do right by others and ideally by reacting with detached compassion or understanding, especially when confronted with negativity. All of this is easy to say, but on a day-to-day basis we are confronted with a bombardment of negative responses from people in situations where there is little tolerance, understanding, selflessness, compassion or wisdom. Negative *Cause* is sometimes translated into negative physical *Effect* and physical evasive action is necessary to avoid a destructive *Consequence*.

Another question: If there is a situation where we have to use physical means to defend ourselves, how can we do this without causing more negative vibrations? I will answer the question by remembering the Martial Art expert and film star, Bruce Lee. In one of his films he was instructing a student in a particularly difficult defensive movement. He made the student do the movement over and over again. The student appeared to carry out the movements perfectly. He became visibly frustrated as Bruce Lee continued to be dissatisfied. Finally Bruce Lee walked over to the student, rapped on his head with his knuckle and said to him simply, *Emotion; no control!* Remember; we are imperfect. But we can aspire always to do better, can't we?

We can do much more in other ways to raise our vibration. This is achievable by trying to link whenever possible to all things which are naturally positive. You must have heard the expression; to have a positive outlook. Positive and negative surrounds us. We inhabit gross vibration and it is easier to deal with the vibration of our flesh. That is why it takes a little more effort to seek the refined way. If we make a conscious effort to aspire to the vibration of our higher selves we can more easily recognise the finer vibrations of beauty around us, even in the sound of silence. So many people are afraid to face a period of apparent solitude or silence. Clinging to the white noise of materialism just reflects an inner disharmony and the need to sustain the imbalance with sympathetic feedback. Solitude and silence even for short periods can allow us to raise our aspirations to higher levels in contact with our higher selves for the creation inner harmony. Here is a personal example:

I was renewing a garden fence. The garden backed on to a disused railway line. A separating patch of rough ground covered in thick bramble, ran from the old tracks right up to the edge of the fence. There was not a soul about and I had been struggling with the stony ground to form new holes for the fence posts. I worked on under the heat of the sun for several hours without a real break. I was only a couple of posts and wooden panels from completion and I was exhausted. The job was starting to get the better of me and I was becoming short tempered. I tried and tried to bash a large stone from the hole I was digging and just came to a standstill. I sagged to the ground on one knee, breathing heavily and cursing my own weakness. I remember thinking to myself, *The spirit isn't very strong on this job!*

As I caught my breath, a scratching noise in the brambles a few inches beside me drew my attention. I kept still and looked to where it came from. I watched in amazement as a Mouse appeared nearby, sniffing and exploring as it went. It stopped and looked up at me and I expected it to disappear in a flash. Instead, from behind it, four tiny young mice also appeared. I registered that this must be mother mouse with babies. I was transfixed. The mice continued with their tour, cavorting exploring and jumping about together. They were no more than a few inches from where I was crouched. They stopped several times to look in my direction but showed no concern or fear. They played around for several minutes completely at ease. Eventually they disappeared off together into the undergrowth. My legs were cramped and it took me several seconds to stand with comfort. I had however completely forgotten about the tedium and difficulty of the job. My spirits were very much lifted as I considered the privilege I had just been granted. I would never have harmed the creatures and they would have sensed this. As such they had no fear. They were able to ignore me and carry on as normal. My attitude to the work had been wrong. I had seen the job as a chore. In other words, I felt I was doing negative work and the negative vibrations fed back to me to make me over-tired and impatient. The little mice taught me a lesson. The remainder of the job went like a dream. The incident had made me pause to link back to finer vibrations and this was sufficient to balance my own aura once again. Simple beauty is all around us. We look but don't see. We are so dependent upon the irrelevant white noise of irrelevant activity filling our senses and drowning out the precious moments when we should be getting in touch with ourselves, and noticing them.

The basic inert package of our any person awaiting its new host is preconditioned with prejudice arising from the handicap of the person's new awaiting physical life. This prejudice will demand automatic responses from its inhabitant regardless of the spiritual level of the new inhabitant. The inhabitant arrives to its new home for a lifetime, carrying with it a personal vibrational signature. As stated, the vibrational signature is a measure of the total spiritual progress of the Presence. The Presence joins with the inert package sometime between conception and birth to form a full physically living person. Immediately, the Presence has to cope with the descent from natural higher vibrations and the need to deal with the automatic physical responses tugging at them. Inner and outer conflict is guaranteed. The conflict is compounded by the fact that everyone else faces the same test. On the earth-plane all levels of spiritual awareness are represented and they must all face the test together for their lifetime. All the factors that produce negative vibrations have to be faced and dealt with. There is no escape from the process. It must happen. It will happen, sooner or later. The physical/spiritual/vibrational battle of balance makes sure of it. The Law of Cause, Effect and Consequence, coupled with the Law of Reciprocal Action, are Laws based on processes of higher physics. They cannot be avoided. Sooner or later, the hot-spots of negative energy we generate, will discharge themselves through situations which make us face our inadequacy. The more we fail to finally recognise and accept the fact, the more extreme the situations will become for us until the message gets home. It is only then that we will find our serenity, tranquillity, happiness, and life balance begins to improve.

We can choose to deny our inner voice for what is right or wrong and spread more negative energy by our thoughts and actions. But just like a boomerang they will return to smother us a bit more. We can choose to indulge our ego and live our lives wrapped up in ourselves and our own selfish needs. The natural Law of the Universe will make us face ourselves sooner or later. We can however choose to open our senses to enlightenment. We can show tolerance, understanding and fortitude. By offering positive energy, more positive energy is created and our pathway to tranquillity is hastened. A drunkard cannot reform before first admitting they are an alcoholic!

Think back yourselves over the last few days. Try really hard to recall as many examples of conflict you had to deal with. Write them down on a piece of paper. Recall for how many of those instances you reacted according to emotion. Be brutally honest with yourselves. Now imagine how the conflicts would have turned out if you had dealt with them without emotion, but with more tolerance, compassion or understanding. How many of your incidents generated negative energy and how many spread positive energy. Try to recall the bad things that happened to you. Then think of the instances before them where you had a bad attitude. They link together! If you don't believe me, you don't even have to do a written exercise to prove it. Simply by me planting the seed in your mind here, you will begin to notice it. Every time something you consider unhappy or bad has happened to you, think back to what you could have done recently to have caused it. It really *was* you that caused it, regardless of the immediate Cause and Effect; because one of your previous negative acts was waiting for the moment to discharge its stored hotspot of negative energy. The process is so simple! Again, don't take my word for it. Prove it to yourself. It is just the way it is. Incidentally, the process I have been describing is also called the process of Karma. It is not a fantasy. It is a strict scientific Law governing the attraction and exchange of vibrational energy. And if you can't be bothered right now to give a few minutes to the exercise, I have news for you. You will have to do it sooner or later for the whole of your life. Your decisions will determine if the lesson is hard or easy.

We can move swiftly to other considerations for the incoming Presence. It can be said of us that while we inhabit our physical body we are in control of it during the active state of being awake or passively during sleep. Conscious and awake speaks for itself, but what are the influences while we are unconscious or asleep? During each waking day we are stimulated by interactive experiences plus feedback from our senses. Our physical brain acts like an incredible bio-computer. We motivate it to sift and sort the things from our lives which must be recalled or learned from. On a strictly biological basis, our brain requires body shut-down time to allow the previous batch of data to be assimilated. Like a mechanical computer our physical memory relies on accessing stored data from our brain cells.

However when we sleep, a far more important memory-function is at work. Every experience of the day; every piece of sensory input; every personal reaction, will have created vibrations or impulses. Our Aura or vibrational field is in a state of vibrational flux, but at all times displays an average collective signature-vibration. The standing harmonic frequencies within our field undergo modification from all of the daily sources of new input while we are asleep. Science understands that our brain functions through the command of electrical impulses along our neuron pathways. It is also understood these pathways develop through repetitive signals inducing neuron growth. It is not understood however, how the brain is able to process the infinite choice of Probabilities and for an infinite variety of combined mental physical and reactive functions. We have already laid the ground for the answer here. The biological processes are understood, but when the mind accepts new input however small or large, it has a modifying effect on the vibrational energy circulation of our Presence that harmonises with the brain cells to represent it. Memory *is* our Presence. Our Presence *is* our memory. It is the culminating signature of everything that has ever happened to the Presence. I could say that immediate memory is written in vibrational large print, but the record of all that has gone before is stored in the finer detail. We generally access the bold type on a day to day basis, but the small detail describes the cumulative change in our Presence over the time of our Lesson. We wake each day with a vibration modified by our learned experiences from the previous day. While we are asleep and while this process continues, the Presence is able to journey away from the physical body in the astral to gain experience in higher spheres. There is always an unbreakable link between the vibrational body and the Physical body. The Presence/ person may for instance meet up with their Minder, (guide) to discuss progress or to receive instruction. The vibrational person may simply journey randomly and mingle their experiences with other people doing the same thing. The vibrational person may be driven by a pressing situation in their physical life to create and enact scenarios so they can examine the different probability options. By doing this they are able to come to terms with something potentially traumatic, or arrive at the best decision for action when they awaken.

Scenarios are played out in a simple process. The sleep—freed Presence is able to examine Cause, Effect and Consequence by directly manipulating vibrational substance. Understand it by likening it to a virtual reality holographic suite. The person creates it for themselves out of Virtuality, interacting with their own virtual situations to examine the strength of probability for each outcome. Unfortunately if the person has a particularly strong imbalanced conditioning, then the waking mind will translate the good work of the higher self by remembering the dream scenario which feeds the uncontrolled lower conditioning;

(even though the selected scenario had a weak probability.) The danger is however that in doing so the person will only reinforce their own conditioning instead of improving it. I am describing here how a person may for example remember a weird dream, but will miss the profound message it is trying to convey. It is always better for a person to first recognise inner weaknesses while in a wakened state. The recognition and resolve to change behaviour can be imprinted with greater resolve while awake, from within a reflective, inspirational or meditative state.

If the person's vibration is low it is unlikely they will be able to break free to higher instructional levels during sleep. In this case it is most likely that their sleep scenarios will be inverted experiences. The general vibration, and therefore outlook or attitude of our *any person*, is self-fulfilling even in sleep. These sleep activities create modifying vibrations that must balance their energy within the general field of the person. When the person wakes they may recall no dream at all. This happens if they are either so preoccupied with the physical world and material things, or if the physical body itself is suffering from tiredness or injury. If someone is at ease with themselves they are likely to have dream recall or even the recall of an involuntary Out of Body experience. If the person falls somewhere between the two types then a dream recall is more likely.

We land now on the well-discussed subject of dream interpretation. How can anyone interpret a dream if they don't first understand the process involved to produce it? When the person wakes with a dream recall, the dream will have been produced in their conscious memory as a shadow of their higher sleep activities. The dream will have been the result from some or all of the processes described. Generally speaking, the dream will have addressed one or more issue of conflict in the life of the person. All of those swirling and interacting vibrations or impulses will have fed back to the conscious brain as either a jumble of thoughts, or as the memory of a possible scenario played out in sleep. The scenario may hold clues for the person to better deal with something that is troubling them. The dream may hold the perfect answer to a problem. Please don't lose sight of the fact that for every person there is a Minder who seeks at all times to provide directional arrows of assistance for the person. The help may be delivered through an astral excursion, or a sleep scenario, or by direct stimulation of the person's mind. Sleep is the time when we are able to make contact with our true home. It is the time when we may be refreshed by the input of new finer substance directly from the greater Space around us, or enriched from our Minders who are waiting to help our progress. The person most qualified to interpret the awakening thoughts is the person who produces them. All that is needed is the understanding of the process involved and the will to improve according to spirit.

During sleep, we have the potential to reach for anything every night. The benefits of sleep reach far beyond the rested body. Just imagine again the ebb and flow of turbulence as the impulses sort themselves out in the process—by analogy just like a dense shoal of fish which simultaneously change direction like magic. But there is not one shoal. There are thousands of shoals of fish of all different sizes and types, occupying every possible space; but each still able to change direction independently.

I was standing at the back door of my house the other day. In the back yard, close to my neighbour's wall, I had left a plastic bucket outside from when I last pasted some wallpaper. The bucket was filled to the brim with rainwater. It was late afternoon. The sun was still bright in the sky and it was a little breezy. It wasn't the bucket that caught my eye. Bright sunlight was reflecting from the surface of the water to cast a bright oval spotlight on the brick wall beside the bucket. I stared at the reflection, oblivious to the brick backcloth. The water in the bucket appeared to remain still, but every minute flow of air over the water caused tiny ripples which spread back and forth across the reflection. Some were so faint they were almost invisible. Some were larger, and coursed within the reflection, overlapping the smaller ones. I noticed how, regardless of size, they all interfered with each other in subtle ways to create new patterns of movement. I was fascinated by the sheer speed of movement and the intensity of the overlapping frequencies. Every now and then, sometimes only for a split second, the tiny ripples seemed to cancel each other out, leaving the reflection mirror calm. Sometimes the impulses seemed to excite each other to create quite strong visible ripple patterns. The intense non-stop ballet of movement held my gaze until a small cloud obscured the sun. The evidence disappeared from the wall and the water surface at the bucket continued to appear motionless. The analogy was beautiful. If only we were capable of visualising the water reflections through all dimensions of space, we would have a perfect description for the workings of vibrational impulses.

The outward evidence for the vibrational state of a person is easy to identify. The vibrational field or aura around a person may extend only a short or great distance and will contain many colour frequencies. The distance depends upon the average vibration of the person. People who have a high vibration are not only able to see and read a person's aura, but rarely are also able to see the aura around everything else living or inert. Human traits that are synonymous with lower or higher vibration are very easy to define. A base person will outwardly display degrees of one or more of the following. Sloth, avarice, unkindness, spitefulness, impatience, wastefulness, rudeness, cowardliness, intolerance, vanity, anger, loathing, selfishness, apathy, callousness, arrogance, betrayal, or any other self-gratifying, self-absorbed action. Vibrations arising from these traits collapse inwards as they condense together and their qualities become self-fulfilling.

If a person aspires to willingness, generosity, kindness, goodness, patience, chastity, loyalty, thrift, courage, tolerance, humility, selflessness, fortitude, tenacity, compassion, understanding, grace, or any other selfless non-material trait; then by any of these qualities the person will have a refined vibration. These vibrations expand outwards as they seek to gravitate to the higher levels, and also become self-fulfilling.

To the person of lower vibration, sleep will make little difference to their condition. For them it would be like going to bed with dirty, soaking wet clothes on. For the person of higher vibration, they would conduct their waking physical life with optimistic grace whatever the challenge. In sleep they would easily journey to a more natural higher level to receive instruction, conduct business, or simply to gain extra strength. The lesson for us all is stark and clear. The evidence of truth is all around, and it simply needs the motivation of an unclouded heart to expose it.

Astral Journeys

Astral Projection or Out of Body experience is the ability to travel away in consciousness from our physical body and enjoy objective experiences. The involuntary process takes place most nights for people when they are asleep. If our general vibration is high, we can retain some of these experiences when we unite with our physical body and awaken again. There is an easy test to determine whether a waking recollection is from and full-blooded astral journey, or just a jumbled dream.

If I were to ask you to describe what you were doing at this time yesterday, you would probably remember easily. If I asked you the same question for last week, you would probably still have an answer. The memory would be more faded if the same question applied to six months or a year ago; unless something particularly memorable happened on that day. On the other hand, I'd bet you couldn't remember a normal dream for any more than a couple of days. The memory of an astral journey is as vivid as the memory of a physical experience, and it ages in the mind in the same way.

Sleep projection is a passive journey. In an induced Out of Body experience there is always a complete subjective recall of the experience. This is because the person, in having the ability to project their consciousness, would already be naturally of high enough vibration to recall the content. While on an astral journey we remain attached to our physical body by a vibrational silver energy cord. On a journey we are able to leave sufficient amounts of our vibrational essence with our physical body to keep it functioning in a resting state. Meanwhile our cognitive Presence stretches away.

This is possible, because for our umbilical connection, just as with woven rope stretched under tension, compression takes place to strengthen it. Our astral form replicates our normal physical body. When the ties from our physical senses are broken in sleep and we lose their input. Our Presence seeks to gravitate like a released cork under water to its natural higher level. We could take the descriptions further by likening our astral form to a submarine. As with us in sleep, the craft is able to break free from the highly pressurised seabed to a more comfortable level, depending upon the number of ballast tanks filled with air.

While awake it is also possible to induce astral travel. The process relies upon the subject being in a state of complete physical rest. The trick is to first detach the mind from the incoming signals of the normal senses. Then by act of will, the vibrational energies are drawn up through the energy centres of the physical body and are projected along with the consciousness to a point beyond the physical body. As a word of caution however; the process requires great physical and mental discipline as it takes a person to an almost complete closedown of the body function. Normally the exercise should be carried out in the presence and care of another adept who would guard the physical person and know how to induce a safe recovery. When we finally break free we cannot adopt the same freedoms felt when we are physically dead. In Astral form we are still weighed down by the gross-matter attachment to our physical body.

So, in practical terms what does such a journey have to offer? During an Astral journey it is possible to interact with life at varying levels. Exploration can take place on the Earth plane itself. Beyond this there is literally infinite scope for exploration in other realms or domains such as villages, towns, and cities of the higher planes and with people in different countries or anywhere reflecting the diversity of the Earth plane. The region of free Space closest to the physical plane represents the densest region. This region is home to all the lower forms of human life that are unable to move on. On an astral journey, travel is conducted passively by the pull of our conditioned responses, or when induced, by free power of will. At higher levels we are able to make the link to interact with those who have passed beyond physical death. At all times along the way, if our activities threaten to cause harm or offence, our Minder would be there to offer inspiration for good directional choices. The ability to make such a journey does not give the power to act like a kind of free super-spirit who can interfere with other people. A negative intrusion would produce amplified negative feedback. The vibration of one's Presence would condense and there would be an instant snap-back to the denser physical body; probably causing a jolt and a headache as a reward. If an induced journey is highly motivated, then the result would be positive and beneficial for the traveller.

A Personal Example : From my job of work in the past, I have a special interest in the construction of buildings; or dwellings in general. I had been aware for a long time that for those in spirit with the same interest, the teaching methods are far more advanced than here on the earth-plane. On higher levels, consideration is given to the perfection of technique in every detail. Remember, inspired design work in spirit borne out of perfection, usually filters down through further inspiration into a flawed version on the earth-plane. In spirit, a student would first have to master the ability of harvesting from Virtuality to create new form and shape. Every last detail of every last aspect of a construction for instance would be scrutinised in every way to find the best harmonic union.

I was Out of Body. I met with my Minder outside the entrance to a huge building. I was aware it was some kind of College. Behind us the walls rose to great height in tight jointed blocks of stone. I use the word stone but their texture appeared malleable even though they stood quite solidly like a normal building. The main entrance to the building was a vast tiled walkway framed at each side by a row of piers jutting out from the walls. At the top of each set of piers a perfectly squared lintel bridged the entrance, creating the effect of a high ribbed ceiling way above us. I remember at the time, making a vague comparison in my mind to the American Justice building. I registered this as the best comparison, but still nowhere near adequate. There were lots of people coming and going, totally preoccupied with their own affairs. There was a hubbub, but the atmosphere was modest and calm. In front of us stretched a great paved promenade, reaching out at the sides to wide walkways following the side of the building.

We moved forward together. Sorry, I have to be more accurate. It was not a case of us putting one foot in front of the other to proceed. We moved forward just an inch or two above the ground. It felt totally natural. The promenade led to a wide flight of steps. The steps were very shallow and were grouped in flights of about six or seven steps interrupted with landing levels of about two yards depth. We continued forward, propelled above ground level by natural will, and now following down the flights of steps. We descended about six flights to the lowest level and turned left to follow a meandering pathway. The paving gave way to an evenly compacted stony surface. I remember the surprise as I began to smell the powerful sweet scent from flowering plants and shrubs either side of us as we continued on our way. All the time I was chatting with my escort. I recall only that we discussed many aspects of things current in my physical life. After the experience I was unable to recall the exact detail of my conversation but I could be sure that any directional help given would have registered in my higher mind for best choice later; and in any case I know we discussed vibrational effects, not physical responses.

I became aware I was being led to see something quite special. Presently the path led out to a grassy gentle sloping hillside. We came upon a large natural depression in the ground which nestled into the hillside. The gentle curve into this natural bowl, created an amphitheatre of sorts. From its open side I judged its size to have been about fifty meters in circumference at its flat base. The path we followed joined the base level of the feature. There were many people of all ages gathered there. At the centre of the gathering, a man stood alone, clearly in charge of proceedings. Everyone's attention was directed to him. I remember the feeling of warmth and excitement coming from the crowd. We had slowed as we approached and I also remember thinking that we may be intruding. Without speaking, my friend answered me in my mind. Passing visitors were most welcome if they had an interest. He urged me forward and we took up stance at the edge of the ring of people.

The man in charge was clothed in old-fashioned garments. He wore a simple three quarter length smock, tied at the waist. His hair was impressive. It was a bushy silver grey shock, like shiny cotton wool. He projected unmistakable warmth. His vitality and confidence were tangible. He had perhaps been speaking with everyone before we arrived. However, now he raised his arm and indicated toward the dais beside him. The plinth was raised from the ground by a few inches and was a couple of yards in diameter. On top of it there was a large oblong block, upended, which itself stood one yard tall. Our eyes were drawn to the space above the block. Thoughts filled my head as if listening to someone whispering. I became instantly aware that we were about to witness a lesson in precision; or to be exact, attention to detail in order to achieve perfection with techniques of construction. Everything happened very fast, but it seemed we were all were able to grasp each detail as if in slow motion. It was more a case that our perception matched the speed of delivery. I shall try to describe what we saw even though any physical description would be wholly inadequate to the task.

Can you ever recall seeing computer graphics on the television; let us say for example a car; where the car is built before your eyes, component by component? On the screen it appears frame by frame—each frame showing components building upon components so fast that it looks like a movie of invisible construction. The completed car is then revolved through 360° to allow a view from every angle, and the camera swoops down and into the workings of the graphic for the viewer to see it all in 3D. For us in the OOB experience the components began to appear in something like holographic form. Each was solid but our perceptions simultaneously allowed us to penetrate each added part, to view it from the inside out. Just like a jigsaw with millions of parts they appeared one by one in correct order until a magnificent building hovered complete in the air above the dais. I cannot stress enough how minute the detail was that we saw; from every fixing to every angle of aesthetic consideration. The building stayed a while to be reviewed and examined thoroughly in its completed form before disappearing again to make way for another and another, and another . . . I knew that like the others there I was not just observing the display. I was melded in an affinity with it, as if I was *one* with it and was able to understand it at a vibrational level. The show continued at lightning speed, but not so fast that we were grasping every detail of what we were being shown.

I felt a particular liking and affinity to one construction shown to us. As sub-sections and complete sections appeared, four towers grew, marking the corners of a large square. At first floor level, covered walkways grew, linking the towers together. The entire construction was from wood and as the towers continued to grow for a further elevation above the walkways, I was able to inspect the intricate carved detail over its entire surface. For this and all other constructions I had the feeling they actually existed somewhere. Certainly this one was familiar, and I felt I would visit it one day. I was able to see through it, around it below it and above it. From each of the side elevations the towers and walkways between them formed an entrance to the central area. The towers were huge and had many rooms on each level. An internal spiral staircase linked the rooms and floors, pausing at the bridge to allow free flow of movement between towers. I had the overwhelming sense of many people in a distant place occupying such a building; all joyously pursuing some form of learning. In my mind I stood at the centre of the towers looking out to the panorama beyond the towers and shared in the collective sense of awe at the things we were all being shown. I remember also a feeling of being totally aware of myself as a spectator. I felt humbled and filled with gratitude to have been allowed the privilege of seeing these things. A message entered my mind from my friend at this time that it was right and appropriate for me to be there. At the speed of light one construction began, finished, and then moved to the next one. So many buildings were shown, with so much beauty in their form and in the form of every component. We matched the speed of delivery, taking in every detail at leisure. The presentation was quite literally like nothing on earth. The thoughts of my guide came through again with a prompt that it was time for us to leave. I dearly wished to stay because I knew the lesson had only just begun.

My guide interrupted me and for just an instant he allowed me to feel something vast. For the fleeting moment I made contact with the complete vibration of the place and the promise of everything beyond. I was overwhelmed with the beauty of its vastness, and its singularity.

I still regretted leaving, but I was also filled with contentment, because I had been reminded how natural laws of harmony would ensure a continuation. We left the group discreetly and retraced our route back to the College. Along the way we talked and I remember as much that it was to do with my development. Despite the importance of our conversations, my mind was just bursting with the sights and images we had seen. I was unable later to recall the details of our talk. Perhaps like a pupil allowed into the staff room for a visit, I was prevented from taking too much information away with me. It would however stay at the back of my mind as a modifying frequency when needed. At some stage while we stood at the College again there was an affirmation between us that I must now turn back. In the next instant I awoke in my bed with a huge jolt. I sat bolt upright and wide-awake. There was not the single, solitary, slightest, tiniest trace of doubt in my mind that I had just been privileged to travel out-of-body yet again to experience and learn.

Most times when we journey out of the body, the visit is brief and less profound when we return. Whenever a full journey takes place, the recall to physical can sometimes produce a jolt. Very often the shock of the awakening jolt and the immediate assault from the physical senses blots out the detail of the journey. Most people will recall sometime waking from deep sleep with a jolt, as if an electric shock has been felt. The jolt effect can happen when something disturbs our physical body, then our astral body is snapped back to re-join unnaturally. In another effect which may be recognised by some; whenever the astral body re-joins with the physical body and for whatever reason the two do not perfectly realign, then the person can awake and for the best part of the day feel out-of-sorts. The feeling is as if the physical responses are half a beat behind the brain or the mind. The effect can make a person feel really queasy. If anyone experiences this feeling there is a simple solution which takes a few minutes to put into practice. A quiet private place is needed. I find the best place is the bathroom!

Sit calmly, eyes closed, hands resting on the lap, palms open and facing up. Withdraw the mind into itself and channel your consciousness into your head. Then use what I call a Light Bomb. Imagine in an instant, that an awesome explosion of blinding vibrational light occurs close to you. Imagine the light ripping through you like a vibrational hurricane. Imagine its power to be so ultimate that every atom of your body is penetrated by it, turning the substance of your body to the light itself. Imagine you are becoming a part of the light and that you are *one* with the light. Bathe in it. Yield to it. Claim it, and hold it—even as you open your eyes again to continue the day as a renewed person. Do it right and it works. Don't take my word for it, try it. Using this simple technique raises your general vibration and is useful in many circumstances. Anytime you feel you are under spiritual assault, this method can be used. If your energy is drained from giving to others, you can now renew it immediately. In fact, to use a simple example; if you find yourself in the company of someone who drains your spirit by soaking you with their negative vibration, use the Light Bomb during the encounter. Learn to open your higher channel even as you conduct a conversation. Let your higher mind bring on the Light Bomb to rip through the both of you with perfectly refined energy of pure vibrational light. Both of you will benefit, but the result on the other person will be startling I promise you. I will not spoil your delight by revealing more. Practice yourself first until you have mastered the technique as if it is second nature to you.

Awake when you go to Sleep

We have been dealing in some detail with the influences at work when we are asleep, or more accurately, when our physical body becomes unconscious. When asleep we are in closer contact with ourselves and potentially in closer contact with the spheres beyond. We have already discussed how we could project ourselves to meet with other people familiar to us on the physical and the higher levels. We could seek help to resolve something that was perhaps troubling us while awake. Incidentally, when we are asleep and therefore more accessible to the influence our Minders, we are able to receive higher substance when we are ill. This is the reason why those who are ill sleep a lot. It is a natural defence where the physical body shuts down to allow the Presence to receive life healing energy, directly from higher more natural levels. There are other circumstances when we are able to project away from our physical body. These could include, when hypnotised, under anaesthetic, while unconscious, through trauma or during meditation.

Much mumbo jumbo has been written about meditation. Here is my definition:
It amounts to a retreat from the physical senses, while seeking to heighten your vibration, by expansion of higher awareness. Conscious equates with being awake; unconscious with being asleep, but your Presence is never unconscious. During sleep, your Presence may be preoccupied with the latest effects of incoming impulses. Your Presence will be sifting and sorting; exercising by self-will and determination, a reshuffle of improvement or otherwise which will be recorded by modifications in your energy circulations. The external evidence of this will start with changes in the neural pathways of the brain. During the unconscious sifting process, the higher self is completely awake, and everything which has impacted from the last physical rest time is analysed and played out at the speed of thought. Your Presence either accepts, rejects, or misses impulses of help and guidance from spirit helpers nearby. When someone is vulnerable due to illness, stress or exhaustion, it is possible for spirit dwellers of a low vibration to draw close and influence the person in a negative way. Minders always try to guard against this happening but cannot interfere with free will. However during sleep, at times of serenity, the Presence is able to project elsewhere and benefit from finer vibrations reaching down from much higher spheres. When this happens we are able to act upon inspirations, warnings or general counselling from higher helpers. I have laboured

considerably to reinforce the point that helpers are unable to interfere with our free choice. However asleep or awake they are acting on our behalf. At times when we have to make crucial decisions greatly affecting our lives, helpers are able to manipulate circumstances to give us special beneficial choices. If we send out prayer or wish thoughts for something positive to happen for us, we are actually creating a motivation which has an effect in higher matter. In these circumstances Minders can act upon our request to manipulate things where we can grab a choice that will be helpful. These can seem like incredible favourable coincidences for us. They are more accurately called Synchronicities. If we all could understand how this process works, and if we trusted and our Minders completely, we would all benefit from the opportunities that would be created. Very often, people fail completely to recognise the chances and positive choices that have been arranged for them. Take for example a seemingly irritating break in normal or expected routine and around the next corner a chance encounter leads to a complete new direction in life. Do you really think this happens by chance? Look back into your life with hindsight. And remember the time when you have said to yourself,

If only I had done this, or if only I had done that! I would have prevented this or that whole chain of bad events. Why didn't I choose differently?

Apart from the simple reason of not understanding the process, there are a couple of other reasons why we miss such chances. Firstly, if anyone has forgotten, we are here in this life because we are inadequate in some way. In other words no one is perfect. So we make mistakes! We choose to learn our lessons by following meandering pathways of probability and we then must come to terms with the effects and consequence to modify our future reactions for the better. Secondly, we hold ourselves so closely to the denser vibration of the physical world that we miss or ignore signposts laid by our helpers, showing the best choices to make in our lives. Think back to Gan's story. The helpers there were manipulating circumstances big-time to create the positive synchronicities that would preserve his best pathway. But they were still acting upon his plea and command.

What is prayer? What does it have to do with synchronicity? When we send a prayer from the mind to a higher authority, we initiate a process which must return with a conclusion. The depth of the prayer can be measured as totally selfless and heart-sent, or as a simple concentration of thought to solve a meaningful problem. Both options create a refined vibration or impulse within the vibrational field of the person. The power of the prayer depends upon the force (Cause) behind it. If there is sufficient cause, the impulse breaks free from the person's vibrational field to rise like a cork to the higher level most natural to it. Helpers there are able to intercept and decipher these requests and act upon them. Even if the impulse is weak, provided it is meaningful to the life of the person or someone they represent, it will not be lost. Helpers at every level are able to detect them and act upon them accordingly. By this I mean a helper would have the benefit of being able to see the whole intention of the person's life. The helper would work in conjunction with any other helpers concerned with the person's progress. All opportunities to help are acted upon. All chances to produce a beneficial synchronicity are taken. I have been asked: If all prayers are picked up to be acted upon, then what is the point of tying yourself up in the mental effort of deep prayer? The act of praying, initiates a Cause, or motivation, which inherently produces finer vibrations. A stronger prayer produces stronger impulses, and makes their urgency easier to detect. The stronger the prayer the higher the message will reach and the more impact it will make. More helpers along the way will definitely become involved to respond to its importance. Then there will be a greater positive outcome for the sender and the subject of the prayer. Otherwise, a prayer is the Effect of Free-Will being exercised in a request or command.

The natural question for daily life would be: How can we improve our chances of doing right by ourselves and those we interact with? First and foremost it is to seek to perform according to higher vibration, or inner conscience. This means thinking and acting selflessly and with pure motivation. Do this and you will see how enlightenment and tranquillity follow. You will recognise the synchronicities. You will discern the opportunities offered by them leading to betterment. Secondly raise your vibration by sending out prayer-thoughts for the benefit of others; and even for your foes and enemies. Consider this for example: In a negative exchange if you throw a negative reaction you are producing resistance, which leads to the possible conflict of negative reciprocal reaction. The situation escalates to become self-fulfilling. By another method, you may still have to stand your ground, but this time if on a higher level you throw a light bomb at them to dissipate their negativity, their negative effect could be neutralised, changed or diluted. Try it and you will see I am telling the truth. I absolutely know it works. Prove it for yourself.

Synchronicities are created for us all the time and it is up to us to recognise them and act accordingly. You may find yourself with someone and unexpectedly out of the conversation the other person reveals a difficulty which you coincidentally have the skills to resolve. You may be on route somewhere, following a tight time schedule. Something happens to delay you. You work yourself up into a negative frenzy, cursing and blaming everyone for what has happened. You get to work late and take it out on everyone you see. Your negativity to others returns to you fulfilled and must be discharged somehow. Later in the day you miss your footing and trip to the ground, grazing your knee in the process. You return home exhausted, still blaming and being miserable. How different if a wise, wider viewing point had been adopted. Faced with the unexpected and unusual delay, higher awareness would have revealed that without the delay you would have been in the right place at the right time for something terrible to happen to you. Synchronicities were arranged by higher helpers to ensure you suffered the delay to save you. If you accepted the delay with good grace and understanding, then no negativity would have been created by you during the day to spring back and strike you later.

Whenever a prayer is issued, it is always answered. The answer is rendered according to a wider viewing point. For someone who does not grasp the process involved, it may sometimes seem as if the prayer has not been answered. All we have to do is pray to those in Spirit and yield to the perfect workings of the source. Otherwise, when an unusual coincidence occurs for you, or when there is a strange twist of events leading to a situation, or if you are presented with an irregular encounter with someone, or if your routine is interrupted; then you owe it to yourself to do two things. Open your awareness to an understanding of why the forces may be working in such a way. Try to determine if you originated the sequence, or how it came to pass from another source with good reason. Follow things through with grace to a conclusion. The results may seem to amount to nothing; but they may also be life changing and spectacular. Self-analysis and the analysis of situations around you easily becomes second nature with practice, even though the relevant factors may be complex. At all times you must recall the basic workings of vibrational forces. The process for self-analysis must take account of the difference between Synchronicity and Reciprocal reaction. It is possible when minor mishaps occur or when negative events block our pathway we can mistake them for Synchronicity. However when such things seem to present us personally with a life obstacle, they happen as a result of Reciprocal action. If we are honest with ourselves we can clearly recognise the consequence of Reciprocal action. It is quite simply the positive or negative consequence from a Cause and Effect we initiated.

If we overburden ourselves with negative impulses, our energy circulations become condensed, and our higher essence becomes suffocated. The pressure can only be rebalanced when the oppressing negative vibration has grounded its excess energy. This occurs when we are soon harmonised to an apparent negative situation or turn in life that we have to face and deal with. Just like a storm cloud full of electricity, the excess power must discharge itself. In our own case as the discharge takes place, the lightning strike is internal through the sharp lesson of a negative situation which must be borne and overcome. Long term affinity with lower vibration has a negative effect upon the tissues of our physical bodies. As the energies flow throughout our bodies, unnatural negative impulses, or vibrations, have a disrupting effect upon our physical organs. Don't forget, we originate these negative vibrations and through Reciprocal reaction we harvest the results.

General negativity can so easily become self-fulfilling when someone has a dependency on something or someone; or when negative behaviour becomes a habit. The behaviour of such a person will always be directed through Cause, to produce an adverse Effect in others, which the person uses as reinforcement to their own originating behaviour. By denying the responsibility of Consequence, they deny responsibility for their own vibrational state. Denial and the absence of Personal Responsibility walk hand in hand. The Cause, Effect, Consequence formula spirals inwards as a result and the condition becomes self-fulfilling for the person involved. Instant karma is a reality. Did you stub your toe since you were mean to someone? Did you even notice there was a connection? Did your computer just crash since you were recently unfairly in conflict with someone? Did you just have a really foul day, when in fact you have been a bit of a bad person yourself lately? Have things been going badly for you when you have been the reason for the same thing happening to someone else? The connections are there if you have eyes to see them. Don't you see, our whole life conveys an awesome responsibility for us to do right by everyone and ourselves if we wish to progress in a positive way. Sadly people deny responsibility for even their smallest bad action. Little real thought is given to Consequence when negative Cause is activated in the mind. It will be so, until everyone realises that even the tiniest Cause has an Effect and Consequence for them.

From sleep we awaken and immediately we are under assault. The disturbing sound of the alarm clock may fill our ears. The sensations of our physical body return. We may be suffering aches from sleeping awkwardly. We may be too cold or too hot. We may itch, or be thirsty. We may be ill. We are engulfed by our agenda for the day. We may be preoccupied with problems in our private lives or at work. The night air may have been stale and our blood may not be refreshed. We may have an attitude to laze in bed instead of getting on with important matters. All of these things and many more conspire to anchor us to the physical; and all of this exists as a turbulent barrier of sensation to prevent us recalling important information from our sleep time. Our Presence is caught between the expansive state of sleep and the constrictive demands of the physical day. So what advice could be given to prepare for the new day? Let us first state the obvious. Get to sleep earlier and more regularly! Before rising from bed and ideally upon awaking, make a conscious effort to remember any thoughts or strong impulses from the night. Even better to keep a notepad by the bed and log everything when you wake. I know all this sounds like a real chore, but don't knock it until you try it for a while. If you are a general sceptic, this will be a way that your attitude could be changed forever. Review the log regularly to see the insights you may have missed before. Over a period of time, you will see the connections you will have received during the sleep state. This is especially true if you send out positive prayers for help on a problem before sleep. Those impulses will register and be acted upon through our higher selves and the involvement of our Minders.

Waking Up

Upon waking, your Presence re-joins with the physical/conscious mind. Your Presence has to put up with the total restriction of the physical brain and the distraction of new data flooding in. Dreams remain for a time, tangled up with all of the other activities of mind and spirit during sleep. The mind awakens, cluttered with dream scenarios of probability from previous waking events. All the possible outcomes would have been explored. These would have been modified by the vibration of previous memories and experiences. Random neuron activity in the physical brain mixed with conditioned interpretations of the probabilities reviewed in sleep all combine to give us a waking picture we must somehow make sense of. Why should we have to go through sleep to have to face this every morning anyway? This has already been answered, but I will try again with another analogy: The bath tub is filled with water which is always in a state of movement. As we gather experiences from the day, turbulence builds up within our vibrational field. The incoming impulses cannot discharge their influence quickly enough. We reach a point of saturation, or like the bathtub with the water gradually filling to become agitated, until it is sloshing about and risking a flood if it spills over the edge. We need sleep so that our vibrational field can absorb, ignore or reject the rippling influences of the day. Through sleep the sloshing water in the bathtub is allowed to settle down; the Presence is enabled to receive fresh input from a new day. The fact of wishing for just another hour of waking time, may allow progress with something that is totally irrelevant in the greater scheme of things, but it denies recovery time for the real vibrational body. Dwell on this and ignore it at your peril. Also, in a waking state if you use your physical body or conscious mind to the point of exhaustion, your physical senses produce a massive assault of vibrational input to your existing vibrational field. This overburdens and binds your Presence to gross matter in order to cope with the negative input. Any other abuse of your physical body has the same effect.

I have omitted the most important thing in the whole sleep to waking process. Somehow through all of the turbulence, inspired help from higher levels has to find a way through. Serenity before and during sleep allows clear passage for higher inspiration. As already explained though, any received inspirational thought is usually locked into the jumble of other thoughts and images from the night. Helpers often choose other ways to convey an answer to something. Direction may be given by symbolism or as happens often in my case I awake with a totally obscure piece of music in my head that I may not have heard for years. I have learned to recognise that the lyric conveys for me a message of significance in a current situation and with deadly accuracy. Once again I challenge you to try. Don't take my word for any of this. Put it to the test yourself. Before sleep, try to lift your mind above any negativity of the day. Discharge it in your mind and lift to higher awareness. Try to close any issues on your mind, and yield them to your Minders. Convert outstanding problems to prayer. Listen to relaxing music. Do anything that will raise your vibration in order to free your Presence for better things. Gradually with practice, stunning positive results will appear in your life; and the positive message will also be self-fulfilling.

One tip is to re-live your day and reconcile any bad thoughts or outcomes you may have assisted—by first transmuting them in your mind to light and forgiveness, and then letting them go. You will then not be encumbered with these issues in sleep, or with the task of examining the infinite strengths of Probability for a later outcome.

What about Karma?

I have been asked many times, if we have lived before and we can link with other knowledge through Astral Projection, why is it so hard to recall the detail of our previous lives? The answer is very simple but I must link you back to the whole picture of how energy is interacting at vibrational level. In the form of our Presence, we comprise a coherent field of vibrational motivated energy. We maintain our individuality because each person is a divine singularity of motivating force.

Try this idea with me as an analogy. You are standing in the shallow end of a normal public swimming pool. The filtration system in conjunction with the pool heating system is circulating and refreshing the water in the pool. As you stand there, your legs and body have become normalised to the ambient temperature of the water. Suddenly, and for a few moments, you feel the rush of warmer water passing over your body. Then it is gone again. It is noticeable because against the background lower temperature, the feeling is comforting. The heat difference may have only been slight and fleeting, but you are clearly aware of it. These warmer pockets of water circulating in a swimming pool are a normal effect that many people will be familiar with. The pockets of warmer water may only be tiny, but they are real. They do not float around in the pool like balloons filled with warm water. They are coherent but are also *of* the substance of the pool water. So it is with us. We are vibrational singularities in a vast vibrational pool. From our previous lives, it is not the detail of the journey that is important to our vibrational memory. It is the cumulative effect of the journey on our Presence that counts. Those who are preoccupied with knowing detail of their previous lives completely miss the point. It is much more important to understand your motivations right now, for they are a product of your free will in all that has gone before. There may be a need to correlate evidence of reincarnation for purposes of evidential research. However if we were all developed to a much higher spiritual degree of refinement, then gnosis, or understanding, would render the exercise irrelevant. Karma describes the process further. In a nutshell, our Karmic status is like a unit of vibrational measurement. It equates to our measure of excess energy that must still be discharged to achieve perfect vibrational balance. Our Presence is trying at all times to gravitate naturally to a higher level. By the action of our free will in all that we motivate through our own initiating thoughts, our own vibrational progress becomes modified. This modifying process can be viewed as the harmonising of incoming impulses to produces excess positive or negative energy in the form of vibrational hot spots within us. The finer vibrations form a bridge to higher levels of refinement, while the lower vibrations conspire to hold us to gross matter. They seek every abstract opportunity to discharge themselves as they gravitate to gross physical matter. Along the way, both refined and gross energy has an effect on us personally, while creating a second reciprocal effect that must also be balanced out. The balancing out of these vibrations and impulses are manifest through the interactions of our life. This is the working of karma. If you have managed to completely understand it then stand-by for another consideration. I will introduce it with a proposition and question. OK. So we are all forging a spiritual pathway. Our Presence equates to the complete *us*. We create a bow wave of resistance in front of us and a drag behind us. This is our Karma. We are bestowed with absolute responsibility for our own individual actions and hence, our speed and route of progress. By the law of Reciprocal action our own decisions are balanced against us for good or bad. Our own free will is sacred and discharges itself via the Cause, Effect and Consequence formula. The whole process is personal and individual. Blame can never be laid at someone else's door. So does this mean then that personal responsibility negates collective responsibility? The question presupposes that when we move way beyond the lower planes to sublime levels, we all remain as individuals. A silly notion springs to mind of a sublime realm filled with sublime individuals, all maintaining an identical sublime individuality, milling about bored and looking for something to do!

At sublime levels nothing could be further from the truth. At sublime levels there is still a hierarchy of purpose. Work of creation on a Cosmic scale takes place. Consciousness aspires to an even greater Cosmic Godhead. Suffice for the moment to explain that where souls have elevated to much higher levels; and where the refinement process has brought everyone to closer harmony, tasks are carried out in greater unison. Individuality of the Presence is always maintained, but harmony of purpose is more easily achieved. At much higher levels, and even during the journey through lower levels, a Presence would expect to meld their experience with that of others in a soul group who share their harmony of vibration. All of this is to indicate that our journey from gross matter may be individual, but it is also inseparable from the journey of every other individual. We originate from collective consciousness and return to it. As such, we share responsibility at domestic level, community level, national level, continental level, global level and cosmic level. The interaction of influences at each and all of these levels produces a karmic response which must also be discharged in the same way as individual karma. I wish to deal with this topic more fully another time. For now it is enough to understand that Karma works for any collective of people in the same way as for an individual. This is as true for a small gathering as it is for a city, a Nation or for the whole planet.

The scope of our viewing point is widening as I now hope you appreciate the awesome collective responsibility we share. Personally and collectively on each level, we are like a dirty car going through the carwash. The car is ingrained with dirt. It takes many visits and a lot of time in the carwash to remove it. Slowly the car emerges from the other end. Inch by inch it appears, bright and clean. The car will become dirty again as it continues to be used in a dirty environment. Every time we take the trouble to give it a good coating of barrier polish, the cleaning effort is reduced the next time around. We first have to recognise that we are impure, before then making sure we keep ourselves clean and polished. A final word to move us away from this section; remember, your actions and their consequence begin with Cause which is Thought. Guard your thoughts. Refine your thoughts. Seek influences which will elevate your thoughts. Do not base your thoughts on prejudice. Know that the result of prejudice is bad Karma. Break bad Karma on all of the levels mentioned.

Understand how it works. Develop a desire with your whole being to recognise the originating chains of conditioning that led to your negative consequences. Understanding will bring recognition and armed with these qualities the effects of external bad Karma will be repelled, and the effects of internal bad Karma will be controlled. Thereby, the greater good will is produced for yourself and everyone.

We began this whole section seeking to explore the nature of a standard *Person to be* and the nature of a human Presence inhabiting the physical package. The influences are many and varied. Yet there is one more standard influence of great importance.

Conscience

If we visit a local modern superstore and try to walk out with an item that has not passed through the electronic checkout, an alarm sounds alerting staff to potential theft. Conscience operates in a similar way. We may enter an uncertain situation, and with free-will we determine a response. The consequence will be negative or positive. The consequences will be amplified through Reciprocal action. The new situation carries with it a vibrational signature. Our Presence has the ability to determine how this new set of impulses will affect our own field of vibration. As we consider the consequences of our decision, (if we give ourselves time to go through the process,) we are, by analogy, taking the item through our own built-in electronic checkout. If our decision is to act in a way to produce a negative consequence, our Presence will be aware of the impending negative intrusion. Our conscience, i.e. the warning alarm, is conveyed from our vibrational field to our mind in thoughts of apprehension or caution. We follow through with a final decision according to our own choice. We can look to no one else *ever,* for the consequence of our own actions. The world is filled with people who deny responsibility for their actions, personally or collectively. There are so many who choose to ignore the reality and warning of their own conscience. The darkness of this self-fulfilling trend reaches from the most innocuous act of unkindness to heinous crime. It denies the right of others to be themselves. On a national scale we are all aware of examples of the corporate and political greed that feeds vested interest. Obvious contradictions appear, like the sale of armaments to a nation where their leaders live in luxury as the people are dying of starvation. We dare not say it has nothing to do with us, or that we not have the power to do anything about it! Recognise conscience. Act upon conscience in whatever way you can, however small. A single voice raised in protest is a whisper, but a thousand whispers raised in unison become a deafening roar. This is the Cause which can bring a beneficial Effect upon the world—having a better Consequence for all. The natural flow of the Universe; the natural Physics of the Space and the gravitational pull of the godhead all demand this of us individually sooner or later! And by the way, we must never ever feel guilt! Conscience is our built-in system for the awareness of right and wrong. When we go against conscience and recognise the wrong in our action we feel guilt. However, the vibration of guilt is simply a way-station to allow us the diversion of diminished responsibility for the actions that led to it. Guilt diverts from us recognising and showing we have accepted our poor judgement by doing something immediately to redress the imbalance. Ignoring conscience implies already that we knew we were doing wrong. Guilt seeks benediction from the victim before redress.

Far worse is to wallow in guilt. This produces more negative vibrations that compound the original behaviour. Prolonged guilt is intended by the perpetrator for the victim to share their vibration of guilt and salve the perpetrator through empathy from the victim. It is an attempt by the perpetrator to justify their bad behaviour and deny responsibility as they continue with the downward negative spiral. If you recognise your wrongdoing you must take full responsibility for the negative energy you created, so do something about it immediately. Carry out a positive selfless action, preferably for your victim. This is the only way to deal with your own recognised wrongdoing. Remember this: Conscience never forgets and never lets you forget. It has its own vibrational signature and the power of its actualised impetus. It *must* be discharged, willingly or unwillingly!. You should have understood by now, the Law of Reciprocal action is waiting to pay you back with interest for your every action, good and bad. You can run. But never ever hide from it. You can never hide from yourself, even if it takes a lifetime of lifetimes to realise the fact. We now have sufficient information to view all the influences that form our *Person to be*. The following illustration shows how all parts work together.

THE MAP OF LIFE FOR ANY PERSON

SOUL SELF or ETHONIC PRESENCE

INADEQUATE but MOTIVATED

with a

? BIRTH PLAN ?

Wishing to Progress by
DISCHARGING NEGATIVE VIBRATION

through
LESSONS and EXPERIENCES

in a
New Physical Life

Ethonic field or Aura

Helpers from Higher Levels, with Departed Friends and Family, giving Guidance, Inspiration or Warnings, and creating Positive Synchronicities

GREATER SPACE

The Higher Levels of Reality

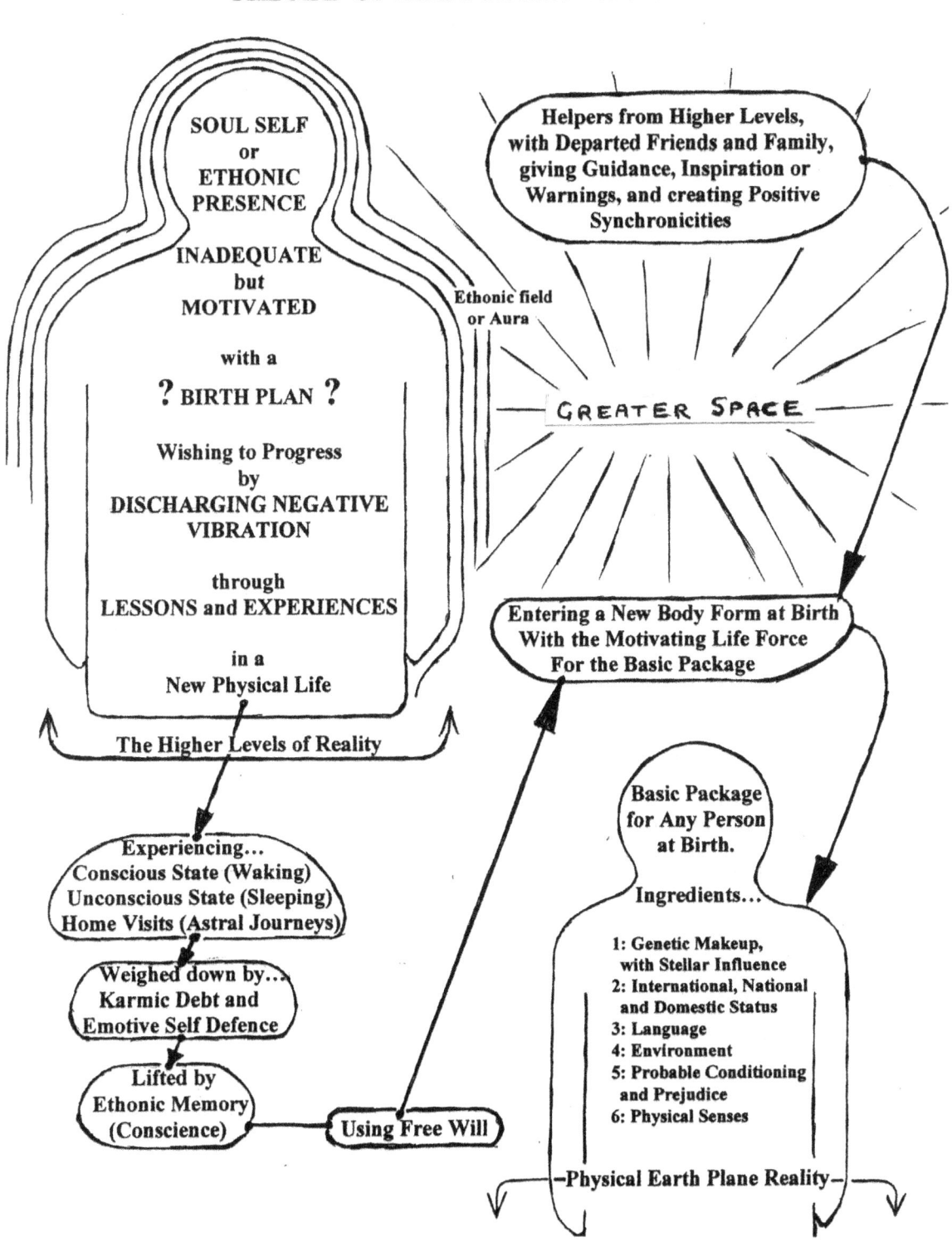

Entering a New Body Form at Birth With the Motivating Life Force For the Basic Package

Experiencing...
Conscious State (Waking)
Unconscious State (Sleeping)
Home Visits (Astral Journeys)

Weighed down by...
Karmic Debt and Emotive Self Defence

Lifted by
Ethonic Memory (Conscience)

Using Free Will

Basic Package for Any Person at Birth.

Ingredients...

1: Genetic Makeup, with Stellar Influence
2: International, National and Domestic Status
3: Language
4: Environment
5: Probable Conditioning and Prejudice
6: Physical Senses

—Physical Earth Plane Reality—

PLATE 2 : The Living Map for any Person

The Living Map

Take time to study the Map of Life. You will soon get your bearings as you recognise the subject areas we have covered. The map should allow you to see more graphically how they all fit together. Within the Standard Package of handicaps for our any *Person-to-be*, the objective influences of handicap await the subjective influences of the incoming Presence.

Beyond the person are all the avenues of connection and interaction with the higher home that the Presence will temporarily leave behind. Merged together, a living physical person is thereby created. On the map you will see a question mark remaining above the Birth Plan header.

I will turn to another analogy to explain what it means. Let us represent the Standard Package as a custom-built and highly personalised car. Let us represent the incoming Presence as the driver of the car. If car and driver wished to embark on a long journey together, they would need a route plan, destination and some kind of strategy for tackling the journey. The question mark represents in the drawing the specific reason for the journey, plus the route plan and the intended destination. I cannot reveal the deep nature of the question mark yet. I must ask you to be patient with me because there are a couple more crucial processes that must be explained for the question mark to be fully understood.

All of the influences producing the *Person to be*, interact together as fields of vibrational energy in a constant state of flux. The energies flow in pathways of circulation within and beyond the physical body. Within the physical body, the energies flow in a major circulation which is divided through several smaller circulations. These are the Chakra circulations, carrying and transferring the energy in a helix up through the physical body. If all circulations were operating in total harmony together, the person would be in perfect physical health and balance. He or she would be a person with great power. Their aura would be extensive, blindingly bright and very stable. In almost every case, we are here because we are inadequate in some way and correspondingly our energy flows are imperfect. Dysfunction in the physical body corresponds to local blockages of energy flow. A perfect chord can only be sounded when all of the tuning forks work in unison. Individually, the hotspots of energy correspond to frequencies of vibration, which in turn are visually represented as colour and extend well above and below the normal visual ranges of the colour spectrum. Generally speaking, the darker and deeper the colour, the more dense the vibration. Physical illness or bodily dysfunction would correspond with dark and chaotic circulation. When the expression is used: *Heal thy self,* there is much truth to it. When a person is feeling out of sorts or is genuinely ill, they can help themselves considerably by linking to higher positive energy. If an attempt is made by the person to increase their general vibration, this assists in the re-alignment of disrupting negative energy in the body and speeds recovery. Illness and physical dysfunction have their roots in our own imperfection, but this can be much better explained. If illness and dysfunction are representatives of negative and/or chaotic vibrations, we need to understand where the negative vibrations came from in the first place. Our Presence comes to the Standard Package as a divine soul which is already an accumulation of experience. Our Presence is the sum total of that experience and reflects the vibration, (degree of refinement) of its progress. Along the road to experience our Presence will have built up a deficit of negative energy which will be awaiting discharge. This personal karmic debt modifies the general vibration of the person. When the Presence joins with its Standard Package, a two-way exchange takes place. The vibrational level of the Presence will be operating below perfection and will not be able to sustain a perfectly operating physical body. The physical body, plus feedback from the physical senses and the responses of an imperfect Presence, will ensure that the person's vibration will be in a constantly improving state of flux. Imperfections will show up as physical infirmity, illness or in the grouch/bad attitude of the person to those whom they encounter.

When a body is inhabited by a motivating Presence the host body is subject to the effects of the vibration of the incoming Presence. All of the organs of the body have the potential to operate in complete harmony and produce radiant health for the person. However Physical well-being is subjective to vibrational well-being. This therefore delivers a small part of the explanation for infirmity and illness. The greater explanation must wait alongside the earlier question mark from the illustration which I still have to answer. Nevertheless; whatever the source of negative energy and its physical effects, I can state unequivocally, by free-will we can remove the cause. You can be a negative and pessimistic person, or a positive and expansive person. You have the choice. You must bear the consequences of your own choice. There is no escape. It is the way it is, and therefore it is all the more important to get our daily priorities right. Even an optimistic and expansive person becomes tired. The aura of an optimistic and expansive person would seem bright, large and balanced. When they become tired, the energies forming their aura would not necessarily become disruptive and chaotic. Instead, the vibrational energies become condensed and draw closer to negative thresholds, which could then cause disruption and chaos for the physical systems. We sometimes say we are feeling a bit low, or that our resistance is low. Either way, if the frequencies are not raised, then even a honed athlete for example will suffer a bad cold or some other more serious complaint. I have already described ways you can raise your vibration, but such is the importance of learning to do this that I am going to repeat myself. I hope my sample method and its potential impact will register with you in this time if you missed it on the last occasion.

If I feel my energy levels have been depleted in honourable pursuit, I find private place, usually the bathroom, and open my higher awareness. I create a Light Bomb in my mind. I imagine the awesome, unstoppable, terrifying, sublime vibrational power of creation exploding to me from higher realms in an instantaneous consuming blast of white light. I feel the light at atomic level; each impulse like a spear ripping through any negative energy in its path, driving it out and downwards. I feel and see in my mind how the light penetrates every atom of my body. The explosion complete, I bathe in the afterglow, feeling the new radioactive coat of light around me. I wear my new coat with gratitude. I give prayer with thanks and ask for help to transmit its strength to others. The whole process may have only taken a few minutes but leaves me feeling renewed and transformed with higher strength. By this simple method in humility and total submission, I *command* and *invite* the power of creation to invade and recharge me. It does just that always and never failing.

I will tell you of another very simple exercise that justifies me repeating myself again. Our progress depends upon the formula of: Cause (motivating thought,) Effect (the action carried through,) and Consequence (the reciprocal outcome of Cause and Effect.) Our progress therefore begins at all times with Cause (thought.) Nothing ever occurs but that someone somewhere has developed the motivating Cause for it. Nothing is more important than having the correct thoughts in your mind at all times. Your thoughts motivate impulses that will draw upon the virtual substance around you. The vibrational substance develops a hotspot of excess energy, which initially becomes self-fulfilling within the vibrational field of its host, but eventually must be discharged as a negative or positive action. By Reciprocal Re—Action the negative energy rebounds to harmonise with, and amplify the original impulses. No one is perfect. We are all bound to have bad thoughts from time to time. How do we control them before they control us? My method: Become practised to be aware of your own thoughts at all times. Develop the good habit of *thinking* about *thinking*. Train yourself to regard your thoughts as being a separate living entity. Give them the total respect of being a powerful force in their own right. They originate from you, but after their birth in your mind, they can become powerful enough to stand in their own right as excess hot spots of energy waiting for a chance to discharge themselves. If you now really understand what vibrational processes are at work, you will appreciate how easy it will be to set up an alarm system in your mind—to sniff out any really negative spirals of energy as they form. When I realise I have created a negative hotspot in my mind, I personally use a crucifix of light. In my mind I externalise the whole negative idea I have created. I place a crucifix of blazing white light between myself and the negative thought-thread. For me the crucifix of light is an impenetrable barrier that allows me to walk away from the bad thoughts I have been having. I carry out this exercise as a matter of course in my day to day life. It takes no effort and a split second to do, and is a totally effective way of discharging the human negative thoughts which crop up as a result of our resistances in life.

The Law of Probability

The Law of Probability is a fundamental law of physics that has a direct bearing on all physical life. It affects everything at vibrational level, but has repercussions for everything at gross physical level. If you can get your head around the way it works, so many phenomena of the physical world will be instantly understandable. So once again I have to apologise for the fact that we've got to recount familiar ground to get there. This Law is really important so please follow with me. Hopefully by now you will have formed a picture of how all things exist in a state of vibration. Everything derives from vibrational substance, or plasma. Vibrational substance at Atomic level performs as virtual matter. Impulses not only flow freely within this material, they *are* the material. Where the impulses focus, a hotspot of plasma is created and this is the basis for solid physical matter. Everything exists in a state of vibration and has a vibrational signature. Solid physical matter maintains a relationship with the vibrational reality beyond it. A human is motivated by an inhabiting Presence whose vibrational field extends beyond it to create the Aura. Creative vibration and all processes of transmutation originate out of sentient free will. The never ending interchanges are in a constant state of flux. Their infinite possibilities for modification mean that the outcome can never certain. *Certain* is a fixed idea and cannot apply to an evolving situation. If we need a yardstick, we would have to say that everything occurs as a degree of Probability, and not certainty. An event born out of sublime matter or motivation, journeys through stages of interaction until the event occurs. Even when the event occurs, it is not fixed. It is transient, and only passes through an actuality. It exists therefore as a certainty only for so long as it lasts as a modifying vibrational effect on something else. I will deviate slightly to say, there is a way in which the record of the event can be retrieved. The passing of the event will have had a modifying effect to produce surrounding hotspots of influence. The effect remains, even if there are further modifications. It would be possible to read the modifications to regain the original influences that caused them, like reading a shadow of the original motivation.

Before an event occurred, if we were able to identify the motivating influences leading up to its possibility, we could predict the outcome of their interchange to a degree of probability. These motivating influences would have to include all the minute the factors in the progress of other events for a very wide field of expected and unexpected factors. The greatest difficulty for this prediction process is the action of free will, where *we* are involved. It is a matter of fact that in the higher realms, human activity is preoccupied with the study and understanding of vibrational interchanges and effect. This is not a passive activity because physical creation originates in higher realms. The manipulation of vibrational substance is carried out in the pursuit of perfect creation. From this, inspiration is passed down to us at the physical level; but the outcome from our physical mishandling of things, still has to be dealt with as a damage limitation exercise again on higher levels. For those who dwell higher, it is normal with developed vibrational sight to be able to read a person plus all the influences that have a bearing on their choices. From this, the strength of probability can be anticipated before something is actualised. The process is on-going according to the changes that are constantly taking place. Prediction is therefore possible *to degrees of probability*. For us the process takes place while asleep, and the anticipation of an event is locked into our subconscious mind when we awake. Déjà vu is just that! We visit somewhere next day and have that feeling of having been there before. We have indeed been there before because we have played out the probability of it as one of our most likely scenarios during sleep. The process is not just confined to places but also complex events and interchanges. If we meditated on the process we could learn to programme our minds before sleep and recall the solution to all kinds of problems at a higher level, with ease. People often wonder why prediction is often linked to disaster. When a disaster occurs on the earth plane, a huge knot of negative energy becomes discharged. The infinite factors that lead to a disaster-event can originate in the lives of multiple individuals and events, and can also be tied into the play of Karmic forces at national or world level. As the interchanges evolve, the factor of probability for the event becomes stronger and stronger. As the time draws close for the event to be actualised, the vibrations of probability will be almost overwhelming. The event is never certain, because the free will of those involved in its development can alter the probabilities. However, the collision course of probability causes an increased gathering of negative energy. Remember, the disaster event would occur to discharge a build-up of vibrational stress, or negativity. The whole proposed event might be complex, involving individuals, animals, machines, vehicles or natural earth energies etc. The build-up continues. The event occurs and passes. The aftermath is a complexity of discharging negative and positive impulses.

During the build-up, as the strength of probability increased, the gathering of negative impulses would have signalled a warning throughout Space. Anyone with vibrational sight could detect and interpret the denser vibrations. Someone in physical life but with a raised general vibration would still have a greater affinity with vibrations from the physical level, or from the lower regions of the higher levels. This means that a physical person would have far greater empathy for the probability of the denser negative vibrations building for a disaster event. It's as simple as that!

During sleep, the Presence does not have to try and see with vibrational sight. In sleep vibrational sight is natural. A person not bogged down and preoccupied with domestic negativity could easily foresee events by recognising Probability hotspots for just about anything in wider Space. At higher levels of refinement, it is similarly possible for all interactions and their probable outcome to be studied in full.

The Birth Plan

At last we have enough information to discuss the most important and final missing element in the Map of Life, *The Birth Plan*. If it were possible to step in and out of the communities living in the realms or planes of reality beyond the physical just to observe their general qualities, certain things would be immediately obvious. First and foremost, within each land or community, the people living there would be coexisting with a far greater harmony of purpose. As explained before, the vibrational field of every Presence resonates within a general plus/minus vibrational tolerance for each higher realm. Each state of living in the higher realms is representative of the souls who have gravitated there naturally to live together with others who have a similar vibration. Someone of lower vibration would feel great discomfort in the midst of a more elevated community. In communities closer to the earth plane, the tolerance of harmony becomes much wider, leading to a greater diversity of opposing purpose. Just as a precaution I will remind you that realms or spheres do not imply dimensions stacked on top of each other like books on a shelf. Realms or spheres existing as diverse states of refined vibration could exist in the same way as Continental masses exist on the earth plane. They could exist as neighbouring villages. They could exist as distant states occupying the same space, just as everything beyond the physical occupies the same space as the physical.

On our tour, we would also recognise that members of these communities do not float about aimlessly as bright lights with angel wings strapped to their backs! In fact at every level there are towns and villages and dwellings of all description. People maintain their previous physical appearance, because remember, their vibrational signature is still intact even though they have departed their last physical body. They will have rid themselves of the gross physical vibrations which maintained any physical deformity or infirmity; unless their vibrational signature was of a depraved, base and cruel person in life. In this case the released Presence would still follow natural law and rise from the physical to join a community compatible with their level of evolvement. But a higher observer would see that their environment was a dark, condensed and oppressing place, and all inhabitants would appear as reflections of their dark, ugly base nature. For the average person, their appearance therefore becomes a sound representation of their former self, but refreshed and renewed.

On higher levels there is a difference. The higher the state, the more refined the vibration, and the more refined and harmonious the residents of that state. When a Presence has reached much higher levels of being, there is less reason to maintain the physical human appearance. Individuality is maintained, and can be recognised, but where souls are functioning in such close harmony of vibration, a merging takes place. This has been referred to elsewhere as the gathering of souls.

Busy life continues within the communities. Living is concerned mainly with education and the management of people and processes. At higher levels this also involves creation. Much more at lower levels this involves the application of processes and the interchanges between people. At lower levels, any negative weaknesses are highlighted because they are now transparent to others who have the same weaknesses. This leads from constant outer confrontation, to inner confrontation. The personal recognition of a weakness is the start of a pathway to overcoming it. In any of these communities, the natural laws of physics regulate the driving force behind everything. Negative energy in every form, seeks to discharge toward gross physical matter. Refined energy seeks to gravitate to even higher refined matter. A long-term resident of any community will have formed many bonds and working relationships. They will have proceeded in spirit life, occupied with their chosen tasks, learning about the external world above and below the quantum threshold, and learning about themselves. They will have maintained contact with souls who were once their own family members and where possible, they will have helped or have been helped themselves by some of these family friends. Their passage through continued life will have been monitored at all times by other Helpers (guides) who function as Social Workers. The repercussions of a former life will have taken a very long time to work themselves out. The actions of a single person touch the lives of thousands throughout their physical lives. With the passage of time, friends, family and acquaintances become spread between the physical dimension of life and the higher levels of life. Family attachments and family interactions and indeed interaction with anyone else, will have left impressions or wounds which must heal. Generally therefore, beyond a person's physical lifespan, helpers ensure that the individual interacts where appropriate, to resolve any remaining historical problems they may have helped to create with their former family, friends or contacts.

During this period, which may last for many years, the individual may move several times between communities as they progress. There comes a time however when the individual is still unable to shake certain negative traits. Only one method remains for the person to arrive at the inner confrontation to rid them of a negative inadequacy. The person must return to serve the lessons of another physical life. It is possible also that the person will have built new bad habits. It is possible that their state of vibration is so low that the negativity from the previous life can only be confronted with a quick return to physical in a carefully appropriate life. The racist for example may return as someone who will be racially oppressed themselves. A male may return as a female, or vice versa; a sinner as a saint; a rich person as a poor person. Or it may be that the person requires a tuning of their vibrational energies requiring them only to stay for a short physical appearance! Baby and child mortality is viewed with negativity but there is a wholly more positive viewing point which encompasses the need of involved parents and community to also learn a modifying lesson.

We shall follow the procedure of a person returning to a new physical life by using the hypothetical example of someone who *was* a racial bigot. Our sample person came from a working class background and made a lot of money at the expense of deprived people in his area. He derived pleasure from the misery of others. His tolerance of other ethnic members of the community was zero. This person in spirit, who has reached the stage where he or she needed to return, will have been spending more and more time in a lethargic state not unlike sleep. Higher Helpers would have been viewing for some time to determine by the Law of Probability, what sort of life was shaping to provide the best conditions for the person's progress. Every conceivable possibility would have actualised by natural vibrational-attraction, including all the factors I have already identified to produce the standard *Person to be*. All the things we have examined will have become naturally manifest as having the closest vibrational compatibility with the vibrational signature of the incoming Presence. The country; nationality; region, parents; genetics, etc. All would have become readable as a Virtual blueprint of probability. It is not as hard as it may seem to translate the earth-bound view of random chance in birth match with parent type. It would be natural to assume a vast lottery of chance, visiting everyone in every country of the world for the final pairing of the eventual child personality that will become the new-born. Some factors would be easy to speculate. For example, the incoming person's proposed race or nationality may not have a great probability bearing on the person's future. So let us suppose our returning Presence would be best matched to an inner city life in Britain, as the sibling of a deprived ethnic family. A baby is soon to be conceived by the couple who will eventually become the host parents to our subject. Their probabilities will have been gathering strength, not only to produce the event, but also to determine all the other factors that will go to make up their unborn Person to be. These probabilities and the event they portend will ensure the existence of the event before it happens. It will exist as a virtual event, recorded as a growing hotspot of energy in the greater Space associated with the person and increasingly with the earth parents whose circumstances are providing the best natural harmonic situation to match the vibrational signature of the potential incoming Presence. This coming together of impulses, heralding the probability of the event, will produce a collective vibrational signature.

However there is a *But* in this natural process of vibrational selection. I have already described how the vibrational signature of a person qualifies them to be tolerant of situations which offer a plus/minus variation of compatibility. These variations of prevailing vibration are a normal part of physical life anyway and provide the opportunities of resistance for us to react and learn from the lessons produced. We see it as the pain of a situation, but there is no such thing as pain—only lessons. On higher levels before a new birth, the variations of tolerance usually produce a number of, parent and situation choices which would enable the new-born to make vibrational progress in their new life. This is where those Minders from a higher level who have an interest in the person, are able to intervene. Faced with multiple choices before the final parents are determined, a higher conscious decision has to be made which will direct the incoming presence to their destination life. (The most bestial and low-vibrational people will have evolved to the stage where they will not have an awakened understanding of the process they are involved in.) Most average people either before physical death or beyond will be able to grasp their situation. As such therefore, the incoming person/Presence, will conduct a conference of decision with their Minders. It is at this stage where the strongest Pathway of Probability for each of the potential choices will be examined. It will be the sacred right of the incoming person/Presence to make the final choice. It is where the incoming person/Presence chooses their parents!

For those I referred to previously as the most bestial and base who need to return to physical life again for a harder lesson, the process is fundamentally the same. The variation is to realise firstly that the incoming person/Presence this time would have a low, condensed vibration. Their requirements for progress would produce a vibrational compatibility for example to a family where they were restricted and forced to face themselves in a powerful way. Their pre-options would arise from past choices and their resulting vibrational signature.

The possibilities are endless, but are most likely to include the probability path which would place them in situations of restriction or reliance upon other people. The base person now under restriction would have the choice to learn through more intense reciprocal reactions. They could choose to elevate themselves through the examples of the compassion, kindness and patience displayed by those in whom they are now forced to rely. They may do the same through their inevitable connection and the example of others in similar position. They may alternatively and very often be under the restriction of a dysfunctional family with its inherent adversities and conflicts, as a result of their own bad attitude—which conditioned their siblings to follow with the same behaviour. The siblings in such a case would be on their own natural pathway of lessons and progression in just the same way. Towards the end of the new physical life if the person strays from their pathway of strongest probability; clinging instead to their traits of lower vibration, a couple of things will result. Firstly the continued low vibration will manifest itself in the physiological state of the person's body. They will be unhealthy. Secondly, the person will most likely succumb to mental disturbances where their decision process will be massively impaired. This will place them personally under even more frustrating restriction. The severity of restriction will provide greater lessons in the pathway of others in the family as they deal with the consequence. Thirdly, the person will likely face earlier physical death because the physical body will break down sooner. Finally, the person is subject to immutable natural cosmic laws. These will ensure the person's fast return once again to yet another restrictive physical incarnation for the opportunity to learn once again. It is all about states of vibration. It is all about the vibrational signature of the person and where it places them in the gravitation pathway back to perfect balance. It is all about the divine choices made by the person to determine how long the lessons may continue. It is all about how long it takes for the person to separate and accept the lessons from the pain, and is able at last to free themselves from further lessons of conflict at such low vibrational levels.

If a person is therefore ready for a return to physical life it will not be necessary to research all the factors that may produce best choice. The vibrational signature of the situation that matches their requirements perfectly will already exist and only needs to be read.

So it is then, the ideal match is found. Careful examination of all close and wide factors for the forthcoming life for the new individual will indicate a strongest pathway of probability for them to achieve the task they set out to achieve. A perfect outcome from this process would be if the individual followed their strongest pathway of probability in life and achieved a stage of enlightenment. However, free-will distracts to self-indulgence and it would be rare for any individual to follow their strongest pathway of probability. More likely their free will deviates them from their best route. Every twist and turn will simply modify the strength of probability for all that lies ahead and provide invaluable harder learned experiences and lessons. Whenever possible, when the time is right for our person to return to a new physical life, they are made aware of what awaits them and the reasons for it happening. An enlightened person returning will be a part of the process themselves.

At time of conception, a bonding takes place. The spiritually sleeping Presence is brought together with the couple and an earthing—out of substance takes place between our incoming Presence and the new inert child, yet to be born. The earthing-out between them is possible because of the harmony of vibration between the incoming Presence and the predicted vibration of the *Person to be*. The whole process is like an arranged marriage. The bond between an incoming Presence and the growing, standard, baby package is made at any time between conception and birth. The incoming Presence may be a willing participant in the whole process, but swapping a familiar environment for this new restrictive alien physical environment is not pleasant. Perhaps now you will see why the screams of protest at birth are not just from the shock of leaving the warm environment of a mother's womb. The process of re-emergence from spirit into a new physical life seems complex at first glance, but the requirements of a Spirit Presence creates a very specific vibrational signature which is naturally matched with choices available, because the choices available create cross-matching impulses.

I have focussed on just one set of circumstances for a return to physical life, but there are many more. A higher spirit may wish to return to carry out a specific task or deed. There may be a need to return simply to act as a catalyst in the development of another soul. There may be a need to return simply to discharge a very specific area of negativity. All of these reasons and many more account for the variety of physical life, the life, time-spans and means of physical death. I have lost count of the times I have been asked something along the lines of, *If there is a God, why does he let babies die?* The question is understandable but asked in ignorance of the process involved. A child who dies as a child only gives up a physical body. They have completed their short physical lifespan for a very specific reason. The reason formed part of *their* Birth Plan and a part of the Birth Plan for all those that the early physical death will affect. The Presence, who *was* the individual, remains so in spirit. Their growing—up continues in spirit. The special bond with the mother remains. The child will experience an accelerated growing—up along with other children at the hands of Helpers in spirit. Remember once again, the child came from a previously completed physical life and an extended period as a resident in spirit. In the child-form as they now find themselves, they are a culmination of their progression through previous incarnations. Their vibrational signature does not just represent them as they are now. It represents their entire existence—and all lessons of their past remain captured in virtual form as a part of their vibrational signature now. It is so for all of us. It negates the need except for special reasons, for a person to ever obsess over their possible previous incarnations. We are what we are and also what we ever have been. It is necessary only to recognise the process as such and on the choices which will elevate our spirit/Presence even further.

The person returning to spirit as a child does not carry with them a bag full of individual personalities. They carry with them the merged progress of their earlier experiences. The new modified vibration of the person/child will maintain its link with the same vibrational signals produced by the person/child's family. This means that the person/child will be specially equipped to return with help to family members when needed, and if they choose. The person/child will re-grow in spirit as the lives of the parents and family continue in physical life. The person/child's death will have forced people affected to face something within themselves in different ways. By the physical death of the child, those affected will have been given the opportunity to grow spiritually. The example of a child death is perhaps the best starting point for you to apply the understanding to every death situation you can imagine. A physical death produces shock. The person is no longer there physically. Their physical presence is a great loss. Grief is felt. If there was a deep love bond with the departed person, the grief is correspondingly deep. Deep grief however produces negative vibrations. Negative vibrations are self-fulfilling as they bind their producer to gross matter. The departed soul has become a freed Presence again. Their Presence is just the same as it was when it inhabited the now redundant body. Their appearance in spirit is just the same as when it inhabited the physical form. Their vibration now is no longer bound to the gross vibration of the body left behind. Their unencumbered vibration is more refined. The grieving parents and family, who wish to draw to their departed loved one, ironically achieve the opposite because they cling to grosser vibration through deep grief. It is a response borne out of ignorance for the process which has taken place.

I have attended many funerals and have shared in the sadness at the physical loss of someone. The deeper grief of close family and friends always increases my personal sadness because of something beautiful they are missing. At some stage I always try to open my vibrational sight to higher awareness. The collective grief on one level is tangible, like fog lying in the bowl of a valley. On another level I am always able to link with the visitors from spirit realms. The Presence of the departed soul will not be far away, tended by helpers, family and friends who have passed before them. I experience their Presence as a wind over my entire body. My hair stands on end as if charged with static electricity. Sometimes I can see mistiness in the air. Always I feel the rush of comfort from deep compassionate impulses they issue to those present. Their attendance is always unmistakable. My sadness is for loved ones who could potentially form a much stronger link than me and are unable to do so in their grief. I also always try to blank my mind so it is in a receptive state for inspired thought. I put my mind into an Alpha state. If I am originating no thoughts myself, then incoming thoughts are easier to identify and grab. I often receive messages or inspired thoughts from those present in spirit. I will describe a very personal experience:

I had been estranged from my mother for more than two decades. My sister and her family in a different part of the country had maintained closeness with my mother. I had very recently re-established contact with her and had arranged a visit for us to meet again. My mother would then meet the grown up grandchildren she had last seen as babies. Before the reunion took place I received a phone call to say that my mother was very ill in hospital. She had been ill for a time and had accidentally overdosed on paracetemol tablets. The mistake had not been discovered soon enough and she was now terminally ill in intensive care at the hospital. I dropped everything and travelled the long distance to the hospital. My sister had been keeping vigil along with other family members at her bedside. Soon after I arrived my sister was compelled to leave for a short while to deal with home matters. I found myself at the bedside alone. My mother was deeply unconscious and convulsing. Her body was poisoned and failing. Her situation was terribly distressing. I spoke with her constantly knowing she would hear me on a higher level. I had a deep sense of her pain as she tried to fight the inevitable. As I sat with her a sudden change took place. I detected a drop in air temperature around us. I was immediately alerted to the Presence of others in spirit. I spoke again to my mother telling her I loved her and that she should now open her eyes to those who had arrived and stop fighting in order to leave the pain behind. As I sat there she took a deep breath and her body transformed. She relaxed totally. Her features became normal and she smiled. I was holding her limp hand and I told her not to hesitate but to accept the warm greeting of those who had arrived. Mentally I asked her to signal me in some way if she could understand. As she took her last breath her hand tightly squeezed mine twice and I knew she had finally released. The air within the curtained area of the bed was very misty and I felt the strongest presence of spirit I have ever witnessed. At that moment I had no feeling of sadness at all. My tears were tears of elation as I felt the Spirit Presence of my mother and others caressing me. The intensive care ward was a hive of activity normally. However for the minutes of these events, her departure had been missed on the monitors and no nurses came near. I now stood as I felt the energy around me begin to lift higher and higher. I felt such privilege to have been able to say a spiritual goodbye to my mother as she departed this physical life. At this time I saw through a gap in the curtain, a nurse had finally noticed the main monitor. She called to another nurse and they came running in my direction. As they got to our curtained cubicle I stopped them to say everything was all right. I knew my mother had passed to spirit. They agreed to give me a few moments longer before they came to do their work. I must tell you by the way, as I have been writing this account of my mother's passing; my senses have been filled with the full yeast smell of our old pantry. I recognise this to be the signal of my mother's Presence when she comes to visit me. She would have definitely wished to see how I described the event. Furthermore I am sending a message as I type it, *Mother I hope you approve*. I departed the ward just as my sister returned to the hospital.

Again in my life—and this time on a highly personal level I knew I would soon have to grasp a double edged sword. I was deeply sad that I had been unable to reunite with my mother during physical life. I was elated to have witnessed the profound nature of her passing. In moments the expected wall of grief from my poor sister and other family members overwhelmed me. I longed to convey the experience of my mother releasing to spirit. I knew however, my sister and other family members were not yet ready to understand. I knew my explanations would only cause more distress. I knew I must yet again keep the beauty of spirit in check until others were ready to see it.

It can often be the case where closely linking people pass back to spirit, they retain the bond when they undergo next physical rebirth. The original bond would usually arise out of family ties. Beyond rebirth, two previous members of the same family may find themselves reunited in different roles and as a part of different families. When two or more people come together in this way, there is instant vibrational recognition. The two people may not know why there is an incredible bond between them. They may lead totally differing lives and be thrown together under synchronicity to work some unfinished business out. The incredible bond may be positive or negative. If for instance one member suffered at the hands of the other, in the new scenario, their roles may be reversed. In another example of vibrational attraction, one person may bump into a complete stranger whom they may never get to know in this life. In a split instant as their eyes meet they will have a strange awareness of each other. There will be a compulsion between them which both will notice. The recognition may only last for so long as it takes for both people to simply walk on their way. The impression left however will be unmistakable. If these two people actually meet properly, there is a strong probability they will form a close bond of friendship or even more. The source of this attraction is that the vibrational field or signature produced by both, will be almost identical. In the spheres, before both of these souls made a return to physical life, they would have lived in the same community or at least at a similar vibrational level. I could go on and on with further examples, but do you follow with me now and see how easy it is to start looking around you and recognise the vibrational processes at work in everything?

We return repeatedly over aeons to undergo more physical lives. This is a natural process allowing us with free will to discard gross vibration until there is no need for us to regress again. By then we will have become permanent residents of more refined realms beyond the physical. In a best case scenario many years into the future, all residents of the physical plane will have lost their need to cling to gross vibration. They will be able to change state freely between the spheres, and work toward even higher unisons of spirit. For now the two-way traffic continues. People armed with their own Birth Plan return to realise it. Many fail and must regress. Many only partially succeed. A few are wholly successful and will not need to return again.

Descent or Ascent?

On the earth plane across the world people are making choices. Their choices are based upon Cause, which is thought. The motivation for thought arises from within. Their vibrational signature is a reflection of the choices they have made so far. This status is affected by opposing forces. On one side there is the gravitational pull of sublime matter. This is the gravitational pull of the Source, or Godhead as some know it. . . It is relentless. It tugs constantly at the higher vibrational Presence occupying a physical body. It beckons through lessons to a state of harmony and creation. The route signposted by this force promises an almighty battle with self. The destination demands that self, yields to the *Law of One*, but the reward is sublime and everlasting. The second force is where hot-spots of gross vibration seek to condense further to their origin in physical experience. This force clings to the gross vibrational traits displayed by an ignorant Presence while bound to physical form. They are motivated by ego, or self-satisfaction. This force gives substance to material rewards and sensation. All characteristics based upon self-gratification or the denial of compassion and Spirit, are the rewards for clinging to this force. These rewards are temporary. They are transient. There is a penalty for their constant pursuit. The ultimate penalty is darkness and discontent.

The battle of choice rages across the planet. Our environment is a reflection of our past choices. It stands as proof that we have been collectively condensing and clinging towards the negative side for too long. Wars rage. People are exterminated and catapulted prematurely back to spirit. Nations starve. The Planet is being raped. Creatures are becoming extinct. Developed Societies are declining into materialism. Neighbourhoods are becoming blighted. The youth are becoming hostage to self, and leaders teach self-interest. At every level, gross vibrational signatures represent these activities. As a world society we fail therefore to provide the best model for our youth. Our youth are unable as they grow physically, to grow spiritually. Their Birth Plans are thwarted time and time again as they grow up to worship all the negative traits of a physical life. They pass to spirit with a need to quickly return and fulfil the task they just failed. Their vibration is low and they find ready places waiting for them in the negative environment of the world as it is. Their base vibrational state become self-fulfilling as the negative cycle continues. The danger signs are already there; but how can the balance be restored? If you cannot fathom the basic answer to that question then you have missed the content of this book so far! However the answer can be enlarged.

Everyone is born into a physical life, starting as a malleable, pliable and impressionable child. As the child grows into youth, he or she is able to start making choices themselves. Gradually the inner battle becomes more intense. Conscience, Synchronicity and Reciprocal Action guide the choices on one side. Self-interest, Self-gratification and Derision drag the choices down on the other side. There are two major factors to tip the balance one way or another. These are firstly the example set by the child's seniors, and secondly—it is the old-fashioned quality of discipline. Discipline engenders Self-Discipline. Self-Discipline engenders Respect. Respect engenders Self-Respect. And without Self-Respect there can be no motivation to progress. If the predominant message from seniors is that it is acceptable to indulge in service to self, first, and disregard the consequence of personal action, then the negative trait will be reinforced and become self-fulfilling. The correct teachings of these vital areas of influence are the responsibility of all peers. This includes parents, schoolteachers and members of society generally. When a child behaves badly we can look to the factors causing the child to act in that way. Too often when such factors are identified, they are taken as an excuse. *Reasons* are reasons but they should never be used as an *Excuse* to negate good behaviour. Reasons are used universally to escape *Responsibility.* In modern society or on a personal level, no-one is willing to accept their own Consequence, and we see the low vibration service to self, mess it has created.

A Presence returns to physical life as a new-born child with a Birth Plan. The lifeline of mankind reads like an open wound, and is testament to the fact that we have been following a pathway of no responsibility for too long. Everywhere, people seek excuses. Everywhere people seek to escape from responsibility through materialism and self-indulgence. In doing so, the fulfilment of the Birth Plan for the Human race is denied. In the meantime, children are conceived with disregard, producing the conditions where all the negative traits can take root. A child with the modest Birth Plan of coming to terms with a simple deficiency in character is therefore more likely to develop other deficiencies. A child with the specific Birth Plan of honourably acting as a catalyst for others to improve has a very hard job ahead of them. They are more likely to be distracted and lose their way. There are millions of births across the globe with millions of Birth Plans and millions of good intentions. Every one of them is a potential champion for the advancement of spirit in mankind. Sadly too many of the chances they provide will be wasted. But how often do we take responsibility for our part in its failure so far. All it requires is for us to act with greater tolerance. Billions of people through aeons of time have followed the idea that we are here for a higher purpose. I am not the only one to realise what the purpose stands for. If you also believe in some kind of higher purpose, do you think the purpose would only exist to be followed when it suited you? If you say no, then ask yourself two questions honestly: How many hours have passed since you indulged yourself to sensation in some way? Or in the last few hours, how many ways can you identify where you acted for self-interest? Secondly within the same time period, how many acts of kindness, compassion, understanding or selflessness have you carried out? How are your scales balanced? If you find the questions difficult to face, you make my argument for me.

We could all make a fresh start right now. It does not mean we have to become Crusaders and deny everything material. We must cease right now to view the world and everything through physical material eyes. We must develop vibrational sight and cultivate higher awareness. Until now, these properties come second to self-interest and material importance. I hope you will concede following this book, you will no longer be able to use the excuse of ignorance to prevent you from making far better choices in the future. With vibrational sight, Gnosis becomes clearer. The workings of greater Space become transparent. Our choices so far as a race have led to segregation, division and conflict. All of these differences have been squarely based upon the wielding of power by one country, one group, one blind faith, one community or one individual over another; and in greater reality, their power amounts to nothing. There is room for difference. There is room for diverse personality. Indeed these things are necessary to develop collective experience. Diversity can function with harmony. Each Presence brings vast experience. When each Presence finally arrives at a much higher level, personal identity is not lost. Each personal identity is the culmination of a thousand of pathways. Together at a higher level, vibrations are of the same chord. Together, a million pathways are represented in unison. At higher level there is no longer a need for difference in colour, language, creed or status, and it is where we all came from in the beginning. Kindred souls make use of speech only when necessary. Communication is usually an automatic process between minds. These things are all possible on this physical level if we were all motivated to it.

Belief in God

Beyond this point, what of God; and do *I* believe in God? Well of course I do, but perhaps not in the same way others prefer. Consider this repeated argument again: Many religions of the world say, Our God is the true God. You must acknowledge our God through our particular Prophet, in our particular way. Our God is the one omnipotent being. If you do not submit to this you will be damned, or suffer some other heinous fate. You must worship our God only, or you will be a naughty, naughty, naughty person and we might decide to kill you. If you dare to worship other Gods you prove to us you are a heathen, a barbarian, a lost soul, a non-person, or a misguided silly, silly sausage! . . . and we will kill you and torture you anyway!

Isn't it ironic? All of these religions say their God is the sublime creator; the ultimate force of all life; yet he is selective. But now just a moment! If your God is the ultimate sublime creative being who made all things, then he must have created the unbelievers too. That being the case, if you deny our right, to disbelieve and reject your version of God, do you not thereby deny the omnipotence of your own God? You accuse us of blasphemy but by denying us in our alleged ignorance, you are surely guilty of supreme blasphemy yourself. Surely you are not claiming that your own God is omnipotent only in areas that suit you. In doing so you place yourselves above the God you worship! Religious Clubs are good business, but as a means of uniting the world in compassion and Gnosis, they are dangerously false.

I was watching a T.V. Programme a few days ago. Scientists were shown studying Supernova, (collapsing stars.) They were trying to measure how fast the Universe was expanding. To be precise, over a long period of time they had been trying to measure by how much the expansion of the Universe was slowing down. If the Universe began as the Big Bang, then like any explosion, the debris would finally come to rest. With the Universe, it was expected that a point would arise where the effects of gravity would balance the effects of the explosion. If so, the eventual contraction could be predicted. Different teams of Scientists arrived at the same result. The Universe was not only still expanding, it was accelerating! Measurement of background stellar radiation showed that the visible energy in the Universe represented only about 1/3 of the total energy calculated to be out there. The missing 2/3 energy was termed Dark energy. The scientists are perplexed but have nevertheless drawn a conclusion. They say that the 2/3 Dark energy must have sufficient power to counteract the natural forces of gravity that would slow down the expansion of the Universe. So what could this Dark energy be? I am sure you will enjoy their best theory so far, reproduced below:

The Dark energy is beyond sub-atomic. It somehow flashes into existence to exert an influence then vanishes again. It exists at such a level of refinement that it leaves no material trace and therefore cannot be examined. It both exists and does not exist, at least not in a form the scientists can put in a test tube or under a microscope to measure. All visible matter is subject to mundane gravity, which has not yet been defined. Dark matter, making up 2/3 greater mass must therefore permeate everything. That includes physical matter. It exists as an unexamined potential which is and is not.

If you think back to my earlier explanations does it all sound familiar to you? If not, then perhaps you need to refresh your memory of my opening chapters. The scientists are puzzling over the nature of greater Space, which is where we came in. Vibrational substance existing as a virtual medium, forms the fabric of Space. From Virtual substance, hotspots of activity are created by the interaction of motivating impulses. From these, the first gross vibrations materialise as sub-atomic particles and out pops physical matter. The scientists need to begin looking through the other end of their microscopes. Perhaps then they will perform a Quantum leap in understanding and finally realise the answer is right in front of them.

To even begin to contemplate the vastness of interaction taking place in the Universe and greater Space is almost crushing. Yet the cyclical motion governing all things can be seen for what it is even in our tiny corner of creation, and even in the workings of a single atom, and do I believe in God? I believe in a force that is one with everything. I believe in a force that is the central motivation for all things. The force I understand is indiscriminate. The force I understand excludes nothing and no one. It allows for, and embraces every effect in every representation as a part of itself. It encompasses you, me, the Christian, The Atheist, The sinner, The saint, The Hindu, The Jew, The Buddhist, The Black, The White, The Moslem, The day, The night, The dog, The tree, The alien, The rock, The air we breathe and everything. The force I know is one with all things down to the infinites of potential and non-matter. It represents The Law of One. It is Paramount and all supporting. The power of one force is one with us as we are one with it. If others believe this but want to contain it in the god name, then we disagree, because even the act of applying a name to this natural order is to contain it.

By another analogy I would explain it thus: If I hold a lit bulb in my hand and seek to contain it by closing my hand tight, most of its light is shielded. But even through the flesh and bone of my hand, the photons of light penetrate through and make my hand glow. But now I am trapped as I try to contain the light. I cannot ever open my hand lest the light burst forth. I cannot hold it forever as my hand would tire and my grip slacken to also let the light through.

I hold my grip but realise that from my viewing point as my eyes become accustomed, I can see dimly because of the ambient light that exists all around. I see my glowing hand. The light I seek to contain is of the same quality as the ambient light and of that which is escaping through my hand. The only thing that differs is its strength. The darkness cannot overcome the light unless by *containing* it more. If I do away with all containment, the darkness flees before the light. The light is all pervading.

So it is with religion and all other orders of containment throughout life. They are part of the *whole*, but they are not sovereign *over* the whole. The whole simply is. Containment is our invention in service to self and ignorance. Containment belongs only to orders of low vibration. The light is of the sublime order, and is what we must aspire to and become *one* with.

Over the known and forgotten history of our planetary races there have been Prophets or Divine leaders who have descended from levels of sublime consciousness. By their Presence, a gateway to Gnosis was opened several times. The gateway was a signpost so that everyone could quickly return to join them again at that higher level. As a planetary race we chose to deviate and have since almost completely lost our way. The message of the Prophets was the same. It did not teach subservience to materialism, selfishness and religious doctrine. When the prophets departed, their message was hijacked and used to create exclusive Religious clubs around the world. The perfect message leading to these Religions became corrupt to justify the power held over the ignorant followers of any of them. The prophets did not teach selfishness, isolation and exclusivity and containment. They did not teach oppression. They did not teach intolerance. They offered Gnosis free to everyone. Their basic message was simple then and even simpler now as we come to understand the smallest structures of matter yet again. I have employed the pages of this book to explore Gnosis. You can explore it yourself from here. You don't need a fancy place to do this. You do not need a fancy Temple of worship. You do not need a fancy ceremony. You do not need secret words. You do not have to promise your salary to someone. You do not need any religious doctrine! All you need perhaps are a few lines of summary.

Consider the following story: In a City far away, a Wise man came upon two Priests fighting. He accosted them and bade them stop. Their fine temples of worship stood opposite each other on the square and they competed with each other for the hearts and minds of the population. Each claimed their version of the Truth was more valid.
The Wise man told them,
'Bring your most sacred Altar stones to me and we will settle the issue.'
The stones were laid side by side on the ground and the Wise man spoke again.

'I see a mist around these stones, each of differing colour, and the colours reveal your **Principles of Possession**. *But I look now beyond the mist and I see the similar texture of the stones surface. I see beyond their surface to the mass of rock in the ground they came from. Deeper still, I see the particles of dust and dirt and gas in the Stellar sky that would be the Planet that spawned them.'*

Then before anyone could intervene he produced a hammer and brought it down with mighty force to smash the stones into grains of sand again. The Priests were outraged. They screamed at him,

'You have smashed our sacred Altar stones. You have blasphemed and attacked our Truths.'
But the Wise man held them back saying,

'No! I have attacked your Principles of Possession instead. How can you both claim the Truth when you each claim possession of its one symbol? You both seek to possess the hearts and minds of men in the name of your sacred Truth, and that your Doctrines represent the only path to find it. The stones represent all the experience that has formed them. That is the Truth, and it cannot be possessed. So it is with everything. Your Temples and saints and rituals establish a Principle of Possession only.'

He pointed to the ground and continued,

'Now; each of you gather a handful of sand and go forth together, to preach the truth at last,' and he marched away, leaving them both in deep thought.

Individually we exist as a vibrational Presence inhabiting a physical form for a temporary time. We originated long ago as sparks of potential, created out of the highest sublime levels of being, and uniquely developed the power of motivation ourselves—as free-will. We descended to gross matter, in order to survive and learn from the experience; then to release ourselves from it and gravitate to reunite with sublimity again. We shed the negative part of ourselves piece by piece through lifetimes of following a Birth Plan of Probability. Our Presence is a cohesive field of motivating vibrational force. We react and interact with each other first at vibrational level through vibrational impulses. All effects have their roots in the interaction of these impulses created from our free will. Our destiny as a planetary race is to reach the point where so many people have evolved away from physical matter that the Planet and its people will flourish as a mirror image of the sublime levels beyond the physical. We are at a crossroads though, for there is another darker scenario.

Humankind has shown itself to favour the temporary gratification of physical sensation. If the trend continues we will arrive at a point of no return. As we draw closer to that time, polarisation takes place. Those who are still capable of ascent and who still yearn to return, will become more distinct from others who may never shed their dependence on temporary sensation. If this route is taken to a conclusion of probability, the negative forces will collectively build around the planet and an earthing out will take place through destructions on the planet. Those souls who invite the event will perish by it. Others who by then still retain their attachment to the higher realms will pass back to them to continue on their way.

Taking Stock

We must draw our thoughts closer to home. For you, and you and you, there are urgent matters to consider. Ask yourselves, what vibrational condition do you think you are in at the moment? Is your vibrational field condensed and shaded; or is it expansive and bright? To what degree do you judge the shadows in others, before ever considering the darkness within *you*. To what degree are you able to deny self? To what degree do you consider others first? How many lifetimes will you choose to endure, in order to redress your balance? When did you last do a kindness? When did you last do a favour that did not carry some kind of price tag? When did you last consider the negative effect your smallest actions may be causing others? When did you last send positive energy to an adversary or rival? When did you last show someone you really cared for them? When did you last give something with no demand or expectation of receiving something in return? When did you last take responsibility for the sum total of your own thoughts and actions?

The list is endless; but if you are unable to produce truthful answers to these questions, then your response is the truth itself. If your answers were negative, do not be surprised if your own life is unhappy. Negative energy returns to the one who produced it, and with extra strength. This is the effect of reciprocal action. Please finally understand, your own fate is in your own hands, and the happiness you seek is waiting for you to see the blockages within you.

The Birth Plan you helped to choose for yourself on this trip, may require you to follow a pathway of Probability through hardship and terrible obstacles, but if you embrace the lesson in the pain, your spirit would soar. It may be in the nature of your Probability pathway that you have to face adversity in order to progress. You may have helped choose your own pathway of adversity yourself. Whichever; the pain experienced will be totally overshadowed by the gain. You may have to experience illness, infirmity, deformity, loss, disadvantage, or derision. But, you have the awesome power of *One* within you. You can turn your disadvantage into strength and selflessly benefit others. You will reap such a reward as you could not imagine. The burden you carry is of your own making. Your attitude to it will determine how heavy it is and for how far you must carry it. I am sorry but I cannot say it clearer. That is the way it is. We are of the physical because we are inadequate in some way.

But it is within our grasp to reach the heights of ecstasy beyond the physical, from the physical, through true Unconditional, Encompassing Love, and to reach much further, to become Truly *One* yet again with the Love of the Whole. We are empowered to do this. But who is ready to sacrifice themselves to attain it. There is a price to pay. It is a price we must pay to ourselves. We must be prepared to face the horror of our own illusion to get to the freedom from self beyond it. To yield is to gain all. Such truth is to be found. Many taste this freedom, but most fall back until another lifetime when the chance and choice continues. The continuum of *One* does not record time. It simply records Progress. And what is it to feel the freedom, yet to continue with the Birth-Plan, with you as an intrinsic player in the game?

I know this well. It is to say, I Love you because I am one with you. I have ceased my struggle, but my struggle continues because I Love you, for I am one with you. Now in my freedom as I share your struggle too. I am free. My freedom embraces me, but in doing so it embraces you, because I Love you. My pain was my Lesson. My Lesson is your Pain. But I share your Pain with you, because I Love you. My freedom is my prison, as I choose. My freedom is limited to your freedom, because I Love you. Join me in Love. It is One with Freedom. I know this, because I Love You; because I Love You.

Do you want to change things for the better within you? Do you want to lead a life of more meaning? Then do it. You have the power. It is up to you. Stop looking to blame somebody else, even in the smallest aspect of your mundane life. Stop using past reasons to avoid present personal responsibility. Stop looking for excuses. Change your outlook and attitude. There is always a reason, but reasons can never be true as excuses. Start by constantly looking inward to see what you can see. No longer take for granted the things within yourself that make up your personality. Ask yourself which of your traits produce a negative reaction in others. Determine what quality would be improved if the negative trait were faced and overcome. Look deeper inside yourself. Ask, what was I before to be facing the life I have now? Discover what really drives you. Discover what instinct lies within you for achievement, however humble. Discover your Birth Plan. Be true to it. The change in you will not be immediate. It will take courage and pain before you shake off the conditioning that has controlled you. It takes colossal effort to find the real you within the disguise you present to others.

The change in you will bring surprises. You will find yourself constantly questioning. Is my response to this situation by my own choice, or is it as a result of my conditioning and acquired prejudice? In other words, Is this really me? If Cause is thought, you will need to be vigilant in your thoughts. You will need to begin thinking about thinking. You will need to guard that your Cause and Effect do not have a negative Consequence for someone else. You will want to prevent any more negative impulses through Reciprocal reaction doubling back to disable you. You will now wish to be free of material. Materialism is only necessary but in moderation for your needs. Separate your life into wants and needs. Recognise your wants are pandering to self and sensation. Question yourself in all of your choices. If you do not need it, then don't covet it. When you are faced with a negative Consequence, ask yourself what you did wrong to help manifest it. If you are a part of a negative Consequence you will *always* have played a part in it. The excuses you make to avoid taking responsibility become crutches that help you walk as a cripple; and soon you believe you can't manage without them. Conditioning has taken hold when in fact you were strong enough to walk-tall the whole time. Be true to yourself and avoid their use from now on. You must do this if you really want to do right by yourself and spirit.

Be very aware that when you find the courage to really look into yourself, you will be viewing the Presence that you have been happy to push into the face of everyone else up until now. Accept this, and accept yourself naked in spirit, and you will have successfully started to take personal responsibility. There is nothing more lonely and terrifying than facing yourself in the mirror this way; but you are never alone. Your Minders in spirit will be with you at all times to ease the pathway.

When I faced this point myself, I was blessed with some inspired words:

My mirror like a mask, now moulded neatly to my skin;
precludes the hope of freedom, as it waits and waits within.
My fire of good intentions seemed so calm in dimmer light,
but how clear the mixed vibrations showed through recent astral sight.
No gold reward nor riches, will still this troubled mind,
as the spring lies coiled and waiting for its moment to unwind.
The balance sheet will start to show the credits to my name,
in facing karmic debts to seek a higher brighter flame.
I turn to face the wall now with my judgement quite complete,
and I stare out through the madness to taste my bitter sweet.
The closing chill of night brings a focus to my shame
and I startle at the sound, for it is I who called my name.

You see, Gnosis, is a blessing and a curse. Understanding does not free you from the game. It simply intensifies the process. From the point you know you are wide awake to the consequence of everything you think and do. You know what to expect if you ignore a negative Consequence. The change will be that you will realise for evermore, you have the choice to make a difference!

Chains of Conditioning

When we finally look inside ourselves to begin tracing the roots of our conditioning we discover that many of our responses are as a result of the way we were treated as a child. We all have a higher Presence, but the personality we present as we grow is only a persona, and masks the real person inside. It is simply the image we project to the world. Our parents work hard in their ignorance to set us free to the world, but succeed only in making us blind to ourselves from *their* conditioning. Of course the process is all part of our selected Birth Plan of Probability; but this does not mean there is not a lesson to be learned in its exposure and in the escape from our acquired conditioned responses.

A sensitive child brought up by strong parents may be required to overcome a resulting sense of inadequacy. An average child brought up by an uneducated bigot, may be required to face and deny the ignorance of bigotry. The child of preoccupied parents may be required to learn qualities of compassion. A child of poverty may be required to learn the will of betterment in the face of adversity. A child of no parents may need to learn the quality of service to others. The list is endless. But in every case it would be so easy for any child to blame their parents for the way they are. Part of the way they are may well be the result of conditioning imposed on the child, but if the parents are to be blamed, then we have to look hard at the motivation of the parents. The parents were children themselves once upon a time, and as such they were subject to the conditioning imposed on them by *their* parents. The same is true of the grandparents and their attitude to life. Where does it end?

The answer is that if we understand how *Chains of Conditioning* reach back before the dawn of time, we can no longer apportion blame. The chains of conditioning are past reasons and not future excuses. However by exposing this process and understanding how it works, we need no longer be a slave to it. We can at last see how we joined our own particular chain of probability and conditioning for a reason. We can seek within ourselves to find the reason, and it is signposted by the positive traits within us that we had the choice to develop as a result. I gave a few examples at the start of this section, but it is for everyone to discover these for our own particular life pattern. Yes there will still be scars from our childhood—experiences; and yes there may still be pain from a poor childhood. There may have been a charmed childhood, but have no doubt, there would be a lesson from this experience too. For every example, it is necessary to return to yourself as a child to absolve yourself of any responsibility for actions that came from the motivation of an adult. By the Law of Reciprocal action, an ignorant or bad parent will have to pay for their mistakes in double measure somehow, some way. It is simply the way it is. Beyond that, the blame must be lifted and replaced with an understanding of how the *Chains of Conditioning* work. This exposure removes the cage around you. At last you will be able to freely move forward, closer to your true self, and grateful to have benefited from the lessons learned from the experience. If you hang on to blame, you are simply standing still with the past as a poor excuse, and refusing to face the inadequacies within yourself. Remember, you helped to choose your own pathway yourself!

A Time to Die

Then comes the time to face transition through physical death, leading to the question I have often been asked. Is death predetermined? In so much that everything is pre-determined or pre-recorded in the Probability impulses leading to an event, the answer is yes. In so much that time and means of death, are a prerequisite to someone's Birth Plan, the answer is yes. In so much that the pathway of Probability for a person, dictates a strengthening Probability for means and time of death, the answer is, eventually yes.

When we physically die we are actually being reborn to spirit, and this time not with the protesting kicks and screams of a baby at physical birth. The terms birth and death are entirely subjective. Under all circumstance as time approaches death and by whatever means, the probability factors and strengths will have been building in anticipation of the event. The spirit Helper of the person will have read these signals in good time. Aides will be waiting alongside friends and family to assist the new arrival as they sever the link with their temporary physical body. Beyond physical death, every single individual has their own particular need of care and direction as they come to terms with their new state. I will describe a few examples, but bear in mind, my examples are just generalisations. I'm sure you will get the idea and take it further yourself. And by the way, if a person has a complete appreciation of the continuum process for life, then the timing and means of physical death are irrelevant. In this case upon physical death, the person would literally brush themselves down and get on with things. Well almost so!. I have hesitated here, because no one is immune from yet another process of rebirth to spirit. During the transition, (or perhaps held-over until some while later,) every person undergoes a review of their life. The review is an internal process. All events and their repercussions are seen and felt. It does not stop there because where the consequence of an action has brought joy or misery to someone else; you re-live their pain or joy yourself. It is simply a matter that upon return to the pure conditions of higher vibration, a person is subject to the reciprocal awareness of their own entire vibrational field—and crucially the origin of each pattern. How many readers will have their eureka moment from that?. In other words, not only every act and deed we ever motivated, but also the reciprocal effect created as a consequence is re-lived by us. We feel the joy we have produced in our lives. We feel the pain we have produced in our lives. It is part of the natural reciprocal lesson and is unavoidable! Whatever the good or bad consequences arising from your motivation—through every moment of your life; you will relive their effect in *your* life review as if they were your own. You see, it is impossible to escape the consequence of your own actions! If this fails to bring you greater wisdom and understanding, then in due course an appropriate return trip is guaranteed. Each time however, in all Probability, the lessons will become harder and harsher until you finally get the point of it all. Here are some simplified examples for the crossing-over event:

At the death of an average person, having lived a non-extraordinary life; they are likely to be met by their Minder and greeted by former family and friends who passed back to spirit earlier. In this case there would be more chance of the new arrival being persuaded quickly to accept their new state and move on.

In a Terminal Coma Patient who dies while unconscious where the Presence was not able to synchronise and re-join properly with the physical body before death; the reason may be from physical damage to the body. The event may be a required experience as a part of a Birth Plan, in which case the Presence will have been in on-the-plot. If so, the Presence would have been in an accompanying sleep state with the physical body, and upon death become fully awake in spirit; soon to be working with Helpers for those left behind.

At sudden death, the Presence would be held in spirit-sleep state upon release from the physical body. Their vibration would be artificially raised and they would be gently awakened to spirit. The raising of vibration would be like giving oxygen to a physical person and the slow awakening would soften the trauma and realisation of their physical death. Such a person would need time to adjust because the sudden transition could have a traumatic effect on their vibration.

A despicable or wicked person would have a very condensed vibration/aura. Their awakening would be stark. They too would have to re-live their life, feeling all the trauma and grief of their own Consequence. They would carry the burden of every bad action they manifest for others. This type of person would be most likely *not* to accept their changed state. Their first impression would be of a desolate forbidding environment, filled with other scoundrels just like them. Helpers would be on hand, but the person would be unable to see them. They would have to progress through their new miserable environment, competing with others of their same vibration until they faced the wrongs in themselves.

The deceased child would be received into the equivalent of a child nursery appropriate to their age. The conditions of their passing would be temporarily suppressed. They would meet with other children. Familiar *dead* family members would be present as well as the child's Helpers. A child will not have suffered a full physical lifetime accumulating conditioning and prejudice. They will have maintained the innocent connection with spirit that adults lose as they grow and become grounded to the material things in their life. Children therefore are quick to appreciate and accept their new state. Children continue in spirit through a cycle of growth to adulthood, but at a vastly accelerated rate. When a mother or father later returns to spirit themselves, the now adult son or daughter in spirit, sometimes have to take on the appearance of its age close to when he or she died to help the parent accept *their* new state. This would not be necessary of course if the parent was enlightened already to the process. Children passing back to spirit prematurely are most often older souls who undergo the experience to help provide a lesson for those left behind. Their mission therefore does not end at death. It is in the nature of things in these circumstances where a parent/child bond has been established, that the child will play a vital Helper role for their parents and family which were left behind.

A Suicide is a person who very often is not a completely bad person. The act of suicide is committed as a lapse of judgement and character. However, the flaw is serious and usually deep-rooted. The suicide act produces damaging negative consequences for many people. The person commits the act of suicide simply as a mistaken alternative to the perceived horror of facing themselves. They confuse need with want. When the person allows unfulfilled *want* to consume them, then by self-absorbsion they become blind to the difference of a more humble need. Suicide is carried out to fulfil gross inadequacy in self. The act of suicide is therefore usually a supreme act of selfishness. The vibration of the person may be blighted by a hotspot of negative vibration that is as black as night. Beyond death, the person will gravitate to a region harmonious with their vibration *at the time*. They will find themselves therefore in the same bleak desolate environment of souls who are thoroughly more despicable than them. Suicides will have condemned themselves to a very harsh lesson in self-awareness. They will either learn quickly among their dark new neighbours, or they will be lost to despair forever. In this situation, senior Helpers become involved in order to give every chance for the suicide to reform within. But, the choice as always, is down to the free will of the individual. If however, the suicide has been committed by someone trying to escape the consequences of a heinous act, there is no escape. They will suffer the lesson that every dark person has to learn in a region appropriate to them.

Death from injury or sickness. In spirit, the injury continues only for so long as the person is unable to accept their new wholeness. Helpers, family and friends would be active to try and awaken the person to their new situation; which would bring wholeness again. But there could have been a host of reasons for the illness. Most would be related to vibrational deficiencies manifest in the person, and those deficiencies would not automatically disappear. It is most likely therefore following a controlled awakening, the person would transit through a period similar to sleep, and then to the regional level of reality where they will continue their learning journey. The same rules apply as always, where the new situation and environment would reflect the vibration of the person. It is even possible that helpers known to them would not even be recognised by him or her, due to the differences in vibrational quality. That would wait until the person had progressed further. Conversely, a person may have accepted the Probability of illness as a part of their Birth Plan in order to provide the circumstance of a lesson to others. For others, dealing with an illness or disability from birth could also be an accepted task. The fortitude and courage of a child so often provides an inspiration for great things to be motivated through someone else. Children born into disability or illness are usually old souls with a beautiful vibration. We can all recall the frequent occasions where the strength of spirit in a disabled child subdues arrogance in others, and links us to the higher vibration of humility.

If someone dies in sudden or traumatic circumstances, the reasons once again will be centred on the need to provide the best lesson for those left behind. This is true for all ages because the impact of a sudden death has a more lasting effect. Innumerable campaigns have been started to improve things in the world; by parents or friends who have been motivated by the seemingly tragic circumstances of a sudden traumatic death.

The examples could continue forever. When a person physically dies, their thoughts are preoccupied to understand their new condition. They would usually remember what they had been doing just before death, but would be perplexed to find themselves in a completely new place which was as real as the one they remembered from a few minutes ago! If the person realised what had happened, second thoughts would turn to the loved ones left behind. There would be a compelling urge to be near loved ones or to try and communicate with them. Now however, the ones left behind would seem as shadowy forms to the person departed. The deceased would be of finer vibration occupying a place of similar finer vibration. The grieving family and friends would fade further from the sight of the deceased as the differences in vibration became consolidated. By free will, the deceased decides how long they wish to hang around people and places they have been attached to in physical life. Higher Helpers would only directly intervene if the deceased was sufficiently strong to interfere with anyone left behind. Normally the Helpers would compress the vibration of the deceased sufficiently to allow them to draw close and give comfort to their loved ones. The comfort would be on a vibrational level. I have explained previously how deep grief actually prevents communication between the departed and those left behind. Grief condenses the vibration and widens the gap between the state of the departed and those who are grieving . . .

We must have a few words about departing souls who still have a score to settle with someone left behind. The issue can be easily explained if we switch to vibrational sight again. The deceased occupies a different state of refinement. Their motivations will not be powerful enough to manipulate substance to affect someone on the physical plane. But the dark vibrations of a vengeful deceased can attract other similar souls to build negative strength. One solution would be if Helpers assumed their own natural higher form. Their heightened vibration would be as a burning light that would be far too distressing for lower souls or entities to approach. This rule is worth bearing in mind for anyone wishing to protect themselves from negative influence. Simply raise your own vibration! It will produce conditions that will always repel anything of a lower vibration. If the deceased is determined to cause harm to those left behind, their vibration will correspondingly be so condensed that they will be denied contact completely. Their own low vibration will guarantee a fast trip to their new vibrationally matching home.

So after the funeral, what happens next? The answer is of course that life goes on for all concerned. The recently deceased will be helped as a willing subject; or unconsciously as an unwilling subject, to gravitate to their compatible region. Their reception committee will be awaiting their arrival. As a new arrival, they would be advised of tasks and duties they could become involved in. But they would still be faced with making their own choice as to how they wished to proceed. In between are the innumerable permutations for the types of people we did not have the time or space to mention here. In many instances, the transition is accompanied by a period of recovery. For people of lower quality this could be similar to a long period of sleep; and for the opposite it could mean a time of rest in a place like the jungle scene I described earlier in this book. The most important lesson for anyone to understand is that by knowing and accepting the process, the death transition can be as normal and ordinary as drawing breath. Death then becomes something to embrace when the time arrives to be reborn again at last to spirit.

The Future is Now

We may not realise, but we all set a standard by which we judge others. The standard we set is the product of our conditioning, our inherited prejudice and the prejudice of our own ignorance. We are selfish to our own standards. We guard them well. We cling to the arrogance of our personal right to act in our own self-interest in every tiny way against the interest of others. We go through life in a state of conflict, where we constantly bump into the same attitude from others. The effect is indiscriminate. It can happen at work, at home, with a stranger, or with a closest loved one. We disguise our wants as needs in the false belief that if our wants are satisfied, we will be happy.

Compromise is held as weakness against selfishness, because compromise does not serve self-interest. We are never truly happy because in fact, we have completely missed the point. Our wants are materialistic. We like to get our own way. Our wants have to be satisfied; but what about our needs? Do our needs stop and begin at material comfort and self-gratification? Material gains are transient. The satisfaction of material gain is momentary. Ask the money rich if they are content. How very often do we hear of money rich who end their days in sadness and tragedy? Of course it's nice to be materially comfortable. Material comfort however is no antidote for restlessness; and restlessness arises out of inner conflict from the resistance of an unbalanced Presence. This can only be addressed by discovering far more important inner needs. The needs of the spirit can only be found by looking within. It is a need to replace any selfish motivation with selfless energy. This is the only way to find true happiness and tranquillity.

Stronger values and higher standards are achievable if we cared. If we want a better future then we must make a stand for what is right. If you have been a careful reader of this book won't ever be able to plead ignorance again. The message will stick in your mind and the evidence of your own experience will provide its own validation. For you personally I hope for evermore you will examine your every motivation, and forever think about your thinking. However enlightened we are, we still carry negative baggage. It is the reason we are still here learning a physical lesson. The negative baggage (karma) must be discharged before we know lasting peace and tranquillity. That karma is a weight we carry that we have created ourselves. It is directly proportional to the form of our Presence, and as such can never be harder to bear than our ability to carry it. If we falter, it is not that we are unable to carry the load; it is because we *choose* by our own free will, not to face it and make it bearable. Whatever the weight of negativity a person is carrying, the load can be lessened immediately if no more weight is added. By exposing our inadequacy and accepting it, we externalise it and it no longer controls us. We can learn from the mistakes that created it and move forward with greater wisdom.

At this point I would like to take you on a diversion that is entirely relevant to the points I just covered. I have a folder of what I prefer to call inspired didactic poems that I receive in a peculiar way. It is usually the case that I have been preoccupied with thoughts of spirit in some way. My vibration will have been lifted. I always get the sense of impending arrival. It is as if I know the postman is about to arrive and I am just waiting for the letter to drop through the letterbox in my mind. The contact can happen immediately or days later. When it arrives, it is as if someone thrusts a sheet of paper into my head with a message written on it. I only have a few seconds to grab the writing from the sheet in a hurry to record the words before they disappear. It is only afterwards when I read the words I have written that I become consciously aware of what I have copied down. I always carry a pen and paper; but in the past I have grabbed for torn bits of newspaper or anything to use. Many times I have been impressed to present the resulting message to a particular person, and always with dramatic effect. I called the following example: *Lifeline to a Friend*.

I was strolling through a field when I saw him standing there.
He stood before a painting of the man from Galilee,
As if to reach in silence for some distant clarity.
Quite lost in thought he trembled as his face set with a frown.
The painted man gazed back with love, though blood flowed from his crown.

This strange affair drew me closer for I saw the man had something on his back!
He faltered with the weight—an evil black monstrosity,
Its claws gripped tight his shoulders in obscene profanity.
The man stood bent and silent, hypnotised to search his past.
I marvelled at the length of time he'd let such torture last.

I could contain myself no longer and called across to him.
He jumped with fright and shaking, turned to meet my puzzled face,
I said 'How long has that monstrosity been clinging in that place?'
I pointed and he turned to look, to see if it was there
Then screamed in pain, 'Each time I look it pulls hard on my hair.'

Well! You can imagine, my attention was caught and I had to know more.
His distress was quite apparent and I sought to comfort him,
I asked him if his creature was his payment for a sin.
Through tears he said, 'I know not how it grew so gross and black;
I felt it as a child, quite small, unnoticed on my back.'

Clearly his memory was sharpening. He moaned, but I urged him to continue.
'It was only as an aged man when I realised its size.
I tried hard to conceal it using barricades of lies.
The more I tried to shake it, the more it held on tight,
And the lies I dreamt for others, plagued me each and every night.'

Remorse and sadness true; but seeing light around the corner, I tried to interrupt.
I said, 'It's time to realise, you get a second chance.
Just give the man from Galilee a thoughtful second glance.'
His weary eyes were shining as he saw how light was there,
While his monster slowly lifted and diffused into the air.

I decided it was time to leave him, standing muttering to himself.
I knew his heart was heavy, but he stood up tall and straight, saying,
'I must turn back to my family, to mend the hurt and hate.'
I glanced back at the painting of a man for souls to seek,
As a perfect golden teardrop, trickled slowly down his cheek.

It is clear that we must therefore discover our Birth Plan; but how can anyone recognise what his or her Birth Plan looks like? There is actually a very simple yardstick that would point in the right direction. Firstly there is a need to appreciate the difference between satisfaction and fulfilment. Satisfaction can be found easily. It is the pleasant feeling of a job well done. Satisfaction is food for the ego. It is a personal pat on the back for something well finished, even though the job is only temporary or half done. Satisfaction is introvert. Fulfilment is wholly different. It is the contentment of personal progress despite hardship. Fulfilment is achievement when an unselfish goal has been reached beyond adversity. Fulfilment requires focus and commitment. Fulfilment is expansive, but the price is much higher. It yields happiness in exchange for scars! A Birth Plan brings fulfilment and the route to it is in the higher urges and affinities we have. We can identify our Birth Plan therefore if know from our interests, skills or ideals, where we could achieve balance in their success.

Often the lesson is in the barriers that block our way. It requires a huge commitment to pursue our interests, skills or ideals in a single life mission. Your pathway will surely force you to examine yourself within and test your own motivations. You will know you are on your right pathway when you have begun to reject the conditioned responses within you, along with years of prejudice. It may take years to achieve, and you will have had to dismiss any thoughts that the task is beyond you. But from the point you recognise your directional route; your devotion must be to its fulfilment. In the passing of years, it does not even matter if you don't manage to reach the final goal, for just like two paired atomic particles, the goal and the struggle are one and the same thing. They are inseparable.

There is another tool that can help considerably for anyone to realise their true plan in life. Every vibrational energy system is cyclical. It is not exclusive to the chakra system. Cycles function similarly on a vast scale in the Cosmos. Cycles of Probability also function during the course of our physical lifetime. You can follow with me now and try to work this out for your own life. The idea was highlighted in a lucid dream many years ago but I have been impressed to include it here.

This study works more instantly for those who have already travelled a few decades in their life, but a younger person can try it also and update it along the way.

It is very simple really. You trace a line up through the centre of a piece of paper, marking equally, the years of each decade starting on the one before birth; such as 1970, 1980, 1990, etc. You then have to consider through your life, the most traumatic or dramatic *turning points*, and mark these positions off from the central life line. Look also for any other regular trends or distinctive periods, or location changes, for example. Or even look for specific year numbers that appear regularly during your life. Mark them all off on your life line and the cyclical patterns will emerge. Look for all the repeated patterns. It is then possible to determine with a greater strength of Probability, what influences are likely for you in the future. By doing this, it will enable you greater choice to take even more responsibility for your Birth Plan. It will give you more control to follow your Plan.

For my own example, born 1950, I have noted a clear ten year cycle, with a lesser three year cycle centred on the turn of each decade. Every time this has included an emerging from consolidation for several years, going through a period of upheaval, and the entering of a distinctive new phase out of it. Each time there has been a dramatic shift in work direction, along with a change of residence, and the involvement of, or to another country. I am able to predict therefore with strong probability the next shift; where it will place me, and involving predictable work activity which I have been consolidating and aspiring to since my last shift. I am confident of my pathway of strongest probability for the next few years and where it will lead. This helps me to take every step in harmony with my life cycles and hasten a fulfilment of my Birth Plan.

There is a supreme irony in our nature as custodians of our own planet. New born children enter the world as old but imperfect souls. This whole book has been directed to those of us who are out of childhood and wish to move forward from the conditioning and prejudice it has saddled us with. As children we entered with eyes wide open. As adults we have become blind, yet we are supposed to be in charge and ready to teach the next generation of innocents! We only need take another look at life, society, countries, and the world, to see the mess we are making. It does not take much effort to see we are getting it all wrong. We, who are in charge, are setting the standard for new-born generations of children to follow, and the betrayal is enough to make anyone weep. Returning souls arrive to be guided and judged through the conditioning chains of their seniors. Parents wish their children to progress and be free, though they are completely trapped within themselves in ignorance. Their prejudice, conditioning, flawed values, lack of fulfilment and intolerance are all passed down to siblings. Children are taught to aspire to self-interest. When will the change take place so children are no longer viewed as heirs to prejudice? When will children be viewed correctly as individual souls returning to the classroom of life to try and do better this time?

Will this book be your inspiration to change, and if so how genuine will the change be? Will it last for one week, or one month, or will it be fundamental. Will it instigate the biggest battle you have ever fought for the control of yourself? Do you care, even when the choice and consequence is truly yours?

Reflections

We have covered much ground from Quantum through life beyond life, to the personal role of everyone in the scheme of things. Every area discussed could have been expanded tenfold, but that expansion must take place in the mind and motivations of the seeker as you test my words through your own experience. For me the testing continues. My eyes were opened to Gnosis, giving me a back to basics understanding of our existence and how it functions. My understanding is in no way based upon reported belief nor blind faith. It is based upon the awakened delivery of my *Event*. It is based upon my tested experience ever since that day. The outcome forms the basis of my free conviction. I am aware of the fact that convictions are not transferable. I am also aware that no one should take any of what I have explained at face value. Convictions should be arrived at through solidly tested *personal* experience.

I ask you therefore to view my words as a challenge to your own experience so far. I ask you to test my explanations yourself and let them prove themselves. As *you* may go forward to begin the challenge, I also continue to challenge. Truth cannot be contained, nor can it be claimed by any dogma. It cannot be exclusive. It is simply a message that will stand any test. The messenger is of no importance. The first conclusion of my Birth Plan ends with the publication of this book. There was a period in my life when I wasted so much life-time kicking at doors that would not open to me. I had not learned then, while I kicked at locked doors there was always one nearby that would have opened easily to me. I was too narrowly focussed to see the truer path. I have learned my lesson, and now the doors open automatically when it is right, proper and timed according to the plan of spirit for them to do so. It can be exactly the same for you. Good luck on your journey

Heading for the Chamber

I have spoken enough about Birth Plans; so where do we go now with this exposition? The answer is that we have to provide you with a description of how the pathway of *our* Birth Plan unfolded next!. Hopefully its example will show you how you must look for the connections in *your* life so far; and thereby determine the strongest pathway for you to concentrate your efforts in the future. We are still waiting to see exactly what our culminating experience will be, but we are in no doubt of the validations we have received so far and that we are on our strongest path. We are many years removed from the experiences and lessons I have shared with you in this book. Our lives now are steeped in concerns for the discovery of the knowledge left behind by our ancient ancestors. Our lives are entwined with the betterment of the animal life in Cairo and Egypt. Our journey to this destination has been intuitive and would have been impossible without the understandings gained from our higher schooling. Our ability to listen and follow the higher signals of direction that have been intended to guide us on our charmed journey would have been equally impossible for the same reason. Our ability to be sustained through danger and hazard would have been impossible without the higher understandings. You will see the proof of this in the concluding section of this book. We have carried the understandings of the universal workings of life with us at all times. We accepted the hierarchy of life both in the physical and the equally valid states beyond quantum. We accepted there were those on both sides who had the ability to function normally despite the illusionary barrier between the two. We accepted also the truth of other sentient beings in the universe, some of whom had been instrumental in producing us in the distant past through DNA manipulation. The journey has been a lonely one for those of us who were aware from an early stage.

In the meantime the world has made huge advances to catch up. Personal validations in the final part of our journey have been strengthened as old texts and new experiences have poured from modern media outlets. Social communication has allowed those like ourselves who thought we were alone in a strange world to find and link with others on a vast scale. Little by little, the conditioning from thousands of years of elite social control is yielding to higher awareness. The process has been an inevitable pathway of higher gravitation.

On a personal level, I guess our validations have been like stepping stones in the direction we should be going. We were inexorably drawn to go to the Great Pyramid and just knew our destiny was tied to it in some way. We carried out an (interrupted) experiment there, and you will read of it shortly. But it provided a solid validation of our route, as did a host of other experiences around it. We were steered elsewhere on the Plateau above and below ground. We struggled to understand why it was, after being enabled to taste the ultimate possibilities within the pyramid, that we were then hindered from making immediate progress in that direction. For a time we did question why we were being steered elsewhere. However we always pulled back to our basic stance. We wished for clear direction, experience and discovery, but then let go and were happy with whatever happened next. Every time we were rewarded because each new experience turned out to be just as mind-boggling as the one before. Also most importantly as we constantly looked back we could see how those experiences taught us something new, or introduced us to people; both of which were necessary to prepare us for the next fantastic step we should make. As such therefore, every event was a learning experience steering us to whatever still awaits us. This helps us now as we seek to share our last-chapter pathway with you. You will see as we did how each event linked to a later experience and placed us with perfect timing for the next lesson, and pointed to what we believe may be our ultimate task in Egypt.

Before you join us on the journey of the last decade in Egypt therefore, I offer you a middle book section which addresses a host of questions put to me by correspondents who know of this book content so far. I hope the questions and answers will be a summary, and seal many gaps in your mind as just as they did for me when I first asked them of myself

Part 2: Key Questions and Answers

Subject Keys

01 Suicide……………………………177	25 Within…………………………….213
02 God………………………………180	25.1 Intervention ………………………214
03 Absolute Self……………………181	25.2 Intervention. ……………………..214
04 Absolute Truth …………………181	25.3 Intervention. ……………………..215
05 New Truth ………………………182	25.4 Intervention ………………………215
06 Meditation ………………………182	25.5 Intervention……………………….216
07 Meat ……………………………184	25.6 Intervention. ……………………..216
08 Pain ……………………………188	25.7 Intervention. ……………………..216
09 Joy ………………………………190	26 Comment……………………….216
10 Peace ……………………………191	27 Music……………………………220
11 Mentality…………………………192	28 Differences…………………….223
12 Transplants……………………193	29 Murder………………………….225
13 Experiences …………………..195	30 Self Service …………………..227
14 Insecurity………………………196	30.1 Comment……………………….228
15 Channelling……………………197	31 Prophet ………………………..229
16 Wind……………………………199	31.1 Comment………………………..229
17 Sexes …………………………201	32 Automatics…………………….232
18 Schools…………………………202	33 Didactics………………………234
19 Mistakes ……………………….207	34 Animals ……………………….235
20 Workings ……………………….207	35 Crystals ……………………….236
21 Time …………………………..209	36 Quoted…………………………237
22 Falsehood …………………….211	37 Connections………………….238
23 Love……………………………212	38 Karma………………………….239
23.1 Intervention. ………………….212	39 Consciousness………………239
24 Intent ………………………….212	40 Consciousness………………240

Epilogue …………………………………………………………………………. 243
Heading Underground at last ………………………………………………….. 246

Part 2: Questions and Answers

Introduction

It is more than twenty five years since I had my profound Event and this book is the consequence. In that time the computer and Internet have taken over as a prime means of communication. I have discussed many of the issues on forum threads and especially through our original Website. It seemed entirely appropriate for me to share some of my question and answer sessions with you. I have edited and abridged them to make them anonymous and more concise. Thank you to all the good souls who contributed. Some of *your* questions will be answered therefore in the following pages. I hope to be able to deal with many more from your continued feedback. Let the Questions Begin.

Question 1: *A lot of people get so low, they just want to commit suicide. What happens to them if they go through with it?*

Answer: The famous British Medium Doris Stokes had a saying: You can't die for the life of you! She was so right. Unfortunately most people have not had an extraordinary experience to validate the fact. There is a good reason for this. We are here in this life to learn lessons because we are all inadequate in some way. This is to say, the vibration of our Presence is still in a process of refinement. It improves in direct proportion to the discharge of our lower vibration through life's trials, and the speed thereby that we gravitate back to the higher vibration of our permanent place beyond physical.

So, convictions are not transferable. We each have to learn individual lessons and arrive at our own convictions through our own tested experience. The experiences occur in absolute direct proportion to the negative energy within us that we must still discharge. This is an immutable fact of life and science. We stub our toe, and you can bet that a short while before, we were having bad thoughts or we were doing a bad deed of some kind. It is simple instant karma.

For some on a gross scale, the pile-up of apparently negative experiences in life, sometimes crowd in to suffocate and appear to leave no way out. These represent a huge build-up of negative energy from personal bad choices and thinking. It becomes a huge negative hot-spot of energy seeking to be discharged. In real terms this is what happens: Negative energy (energy of a low vibration,) generated from the wrong thinking and directions we have taken, condenses or compresses our aura or Presence. If you could see someone in this state using a higher vision, their aura would appear shrink wrapped to their physical body almost. It would appear dark, discordant and confused. This does not mean that the person is bad. In fact the opposite could be true. The person may have a very high soul-Presence, but wrong directions in life may now have left them with their higher light squeezed deep down inside them.

It may seem impossible to believe there is life beyond life. I can tell you there is a multitude of extraordinary ways that people receive solid validation. The most powerful of course is through an out of body experience. This is when we detach from our physical bodies in astral form to enjoy conscious experiences elsewhere; then to return to the physical body and subjectively retain the whole experience. Validating evidence for the journey can often appear later, and the effect is profound. So many people have these experiences, and almost everyone has them involuntarily while asleep. My convictions are not directly transferable, but at least trust my sincerity if you have ever entertained suicidal thoughts. Judge it in my words. The physical body is a product of the physical world. It goes through a cycle of birth and decay. It would just remain a huge inert lump of cleverly joined minerals and chemicals but for one thing. It is inhabited at birth by a motivating Presence with a mission, (A Birth Plan.) Our Presence grows and modifies along with the physical person we have become according to the pathways of Probability we choose to walk, which depend on our own sacred choices in life. When we leave the physical body at natural death, we take stock, we rest, and we get on with life in a higher, enduring, and much more valid dimension. Later we prepare to return once again for another, and another, and another life; and in fact for as many lives as it takes to modify our vibration at last.

On the higher levels of reality, life continues as it does here. There are good places and there are bad places, each according to their more polarised vibrations. Here on Earth-level it must be a pretty low vibration life to live under the regime of a dictator as part of a starving nation. Conversely it would be idyllic to live the life of ease in a free tribal society on a sunny pacific beach. The first example would be hell and the second one would be heaven, metaphorically. On the higher levels it is no different, only a whole lot more intense! Commit suicide, and you will wake up in a place that will reflect the state of your vibration at the time;

which would be pretty ghastly. It will be real. It will be tangible. It will be in a place which has substance to its inhabitants just as the physical world has for us now. All you will have done by your suicide will have been to change your environment to another one more suited to your condition; and guess what? Your new life there will be ten times worse that the life you tried to run from here, for the simple reason that everyone you encounter in your new home will be of a similar compressed vibration to you.

If you end your lifeline of probability through suicide, it just means that once again your new circumstances in higher life will present you with situations sufficiently hard, and balanced to the vibrational resistance you have, for you to face them and learn the lessons you must learn by your own choice! However desperate or bleak your life seems now, there really is a way forward; and I am going to tell you what it is in a moment! But first I just want to convince you I know what I am talking about with a little more of my own validation.

Previously in this book there were full details of when I went through the process in my own life. I have been there myself. I have seen the video; got the t-shirt. I have been to the abyss and beyond. The wrong I did to myself in that state should have been enough to kill a buffalo! By all earthly rules I should have succeeded in my misguided act. However in my case, my Birth Plan called for me to remain here and face the dirt pile that was my life at the time. My path of Probability had been planned (with my correct choices,) for me to do far greater things in my time. It was too valuable for the chance to be wasted. My helpers on the next level intervened and worked on my physical body overnight, so that next day I woke from my suicide attempt feeling like I had returned from a good holiday.

So how was it they went to so much trouble to save me from myself? The answer can be *your* final answer too. In a state of vibrational compression, that part of us which is of higher vibration is also highly compressed within our Presence. In my last moments I screamed out to higher authority for help in a final cry of abject despair. I had made a last choice. I had expressed my last will. I thereby empowered my higher helpers to intervene. They did so. It was such a dramatic intervention that it provided its own validation. Beyond it, I still had to face the dirt pile of my life, but in my mind I now knew that by yielding my problems to them and praying from my Soul for guidance, the escape route to sanity would be shown to me, even though I knew I would have to go through much more pain to emerge at the other end a stronger person. I learned that the pain we are faced to carry is directly proportional to our ability to carry it, if we choose. I have written previously:

My pain was my Lesson, and my Lesson is your Pain.

My meaning is that the only pain you now have to face is the understanding and the acceptance of what I have explained to you. The rest is just a process of getting on with what *you* helped choose for yourself in this life.

Question 2: *What is God ?*

Answer: The answer can be found in a few questions of my own:

Can you dangle your feet into the ocean and let your mind travel to its farthest connection. Can you reach in an unbroken thought, to miles below the deepest surface, and feel the crushing pressure. Can you reach to hundreds of thousands of rivers and inlets, and feel the differing quality of the water rushing to join. Can you leap to the rain and the tempest raging in its many degrees. Can you return from the atomised spray in the air across the globe, and feel the difference as salt turns to fresh ice and the vast frozen sheets. In your mind-sense can you make those connections?

Can you stand in a forest after the storm, and hear the water sucking into the ground. Can you hear the trees and plants heaving as they shed water and lift to the sky. Can you touch a tree and hear the sap transforming in its leaves. Can you plunge below the earth and see energy sharing from the soil. Can you see how the roots of all life mingle across the world. Can you embrace a tree and share its link with all that it touches and connects ?

Can you stand in a crowd, and step out again while still there. Can you see the packages of life that everyone displays. Can you see the attributes and movement these produce. Can you see how their interaction is derived from the resistance between them. Can you see the unbroken thread which is woven in a blanket of consequence to all things as a result ?

Can you reach beyond your own senses. Can you hear your own heartbeat and the blood pumping through your body. Can you take your awareness beyond your body, and travel to places beyond yourself. Can you interact with others who live there the same. Can you look back and see the limitations of your material self. Can you appreciate the difference?

Can you imagine the qualities of a Mobius Loop and travel its length. Can you conceive its infinite nature. Can you visualise its expansion into Torus. Can you continue your mind-sense movement in the spiral of compression and expansion within its flow. Can you see at its core, how matter is actualised from Virtuality. Can you see how Motivation drives the process?

Can you fill your lungs with air and feel how you are drawing the cosmos into you. Can you feel the Torus working within you by your own motivation. Can you fly forth and trace it back to our closest source in the Sun. Can you connect to its core and feel the Torus there too. Can you stretch out in every direction and touch the fabric of other planets. Can you take your awareness there and feel their quality in your breath?

Can you go beyond that, to the millions of other systems in our space. Can you conceive their shared connection in the transformation. Can you grasp the Infinite millions of endless star bodies and their planets. Can you see the motivation in their movement. Can you see the motivation in your own movement. Can you see your own thoughts. Can you see the responsibility of your own cause?

Can you see the creative movement within yourself. Can you grasp the creative movement beyond yourself. Can you see the whole intrinsic connection with your own Presence. Can you see the greater motivation from infinity for all things. Can you see the vastness. Can you see it also dwelling within you? Though convictions are not transferable, if your answer is *yes* to these things you need no longer ask: Who or what is God.

Question 3: *What is Absolute Self and Spirit?*

Answer: I see two questions here in the description of absolute Self and Spirit. I would describe Spirit simply as that part of ourselves, our vibrational Presence that inhabits our physical body—vehicle for the duration of its stay. In the broader sense it is a name to describe the equally valid and greater reality of coherent realms beyond physical, continuing to infinity.

The Absolute Self is something more different and specific. The term Absolute Self, is a contradiction in terms, because to imply Self is to impose a human restriction. Anything Absolute, in this context, cannot be contained by a human restriction. Self is self. Absolute is Absolute. When the condition of our Presence reaches a point in development that breaks us free from the physical, we become part of a collective consciousness, retaining the cohesion of our experience as an intrinsic part of the collective experience of all. We continue to progress through the ever greater awareness that joins and extends beyond our Earth experience; always moving forward towards *Absolute One*

Question 4: *What is Absolute Truth?*

Answer: Truth is subjective, because when a state is reached where Absolute is known; there is no need for the question. Truth is simply a snapshot of known experience in direct proportion to the distance a Presence has progressed in awareness. The absolute condition is a state of oneness with all, where neither questions nor answers are necessary, because we are one with ourselves and everything else at the same time. Then we are singular while also infinite, and are *one* with the questions and the answers to everything.

Question 5: *What is the discovery of New Truth?*

Answer: Truth is dynamic because, that which is taken for Truth is only the reflection of a stage of awareness. The stage of awareness depends upon the viewing point of the observer. If our level of development means we are unable to interact in full consciousness to be able to *see ourselves—seeing ourselves*, then our truth can only be taken as a dynamic snapshot *within* our own limitations. By us forgiving our own inadequacies, thereby to break free from them, we hasten our progress to greater Understanding. Each stage of dramatic inner revelation allows us to leap forward to a New Truth. This becomes our new position; but it too, waits to be tested the same.

Question 6: *What is meditation?*

Answer: First it is the simple ability to detach one's mind from the sensational input of our physical senses. The practice has itself been turned into an unnecessary mystery by many. There is no mystery. It does not require a position of great comfort, nor exotic aromas. It does not require the presence of sacred objects or crystals. It does not require the use of complex mantras or other sounds. It does not require the presence of other gurus or adepts. However all of these things can assist the preparation of the mind in readiness for successful meditation. The latter is necessary where a person is ready to project their objective consciousness out of body, and ideally needs a watcher to safeguard them physically; or an adept who can assist them to return to the physical.

Our conscious mind is filled at all times with chains of responsive thought stimulated by our physical senses. Through meditation it is possible to detach ourselves from these responses and take ourselves to a point of nothingness, or yielding. In this state we may interact with our higher consciousness, or that of others including our Minders on a higher level. At a higher developed stage we can proceed to full conscious Out of Body projection. At a lesser level when deep stillness is sought, there are stages we have to go through in our mind. Words, images, or thoughts that penetrate the nothingness, have to be tested to see if they came from an inner prompt. Detached thoughts can be retained because they may have been inspired from the higher self or from an external source. In all meditation, a prime objective must be to raise one's vibrational frequency. This is necessary for personal wellbeing but importantly is also necessary for psychic defence. In deep meditation we can be vulnerable to attack from other lower source. A vibration raised by preparation exercise makes certain that lower energies cannot interact. The process also brings healing.

With much practice it becomes possible for a person to switch to a higher alpha state at will, and thereby benefit from the tranquillity there. In reality during a busy life it is best to set a regular time aside for meditation, when no distractions are expected. There are a thousand techniques taught but all basically come back to the same thing.

Consider this: When we are thinking, our thought patterns evolve in chains of thought. A conversation may remind us we have to go to the shop to buy something; which reminds us we will have to stop to fuel our vehicle; which reminds us that we have to stop to pick something up from a friend; which reminds us we don't have time because we have to be back for another appointment; which leads to us speculating a fresh arrangement to see our friend; and so on and on. My examples are simplistic but if you take the time to think about thinking, you will see for yourselves how we all think in complex chains of thought all the time. Even when we are supposed to be resting, we allow our minds to be cluttered with chains of speculative thought. Watching a movie or listening to radio chat does the same thing, even if our attention is not fixed directly to it. Falling asleep for example while the television is still playing in the background is a terribly harmful practice. The effect all of this has on our vibration is to clutter it with a tidal wave of new vibrational input. We begin to feel tired because our Presence is becoming overloaded and needs time to balance out all the new input. Our conscious brain is forcefully signalled to slow down and finally we are forced to shut down our sensory organs to allow our Presence to catch up. We fall asleep. For ideal meditation therefore, our minds must be calm, uncluttered and rested.

Next we must be in a comfortable position so that our physical senses are not triggered to distract us with fatigue or stress. Finally we must control our thinking and focus to a single point of nothingness; or light. As thoughts or ideas inevitably infiltrate our minds, we must grab them individually as they occur and test them to see if they were preceded by another thought as it fought to start another chain. If we are able to identify spontaneous thought or ideas, we must grab these also, because they may just be the inspired thought or idea we needed to help us with a problem or direction in life. It is the spontaneous thought that will have been fed to us from our higher mind as an answer to a prayer plea, or as guiding inspiration from one of our Minders. In fact with much practice it is possible to be in touch with this discarnate thinking process while consciously engaged in mundane conversation.

Such is the ability of a clairvoyant or psychic, and it is also the process that leads to abilities of automatic writing.

With much practice, the process of thinking about thinking becomes second nature, and ultimately can allow us to function with inspired calm and wisdom in any situation. There are other endless beneficial applications to be gained when we set a regular time for meditation. Such is the power of meditation.

A word of caution however. It is always advisable before entering a period of meditation to motivate a higher shift in general vibration. The easiest way to do this is to manifest the idea in your mind that you are surrounded by incandescent white light, or that you are taking up position within the centre of the sun for example. Imagine you are infused with the fabric of the light; that you have become one with the light. This simple act will raise your general vibration and will guarantee during your meditation that you cannot be approached by the energy of anything of lower vibration to cause disruption.

Do not be surprised during this process also that you experience a brief feeling of spontaneous sexual arousal. As described earlier for techniques of astral projection, the effect is normal and relates to the rising circulations of energy through your chakra centres. As the circulations expand and rise up through the body, the areas governing sexual response have to be overcome. By not allowing your thoughts to be triggered by this physical reaction, you will ensure your energy does not get bogged down before it rises to the crown chakra and beyond.

Question 7: *Is it any different eating a potato from eating meat. After all they are both living, and only the form differs.*

Answer: The subject cannot be explored properly unless we examine our core motivation as a species. The debate runs back and forth on the question of whether we should eat meat. Our physical bodies seem to be designed well for meat consumption and although we are able to survive perfectly well on a non-meat diet, our design does seem to be Carnivore. The question is posed therefore: Why *should* we aspire to become Vegetarian? By my Understanding, I would tackle this from two perspectives. First to appreciate how it is that as spiritually upward mobile entities we seem to have the contradictory trait for eating the flesh of other conscious creatures. Secondly to understand at a vibrational level, what effect this trait has on our Presence and its implication for our future evolvement.

Just as with any simple question on the nature of our choices as sentient beings, we have to go back to the start of our pathway on Earth for a more precise understanding. In a time long past, when the chemical evolution of creature-form on our Planet was in its infancy, nothing had evolved with a conscious appreciation of self in any way. Reaction and interaction were based upon instinctive response. *Question*: What is instinctive response? *Answer:* The automatic reaction and interaction of vibrational energy, motivated by the living process of the plant or animal; producing harmony/conflict and change, from quantum to gross level.

Our Planet became the focus of attention from highly evolved Star travellers inhabiting systems elsewhere in the Universe. We became an experimental ground where DNA manipulations were commonplace. Natural selection was given a huge kick start at the hands of these Star travellers, each working to their own agenda. The age of the Dinosaur was a spectacular success. Dinosaurs ruled for nearly 200 million years—40,000 times as long as recorded human history; then suddenly disappeared at the end of the Cretaceous Period, circa 65 million years ago. We were visited during this time period, and many of the designs of Dinosaur resulted from DNA experimentation. Natural selection was not always so natural! Listen to this abridged extract from Saint Germain:

'So, in the times before Atlantis during the formation of the world, when matter was becoming more and more dense and solidified, sources of consciousness projected into various forms and matter, and idealized forms of creation and matter came into being. This predated Lemuria and the Atlantean civilizations. It predated what you call Earth in its 3 dimensional density. Earth was indeed a 5th and 4th dimensional being at that time and so it was possible to mould and shift matter just by merely projecting thoughts in different ways.'

To know the mind of God rather than the Spirit, as is the Left Hand path if you will, is to understand the crystalline nature of all life and that everything is geometry.

And in that patterning you projected yourselves, even into these different forms and created new forms from the geometric matrix. And so from that, God saw in its wisdom (and is not of gender and therefore is also Goddess,) that there were forms in which certain information could be stored and certain resonance could be transmitted. There was a way to receive and give information as well as transmit data that would not require biological electromagnetic fields. And so it was decided by many entities to create new forms of beingness; first in the outer reaches of the galaxy in a different dimensional time/space continuum.

First it appeared in the Arcturian and Andromedan systems and gradually as the forms became more complex and more solidified they became known into this realm. They came to Earth, as Earth herself also began to birth different crystalline forms just by her cooling, and her densifying of matter, The geometry and the materials and the silica and all the different chemical compositions evolved, necessary to support this, And so you have now a situation where consciousness has inter-penetrated matter and is projected into it and is beginning to direct its own matrix—within the matrix of the form, you therefore now have the situation of course, that is commonly called the Fall. And it is not a fall from high to low; it is a fall in vibration from quicker to slower. And you have the projection of many souls into these various kingdoms of animal, plant and mineral.

'So the first incarnational experiences in this world were ones that were not in bodies such as you now have; and indeed when you were floating in the ethers and the mists above this world, before it became more solid; that was your true nature, your true geometry, your true bodies. It is what you would call the light vehicle or the Merkaba. Now, as these densifications continued; as consciousness became more and more separate and forgetting of its Source; then it became necessary by the design of the Angelic forces and by the design of the Creator Lords, to find a way to keep in contact with the forms that had lost touch with their own Source. One of the ways to do that was through the plant kingdoms with their oils and their fragrances. Another way to do that was to project consciousness or information into the forms you call crystalline and mineral, and to have them be archetypes unto themselves. These then would be to contain information; to be able to transmit information; to be able to activate bio-electro magnetic and chemical forms of life into remembering their connection with the Unity of all life.'

The point of all this is to show that we devolved from a higher collective state through a cycle of experience to our present state. We continue on the cycle, striving by our choices and due process, to gravitate back to our original form. As a part of the devolving process, and as we took up solid Human form, our solidified bodies had separated into gender. Our solidified bodies needed nourishment as a part of the natural process for chemical survival. Our bodies *then* had no need of meat. As we descended into a state of complete sensation, the power of the new experience was such that we soon forgot the process that had brought us here. We had examples all around us of non-sentient creatures who followed cycles of development at instinctive level, and who followed natural chains of survival, each forming a food chain for another. Our bodies could have quite happily survived with Vegetable nourishment, but in primitive ignorance we copied the lower forms! The long pathway of natural selection, plus some external DNA manipulation; eventually produced the physically intelligent/ partially re-evolved creatures that we are today.

Our bodies may seem well designed to cope with being carnivore, but it was not always so. In truth, as the cycle continues it will be necessary for us to un-learn the need for eating the flesh of other intelligent creatures. Now here is the real focus! It is not specifically the act of ingesting flesh that is the problem, (though there are reasons why this is not a good thing') it is the fact that to support such a process, we must procure, gather, and end the physical life of the creatures we eat. In a perfectly balanced world *all* intelligent creatures would exist in a harmony, where even at 3rd. density, survival would never depend on carnivorous nourishment. We have an evolved intelligence, but we still sacrifice and slaughter other thinking creatures in the name of sport and food. We have forgotten, we aspire to a condition where we shall once again function as greater beings with no need for physical food intake. We shall eventually evolve again to a state where we exist and interact with equally valid levels of reality at 3rd. density and beyond.

The physical cycle we inhabit is a temporary illusion. Our vibrational Presence, (the real us,) survives forever beyond the time when our temporary physical form can no longer function. This is true for every life form. Living forms of a lower order also survive their 3rd. density manifestations; but they survive through transformation of energy. In ourselves we fight a barrier of our own making, which inhibits our ability to evolve speedily back to our natural state. Part of this barrier is our attitude to other evolved forms of life. Animals are either regarded as pets, or food, as it suits us. Our attitude to animals is often barbaric and totally hypocritical. In the act of sacrificing or the killing of other thinking life, we entrap that life along with us, to a cycle of lower vibration.

Every form of matter has an inherent energy. This energy remains beyond the time that an incumbent energy has departed. For example, if a human body is riddled with cancer, the departing Presence does not continue to have cancer on a higher level. The Presence may still retain the energy patterns of inadequacy that led to the cancer manifestation in the physical body, but the discarded body, riddled with cancer will adopt a new energy pattern of its own as it performs a cycle of decay. So it is with any flesh. We consume the portion of meat, and we take upon ourselves the energy vested in the meat. The vibrational level of the ingested meat will usually be of a lower order, made more so by the imprint left from the fear or conflict in the unnatural death of the living creature it belonged to. Our Presence has to balance out every interchange of energy it encounters. These myriads of interchange, like water slowly dripping over decades and lifetimes, are gradually filtered by our choices, as we travel the cycles back to source.

So what is the difference between the consumption of flesh, and the consumption of vegetable matter? Vegetable matter, or the fruits of vegetable matter, are motivated from higher levels, but evolve in lower physical cycles. They evolve at our level also in a battle of resistance with the elements, and interact with even lower life forms in the insect and microscopic world. They too aspire to perfection of balance; and if anyone has been blessed to the vision of their counterparts in higher spheres, they would know of the sublime difference in state awaiting even them. They exist here in lower cycles carrying a vibration as close as possible to the natural force of creation, and as far as can be found from sentient life. Their vibrational energy is closer to source and can only raise our own vibrations, but not at the expense of more conflict in our own Presence.

Do I eat meat? Yes I eat meat. But, I do so in the stark knowledge, realisation and choice as someone still battling with my own conditioned inadequacies. I aspire not to eat meat, and would convert tomorrow to a vegetarian diet if I had better control over other aspects of my life. I look forward to that goal. In an ideal world, we will progress beyond the need for material food once again. However for now, the refined energy from fresh Vegetable matter and fruit, is the best means of sustenance for our physical bodies, and for our vibrational well-being.

Vegetable versus meat, from a slightly different angle.
Further Questions 8: *We cannot know live without knowing death. Ultimately there can be no light without dark. To know of one we must know the other. In exactly the same way, how do we know what joy is if we do not know pain; and how do we know of both truly, by experience alone? Words cannot convey the feeling, so pain is equally as important as joy; for without knowing of pain how do we know what joy is? Therefore, you can safely say that any living creature born of this world will experience all of these and more. To that end does a potato feel pain? Well, if it is here to experience joy—which is ultimately living, it must feel pain. I ask you this question then. Would you then deny a being the experience of pain, or more importantly, would it be possible to do so? To that end, what is the point of feeling guilty about playing our part in it all?*

Answer: First, we should understand what we mean by Pain and Pleasure. We must take these conditions to their basic components, which of course are Conditions of Vibration. Let us once again take a look at the nature of our Presence. I refer of course to the enduring part of us, which inhabits and motivates our physical body. Our physical body is a condensation to Gross Matter, of energy existing originally in virtual form as part of the dark matter filling the Universe.

In a Physical life-cycle, our Presence amalgamates with the physical form and extends beyond it, so far as our Aura field reaches. The energy of our Presence is in a state of Flux. It is constantly changing according to our reciprocal interaction with all other forms of incoming vibrating energy; and importantly, according to the motivational choices we make which regulate the nature of the interaction. The energies within our Presence function within connected circulations centred on our Chakras. An elevated onlooker could read our Presence to provide a snapshot of our condition at any time. This is our Vibrational signature.

An elevated onlooker could also view incoming interactions as packets of vibrating energy. The frequency of the incoming energy packet would depend upon the thought motivation behind it.

If someone were about to slap us hard on the face, they would have already done so in virtual form before the event was actualised. Thought is therefore tangible. In our present un-awakened state, most people ignore the responsibility of creating the virtual event, and only examine the probabilities when the event is translated into effect as the strike is made. An elevated onlooker however would be able to read the Probability for the event at its Virtual stage.

If we had higher vision we would understand immediately how the action directed against us was a packet of negative energy. We would deal with the Actuality of a slap according to our level of deeper understanding, and this could result in wholly different outcomes. If we allowed the packet of negative energy to pollute our own Presence, we would produce a matching, counter-action, and the situation would escalate. But, if we motivate ourselves to remain aloof and loving despite provocation, we effectively maintain a high frequency as in turning the other cheek. The frequency of our vibration would be far too high for the lower energy of the negative event to penetrate and affect us badly. Sure our face would sting from the attack, but an alternative reaction out of wisdom would confound the negative energy. It would find no home in us to discharge itself and would be retained by the Presence of the sender to condense *their* vibration even further.

You may ask why I have bothered to give this laborious explanation. Well, if we are to get to grips with the original question, we must understand that Pain and Pleasure are simply degrees of the same vibration. Pain or Pleasure can be measured in all thinking creatures according to the refinement of our energy, and thus our ability to react with wisdom or the lack of it. For example, a more base person may not think twice if such an event occurred. They may produce a knife and escalate the event into a downward vibrational spiral leading to fatal injury or physical death.

We, as Sentient, thinking beings, stand unique among creatures in that we have power of Discernment. The world we live in is a reflection of us. Other lower life forms follow instinctive patterns, and exist within the temporary physical reality that we as a species have manifest for them. In a perfect world we would no longer be meat eaters. We would no longer have the need to ingest physical food at all. We would gain all the sustenance we need by simply manifesting and modifying our Presence from the virtual matter around us. We would be able to control the density of our vibration at will, enabling us to interact harmoniously on all levels in the physical and beyond. This balance would be reflected in our environment, and creatures who still lived their physical cycles, would no longer do so where the survival of one, depended upon the wilful destruction of another. It would be as it used to be when the higher realms of reality reflected their balance throughout all levels. It is only we humans who have a measure of Pain and Pleasure, and have a need to know the difference.

Of course other thinking animals feel pain. But they are trapped to their cycles *because* of the environment *we* have created for them. It is ignorance for the Human race to think that the downward spiral to lower vibrational levels began before we interfered. We have un—learned the truth. Now we are trying to climb back out again. Plants do not have the thinking process to manifest the same sensations we do; but they are affected by the vibrations we manifest. Plants simply strive by natural process for biological survival and natural harmony in a hostile environment that we hold them to by our ignorance and obstinacy. Once upon a time we were one with all things. We were one with the experience of everything to infinity. We were one with the All. We still are one with the All, but it is just that we have put some distance between ourselves and the source, even though the source remains within us all. When we can grasp this and its implication, it is possible to appreciate that Pain and Pleasure are only two aspects of the same vibration. They are also an intrinsic part of the whole, as we are. When we draw closer to the higher vibrations beyond physical, we draw closer to the experience of the vegetable or tree who are already one with all.

Understand this, and we lose the need to place our hand in the fire to know Pain; or the need to seek sensation as a goal to Pleasure. Reaching within, allows reconnection to Source and automatic empathy with *every* condition. But it is also our divine choice to remain ignorant if we will!

Question 9: *If joy is ultimately living, and pain in turn equates to death; with death being our constant companion and guide—how could we find life if it were not for death?*

Answer: There is nothing to separate my Understanding of Tau; (described beautifully in the wisdom of Chaungtse,) and the condition of being *one* with all things. Some have experienced this feeling of oneness through drug enhancement and by other means. I have visited it through deep meditation and spontaneous experiences, and to some extent I always strive for this state through alpha during out of body projections. One thing is clear when we experience the condition; *any* description is superfluous. I have to borrow here from another analogy. When we stick our hand out of a car window we can feel the pressure of air on our hand. We close our fist, and the air cannot be captured. Indeed, the wind cannot be captured for examination because we are not *of* the condition of the wind. So it is with Tau, or Oneness.

If joy is described as the ultimate in living with a need for pain as a yardstick to measure it, then against the nature of Tau or Oneness it cannot be regarded as ultimate in anything. This presents a conundrum, because as Chaungtse so ironically describes, the moment we give this condition any description, we are closing the fingers of an empty fist. My Understanding is that ultimate living, cannot be described through 3rd. level, because to do so restricts it within parameters of our making. Tau or Oneness is a sublime state of being, where awareness blends with all awareness. It is a condition of total grace and knowingness. It is a state of seamless union with the experience of all Virtuality and all Actuality. It is a state of non-resistance in the presence of complete resistance. Death on the other hand, is simply a 3rd. level perception. What to you may be seen as death, to me is the opposite. I understand death to be just another transiting process where we release from the physical form to be born back fully into our more natural permanent higher level. The body decays and returns to matter. We simply continue on our evolving cycle according to lower and higher laws of science. I see the clear distinction between death, and decay. We contain within our cellular memories, the imprint of our origins. We travel this course on a cycle of progression to return there once again. The All is Tau or Oneness.

Beyond the gathering of Souls on a cosmic timescale; which is only a millisecond blink in time but seems excruciatingly vast, the moment awaits when we will return to single Potential again. The anguish of this gross level and our attempts to place tags on everything, is testament to the restrictions we place upon ourselves.

Knowledge and understanding are the keys to progress. Death is as Life is! It is simply a transition where we have control through motivating choice to decide on one thing only: The speed of our return home.

Question 10: *What does it mean to have peace within ourselves?*

Answer: I have found peace within myself through two things. I formed a trust of acceptance within myself. By this I mean, I was able to form a Covenant with myself after my *Event* in particular. I have said before, I realised the Awareness was a Curse and a Blessing. Knowing the strategy of how it functioned did not absolve me from my continuing part within it. Knowing the strategy of it all did not take away from the infinite tactics of its playing out. I was stuck with it and with the madness I felt initially. The noise in my head was deafening until I saw how the perfection of the greater All, contained the lesser perfection of which we are all a part, and that it was all very ok! Before I achieved equilibrium I wrote the following:

A Sharp Intake of Breath:
My mind is, now turning, sharply against mind.
Please shut your mouth my noisy friend.
An undeserving rhapsody, tangential inclined,
Thus delivered from exhaustion in peaceful dire alarm.
Travail to get the better of me Huh!
This Libra so maligned; I grind my sharpest teeth.

My Second covenant to inner peace was through a new honesty. I knew from my *Event* and my moment of total realisation, I would walk for the rest of my life with a mirror before me that would reveal all of myself to me, and from which nothing could be hidden. I accepted this finally. But it was only possible when I accepted also the awesome power and responsibility that went with it. That power was in the knowledge from that moment the entire content of my destiny would unfold by my singular choice alone. My reactions determine reciprocal reaction, and thereby, the Consequence. In accepting how it is, I accepted my own responsibility. I knew I had finally *got it!*

My frequency; my vibration, could and would only ever be determined by my own choices. It had ever been so. Conditioning trapped me; but it also freed me, because the imbalance led to discontent and then resistance. From resistance I sought understanding, and my pathway shortened. Responsibility came from understanding on a balance of humility to my own condition, finally leading for evermore to tranquillity even in the face of chaos.

Question 11: *But the ultimate cycle is surely the Will of the Creator to exert its purpose and in turn unfold its potential upon the physical plane. So does it matter then if there is pain; and why feel it anyway?*

Answer: We are the *expression* of the Will of One, with Divine choice and inevitable Self-Responsibility for the direction of our pathway back to the Source; and explicitly, pain is simply our human measure of conflict between opposing levels of vibration, and is borne out of the Resistance *we* choose to create between them. Pain is one Consequence derived from the effect of our motivating Presence. If a Cosmic event of apparent conflict takes place somewhere in space, do we say that the event causes us pain? The event would certainly arise through conflicts of vibration on a gross scale. When something strikes us for example because of our careless motivation, the Event is also an interpretation of conflict based upon opposing vibration on a gross scale. So why do we record the event in pain? A strike on the arm triggers chemical responses from the conflict of gross matter, and these are transferred through neural pathways to be recorded in our physical brain. It could be said that the message of conflict is transferred by harmonious pathways which carry the vibration of the conflict to our cortex. We receive the sensory input of the event. We motivate a response based upon the degree of resistance the event produces to the vibration of our Presence. We discern the vibrational resistance within us and motivate a reaction accordingly. Resistance = Conflict = Pain! Capacity for Pain is a measure of the Refinement of our Vibrational Presence. We can choose to recognise that fact, or ignore it; which coincidentally is the process of choice repeating itself. Pain no longer exists when we are able to step beyond the sensational resistance of our Gross body and centre ourselves to higher vibration. No Pain is No Gain: No Pain is No Lesson: My Pain was my Lesson. But my Lesson is now your Pain!

'But do you still experience pain on a mental/emotional mind level?'
Answer: We have to agree what we mean by the Mental/Emotional mind, and I can only offer my own understanding as a parameter for the question. Several notes of a musical scale played on the piano each represent a different vibration; or packet of vibration. Some of those notes harmonise, while others oppose. The difference is determined by the degree of frequency compatibility. So it is with Emotion. Each emotion is a packet of vibration, motivated and moderated by our own individual signature. *We* produce these packets of vibration as an harmonic or opposing reaction to sensory input we receive in any situation. Emotions are simply measures of condition borne out of reaction from within the lower vibrations of sensation. If we were sufficiently centred, we would no longer be trapped to the world of sensation, and our discernment would improve. At such a higher level it becomes possible to express *Dispassionate Compassion*.

I contend therefore that where Emotion is a unit of measure from within the condition of physical life, it cannot be described as Mind itself—as in a separated category of consciousness. Pain, as another measure from lower levels of vibration likewise does not exist at a higher level. The same thing is true when we use the word Mental to describe a condition of mind, when in fact it is an Effect! I still feel pain on an emotional/mind level, because I am still in the classroom as a student.

Questions 12: *How are these conditions affected by organ transplants?*
It has been shown in many cases that a person will take on the traits of an organ donor. Which person are these traits part of? If the traits have migrated, who has reincarnated? Is it the recipient, and / or part of the donor? A core consideration would be that there is nothing

migrating but just a singular force of God in constant flux, and it is only our view that can be carved up, examined and differentiated. That is arguably the core point of Buddhism; whereby all our great speculations are essentially irrelevant if we reach enlightenment and experientially find oneness with all.

Answer: Our Presence occupies the physical vehicle of our person during the cycle of physical birth to physical decay. The physical body therefore is a gross manifestation of motivated vibrational energy. Every component of our physical body functions biologically through the transfer of motivated energy from our Presence during occupation. When a physical organ is removed, it does not lose the vibrational matrix of its donor. After it has been transplanted it can be possible for the recipient to detect the old energy pattern before they impose their own vibrational energy pattern on it.

It is like when one computer programmer builds a software programme, and then another Programmer comes to use the same computer. The new programmer is able to make use of the first Programmer's software; and can explore the style and method of how it was formed. He can read the signature of the first programmer but is then able to rewrite the software to his own liking. This does not mean however when the new Programmer starts to use the computer, that they will *become* the personality or Presence of the first Programmer. The Effect of the donor vibration may live on for a time in the recipient, but the traits behind them remain a living part of the original donor only.

On the second point about the migration of senses beyond physical death and its relationship to Buddhist thinking: I would propose that senses themselves cannot migrate because they are not a singularity. They are an effect which belongs to physical sensation. The transformation of physical rebirth is a manifestation of the Law of One, and the process is unshaken by our divinity of individual experience. We have the ability to return to being One with the Source while still able to retain the singular memory of our divine experience.

I understand a different ending to the Buddhist ideal. Buddhism teaches that we must become one with all things through enlightenment, and that beyond this aspiration; all our speculations of grand design are irrelevant. I see this to impose a conclusion. I believe that there is no conclusion, because at such a level we are part of the Mobius loop, the spiral torus, and the continued transformation to infinity.

I understand that the divine motivation we carry allows us to be one with ourselves, but later to also be one with everyone and everything else. By being one with ourselves we automatically make the connection of understanding to the condition of collective oneness. We become the inhalation and exhalation at the same time. Ironically, there is no such thing as a singularity anyway because everything *is* the singularity. Even to describe it so, is to contain it; because *it* encompasses all.

Question 13: *How do we know if experiences are spiritual or delusional?*

Answer: Compare a dream from last week with the memory of a physical event from about the same time. The dream may still be remembered, but the memory of an important physical event around the same time is strong in the mind. Do the same for last month or last year or for any specific date from a more distant time. Once again, the physical experience is remembered, by fading degree, but dreams are usually soon forgotten. When an Out of Body experience is recalled it is a strong memory like a physical event memory. Sleep OBE's are involuntary, but an induced OBE would remain even more powerful in the mind. The memories I have of past OBE's fade in my mind as slowly as important mundane memories. My OBE's always happen in the company and protection of my Minder. They are always instructional. They have a start, middle and an ending. I am always aware of myself within the experience, and they are always very positive. These factors are the yardsticks that govern my memories and help me to focus on the important ones . . .

How do I know that I don't subconsciously produce the automatic writings and didactic poetry myself? Well, practice brought confidence; but in the early days I allowed my conscious mind to interfere and second-guess the words given to me. The results were flat and contrived. When I meditate to an Alpha state and when I am totally passive to incoming information, the process happens in two different ways. Firstly, if I am actually sitting to practice for automatic writing, I detach myself, from myself. I don't even look at the paper; or at my hand as the words flow from the pen. The words flow almost faster than my hand can transcribe them, and I am totally unaware of the words or the subject matter that appears. It is only later when I end the session that I study the material I have received. The writing is always continuous without punctuation and usually untidy on the page; but is always legible, and instructional. It always reads to me as a composition from the mind of someone else.

Secondly, for the receipt of didactic poetry I first get a sense of something on a higher level building up. I can feel a static energy around me, and I have an inner knowingness of something about to appear. When it actually happens, it is as if someone has thrust a brightly illuminated page of text before me (in my mind's eye.) Then it vanishes; but like the imprint of light from a blinding photo flash, the shadow image of the page stays in my vision in just the same way. I have to grab for the nearest piece of paper and pen, and scribble the words furiously from the fix in my mind before they fade away to nothing. The arrival is from an external source using me internally. I am always humbled by what I have been blessed to receive. I am also usually impressed to know where, or to whom I must direct the text. The reaction of the recipient gives me a validation of the quality and accuracy.

There are those on higher levels who have a better viewing point than me. They have infinitely greater wisdom than me. They have my very best interests at heart, and they are waiting to help me. All I ever have to do is to live my life with crystal honesty, then yield to them, ask from my soul for their assistance, and be sufficiently aware to recognise and act on their response. To do anything different is to act through angles instead of curves, just as Thoth warns in *The Emerald Tablets*.

A Further Question 14:

I understood a little of what you meant perhaps. What can I say! Only that these thoughts seem to hound me down and I feel they arise due to doubt/insecurities, which can only exist in one place, with me. I doubt others, but feel that this is a mere projection. My relationship with others was not good at a point, but now I am working on it and it is improving. It must be said also, if you can't see, how do you know what to look for? I only have this to offer at this stage! At times I hold on by my finger nails and my strength keeps me afloat. These thoughts I dare not share with others for what they would think of me. I do not want them to fear me as I feel they would. There is absolutely no chance of me following these thoughts, but still they can be all consuming at times.

Answer: I know now that when we return to a physical life, and indeed the life we helped to choose, we set ourselves up for conflict. Conflict is an absolutely necessary part of the process towards enlightenment. We carry the baggage of our past lives, as grades of energy within our Presence. These energies are in a constant state of flux, but evermore, the lower energies are trying to discharge as hotspots to the material plane; while the higher energies within us are straining like a cork trapped underwater to rise to the higher planes where we came from, and will return to. We cannot be freed until we shed our physical body upon death. But this is only a rebirth to our true higher level. In the meantime here, as we face the inadequacies within us we are facing the negative energy which prevents us from being free completely from the physical plane. If we are reluctant to face the lower energy traits within us, as that energy struggles to discharge itself to the material, the conflict arises within us. We become discontented. Negative things seem to spring up in our pathway. We label them as bad luck without ever realizing at the time we are creating it for ourselves!

As we step on the lower rungs of understanding, the conflicting thoughts in our head give rise to unusual behaviour, such as in extreme cases the will to self-mutilate. This is just inner conflict externalized. However if you hold always to the trust that a higher force is at work, you will be shielded from yourself before negative actions of self harm or otherwise, become too overwhelming. If you always seek in your mind to link to a higher guiding energy, and ask in silent prayer or thought for help to understand; then trust to the process; the teacher or the lesson is always placed before you to absorb and move on. You will opt to recognise and act upon it by your own choice. This is how it is. It is as I have understood, experienced and tested it to be. But never take my word for it. Put it to your own test! Just remember that a single selfless thought to Spirit for help will always be answered. Our Minders and Helpers on a higher level are around us always ready to guide. We have to be ready for it. We have to want it. We have to be ready to face ourselves with open our eyes to receive it.

Question 15: *Can you make sense of the hundreds of alleged divine sources that seem to be offering Channelled wisdom on web sites everywhere? Which of them are true and which are false?*

Answer: Every week on Internet sites, we are presented with dozens of Channellings from alleged higher sources. A proportion of these, from separated individuals, even claim to have been delivered from the same Divine personalities! How do we make sense of this? Channellings can manifest through Automatic Writing, Clairvoyance, Transfiguration, Trance, Hypnosis, or apparent direct inspiration. We can't even begin to discern the strength of any form of alleged Channelling unless we first understand the mechanics of how the process takes place! By the Understanding given from my *Event* therefore, I'd like to offer a comprehensive explanation to this so we can move forward to appreciate what is really happening.

We start on the basis that we inhabit what is termed 3rd. density; or put another way—we inhabit the physical universe. We start on the basis that when we refer to we, it is not just the physical body we refer to, but our whole personal package at this stage of our progression. The physical body evolves out of basic physical matter, which grows from conception into an ever-aging adult form; and after a physical lifetime of use, it decays back to basic physical matter again. The physical package does not constitute the real us before or beyond the physical process. We start on the basis that we comprise a motivating Presence, which inhabits and controls the physical body for its duration. Our Presence can be detected by some individuals who are sufficiently raised in vibration. They are able to see the aura, which is the extended energetic field of energy from the Presence.

The flows and densities of energy within our Presence mirror the frequencies of the electromagnetic spectrum and they represent themselves through every colour of the spectrum. The Presence is in a state of evolving flux. Our Vibrational Signature would be a snapshot of our Presence taken at any one time. The refinement of our Presence becomes modified by our choice of interaction to the incoming packets of sensual energy. This is true even of Channelling, because the last filter for higher contact is the limitation of our physical senses. The biology of our physical body and in particular the neurological process of the brain, places a huge limitation on our ability to interact with incoming signals, and stifles our ability to receive any pure information from higher levels.

We function from within 3rd. density, refining our vibrational frequencies for the benefit of our higher enduring Presence. Our lack of appreciation for the process delays us from making better progress. Our higher mind can be almost completely distracted by the input from our physical senses and from our physical interactions.

Most especially during sleep, our higher mind is again almost completely blocked by these influences. In the daytime, we pick up packets of energy with thousands of multiple frequencies. In sleep, just like a tub of water sloshing about, our higher mind wrestles with the input from a physical world in an attempt to bring calm before we wake again for more. During sleep, our mind is occupied at several levels of consciousness. The process of meditation, or centring, or achieving alpha state, is where we train our immediate mind to go to sleep while physically awake, so the insight of our higher mind may become accessible to us.

The question begs: *'What does all this have to do with channelling etc?'* Let us take it all a little further! In a nutshell, a person can interpret the information in their head as being either from their own conscious working mind, or originating from the higher mind where sensation plays no part. Or they can interpret it as originating from a genuine external higher source. Or they may think they are receiving channelling from a famous departed guru, saint, or God source which has chosen them personally as an emissary! If we agree in all of these cases it is the message and not the messenger that is important, we have to ask ourselves, who benefits from the Medium being hailed as the channel for a famous divinity?

The truth in any message will stand the test of anything that challenges it. So, if a big deal is made about the originating source, it can only be to feed the ego of the messenger. Any alleged divine source would be perfectly aware of this and by their nature would have no part in their own glorification through the Medium. I contend therefore, that for the vast majority of alleged channelled information, the information may be nobly motivated, but the message is lost to ego when the Medium claims it is from a fabulous or famous source. At a higher level they would know this and would not willingly supply food for the ego of any earthbound pretender.

We need to take heed of the lesson in this because of the profound period of energetic change we are all entering. The vibration of everything and everyone is being affected already by the incoming interaction with Space Matter of a higher order. The planetary bodies heading for a rendezvous with us are still distant but the vibrational interactions are so powerful that the process of realignment has already begun. Every Planet in our system is undergoing profound and massive change, including Planet Earth. The changes manifest themselves through the obvious polarisations of energy that we can see within us and in nature around us. There are those whose vibrations are being raised and are finding enlightened understanding at last; and on the other side there are those who align themselves to the darker side and are behind the increased venom of conflict in the world. Like is being attracted to like with strength never seen before. In nature the same thing is producing huge planetary changes that can no longer be ignored.

Inspired messages are reaching the people who have responded to the higher calling. But these messages still have to go through the interpretation of their imperfect host. If inspirations are not examined with cold blooded honesty, there is a danger that ego will take over to try and make the Medium as important as the message. Remember, truth stands alone and does not need a famously named sponsor to boost its importance.

Question 16: *I was just sitting here trying to relax and connect to the light, whilst grounding to flush some obstinate knots out, and felt the usual Goosebumps run up and down my body and wondered why I'd never brought this up before. I remember you, Richard, saying how this was a sign for you that there was a Presence or connection operating on you, and I wondered if you might expand a little on this. I've always felt this when focussing my thoughts on uplifting matters, even well before I believed consciously in anything spiritual, and have been making this connection myself for some time now, but well, the doubts creep in and pick away as they like to do. How can I really know what is happening or why my body sends shivers up and down? Yet I could always induce this just by thinking in a certain way, so it's not really a reaction to temperature change, I would think. I also wonder if others have this little signal too. Sometimes I feel less sceptical and can almost sense a pushing in my back, although family strife over the last year has meant this has been rarer, but that's mostly due to me just not taking the time very much to actively seek out this kind of mental activity. Anyway, I was just wondering what to think of this?*

Answer: I will do my best. First with a couple of simple analogies: If we step out of a warm house to the crisp air of a winter evening, we feel the temperature change all over, even if wrapped up. At a more subtle level, if we are standing in a swimming pool and a pocket of water, fresh from the heat-exchanger circulates past us, the tiny temperature change registers to our skin as a big temperature change. In simple terms I understand we register changes in vibration around us in just the same way as the physical senses register temperature change. We are physical vehicles, motivated from our inhabiting Presence; which in turn is a cohesion of complex frequencies of vibrating finer matter. It extends in an Auric/energetic field for a fluctuating distance around our physical body. Our Physical body is also a cohesion of much more dense vibrating matter. Our physical senses are preoccupied with the action and reaction to/with physical sensation, whereas our higher senses are preoccupied with action/reaction to/with higher levels of reality; and all according to the vibration of our Presence.

To me, *everything* can be broken down to an understanding of the interaction of vibrational energy. It may be in a Virtual state awaiting motivation. It may be in one of infinite states of static cohesion, such as with inanimate matter. It may be in one of infinite states of motivated cohesion, such as in the makeup of a Presence. It may be in one of infinite states of all of the above, represented throughout the higher realities that our earthbound senses prevent us from remembering. But the understanding begins with the knowledge of what is happening within *us* at a vibrational level. I deal with this comprehensively earlier in the book. But to recap: The circulating energies of our Presence centre individually around the Chakra points of our physical body. All circulations are linked. At the root Chakra, fresh energy is actualised from the Virtuality beyond us by the will of our own motivation. At our crown Chakra, the energy flow leaves us partly to enrich and return to feed us at our root Chakra, and partly to hold the connection from us to higher realms of energetic reality. Our general vibrational signature is modified by our response to incoming stimulation. I understand therefore when I feel a rush of Spirit it can mean one of a few things.

If it has been triggered by an inspiration of some kind, like a piece of music; a beautiful scene, vision or thought; an act of compassion, kindness, selflessness, or sacrifice etc., I will have been stimulated by higher energies to actualise similar energy. I will feel the rush of that new energy. At the same time, the presence of the inspiration itself has form. There will have been a vibrational handshake between my Presence and that of the inspirational source which will add to the spiritual rush.

If I am in a meditative, contemplative or alpha state, I am detaching myself from my physical senses. I am thus making conscious contact with my higher self.

If I make firm contact, I recognize myself at that refined level and I become immediately open to higher non-physical senses. This would again register as a spirit wind of recognition around me.

If my vibration drops out for dire reason, such as from an argument; or from dealing with someone else's bad energy; or from negative introspection; or from my own bad reaction to incoming energy of any kind etc., I will have motivated my own energies to condense in instinctive readiness for physical protection. The consequence conversely, would not be as a spirit wind. It would be as a headache perhaps, or as a number of other physical discomforts. But ironically in this state, I would be wide open to allow those of a lower vibration on a higher level to draw near to me, and their malevolent presence would register to me as an uncomfortable spirit wind.

It is often asked: If we have Guides, Minders, Spirit Social Workers or even qualified family members who have returned to the levels of higher reality, how is it that they don't come to us more and prove their attendance? Well, anyone visiting a person on the Earth Plane would bring with them the intensity of their more sublime vibration. This would be felt by the person on the Earth Plane as a sudden spirit wind blowing over them or around them.

The bottom line is this. The quality of whatever or whoever you detect has everything to do with our own state of vibration. We will feel the interaction any other stimulating vibration depending upon the status quo arising from our own vibrational signature. When we yearn for example to feel the higher presence of a departed loved one, it is not that they do not come to us so we can feel them, it is just that we *choose* to hold our vibrations too close to physical sensation. Incidentally, this recognition of difference of vibration takes place between every individual on the Earth plane. It is the reason why we instantly like or dislike someone new. It means we are simply recording the higher effect and consequence of vibrational recognition.

Question 17: *Why do men and women think differently?*

Answer: In simple form it must be accounted that Men (as hunter gatherers) are genetically programmed to think strategically, while Women (as nurturers) are genetically programmed to think tactically. This ties Men to think more of the application of action at the expense of its effect, while Women are tied to emotional response at the expense of the bigger picture. It is a wise Man that can understand the roots and implications of emotional response; and it is a wise Woman who can step away from emotion, to see the bigger context of its preoccupation.

The path of greatest Understanding and expansion comes from a position where both are acknowledged with equal importance.

Question 18: *Many esoteric explanations seem to come from the Mystery schools of thought, and a lot of what you have written has the same flavour. Have these teachings influenced you. Can you explain?*

Answer: I want to talk generally about these things. So: The Mystery Schools. What exactly do we mean by this? We describe something as a mystery if it falls outside of our mundane experience or understanding; yet we are prepared to accept transferred faith as fact from others on Godly matters; or from untested personal experiences. Supernormal things may happen to us, and it is by the testing of these that we are able to leapfrog forward in our general understanding of things. For myself, and following a particular occasion many years ago I call my *Event*, I came to realise it is not possible to really understand the nature of things beyond us until we have fully understood the workings of matter itself. I can't condense the explanations of tens of thousands of words here, but it is possible to plagiarize my own work to describe a few conditions that arise from the Understanding that was returned to me. It will be up to others to put it to their own test. For a start, the Truth simply *is*, and the final Actuality of everything simply *is*. At our level we have a limited Viewing point. We describe all unknown truth as Mystery to reflect this. The word Mystery is almost to say, *beyond understanding*. However, the great Mystery as a description, allows us to form a comfort zone that is also a salve to our inadequacy; and unfortunately empowers a whole bunch of control mechanisms that help to perpetuate our ignorance.

If one person, or a group, appear to hold knowledge that others do not have, then the dependence of inadequacy vested in the seeker, will empower the so called keepers of the knowledge. The seeker will then have an excuse to dwell longer in ignorance because the so-called keepers of the knowledge are able exercise control over them by their implied superiority. The situation worsens when the so-called keepers of knowledge encourage their own loftiness. Before long we see Mystery Schools or Grand Religions holding power and sway over the minds of the masses. Jesus as a counter-example did not have a toll booth or a grand teaching academy or Church when he taught the Actuality of Truth.

Years ago, when deep coherent messages first flowed from my pen while meditating, I knew they appeared from beyond me. Those were the days long before the Internet, with its thousands of examples of alleged channelling from alleged entities and angels from a higher level. I don't say that to put them all down, because the law of averages dictates that some of them are likely to be quite genuine; and many more at least inspired and sincere. However back then, without the stimulus of the Internet, I looked inside myself for an answer. Now I know, I was answered by guided synchronicities on a pathway to my Event and beyond, where their source then became clearly understood.

When working at higher levels with someone of Earth concern, or even from more distant places, there is a regular occasion where the seeker encounters a particular conundrum. It is where the seeker wants to know the name of the person or entity they have contacted. A common reaction is to be told by their source that it is not important to know. Yet those who understand, appreciate there is very great importance in a name. So why would a genuine contact wish to make it seem unimportant? When there is Understanding of the whole vibrational interaction of matter there is also appreciation of the energy represented in its smallest component parts. We all have names, given to us at birth by our parents. Our parents are people who themselves are on a journey to realise and fulfil their own Birth Plan. They each represent a Presence locked into a physical vehicle, but interacting together. You helped choose your parents and the Birth Plan you would contract for yourself. The very act of this process guaranteed as one small element in the whole thing, that your choice of name would end up as it has. It guaranteed also thereby, your name would carry the vibrational signature appropriate to you, and perfectly delivered out of your parents. When we shed our temporary physical form and return to higher reality, or especially, progress to even higher levels of state, we may still have an identification name. The process is no different there. The name would no longer be the Earth name that the person held in their last incarnation, it would be a name that represented the culmination of *all* their experience. It would nevertheless still represent the vibrational signature of the person.

What's in a Name, via a small diversion . . .

All here know me by my name as Richard Gabriel. I have never made a secret of the fact that this is not my birth name. Even as a child I was not happy with my birth name. I carried it unwillingly. When my adult-life journey to enlightenment began properly I was already married and with children. I was so young then and badly prepared! I spent all of my higher thought process in an obsessive effort to try and figure the answers to seemingly imponderable questions. One of these concerned my birth name and why it was that I had such an antipathy towards it. I always thought my name had been a mistake! I always however held knowingness that I had another name. I had just turned 30 years and I had dwelled on this conundrum for some time. I sent out prayer thoughts for inspiration. I remember one day in my work I was reconstructing an internal corrugated flat roof for a friend and customer. The job was particularly difficult and I had been working hard for some hours to beat forthcoming bad weather. The work required intense concentration as I was working very unsafely at height. I arrived finally at a stage where I could take a break. I had a drink and sandwiches with me and found a comfortable spot on the roof well out of sight from anyone. I guess as I sat quietly, my mind instantly returned to my current higher *name* conundrum. Instantly I broke a dream I'd had the previous night. I remembered I had been with someone familiar who was explaining something important to me. I had been aware of myself as in a lucid dream and more importantly I was aware of myself under the name you now know me as.

The story does not end here though. Inexplicably as strongly as I knew I had been given a birth name which sat badly with me, and despite the fact that I felt my new name was correct—I also did not feel right in its use either.

It was only at my *Event* the following year that I understood. Even a name represents a vibrational package. The predetermined birth name is the name which is a reflecting vibrational identity of the person who bears it. Through my early life I had been aware on a higher level that I was on an accelerated journey of probability which would provide me with very difficult lessons. I arrived at an elevation where my later name would become apparent to me, but still many years from the time when I was sufficiently enlightened to wear it. It was nearly 20 years from the time I was made aware of my evolved name that I knew I could begin to use it. In my mundane life, my birth name endures and I am often asked why I do not make the full legal switch.

Apart from the legal rigmarole, the real reason is that my mundane work—although giving me great satisfaction in a job well done, this work still belongs to the progression of my earth-bound journey. My enlightened journey and the purpose of my Birth Plan is where my fulfilment remains to be claimed. On the day I am enabled to make the transition to full time working in this direction I will cease to use my birth name completely

Beyond a certain point of progress, people of similar vibration would have no need of named introduction because they would automatically be able to meld with the experience of the other and know them anyway. While bound to this lower level we need to know a person's name to be able to hook their identity, without even remembering it is possible to know them truly by a deeper method. Dependence on our need to obtain the name leaves us wide open to deception. The process of interaction between our perceived reality and the equally valid greater reality occurs by laws that simply *are*. The strategy of that interaction simply is. However the tactics of interaction are determined by our motivation, (thought.) *Like* vibration gravitates to *like* vibration. Lower physical matter condenses to other physical matter. Within us, our Presence strains against the constraint of physical matter to link with higher levels. The binding cement is our dependence on sensation and the ego that drives us in ignorance to feel better among peers as the process unfolds. Eventually the physical vehicle will be left behind to complete with its cycle of birth and decay. Meanwhile our Presence pulls us inevitably in the direction of our enduring home in another state.

Those who are less dependent on sensation hear that calling more loudly. There are powerful Cosmic reasons why that calling is becoming louder across the world right now. We have to be reminded though, that on levels of reality beyond the physical; there are vibrational levels where even the dregs of society live. There are regions also where less pleasant entities exist. Many of these are motivated projections from the darkest recesses of sensation in the physical world. Someone who heeds the higher calling, but who has not yet turned into themselves for answers, is a prime prospect for the deceit and self-deceit I spoke of earlier. The reason for this is very simple. If we are still dependent on the pull of sensation, we will place importance on the name (as we presently understand a name!) to nurture our ignorance. Those people and entities beyond physical who seek to feed on the forlorn attachment to physical, will try to enact the sensation they need through the reaction and energy of misguided seekers on the physical level. So they will gladly give a fantastic name, or portray themselves as a sensational or grandiose manifestation in the mind of the foolish seeker. When the seeker is caught out by this, it is easy for the low entity to keep them hooked by feeding whatever vision or false information is needed. This keeps the seeker enslaved and dependant on low vibration. I despair of the times I read from yet another misguided soul claiming to represent another highly named angel, and who seeks followers to their unquestioning bland messages. The messages are all the same and appear lofty, but usually do nothing to explain the truthful unassailable process of the way things really exist and interact. If this were so, then we would have returned to whence we came, away from physical Earth eons ago.

In the scenario I describe, the seeker is held back by interdependence with whosoever or whatever has caught them at a lower level of higher vibration. Otherwise, seekers may hold themselves back where they have risen to be able to tap into their higher self, but then fall back to feed ego through a self-manifesting entity with a comfortable false identity. In this case, their source is intended to impress others—so that the attached messages or information are given credibility; and so the process continues! Self-deceit is also evident when someone purports to offer lofty information that has been plagiarized from other sources; when in fact a lazy Presence is answering the higher pull within themselves simply by association. There are many other versions where the message is lost because of our own clouded interpretations.

By my Understanding: Entities from the highest levels would manifest in their natural state at a vibrational frequency that would be utterly blinding to us here. People, who go about their business in the myriad of other higher levels, (remember from the teachings of Jesus, *In my house there are many mansions*! and all have frequency levels which are far brighter than ours. If I wish to meditate and align myself to levels beyond myself, I project my awareness beyond the vibration of physical to levels that appear as pure light to us here. Such higher vibrations are actually harmful to any form of lower vibration beyond us that may try to draw close. To them it would be like drawing close to the full force of an electric fire. I know by simply reaching to the levels of light, I will receive contact, help, guidance, inspiration, direction, information, protection and tranquillity every time. I know at any time whatsoever, if I intuit the negativity of a lower vibration, whether it is from the projected vibration of a physical lowlife, or from the presence of a bad entity at higher level, I simply need to explode a light bomb in my mind where I am at the centre of it—and anything or anyone of a lower vibration will be banished or forced far away from me. This is quite simply in accordance with the natural law of things. It simply is. It is the reason as you will read of later, why there was no fear to be felt within the depths of the underground cave system of the Giza Plateau.

When I wake with seemingly prophetic dreams, or if I awake from meditation with thought forms that are not immediately clear, I send out a prayer message to the levels of light, knowing my vibrational message packet will be picked up and acted upon to the best purpose from the highest levels. We are charged however to learn lessons ourselves. We must first channel the information back inside ourselves and *test it*. We must learn to align with our greater Presence so as to read the information; but not like someone earthbound seeking to know a name, rather as someone who does have the innate ability to feel what is truly behind the message.

As to the name of one Presence who regularly helps me. Well I am satisfied to call him my Minder. There are probably several, as with anyone, depending on the circumstances. So it is with the process of vibrational identity and interaction. So it is when something new is presented for us to consider. So it was when I read the words of The Emerald Tablets. Their source can and will be argued. Was it from Thoth or wasn't it? Who cares! I read the words and feel the rush of Spirit-wind every time. I draw into the vibration of the words and feel the surge as I am automatically lifted by their genuine power to a higher level. I draw deeper and deeper every time to feel and know their meaning. So it was meant to be. I have made my own choice as to their validity; and it would not have mattered if the cover claimed Popeye wrote them! So it is also with The Wave writings from the Casseopeans. These are argued to hell as being genuine, or not. I have made my own mind up to the great worth of their teaching. Let others do the same, or not! But at the end of it all; if the teachings are to be shared with others, then there must be a proviso.

Any such explanations on the exact nature of things, (and this particularly includes for myself the explanations of my own book,) must never be offered as the final word. They must be offered as an expose of understanding that is intended for others to test against their own experience, before reaching their own conclusion. And finally, the source of these explanations must avail themselves to any challenge or enquiry, as I gladly do with my own contributions.

Question 19: *How can a person plan their own future if there are so many mistakes they can make along the way?*

Answer: So often we seek excuses for things not happening as we wish when in fact it is our own misguided motivation which stands in the way. I have used an analogy for many years regarding staking your own future, and it all begins with our own single-minded motivation of thought. I examine the Probabilities for long term goals. I decide upon the one I wish to Actuate. I march into the future in my mind with a hammer and a stake. I drive the stake hard into the ground. I return to my place, knowing my Virtual future is already formed! I simply have to keep moving toward it one step at a time and it will be mine. It will also be my choice to discern along the route whether the closed or open doors I encounter are obstacles meant to deter a wrong path; or to provide the inner tools for best use of the prize when it is claimed. An overriding consideration must be if the target prize is sought with truly honourable motivation, and for truly honourable purpose. Is it serving a need or a want? Is it for service to self, or for service to others? These factors will have a major bearing on whether the goal will be achieved, or if the scars of the journey will form a better prize.

Question 20: *Can you give a bit more detail of the workings of Spirit within you on a mundane day to day level.*

Answer: This isn't easy to describe. Everyone knows the feeling when you are busy with a mundane a task and your higher mind goes off on its own in a bit like an alpha state. I have found over the years as my awareness and link to Spirit strengthened, I began to function more and more on a split mind level as a matter of course. The difference was that I no longer needed to give these higher thoughts any direction. It was as if a part of me was permanently outside of myself. I acquired a constant split perception. On a mundane level I go about my mundane life. On the higher level my perceptions are from a viewing point outside the physical. All the things that happen to me on a mundane level are modified by the higher perception. If someone does me very wrong, I may have a short mundane reaction but in a moment I am able to transfer my sight to a far wider viewing point and see the encounter in vibrational terms. For me as an individual, the wrong that someone does to me is not as important as my reaction to it. I refer again to the formula of Cause, (Motivating thought,) Effect (Action carried through,) and Consequence (The Reciprocal Reaction.) If someone does me a great wrong their Cause has been negative. The Effect may be negative. The Consequence however will only be negative to me if I accept the Effect. To do this I would have to allow my vibration to condense sufficiently to match the incoming negative energy. For the Originator however the Consequence would then be negative, because in creating and delivering a hot-spot of negative energy, their lowered energy field would condense further. The final consequence for the Originator would be a forthcoming negative situation for them to deal with as their negative hot-spot of energy discharged itself. The effect is commonly known as the *Law of Reciprocal Action* and has its basis in higher Physics. It is a real effect. For me as the recipient, if I maintain my vibrational link to higher levels, the incoming negative energy will have no great effect. My body may bleed but my spirit will grow stronger.

We can take it a step further. The more I yield to the flow of higher spirit, the greater I can tap into its awesome power. With such energy it is possible to control any negative energy encountered. Here is an imperfect analogy, but which does convey the point. If I, as an unawakened person, am like an electric fire with one bar lit, people of all levels will congregate comfortably around me to do what they will. If I, as an awakened person, am like an electric fire with six bars of heat blazing out, then only others who themselves are of the quality of fire will be at home with me. All others of lower vibration will be afraid to come close. So it is therefore, as I strive at all times to build a stronger link to Spirit. Sometimes it is necessary to command the power of the Source and Spirit to flood through you, to drive negativity to earth and to embrace all with the higher heat. Remember that the path being walked by someone else, is a path you have walked before or are due to walk in the future.

My ramble leads me to address the workings of spirit in the lives of bigger groups. The Cause/Effect/Consequence formula does not confine itself to individuals. It can as easily be applied to Nations. Each Nation of the world operates with a lower and higher consciousness. At lower levels, the mundane path of progress traces like a jagged lifeline. This is the technological development, and the effect it has on a nation and on its attitude to others. We can see in the world how national and collective global control is at the root of so much unnecessary death and suffering. But they do this because the masses allow it to happen. Our global race is such a bad student. National and international *Cause*, is still controlled through

Service to Self. The Effect and Consequence are disastrous, and a change seems impossible by the hand of any one individual.

Nothing could be further from the truth however. If we step back from it all once again and think in terms of vibration, a higher reality emerges. It seems a long time ago in this book since I described the interaction of matter at quantum level, but this process of interaction takes place just the same on a planetary scale. It is all about circulations and the balance of frequencies circulating within them. Our globe has a frequency that is directly proportional to the motivations of every individual who occupies its surface. Every single motivated thought affects the whole world. It affects the environment above and below ground. It follows as a plain fact therefore, if only a small percentage of human life could raise their vibration toward spiritual levels, it would have a dramatic effect upon the convulsions of protest that the Earth is making at the moment. Furthermore, the effect would be dramatic upon the collective higher consciousness of the earth. At the moment everyone is carried along on waves of fear. When a grasp of the pure interaction of vibrational matter becomes a conscious reality in the mind, all the bullshine of conditioned responses and ideas generated by mankind to control mankind, falls away forever. The fear then transfers to them because they know their power of mystic illusion has been shattered.

A new mental attitude of awareness to the universal simplicity of creation would lead to a paradigm shift towards tolerance. The sole responsibility lies with every single individual. The process to Planetary balance is slowed every time someone casts a bad thought; every time someone thinks an unkindness; every time someone misses the opportunity for compassion or selflessness; every time a good turn is missed; every time love is withheld; every time understanding is not given. every time an animal is wronged and on and on and on; because all of these things and more, create negative vibrations that tip the scales in the wrong direction. We can all do the right thing, but we must first be able to look into the mirror and judge the Cause within ourselves.

Question 21: *What is time?*

Answer: Time is measurement of the interval between two or more points. The condition of time is a pre-set necessary only to Homo sapiens, helping us to judge our interaction with the limited world we perceive around us. Today/tomorrow. This week/next week! Next week is a point of Probability and is wholly flexible. Its outcome depends upon the Actuality of yesterday and beyond. We have the free will to shape it. Today, is a moving point, and is thus an illusion of time. But even these parameters are borne by a material world where we hold our consciousness to the straight jacket of mortality. We constrain ourselves with the finite illusion of physical birth and death. If we could grasp the greater viewing point of a vast cyclical cosmos where we too play a role, we would break free of the measurement of time and begin to judge the transient nature of all things. Our role is never ending. When we pass beyond the illusion of death it comes a shock to most to be reminded that we are an integral part of a continuum.

I said earlier we have the free will to shape the Actuality of all Probability before us; and that all must be understood beyond the constraint of physical birth and death. Free will takes the form of Thought, for thought is the motivation for movement, or vibration; and shapes all Probability. So what is thought? It is the condition where we provide the motivation for Potential to be actualised. There is greater power in the process than any Presence could possibly realise while tied to the viewing-point of physical birth and decay.
The words say,

In the beginning there was eternal thought. In the beginning there was Potential. In the beginning nothing existed; but all things existed in Virtuality. Both states were one. In one lay the other. In the other lay the one.

But then from the Potential a new cycle of Probability opened where movement occurred. This motivation to movement was as *thought*. From Potential and eternal thought, Virtual became Actual and condensed to the physical vibration of the Cosmos that we can or cannot see now. The words say,

Know ye that even though in the time ye are separate, yet ye still are One, in all times existent.

So it is that we, as children of the whole, having the individual Will to produce from Potential . . . .
(A) Cause/which is thought . . . .
(B) Resulting in Effect/which is Actuality . . . .
(C) Resulting in Consequence/which is rebirth to Potential through Reciprocal Action.

Nevertheless, for all of us, we exist within the whole as the whole exists within us. And as the cycles of Probability opened with infinite Probability for all matter, so, the interval of movement could be measured. Between two or more points the interval of time depended upon a fixed state. But what impression of time could be exact where all points are transient.

In this we can find understanding of the illusion of time. Of what use is time, where all things are eternal. Yet the eternal itself implies a measure. The answer is that there is no answer, nor any need of one. Eternal indicates in truth, a cycle. Our illusionary concepts of time are a necessity of our self—imposed state. We can choose if we wish to follow the curves of the cycles and break free from the constraints of our time. Then even though bound to a physical body, we would be capable of travelling to all parts of the whole, faster than the blink of an eye. We would be capable of becoming one with the whole again. In time; beyond time, we will all eventually understand again.

Question 22: *Some-one said to me today that is it not for every-one to see for themselves what truth is and what falsehood is. My initial response was to question this point, but on further reflection I now believe it is for each to see the truth for themselves . . . Do you think we truly only fool ourselves?*

Answer: If we examine a Rock; down to the molecules, down to the atoms, down to the neutrons and protons, down to the quarks, down to the gluons, down to vibrational matter, down to Motivation, we are at the threshold of Creation and Truth. But Truth is not only present at the birth. It describes the Virtuality and the Actuality of the whole process, and is in a state of constant flux. Quality of truth is movement, which is vibration. We can only grasp at the lesson from Truth when it has passed from its Virtual state through Actuality, to recycle again. We have the opportunity to learn from its Consequence. We look at the Rock. We understand the gross implications of the Rock. But if we were to understand the implications of its very fabric; or if we were to read the cycles of vibration which are its Presence; our Truth would benefit from all of its experience. The Rock is not just a Rock. It represents a vast Consequence. But we only see a Rock! So it is within our own experience. We only see the gross material. The condition of Truth reflects within us the dynamic stage we have reached in our evolvement. If we journey to the essence of what we are, we discover Vibration. It too could be read collectively for each of us to reveal our signature; like the Rock, reflecting a vast Consequence of all we have been or experienced before.

Truth is dynamic. But in the ever-turning cycles of existence through Virtuality and Actuality, every Rock and every Person and in fact everything, is connected. We continue to view just a Rock and our viewing-point is thus fixed to a position just in front of us. This limits our scope for expanded Truth. If Homo sapiens could only appreciate that we must first understand the whole nature of our own personal Consequence, we would make the connection to all things. Then at last we would be able to all join at a viewing point of harmonious Truth; light years beyond our present collective viewing point.

Question 23: *Re your comments: Quote: If we constantly examine the motivation of all that we think, we will surely draw closer to the harmonies of Spirit; especially if we can separate and discard those thoughts borne from emotion.' What of love. Is that not emotion?*

Answer: For us to tackle this question, we must first agree common ground. I cannot presume your interpretation of Love. To me, when I say *I Love*, I am reaching beyond the constraint of physical mortality to that state where we may be one with all.

Human notions of Love are so often restricted in truth by Service to Self. Love in this context fulfils an inadequacy within us that we have not yet faced. It is only when we reach beyond ourselves that we are able to feel the higher Love of connection to all things. This can be more deeply explained as a state when our own much raised vibration is able to meld with the experience of everything else

Reader Intervention 23.1: *I speak of the chance we grasp or let slip if we are not aware; as when we fail to see the power in the moment; or when we let the potential in any experience pass us by, for it is fleeting. That moment would then become an eternity, with ripples sent forth, and further experiences generated.*

Answer: Yes I agree. The less refined energy that is a part of our signature represents the hotspots of inadequacy we carry. As like attracts like, those energies bring us to situations where there has to be confrontation. The confrontation forces us to re-evaluate our viewing-point and progress if we so choose. If we decline, the energies build with increased force to ever greater confrontations until we *do* learn and rise out of our inadequacies. As this happens, the gross vibrations become discharged to their own kind and we raise a bit more, returning closer to our own home beyond the confines of the material world.

Question 24: *Are you saying that Love should be our expression of Intent?*

Answer: An old saying sprang to mind that the pathway to hell is paved with good intentions. I think there is a subtle but important distinction to be made between intent and motivation. (Motivation = Cause to produce Effect and Consequence.) If I say I *Intend* to do something, this just expresses a desire within me for the particular thing to happen. It does not convey my actual Motivation to make it happen. Desire can be externalised and give reassuring signals to others only of our good intent. The power of true Motivation to create a beneficial Effect is something which is internal. It is something deep within our Presence which no one outside of us can see or judge, no matter how many fine intentions we express. Another saying says actions speak louder than words; but this can only occur when we motivate our intent into an effect that will have consequence.

Question 25: *You wrote; 'It is for each to find their own truth and tranquillity within.' So am I right in making the assumption that all of us have our own personal truth? In essence is my truth different to yours and to everyone else's?*

Answer: How *shall* we define Truth? Truth is a condition where no further interpretation or understanding may be gleaned from its nature. How shall we recognise Truth? First, let us consider the viewing point of a Presence who is one *with* Truth. We shall grant this Presence the status of perfection, which implies a oneness with all things. This is the only way they could embody such an immaculate condition.

Such a Presence would form no judgement of our inadequate state. They would understand we were simply reflecting a lesser state. We would not, and could not be viewed as imperfect, because we are an integral part of the whole. Their immaculate Truth would include a complete awareness of us and our condition. They would fully understand! We can only aspire through limited perception to this truthful knowingness of complete connection.

So how shall I reconcile my truth with that of immaculate truth, and with the truth that others cling to? I am qualified only to judge myself; therefore I must be my own starting point. I must first reach an awareness of the limitations of my own viewing point. I must recognise that my condition conveys no status; for status conveys exclusivity, and immaculate truth would have no barriers. If I am to know tranquillity in this, there can be no resistance, even though I occupy an inadequate state. I must strive at all times towards the higher awareness, because awareness draws us closer to the immaculate position. I can look within myself. I can build upon my own evolving awareness. I can think about thinking. I can examine all of my thought processes and guard the Cause I create. I can thereby get to know the Effect that is mine. I can strive to understand all Consequence for which I am responsible. And if I hold to the vision and the certainty of a higher immaculate truth, I will be satisfied knowing even though I remain inadequate, my aspirations will take me as close to it as my condition will allow. I never lose sight of the fact also that I am an integral part of the whole; and such is the source of tranquillity.

Immaculate Truth is immutable. Your truth or my truth? It is a temporary condition. It is transient. I can only ever offer my truth as a catalyst to others. How shall I hope to be viewed then by others of my kind? In hope, as someone who can demonstrate that the truth I offer is truly tested within my own experience. That it is never claimed as the last word on anything. That it is offered openly to be accepted or rejected by anyone. That it is offered to be tested through the experience of anyone else, and with the hope that it may assist the transient process of evolvement in others. It is for each to find truth and tranquillity within, not to imply a difference, but to encourage the awareness.

Reader Intervention 25.1: *Truth is not absolute and neither can it ever be, for it forever evolves.*

Answer: Your understanding comes from the parameters of your own conviction and I respect that. I claim an altered understanding as a direct consequence of my own tested experience. I see your words, and address the task of marrying the two perspectives under a single viewing-point. In my previous reply I simply tried to set a universal parameter for the condition of immaculate truth; this being a representation of oneness with all things. Quantum physicists wrestle with the Uncertainty Principle whereby to measure a quantum particle, the act of placing it in a measurable condition alters its original state and defeats the object. By analogy, we likewise, cannot measure the state of wind. We can measure its resistance. We can examine the components of the air which conveys it. But we cannot close our hand and capture the essence of energy which motivates it. For the Physicists and for us, the conundrum can only be solved if we were able to adopt the quality of the air itself. The analogy equally applies to *all* things beyond the cutting edge of material (scientific) understanding. The fact that higher understanding stretches beyond earth science does not invalidate its probability. Higher understanding is simply qualified by higher laws of physics which earth science by its limited viewing-point, cannot yet attain. So it is with immaculate truth; which is surely omnipotent in that it has no boundary and encompasses all things.

Reader Intervention 25.2: *Truth cannot be interpreted by the rational person.*

Answer: But it *can*; for to say that any condition, including the concept of immaculate truth (oneness with all things) is an irrational thing, is to put all that is outside of earthbound understanding beyond the reach of understandable physics. This clearly cannot be so. The cutting edge of quantum physics has reached an impasse for the same reason. The next scientific advance will occur when the scientists make a paradigm leap in their thinking from material to the possibility of realities beyond.

The door of serious enquiry must be seriously opened to areas that were once considered to be lunatic! Already in the last decade, scientists embrace the idea of a multiverse universe. They are beginning to realise the possibility for extended realities within them. Many scientists embrace the probability of intelligent life elsewhere and the certainty of a vast, advanced civilization, many thousands of years before our own sorry planetary race. Hitherto, our supreme arrogance as a global race decreed that those who practiced affairs of the Spirit would be persecuted to death. For the people out there who share valid personal experience of effects beyond current earth science; *their* conviction is a blessing and a curse. It is a blessing because they carry a certainty of the reality beyond the physical. It is also a curse, because enlightenment doesn't grant exemption from the lessons that have to be learned along the way. Convictions aren't transferable, but even so, it is wrong to suggest to someone who has had supernormal experiences that their conviction comes from irrational thought!

Reader Intervention 25.3: *We can at best try to adjust our perception and listen to our feelings to gain the knowledge or the part of the truth required in the moment—for it cannot be directly interpreted by the rational.*

Answer: Don't you see. Each perception is OK within its own parameter. The mistake is made when they are held to account against each other. You seek the conflict of debate while within me, I have no need for it. Within my Understanding, I would be wholly wrong to demand your acceptance of my perceptions. Within my understanding, I would be wholly wrong to claim any advantage of truth. We are here now exchanging thoughts because I invited you through the Book to study my experience and not to just take its content as the final word. However from my experience I can tell you, only one OBE is sufficient to persuade anyone of the rock solid higher realities. I have felt the merging of experience with other living and inanimate things. The awakening experience provided by my *Event*, gave me the explanation of the physics involved. My experiential journey continues to provide the validation.

Reader Intervention 25.4: *I too seek the truth and this means resistance, be it positive or negative.*

Answer: Within Harmony there is no resistance. Resistance resides within *us*, for it represents the conflict of inadequacy we individually carry and nurture or oppose; depending upon our will to progress spiritually.

Reader Intervention 25.5: *There is simply no way to avoid confrontation, for the evolution of awareness would cease without it, and so would life as we know it. Only chaos would rule!*

Answer: Human awareness evolves collectively in direct proportion to the sacred individual choices made by individual Souls as they eventually face the horror of the perceived chaos within themselves. In the overall picture, there is no such thing as chaos.

Reader Intervention 25.6: *It is my Intent to resist positively, to find harmony through conflict and discrimination, If you see it any other way then that lies squarely on your shoulders not mine. Basically I try to find the truth by eliminating all that is not desirable. Therein lays the true nature of the rational mind.*

Answer: You make the point for me. You say, It is my *Intent* to resist. Resistance requires an opposing force. You are *dictating* your parameters. I am *offering* mine. If you still feel resistance, it comes from you, within.

Reader Intervention 25.7: *The truth of the matter is that we cannot avoid our fate, whether we are dragged along kicking and screaming or accept it willingly.*

Answer: By my understanding we cannot avoid *ourselves*, whether we are dragged along kicking and screaming or accept ourselves willingly.

Reader Comment 26: *You talk about changing our fate and how you see the science behind it, but you haven't really written about how it worked in your own life relationships. I wouldn't expect you to write too personally about it but you would make it more understandable if it got a bit more personal.*

Answer: Hmmm! That sounds like a bit of a challenge. But if I am to be true to my own words I have to answer you. You might expect me to say that it was all rosy for me after my *Event*, because I presumably knew how everything worked from that point on. Not so I'm afraid! I'd just like to restate: From the Event I recalled the strategy of how it all fitted together. It taught me also however, that the strategy of life and everything was supported by the infinite tactics of how all vibrational energies played out against each other in the scheme of things; on every level, for evermore.

The tactical pattern of my own life and pathway of probability was still subject to *my* inadequacies. I understood how I had moved first through a karmic relationship, but then I misunderstood what it represented. I then went through a second Soul relationship, but not the Twin Flame relationship I desired. Deep rooted inadequacies still blocked my understanding and acceptance of the difference. These confusions had been seeking to work themselves out within me for the whole of my life to that point. It was so important to my Birth Plan for the matter to be resolved finally. The build-up of negative energy I created trying to force-fit a square peg into a round hold in what I perceived to be the perfect second relationship circumstance, finally found a way to completely discharge. It was traumatic and dramatic and steered me to the darkness of the abyss; but ultimately cleansed me. Almost overnight it seemed, my Soul relationship ended, I lost my beloved Business, I lost my home, I lost my whole friend contact base, I lost all possessions other than my work trade tools, I had experienced crippling betrayal in love and in business, I had survived my attempted suicide and later a humbling breakdown. But with the help of my Minders I finally emerged knowing I was free of myself at last.

I immediately asked myself and my Minders in Spirit, Ok so now at last I truly understand about the connection of gender energies and I truly understand about choice and responsibility, so throw me what you will, because I am ready. Despite my awareness I was still utterly shocked that within only a couple of weeks the path of my Twin Flame from the opposite side of the ocean converged with mine. It did not matter that we lived half way across the world from each other. From the very first encounter I was given a vision of Probability for the fulfilling task of our Birth Plans. Its importance will be explained in the next section of this book when the Egypt and ET connection unfolds. I remember being so struck with the seeming perfect irony that I laughed out loud with a surety that my Minders were sharing the delight also. I had got what I asked for; because after all, I was now ready and equipped to make the choice that would set my correct pathway for the rest of my time in this life! Some while later when I reflected upon these things and words came to me that summarised my whole life and relationship pathway to that point. Please judge for yourself.

From Darkness to Light

Two abiding memories formed the summary of childhood experience for the little boy as he now stood at the Marriage altar. One was of his awareness of something greater and good outside of himself which also filled him to the brim when he thought he was going to be broken; then made him feel stronger than anything. The other was of the familiar ritual where he had to drop his pants, bend with his head low and reach out to grasp the sides of the door frame, as his father spilled blood from his skin with lashing strokes from a leather strap. These two experiences were replicated in many dramas, which produced a young man with an iron grip to Spirit but with a mundane head that was totally screwed up. But now he wanted to prove to the world and his father that he was worth more than the dirt he believed was his value. He went for the big one. He excelled. But soon his conditioning dragged him down to fulfil the failure instilled in him, and his time with the Elite of the Military came to an end. He was sorely inadequate. Now he needed to start learning how to get in touch with himself. He needed support for the journey toward light to begin. He needed a partner who would tell him how to tie his shoes, how to feed himself, and how to draw breath.

At the altar, his partner was happy. For 18 years she had lived in the shadow of her several brothers and sisters as the last sibling. Always getting the cast—offs. Always the last for attention. Always least important. But now it was different. She was in charge. She had found her perfect partner, and all he wanted was somebody to be lovingly in-charge. At eighteen and nineteen years the nearly two decades of run—in to divorce had begun. That is how long it took for their journeys to play out within each other, and for the wheel to turn again. At the end, they were as strangers, unable to understand or tolerate the Alien presence that each had evolved into for each other. Their scars showed the depth and the distance of their experience together; and were a measure of their evolving pathways. The Lawyers were good. But his Lawyer was less good. Two good following years she had in life with the man a neighbour who had been there secretly and truer for her, before a heart attack reclaimed her to Spirit. Two years on and our journeyman was living the fact of losing family, home, job, possessions, esteem; but never Spirit. The lesson was delivered, showing the futility of coveting material and clinging to hurt—which never charged a fee. The wheel had turned.

But then what was this from a chance meeting. The young man was in total confusion. Here was someone with whom he seemed able to telepath. It was quite funny. It went beyond funny when they found they shared the same unusual birthday, and that the detail of their life—journey so far had played to perfectly parallel tracks. He felt a conviction of Spirit that here at last was someone who was there to share love at a Soul level first. But for many years he denied in his foolishness the fact of her journey on parallel tracks; but on a track that had not yet been laid equal in distance to his own. The perfection of agony spiralled for years as he strove to defy the interval between them. The build of frustration as she in turn; many years unready to share at Soul level, finally delivered the severance blow of betrayal, and the wheel turned again. For the second time he turned his face to Spirit and walked away from the efforts of his devotion; his home, job, family, possessions. But not his esteem this time, and still not his Spirit; never Spirit. Twice he had returned from the dead. His lack of understanding showed him to the edge of the abyss. Two times he had faced the abject despair of grief, rejection and betrayal. Two times he denied his Spirit. Two times by any of the rules that hold for anything, his suicide actions should have ended his life. Two times, through the intervention of higher watchers he was saved from himself with his ignorance forgiven; and the wheel turned again.

The elements were all in place. He had served two long terms in the classroom. Would the pattern of his scars finally yield his lesson? He had been a perfect mismatch with his wife. Their coming together was perfectly timed. But evolvement to understanding requires conflict for the inadequacies to be confronted and dealt with. The conflict was temporary, the lesson was permanent. In his second relationship he was almost ready to make bonding contact at a vibrational level first. His partner was not. Even *he* was not aware he was not ready for this merging of Spirit. For each of the Souls involved, the same evolution was taking place, but in different frames. The time approached for him to emerge with clarity. At last his sight cleared and he saw the chains of progression . . .

The father, raised by a substitute himself; striking out at his own conditioning in brutality to an innocent child, instead of confronting it within himself.

The wife who understood only her unhappiness at the complete lack of affinity with her partner; and the seal of her true sacrifice as she returned to Spirit early, having fulfilled her Birth Plan to be a catalyst for positive change in others.

The partner who could not understand the power coming from the spiritual fire, which her man had raised to full heat; and her gnawing desire to learn the use of her wings discovered during the relationship. The elements were all in place and Understanding was his at last. He returned in his mind to the little boy and forgave him the way he felt. He returned in his mind to bless and thank his absent wife for her sacrifice in his pathway. He returned in his mind to wish Love, direction and Peace for his former partner as she continued with her Plan.

Finally he looked to himself in the mirror, and realised that beyond the illusion there was a greater prize. This was a prize of Spirit and it was everlasting. This was the Ultimate prize; to be *one* with all things while still of the Earth Plane. To be *one* with the true power of everlasting Love. To be blessed as a conduit for this force. But a question rose in his mind. How could this be so? His lessons revisited him. Mind, Body, Spirit. He was of the flesh, and all energies must be balanced to claim the prize. Mind, Body, Spirit. Balanced Male, female energy with no more conflict. The initiate could only dream of that role if these were not in balance. He accepted the understanding but a burning thirst remained for the final connection. Was his energy really meant to be balanced by the matching opposite in true harmony in this life? He yielded all in a question to his higher friends for an answer; and the wheel turned again.

He looked back to his distant horizon with Love, compassion, gratitude and forgiveness. He looked to his future with hope. The doors were opening before him. Some way ahead he recognised someone. They looked familiar. Very familiar. It was a stranger. But the stranger looked as his own image. In all of humanity, could she possibly *be*; really *be* his true balance. He called to her; and the wheel turned again!

An ocean and half the world stood between them, but their common purpose and task in Egypt beckoned. It had been many years before birth since they agreed their plan together. Their respective births to this life had sealed its direction. Their choices sealed the probability of its conclusion, and now it was time for the cycle to mature. And you will read of how the plan played out in the last section of this book.

Question 27: *Can the music we listen to determine our vibrational level?*
Food affects our vibration, so sound must surely also affect it? What exactly is our vibration anyway?

Answer: Everything can indeed be broken down to an understanding of vibration within us and beyond us. The modulating effect of sound at every level can heal or harm, and is illustrated by two images. In the first image, a musical Tuning Fork begins resonating in harmony with another which has been struck nearby. The second image is the sight of a glass shattering when its vibration is raised to breaking point by the presence of another more intense sound. Vibrations reach on out!

Recently I was pondering the implication of sound vibrations. A radio programme prompted a new chain of thought that has a circular connection to the question in hand. An author was being interviewed about his book. In it he examined the origins of good and evil. The journey disappeared to automatic as I locked into the conversation. The author was responding in an unsurprising way using classical origins to describe the two conditions. I wasn't so much captured by their conversation as by the thoughts that were being triggered in my mind. I was trying to respond to the interviewer as if I were in the shoes of the Author. I asked myself, what I would have said to that. My answers would have been much different. The Author explored human psychology, and justified much from brain patterns fixed by

DNA. But I got to thinking! What constitutes an evil act? How about: A motivated Cause, producing destructive Effect. As usual, my mind meandered down the road of a string of questions and answers until I got to the crux of the matter.

What is a destructive Effect? It is an Effect that disrupts the natural harmony of something else. What do I mean by the Natural Harmony in something? Well, if anything can be examined down to quantum, I know we would see how at sub-atomic level and beyond, energies cooperate to repel or to form amalgamations. These combine at greater and greater levels to produce for example, a physical person at the end of it. So, a physical person is in fact, a grand amalgamation of condensed finer matter. Why then does it not just remain as an inert lump? As the book discusses, our inert lump becomes a person, because it is given life through the motivation of the Presence. However a person is made up of many individual amalgamations of physical matter, cooperating together because the energy fields of each package and its components react and interact in vibrational harmony. The vibrations are compatible! The Life motivation comes from the inhabiting Presence. But what is the Presence? The Presence, otherwise known as the Soul of a person, is also an amalgamation of higher energetic matter; but operating with harmonies that reach proportionately to the highest refinement. If the Presence were suddenly to vacate a human body, the body would just become a collapsed pile of amalgamated physical matter, just like having had the batteries removed from a toy; which coincidentally is the same as a description of a dead body!

The Author said that evil generates solely from within the brain or mind of the individual? Are we to agree and say only that the neuron pathways of the brain—determined by DNA performance, decide if the individual will produce Cause leading to destructive Effect. Or are we to accept there is a motivational Presence inhabiting and directing the physical body, and that the motivating choice of the individual determines the path they will follow. And even accepting the latter, we still only touch upon a fraction of the wider understanding needed to square the whole picture. What about past lives for instance? By my understanding, the Presence progresses through the experience of multiple lifetimes, with each physical lifetime providing the lessons needed for the Presence to develop. What do I mean by, *progress*, and *develop*? As always I tell myself, Get back to vibration again for the answer.

A snapshot of the Presence would show energies in a state of flux, responding from within to the input of stimuli from without. Each new input would trigger an Effect and Consequence to the Presence, modifying the vibrational frequency. Incoming energy (like music,) condenses, or excites the vibration of the Presence, depending upon the person's choice. If the person motivates bad reactions, this also manifests hot-spots of more condensed or negative energy within them. Remember, negative hot-spots of energy always seek to discharge to like-kind; while hot-spots of higher energy always seek to gravitate to like-kind. This translates from a negative act committed by a person, to the negativity becoming self-fulfilling as their own circulations condense.

Amen! . . . so now we have got to the crux of the question! Negative energy is much more condensed, or compressed than positive energy. If a Person is the type who clings to negative energy, then there is no way they will be able to appreciate the kaleidoscope of opportunity in the higher energies waiting to interact with them. This will compound the negative person's situation, because of their natural affinity with negative situations. In every negative act committed there is a like for like consequence. By the law of Reciprocal action, an equal opposite effect returns to bite the one who produces the negative Cause in the first place. It is only when the person realises these direct connections that they are able to progress.

The process of interaction and consequence is no different for music. *Sound* in the form of music is just another form of vibration. Depending on the composition, the vibrational frequencies in a piece of music may be harmonious or discordant to someone, depending on how the music harmonises with the vibrational signature of the person. In effect, depending on how positive or negative the music is to a person, negative or positive hot-spots of energy are actualised by the music; then to be absorbed into the frequency of the person.

Most times, music accompanies the words to a song, and the song also reflects the mood of the music. However in modern times it is often possible to hear a song which is harmonious; but if the lyric is examined, it is found to contain a damaging message. The words have a modifying vibration also, and it is worth remembering that even if the sound seems good to the ear, there may be a negative vibration in the message that can have a negative subconscious effect on anyone listening. Listening to music brings us closer to higher levels, but if we are seeking help for meditation, it would be wise to choose appropriately, and make sure that any song lyric has an equally high vibration.

People play music to fit their mood. What they really mean is that they play music to fit or harmonise their vibration. This just underscores the fact that we naturally seek situations, surroundings, people or sounds that complement our own vibration. When our vibration is low this may not be such a good thing. If we compliment a melancholic mood with soulful music, we are not helping ourselves to snap out of the mood. Instead if we played more inspirational music it would be like medicine to the system and lift us sooner from our melancholy. When we go against ourselves to listen to music that is higher than our current vibration, our vibration is lifted by association. Inspiration by association lifts our aspirations; but, can there ever be anything wrong in aspiring to something by association?

Well, the main factor that leads us to modify our Presence is simply experience, or more specifically, tested experience. This is where our motivations are tested within us against potential Effect and Consequence; with wise values adopted as a result. We discern, and gradually get better at it. We evaluate the probabilities more before making a better choice. A person who is good at it usually has a persona of quiet authority and they have a self-assurance rooted in an inner calm. Conversely there are as many people whose ego gives them a persona of false authority. This is nearly always sustained by the trappings of association. Others may accept the authority of the person, but if it comes under challenge, they do not have the solid foundation of tested experience to withstand anything. Originally the person may have set themselves high ideals by adopting decorations of knowledge to imply a position closer to their aspirations than their tested experience could support. But they face disaster if someone really challenges their beliefs. They will have no real answers. Even worse is when a serious crisis occurs in their private life and their lack of character leads to them crashing out in some way. They are thus faced with an inner conflict to make them finally face themselves and make genuine progress through their own genuine tested experience.

There is nothing wrong with aspiring to higher vibration. For our own best progress, it is our duty to do so. But when we hang on the words of any individual who is still on their own road to discovery, there is the danger of dependence. When that happens we forget our lesson lies in the testing of our own experience. The same is true if we fall into the trap of dependence on a particular tenet or faith. Remember truth is something that cannot be contained within the boundaries of any exclusive system. If we succumb to self-delusion by dependence on such, then vibrations will balance out through situations that will take us back to basics if necessary. We will be faced with ever harder lessons until we also get-it! Cause leads to Effect and Consequence. Understanding and accepting this process, is to accept personal Responsibility; and this is where real Progress begins. We must test our every thought, before they ever translate into a bad Effect and Consequence. When this practice becomes a way of life, our aspirations need never be carried by dependency or by association. Careful choice of the music or the sounds we listen to can add to the many sources of input to raise or stifle our vibration, and is just another of the powerful modifying sources for our Presence.

Question 28: *Why are there such differences between Male and Female, and why is it that sometimes there is so much human conflict between them?*

Answer: Again we need to take a huge step back and try to understand the bigger picture. In an ageless time past, before the descent of mankind to material levels, the hierarchy of progression evolved through cycles that extended from collective consciousness, down through the condensation of substance towards the vibration of physical matter. Collective Presence then was hermaphrodite. In that distant time, Presence had not developed the will to experience the lower levels of sensation in the physical world. The cycles continued to progress downward into the physical, with the emergence of life on Mu followed over aeons by Lemuria and Atlantis. As we devolved to physical form, it eventually became necessary and convenient for the creation of children, so that even more waiting souls could play host to sensation on our level. The process took further aeons, but eventually separation of gender became defined along with the physical biology to support it. The reproductive process became defined and was attached to the pleasure centres of the physical form. If physical displeasure accompanied the process, then the progression cycle through procreation would not have worked.

As a race, our intellect developed long ago to the point where we could have turned science to the task of proving and reinforcing our understanding of where we evolved from, and how the whole process works. We chose instead to worship sensation and thereby ground ourselves in the physical. In the distant time of Mu, our ancestors, seeded originally from other systems in our Universe, were able to exist and function in a state which to us now would appear as varying between solid and ghostly form. In other words, they were still able then, not only to interact with our physical world, but they retained the ability to interact at far higher levels of reality too.

The cycles of progression however cannot be denied despite our Service to Self-choice. A submerged cork released in water will always rise to its proper level. We as Entities also have a natural level, which is not the physical world. We have forgotten this clear fact. By now, if we had rejected the temporary effect of physical sensation, we would have returned to the position of our ancestors long ago. Our descent has almost reached the end-game. Negative energies have been condensed and polarised in so many of the world population, that babies are conceived who are vibrationally perfect for the descent to our level of darker and darker brethren.

Most have heard of the promised 2012 doomsday scenarios. Well it is not going to be doomsday in our terms. It will be a very short period in time, when new cosmic energies will affect everyone and everything throughout our Solar System. For many of us here now, it will mean a sudden departure to take up a natural higher level of frequency. The counterpart to our physical planet waits to play host to those who make the transition. They will take up residence to seed the world they have been unconsciously developing for years. Those remaining will seem as if they are catastrophe survivors. They will find themselves in the same position as the survivors from when this transition took place last time around. That was nearly 13.000 years ago. The Atlantean cultures were also split in polarity. Their time came as it has for us when natural cycles force a rebalancing through cosmic confrontation.

We could say that the division of gender signalled the start of this cycle, and we are about to come full circle. Sexual indulgence is now synonymous with self-serving physical pleasure. It is used in every form to exalt sensation. But it simply reinforces our attachment to the lower vibration of this level. Rarely, the procreative act can lead to a much more wonderful union. The merging of energy, rising up through the chakras, could allow couples to break out of body and merge in radiant form. This has been discussed earlier in more detail.

Question 29: *Is it murder when a child is aborted before birth, and how about the right of innocent children to life when they die young?*

Answer: We have to detach from the emotion in this question to be able to answer it. That is the only way we can examine the circumstances and reach an understanding. I hope I can reason it out well enough for you with another scenario. First, we are going to profile a Presence in Spirit, while talking through one of their hypothetical incarnations. The person will have been going about their business for perhaps many years since their last physical life. She, for example, could have been involved in many interests. Following her rebirth back to a higher level beyond death, she will have gone through a debriefing and recovery period as she adjusted to her new surroundings. Her vibrational signature would have imposed its own limitations, and she would have felt comfortable amongst others who vibrated to her tolerance. Helpers, or Mentors, would have ensured she was steered according to her choice and needs into activities to help her progress. Her awareness may not yet have included a full appreciation of her condition within the scheme of things. If she was more enlightened it is likely she would have graduated from many learning experiences to help with other family members from many past lives, including the most recent. She finally arrived at a time where most of those with whom she previously interacted as direct family, had also passed back to spirit. Her surroundings would by now have become normalised. Certainly her Minders would have recognised her vibrational refinement was in need of the lessons that could only be won at a lower level. In this person's case however there was a circulation of disharmony in her Presence that would only need a short sharp lesson. It was a lesson, not requiring the complex motivational choice of an adult. It was an anomaly that required only the vibrational modification of a short physical experience. We shall assume our person was in fact from a naturally higher level and therefore privy to the assessment discussion led by her Minders. Decisions would have been made according to the simple process described earlier in this book for her choice of family and circumstances for rebirth. It is likely also that the selected parents or friends to be, would have been part of her Soul group for a very long time. The time would have approached for her rebirth.

Before full attachment to her new parents she would have gone through a period similar to sleep here. But during the equivalent higher state, her higher Presence would have received programming at an even higher level. This was necessary to lock down her memory at a level in accordance with the vibrational frequency she was about to occupy. Then at a variable time between conception and birth, her Presence would have been brought together with that of her parents, for the genetic bond to be consummated.

The adult person from spirit was now a girl child on earth. As a new baby her life was harsh at the hands of parents with low vibration. They were not bad people, but their aspirations were limited severely to sensation. Unkempt living, undisciplined lives, and lack of compassionate understanding meant that the little girl was neglected. As a toddler she was left to her own devices far too often. It therefore came to pass one day when both inattentive parents were preoccupied, the little girl wandered out of the yard and into the path of an oncoming vehicle. She passed suddenly back to spirit.

As a child, the girl did not have the developed power of choice to veer from her pathway of strongest probability. This meant that her Birth Plan worked out exactly as it was meant to do. Her Minders were ready to assist her return. By her choice of action alone her vibration was refined more. It was possible after a very short time for her to recover and be gently reawakened to spirit. She maintained the form of a child, because although she contained the vibrational qualities of all her former lives, she was still a child-form emerging from this short physical life. The big difference this time was that she went to a place where children grew and were instructed. Her growth to the form of an adult was not the same as the time period of someone on our level. Her growth would have been hugely accelerated and she would have been able to reassume her position as a more advanced adult very quickly. Even during the beneficial growing-up process, it is likely that her presence would have provided beneficial help also to the parents and family she left behind.

Now let us look at the situation from the point of view of the parents. The parents would have been traumatised from the tragic loss of their daughter. They would have faced the legal consequences of their neglect, and it would have become the wake-up call in their lives as they came to terms with their own motivations. As they modified their attitude to life, *their* vibrations would be raised accordingly. The loss may have had an extra effect if there were other brothers and sisters still to care for. Either way, the tragic death of the daughter would have had a beneficial effect on the parents and potentially many others in the scheme of things. The same rules apply for any and all similar cases, even down to babies and yet unborn children. No experience is lost, and genuinely, nothing happens by accident. While parents and family are still in physical life, the aborted child, the killed child, the accidental death child, or the death by illness child, are nearly all higher souls who use the short lesson necessary for their own life as a sacrifice to aid the lessons in the lives of others. Beyond death, they are able to return to their parents and communicate with them on a higher level usually during sleep. The lost children are always able to heed the prayers for contact and be there for the caller. It is only the lower vibration of grief that prevents them from joining with the waiting contact of their lost ones.

We rightly grieve the loss of a child, but it is wrong to dwell only on their passing. We should dwell on the process at work, and give equal time to the lessons we should learn from it ourselves. If our children pass from us, they will be there very soon you can be sure to help inspire our own pathway along a better route. We simply have to understand that fact, and choose to move forward with their help. We never really lose them anyway. They have just gone ahead of us to make our route clearer. And by the way; when our turn comes, we will always have the opportunity to reunite with our deceased loved ones anyway!

Book Quote:

'The cycles of progression however cannot be denied despite our Service to Self-choice. A submerged cork released in water will always rise to its proper level. We as Entities also have a natural level, which is not the physical world. We have forgotten this clear fact. However the cycles of process, at the most lowly level and on a grand cosmic level inexorably tick away to the time when confrontation is forced for the shift in balance to take place again.

Question 30: *So what do you mean here exactly by Service to Self?*

Answer: When we travel our memory back tens or hundreds of thousands of years it seems unimaginable to picture the world of our ancestors. Agreed it would be even harder to imagine the birth of Actuality! The answer to the question however requires at least that we try to understand the implications from the event.

So, try to picture a huge blob of thick gunge! The blob of gunge makes contact with the ground. It flows out in a slow flood until its viscosity is spent. It doesn't flow out indefinitely because there is dynamic tension in its structure. If the same gunge were to be poured into other types of less dense fluid, its dynamic tension would be sufficient to draw it back into a blob again. By analogy, in the infinite cycle of universal Virtuality, the blob of thick runny gunge touched the ground to produce the tension of Actuality. In the twinkle of a cosmic eye, everything was Actualised. The same thing happened infinitely, on a smaller scale across the cosmos. Unimaginable cycles in an unimaginable cosmos; but all inter-related and interconnected through the dynamic tension of the Source.

But even as that first breath was taken, it too was simply one heartbeat. It was this heartbeat where we now dwell with our present awareness. We are simply a snapshot within a grand cycle of cycles where the beginning is the end, and the end is the beginning—and so it is for any part of the Whole. It is quite unimaginable but only from our viewing point. If we still had an awareness of Virtuality, we would still be one with an awareness of the Source. But that would require a separation from sensation, and we have not yet re-evolved to that position. For humankind, the blob of gunge flowed, and within it more separations took place. From virtual to actual; motivated from the source; which is the beginning and the end; with the identity of the source maintained throughout; and here we are as conjoined and motivated cycles within the cycle forever.

The gunge flowed, seeking its limit; and somewhere in the process of devolvement, our awareness balanced the dynamic tension in our cycle. We began the long retraction. Awareness conveyed choice as a necessity, and became more strongly embedded to our Presence as we drew further away from the source and closer to the lure of sensation. Service to others is in fact a misrepresentation. It should read, Service to One, as in *Source*. If Service to Self is the choice to prolong the dynamic tension through Sensation (and away from Source,) then *all* selfless motivation yields to One, which *is* Source.

Reader Comment 30.1: *I don't think there is such a thing as a bad choice.*

Answer: I agree with you, there is no such thing as a truly bad experience. However we are stuck with the reality we have motivated. The acceptance of responsibility for our reality conveys also, acceptance of consequence. If we continue to use the gunge analogy, then we too are setting our own cyclic limits. Our divine choice functions through the simple formula of Cause, Effect and Consequence. Cause, is the Motivated thought. Virtuality becomes Actuality and the Effect is its motion. Consequence is the Reciprocal effect, which then becomes Cause for following cycles. Our Civilisation has condensed its vibration more and more, because we dress Consequence as Effect, and avoid taking Responsibility.

Sure, there is no such thing as a bad experience; but if people woke up early to the responsibility of their own motivation, they would save themselves and the world from eons of painful lessons. I was awakened to the process in the same way that countless people around the world are now also being awakened. All the rest continue to kid themselves that sensation is king. But a cosmic clock is ticking away to a point very soon, when the dynamic tension of our entire cycle shall have reached its limit. Like a separating amoeba, the polarised parts our 3rd density will either ground to earth or gravitate toward spirit literally overnight. From the transformation we will all look out upon our new separated worlds that will be a more accurate reflection of our devolved vibration. Those remaining on physical earth will be forced back to the basics of a primeval existence from the land; and the land around them will have been churned from its age of technology, to the rearranged hostile aftermath of catastrophe. Those plucked from this physical life will arrive in their new counterpart home, to enjoy the virgin environment of a new harmonious world.

Question 31: *It looks like we are in a time once again when we need a Prophet to follow. Where will we find one?*

Answer: A Prophet is only someone who understands the mechanics of vibration, and an ability to see probabilities arising from the process. The knowledge is not hidden from us; it is *we* who have hidden ourselves from *it*. You ask where you will find the Prophet to lead you. The answer is simple. You are always closer to him or her than you ever realised. Just look within!

Reader Comment and Question 31.1: *You mentioned about how yourself and your twin flame are hermaphrodite in radiant form. I cannot profess I have experienced that, but I was under the impression we are all hermaphroditic in nature, but have only extended one of our polarities into this world. So if we are male, then our hidden counterpart is female and vice versa. It is when we have achieved totality-of-self; communicating in full with our hidden counterpart that again we experience this state. Is it then necessary that we all have a combined Out of Body experience with our counterpart of gender to know the harmony of our original form? If we do not have such an experience, does it hold us back from fulfilling our fate?*

Answer: I have to untangle a few things from your question. The question opens such important issues that I will take time to explain as fully as I am able. Relationships on this level can be split into Twin Flame, Twin Soul, and general Karmic—bonded relationships. The first occurs when two people are both halves of a whole person on a much higher level of reality. The person complete, is close to the level or condition described elsewhere as *the gathering of Souls*. In layman's terms this describes a level of vibrational existence where personality is still evident, but the Presence of everyone there holds such an harmonious refinement of vibration that they are able to merge all experience within and beyond them.

Twin Flames occur when specific aspects of a Presence need specific refinement that would benefit from a separation of their essence. At much lower levels of vibration on the physical plane, the Male and Female representation of the Presence, invariably are able to help each other through attributes picked up in their separated experience. An example of absolutely perfect synchronicity was presented in answering this question. I tried several ways to form a suitable answer to the original question. Each time I made a complete mess of it and deleted back to the start. I am in the UK. Judith is in the USA. Remember distance is irrelevant on a higher level. So out of the blue, a mail popped into my mailbox from Judith last night. She headed it by asking what I thought of the enclosed material. She had stumbled across an article detailing differences in relationships. In fact the article was *exactly* what this question is about. The timing was perfect and I am unashamed to say I have borrowed from the structure of the article to complete the inspiration for my own reply. Judith had no tangible idea what I was writing about, but our connection on a higher level meant that she was actually not only completely aware of what I was writing about, but unconsciously found and supplied me with the material I needed to continue! That is how it works. Examples similar to this from Judith have happened more times than I can remember. Our twin flame bond is there to provide mutual help, even though we are each working through difficult personal circumstances half way across the world from each other. However when we raise to alpha; when we are in meditation together—we are then able to merge our presence with a power that is humbling and awesome. Despite the chains of lower vibration around us, we have had some mindboggling experiences together on a higher level. We are separated parts of a Birth Plan that intended for us to fulfil a powerful conjoined pathway of Probability and awakening in this life. Thereby we would also hopefully bring understanding to others.

If we return to the reality of the Soul gatherings at a higher level, we can understand the hierarchy of the process with an earth analogy. Think of a business organisation. It is controlled by the Board of Directors. There may be various divisions, each with its own departmental management groups, operational groups, worker groups, and working teams finally. Transpose this to the progression of Souls. From the gathering of Souls, there would be multitudes of divisional separation that deals with aspects of creation, order and teaching. There would be multitudes of sub division to implement the local policy (universal laws) operating at varying lower levels. There would be the groups who function to govern the operations of a continent. Lower still there would be gatherings of Presence to reflect the vibration of a nation, or town, or extended family. The point to understand is that for all of these Soul groupings, their common factor is in the harmonics of vibration. As the groupings work closer to the source, when through their combined experience they have evolved to greater and greater harmony of purpose, it means that for each grouping along the way, a degree of higher collaboration is also taking place. Within the evolvement of a family group for example, their progression may require individuals within it to incarnate through many different roles, both male and female, interacting together over many generations.

Karmic relationships can be viewed a little differently. During the time before a new incarnation for two individuals, the pathways of probability are examined for both of them to be given the choices that would refine their inadequacies. It may be decided that they would benefit each other through close interaction. Their lines of probability therefore may bring them together in a relationship that could be called a perfect *mismatch*. This is to say at the time, their inadequacies would be fulfilled through the imperfect vibration they share, but held firm only by the glue of sensation. In time, as each gather experience and expand from thoughts of physical satisfaction to thoughts of greater aspiration, the real difference of their vibration shows up. Conflict ensues and they most often separate to continue the journey separately; hopefully having learned the lessons they planned to come together to learn. I have simplified the issues into a few explanations, but it does not take much imagination to see there are infinite combinations based on the same rules. With this in mind, let us take it all a stage deeper by entering the subject from a different direction.

Since I was young I found I had the curious ability to produce a voice sound which builds upon itself and increases in volume, even though I am not forcing it louder myself. By the way, I have learned there is purpose to the ability that concerns important things in the Great Pyramid of Egypt; but that will be dealt with in the next book section. I also understand it is possible for one sound frequency to be played against another one to make both sounds cancel each other out to silence. Both these examples demonstrate how harmonics can cancel or increase an effect. Music is just vibrating energy which we are equipped to detect and interpret. The blending of frequency can produce infinite possibilities; but it is also possible to transfer our understanding of sound effect, to understand the interactions of gender in the physical world.

Let us examine an average human being more closely. Let us set Personality to one side for a moment and concentrate on the vibrational makeup of the Presence. It is in a state of excitation, or vibration. Its parts are in a constant state of flux. There are a multitude of influences motivated from within the Presence that cause these changes. Constantly there is action and reaction as the person interacts with the input from their world. We observe the multitude of inner circulating energies, centred on the chakra areas of the body. It is possible to take a snapshot of the average frequency of the person at any time. It is possible also to observe, despite the ever changing state of their energy, that the average frequencies of the individual circulations have a pattern too. This would be true for a male or a female. However there would be fundamental differences in all of their frequencies due to the biological differences in their physical bodies. Their DNA would have ensured a programming for the female to be a tactical nurturer and the male to be a strategic gatherer and protector.

If the male is superimposed upon the female, their programmed differences ensure an harmonic match at certain levels only. Other frequencies would not immediately lock together in harmony. As previously explained in the book, circulations usually harmonise for particular activity such as procreation, and then in a temporary way to satisfy sensation. For the male and the female, the differences in frequency disappear only when each has become harmonised within themselves. By that time they will have evolved to a point where their combined frequencies exalt each other on a higher level as a much higher collective Presence is formed. In summary, the makeup of any Presence comprises a multitude of blended frequencies. These are chords of vibration; some harmonizing perfectly; some still struggling for harmony in a reflection of the turbulence within that person which still has to be worked out. This does not mean that a person is doomed unless they achieve the ecstasy of radiant merging with their perfect twin flame. Each person within himself or herself can seek their own balance. If such oneness could be achieved, they would be at a level where their motivation was not dependent upon sensation at all. The implications are obvious.

I understand it is unusual for those who are incarnating as Twin Flames, to fully come together in common purpose until they both balance the traits they came back to refine. It is their individual sacred choice as to how fast this happens. A premature joining of the two would create a vibrational comfort zone between them that may block the lesson each has to learn. Conversely, Twin Flames may have arranged to incarnate together to fulfil a specific, higher task. Most people need only concern themselves with their own state of balance and harmony. When personal motivation is under control, there will be all the time in the world and beyond to think about other things.

Question 32: *You talked in the book about Automatic Writing and how it happened for you. How about giving us examples of what you got?*

Answer: I'm only too happy to oblige. Over the years I have spent far less time than I wished to allow my development of Automatic Writing. By this process, when the mind is completely still, and the pen is ready to follow a passive mind, helpers can build a powerful link from spirit and send their direct messages through. I sat regularly at the same time over many weeks in quiet meditation before the first meaningful words came through me. It is my own loss that I continued with this long enough only for a few precious messages to be given.

Here are a couple of them. I tidied them up with punctuation after they were received. The first one came to me, **June 1st. 1988 between 12.48 am.—1.18 am.**

Break with the perception of a field filled with flowers which must be plucked from their stems without due regard to the source of their growth. A single flower can only be raised to maturity following infinite pathways of deliberation. Finally it may be enjoyed in its real beauty. There rests no cause to pluck it from its stem, for from perfect beauty, yet more beauty can spring. If allowed to blossom and flourish, its seed will spread the beauty tenfold.

So it is as we abandon our weaknesses and mature to spiritual perfection. Spiritual progress is unrestricted by time. Progress can truly take a lifetime of lifetimes. But for some, as with the plucked flower in the field, there is a need to stunt the pathway of progress by marking the ground. If only they realised the beauty contained in the roots beneath their feet, and within their soul, surely such a vision of beauty to come would urge a greater vigilance toward self-control.

It is however within the nature of things that the pathway to understanding and enlightenment, and thus toward the Source—must proceed at a pace to be chosen by each one individually. It is for those who are blessed with the vision of a field filled with perfect flowers, to set the example for others who continue to pluck at the ripening stems.

The second example was received **May 9th 1997 between 11. 04 pm.—11. 20 pm.**

You think it strange that a man in the midst of turmoil can find a corner of life that encompasses the whole of being. Like a lone sentinel, the flame of truth burns forever and its light penetrates the darkest crevice. None are so dark that truth may not warm the spirit, for it must obey movement. The movement becomes a step forward, and the journey to the Source continues. You wonder when the corners of darkness shall be lost forever. Walk softly my son that you may feel the vibration of arrival. The air will yield strange smells and dizziness will affect many. No one knows the speed of silence save those who dwell there themselves—ready to be woken at the final hour for their work to commence. Heaven's Gate is waiting for the picture to be completed, and those who dwell in darkness shall feel the searing heat of his love as the time approaches. A stable brought the child to a world in need of cleansing. His job must now be done. Go now to that which you know to be right and be guided by the silence of love in the God Source.

Question 33: *How about the Didactic poems you spoke of. Can you give us more about that?*

Answer: I have a folder of inspired poems. I keep these together with a lot of short stories that I have been deeply inspired to write. These are being compiled into a separate book also, which I hope will be published . . . However I will deal with the matter here in answer to the question, and as we were recently examining relationships, it may be appropriate to give an example of something I received while pondering the higher level handshake that happens between harmonising Souls. I receive the poems in a peculiar way. It is usually the case that I have been preoccupied with some aspect of Spirit and its workings. Or I have been in a situation involving a third party that has stimulated deep thought. Questions fill my mind and after a while I when continue to think about the issue in a passive way, I get the sense of impending arrival. It is as if I know the postman is about to arrive and I am just waiting for the letter to drop through the letterbox. It sometimes arrives immediately and other times it takes days. When it arrives, it is as if someone thrusts a sheet of paper in front of my eyes. I only have a few seconds to memorise the writing on the sheet and then scrabble to write the text out before it disappears from my mind's eye. It is only afterwards when I read the words I have written that I become consciously aware of what I have actually copied down. I now carry a pen and paper handy at all times. In the past I have grabbed scraps, or torn bits of newspaper and blunt pencils to capture the words. I am usually impressed to present the message to a particular person, always with dramatic effect. These words about higher relationships however were just general words that came to me. See what you think. I called it: A Mutual Understanding

A crowd of people fills this place.
Two strangers from the crowd collide.
Fate has fixed their eyes.
The gaze of bonded friends denies this shabby place.
Each friendly gaze compelled to pierce the other, in mutual understanding.
One second split. It lasts for now and ever, to control this love exchange.
Instinctive hand is lifted, forward stretched to touch, and the stranger follows suit.
By compulsive force, two fingertips with lightest touch, have met.
Ecstatic force; and no words have passed.
There is no need for words.
The strangers who are friends have spoken truth.
Simultaneously, see, the friends have signed a nod, as they turn to go their separate way.

A final smile to say farewell for now.

They each have whispered sadness at their world so filled with strangers.

Such low resolve to know the love, of mutual understanding.

I sometimes see a stranger but a friend, whose heart and mind are screaming, with mutual understanding.

The beauty of the word.

The need to be proclaimed.

To speak, when first you meet a stranger but a friend.

And there is no need for words.

Question 34: *What is your attitude towards animals?*

Answer: It is said that you can tell the state of a Nation's mind by its attitude to animals. This is a very good test. Only the ignorant could believe that it is right to abuse and torture animals; even when the animals are used as a food source. If animals cannot be kept with dignity then there is no dignity in the people who keep them. It is a tragedy that millions of years of animal evolution are being wiped out in decades by the callous, ignorant, greedy, unthinking inhabitants of earth who are supposed to be the higher sentient custodians of the Planet. The attitude of Spirit and the attitude of Judith and I towards our fellow creatures comes to the fore in the last section of this book. You will see how our pathway gave us the opportunity to speak for the animals. They are also of us as we are of them. Who therefore in their ignorance feels they should stand above them? To do so is to stand in shame.

We have seen examples of cruelty to animals and sights of their wicked treatment in Cairo that would shock anyone to the core. We have intervened many times and brought trouble to ourselves as a result, but our experience there led to us incorporate The Giza Foundation to change these practices and help the fate of animals in Cairo and Egypt generally. Mankind's descent to the levels of bestial ignorant and mindless behaviour to each other and to animals is testament to the depths we have reached as a sentient race. It cannot be allowed to continue in this way. It is also incumbent upon every single person to show themselves and the world which side of the dividing line they stand. Every person could and should help to reverse the trend. Animals cannot speak for themselves. Animals feel pain and anxiety just as we do. When their treatment improves wherever the worst cases appear, then we will know we are improving as a world race.

Question 35: *Do you use crystals or anything else for meditation?*

Answer: I have to say at the outset, there are many people out there who use crystals, or crystal skulls, or many other focal items of energy to help them achieve a meditative state. However as the vibration of the earth increases and more are becoming awakened, it has meant that as many people think they have found a short-cut to enlightenment by possessing crystals. This is true especially of crystal skulls.

There is a problem as always due to a lack of understanding of the vibrational processes at work. Crystal in particular has an atomic structure which produces a very refined vibrational matrix. By attuning to the vibrational field of crystal, it is possible to raise one's personal vibration. Crystal can be used in reverse as a vibrational conduit for helpers on higher levels to reach into the Presence of its user with inspiration or healing. Unfortunately, many users place more importance on the sensational kudos that has been attached to crystal itself. They completely miss the point. They are in fact seeking enlightenment by association only. There is no short-cut. If crystal is to be used a tool to aid refinement, the user must know exactly what they are supposed to be doing with it! In the distant past when a previous civilisation on this earth used the properties of crystal as we use hydroelectric or nuclear power, adepts knew not only how to use crystal, but also how to programme information into the matrix of crystal. Some ancient crystals have been found but there are very few people who know how to access the knowledge they contain.

Judith has a full understanding of the nature of crystal, and works with many different crystal skull matrixes. We have also worked using the sound vibration of crystal bowls. This is what happened in one incident. We were together on American soil, and we had the moment to ourselves within a large lakeside log cabin. On the table sat a beautiful 14inch, rock-quartz bowl. We were meditating to its sound; a perfect middle C. Standing across the table opposite me, Judith ran the rubber mallet around the bowl rim, intensifying the sound, while meditating on its power herself. I held my hands either side of the bowl a couple of inches away, holding a rose quartz in one hand and a double point clear quartz in the other. With my Eyes closed, it seemed like waves of blue light were passing backwards and forwards between my hands like the wave effect of wind over a cornfield. I began to intone my own matching frequency. I could feel the sound intensifying and the timbers of the building started to vibrate in harmony. I remember even feeling the floorboards moving. In my mind's eye, the wave motion of the light was becoming narrower in proportion to the intensity of the sound. It narrowed and narrowed until I saw it was almost like a pulsating blue laser light. The feeling of Spirit presence was huge. Then the laser light brilliantly flashed, just like lightening. At that instant there was a deafening loud sonic boom. The bowl simultaneously exploded into a million tiny pieces, thrown all around the cabin. There were tiny sharp shards everywhere especially in places completely out of reach of the source. But none had touched us! Most of the bowl had been turned to a fine powder which covered the table. We were both startled but intensely aware of the overwhelming spiritual energy in the building. The energy remained for days, and was noticed by unaware visitors who were unable to pinpoint the powerful effect it had on them. Clearly the vibrational energy from the bowl coupled with our own effort, was more than the physical structure of the bowl could sustain. We hope to have a full set of crystal bowls again someday.

Question 36: *You wrote that you got the following from a lucid dream. Can you explain what it means.:* **Quote**:

Would you shun your friend, lest he become your enemy?
Would you shun your enemy, lest he become your friend?
You are one with the World and all things.
Would you then greet the world as your friend?
Why then do you shun yourself?'

Answer: This enigmatic message was part of a far more involved lucid dream. At a crucial stage in the dream when I was aware of my own puzzlement, my Minder intervened. The room we occupied was filled with light. It seemed to be coming from the fabric of the walls. The presence of my Minder emerged out of the light like a picture coming into focus and then taking solid form. The light normalised and I suspect that it was me and the other people I was with whose vibrations were raised to meet his. He spoke in a friendly authoritative voice, filling the air with precision and absolute clarity. Although he spoke for a while, I was only able to understand the explanation in his words and not the exact form he used. When I woke I recorded the explanation I received from him:

We inhabit this physical form, but if our Presence is part of an ever-greater reality permeating vast spheres, we must also accept that we can eventually attain a state of collective Oneness. We regulate the harmony or discord of our pathway along this physical experience by our own sacred choices. We feel separation, but separation exists only when there is conflict. We live in conflict because we have forgotten the nature our original condition. In nature there is no conflict, only transformation. If the world then is our true friend, why do we treat it as our enemy?

Friends or Enemies are still all a part of the whole. The only thing that separates them from us is our choice of action and reaction. Tolerance must be our yardstick, regulated by understanding and arising from knowledge. Separation exists where there is Conflict; and conflict exists only when there is Resistance. This may lead to our friends becoming our enemies and our enemies becoming greater enemies. They are still all one with us, but we have forgotten the Source. We are all one with the whole. To continue resisting this truth is to continue in conflict. To resist this truth, is also, to continue resisting Ourselves.

Question 37: *When do you know if you are making the connection to everything that you speak of?*

Answer: It is something that is really down to everyone's personal experience. When it happens there is no doubt. It is like when using that wonderful saying: To those who believe, no explanation is necessary; but to those who do not believe, no explanation is possible! The best I can offer you is to describe again one particular experience I had. It lasted only a few seconds, but remains with me as if a sharp memory from yesterday. The moment can happen when it is least expected:

On my nightly walk with my dog, my route traced a path along the Avenues at the edge of town. I loved the calm of the night air and the silent activity of the growing plants and trees in the gardens I passed. There was one young Birch tree I passed. Its shape and form were balanced with such symmetry and beauty that I would always stop to wonder at it as it glistened in the light of the street lamp. I loved that tree. One night it was misty and my walk followed the usual pattern. But this time the heavy mist cast a hush, and everything seemed bathed with an ethereal glow. I felt so immersed in the incredible beauty of it all. I reached my tree and stopped to share its spirit. I found myself speaking to it to thank it for its contribution to the world. The same detached feeling overcame me as when I am meditating to Out of Body.

Suddenly I found I was seeing from the perspective of the tree. I felt time had slowed and I was now one with the fibres of the tree. I could feel the sap rising from the ground like liquid energy through me. There was no feeling of separation to the ground and I felt myself being drawn along the connections in the earth, to the life force in other plants and trees nearby. The feeling spread and in a surge which must have lasted only moments I was suddenly one with all that came from the ground. Across the Planet, there was only total connection. I came to my senses again and found I had continued my walk for several hundreds of yards. Tears were running down my face. It was very profound. I was humbled and grateful for the privilege of the experience. You asked how a person knows when they have made the connection. When it happens it is total. There will be no doubt.

Question 38: *Can somebody forgive the karmic debt of someone else?*

Answer: By my Understanding, it is within no one to forgive the karmic debt of another. Within the context of the question, the act of offering forgiveness is only representative of a change in the reactive position of the forgiver, (where they were presumably the victim.) All of us have devolved from the source, and all of us are on a return journey. Every one of us is at a subtly different stage, and our differing vibrations reflect this. Our progress is determined by the scientific principle of the conservation of energy. Our frequencies discharge or refine themselves through our actions and reactions and the situations that arise as a consequence. This is the process we call Karma. It functions on a personal scale and through every other scale back to the level of the source. This will include the workings of collective Karma at family level, ethnic level, national level, international level, world level and planetary level. In fact it functions in the same way at every level imaginable. Karma automatically alters the probability of continuing choices in our pathway. We can accept or reject the lessons made available through them. Rejection leads to new probabilities with correspondingly harder lessons. It is therefore not possible for someone to forgive Karma and deny the right of choice in a necessary lesson for another person. A victim, who forgives the injury upon themselves, rejects the negative assault and takes a huge step back towards the source. For myself I say: I need no one to offer me forgiveness for my Karmic debt because I have identified its nature myself. I take responsibility for it myself, and I exercise my sacred free will to modify my motivation accordingly. I know however most try vainly to avoid the consequence, by not accepting personal responsibility for the consequence of *all* of their actions.

Question 39: *Are you able to summarise how you see the whole life process working?*

Answer: *Ignorance challenged by Change, creates unrest.*
Unrest seeks rebalance through familiarity.
Familiarity requires, understanding.
Understanding requires questions.
Questions, bring answers.

Answers, bring realization.
Realization, generates awareness.
Awareness, kindles faith.
Faith, seeks corroboration.
Corroboration requires development.
Development needs experience.
Experience provides conviction.
Conviction demands strength.
Strength builds, through introspection.
Introspection leaves scars.
Scars are the banner of compassion.
Compassion is the banner of humility.
Humility is the banner of Love.

My Conviction *is* my Faith. It was arrived at through my own tested experience. I embrace the pain of my pathway, for in its depth I find the Love of connection. I challenge my Conviction with every thought, for with every thwarted challenge, the Connection becomes stronger. With every mistake I make, I feel the unrelenting love of compassion from Spirit as my friends elsewhere see me stumble toward them. Every stumble provides greater enlightenment. My conviction; my gnosis, stands supreme for one reason above all. Since the moment of my awakening I knew that no aspect of it is exclusive to anyone or anything. It is as truth is, omnipresent.

Question 40: *Assuming that you want to improve your consciousness, how do you define better to yourself what you mean by agreeing to improve it? Are you really conscious of your consciousness? Doesn't that imply two consciousness's? If one is seeking to improve the other, what is assessing the first one? Can it also be improved? If so, does that not give rise to an infinite regression of consciousness's wanting to improve themselves? Or is it that consciousness can get itself into a self-assessing and self-improving state. If so, how does it do that?*

Answer: Phew, you have been thinking into overdrive with this one. Let's cool it down a bit with a few assertions. We could begin by saying that we are self-aware, and aware of our surroundings. We could refine this and say that our perceptions are inadequate because they do not yet encompass the totality of understanding. Animals are aware of their surroundings, yet very few are self-aware. A sea urchin reacts in an awareness of its environment, but is not self-aware. *We* have not developed to the stage where we can share their perceptions; so we are lacking. We are restrained by self-imposed limits. We progress higher because our sentient nature enables us to learn from our own experience, based on the clues and evidence around us. Our drive to expand is fuelled from an apparent distant memory of something greater within us.

Waves of energy surround us and invisibly pass through us. We accept this by turning on a radio for example. Their probability is strong enough for us to move beyond speculation to acceptance. Science provides more evidence to sustain it. There are realities beyond our physical senses. The restriction of our physical state does not invalidate them. Those who have developed an aspiration beyond sensation, seek to understand the greater reality beyond physical. Those who have the will, discern and test the evidence through their own experience before reaching their dynamic conviction. But, convictions are not transferable and it is within each one of us to follow the same process. As sentient beings, we have individuality. But if we wish to achieve higher awareness and share the experience of all other things, we need somehow to yield our individuality. How can this paradox be resolved?

The problem does not arise for someone who has had a validating experience to prove the reality of higher levels. Their awakened consciousness will have made a paradigm shift to the new viewing point. For others still struggling however, questions of consciousness are restricted because they are contained in a pattern of thinking that prevents the whole picture from being seen. Without the whole picture, the pieces never seem to fit, as with confused questions of consciousness. The higher thinker realises that consciousness can remain singular, even though it is an intrinsic part of the whole. This happens only when a person can see that all perceptions of consciousness are one and the same, and are only separated by different Viewing Points.

For the unawakened person who is still trapped to sensation, the tension traps their consciousness into the belief that their viewing point is the only reality. Nevertheless there would still be a pull in the higher mind to remind them of their higher consciousness—connection. Confusion would be assured! Transformation however guarantees that the lower self-consciousness will be transformed into self-awareness. We need not concern ourselves for the differing nature of consciousness.

We need only accept the responsibility and consequence of our own Will, and nurture the hunger within us for understanding. Then we will always be one with our consciousness however separated it may seem from a different Viewing Point. Whether you believe or not, you are a part of the Cosmic truth. It is by your own Will only that you hold yourself apart.

Epilogue

Our selection of questions ends here, but I hope you will be sufficiently armed at last to see answers appearing to your own questions. If I receive sufficient feedback from this work I will publish a companion book that develops many more of them. I will close by answering a very personal question I was asked. It was to describe something inspirational I received that had a particular bearing on my own life. I did not have to search far. I particularly remember one time when I woke from deep sleep with a profound piece in my mind that summarised my own battle with self. It captured also my Twin Flame potential in this life.

One Time I heard A Song.

Below Diocretes' feet the jagged rock of the pathway narrowed to barely six yards in length. Its steepness signalled warning; with strewn rock rubble and an endless precipice off to the left. His thoughts plummeted with the atmosphere into the darkened gorge below. The thongs of his skirt slapped hard to hinder his laboured steps and rubbed into his flesh with each push forward. Sweat mixed with the rawness of his skin; his tunic stained wet from the flow of his musk. His knuckles clenched-tight the short-sword in his grasp and ignored the bloody scrapes from the rock face as he struggled on. His breath eased but the curses grew; even as the tortuous path turned the bend to finally level and widen.

'Damn you to hell,' he spit, as he reigned back abruptly. His short-sword thrust forward in mortal challenge as an extension of his troubled Soul. Before him a figure stood serenely in simple powder blue robe; the colour of the robe matching his eyes and the thin hue of the sky. The Stranger's gaze was fixed to some far event on the horizon. Arms hung in rest at his side supported on the air as if on Eiderdown. He spoke.
'Why do you oppose me Diocretes?
Diocretes choked on his words,
'Oppose, oppose! I shall be done of you. Is there no place you will not plague me?'

He lunged, and his rage travelled the length of the sword to carry it, penetrating so easily through the body-flesh of the figure before him. Then with the ease of a hand from water his arm drew back; the glistening blade sucking crimson splashes in a neat bloody pattern before him. A slight sway betrayed the stance of the Stranger. Diocretes stared in fascination as a pool of red spread towards his feet. In slow motion, the figure sagged to his knees, palms upturned as they met with the rocky ground and came to rest. His life force ebbed. As the last breath expired from the stranger's chest, his flowing locks parted to his beautiful gaze. His head tilted toward Diocretes and the stranger smiled with Love for him. Diocretes spun from his trance as a roar in the sky behind him tore him from his nemesis. Clouds boiled and in seconds surged toward him like a geyser. The sky parted. Diocretes fell back in shock to see the vision of a beautiful armour-clad maiden in the firmament. She spoke to him.

'Diocretes, what is it you have assailed today?'

He caught his breath and stood forth with instinctive familiarity. He thought her name; Alana, and returned her question,

'I fought at last for peace from a demon who followed me; and now it is done.'

'Oh! Diocretes,' said Alana, *'Know you not, that it is not done. It is only begun. You were lost, my lord and you knew not. You have found your way, and still you know not.'*

Diocretes pointed hard with his short-sword behind him and turned to follow its direction. He staggered as he saw how the figure was no longer there. No stains of blood, no sign of the Presence. He turned again to his vision, her eyes sparkling with Compassion. She spoke again.

'Diocretes for so long you have fled the fear within. Now you face it and I await your thought of me; to be reunited again. There is no cause to battle more within.'

Diocretes turned again within his questioned belief to check the Figure was indeed now gone. Balance tricked him and his outstretched palm fended his frame from the rock face as he staggered back. His mind caught up to his Soul with a Snap! No short-sword. No opponent. *'But, but,'* and he felt a sharp pain at his side. His hands clutched to the sudden agony of sensation from his body. He looked down as his fingers squeezed to stem the blood-flow from his wound. He felt the energy drain from his body to earth and the strength sap from his legs. He began to sink but was held firm by strong loving hands. He looked and saw. It was his vision, now at his side as flesh and beauty. She whispered softly to him now.

'Recover my Lord indeed, for now we may do the work we may do. It awaits us, as it always has done.'

He looked deeply into her eyes and answered her. *'I am not Diocretes am I?'*
No, she returned.
'But you are my Lady?'
'Yes,' she said, smiling.

Heading Underground at last

The wheel has definitively turned year on year; so clearly for several years now, and we head towards a potential zenith of human experience. Attentions are turned from around the world towards Egypt more and more. The conflicts, subterfuge and strife there seem to fit as an allegory for much of what is happening in the rest of the world. The politics churn with predictable religious overtones, providing a violent diversion as ever from the plaintive question of, why anyway?

Evidence stacks on evidence of a sanitising operation at Giza to remove the audit trail below ground that may lead the world to a paradigm shift in belief, but which really would only be a return to when everything was ordered from a common source; the Law of One. Back then, STS won because we were still descending. Service to Self may be putting in a good show again this time; but this time there is a greater overriding cosmic factor which will sort the sheep from the wolves during our future cosmic ascension. And how would we be able to determine this? I speak in the first person singular, as I speak for myself.and my Twin Flame. I speak also for the suffering animals that were surely not born naturally to this cruel world to suffer as they do at our hands—and under the pious banners or wailing speakers of our religious clubs! I speak with my own conviction under a blank banner which was tested—and it taught me the quality of righteousness, because unlike all the other banners it proclaimed nothing.

But the pathway here was rough—as it must be to carry the lesson of experience. The reward is sublime even in the face of those who seek the shadows in others as they ignore the darkness in themselves. And the route brought meetings with friendly strangers who placed us with the evidence. It brought us to events which defied all normal logic and expectation; and the outcome of which opened portals into an ancient time for us. It brought us to the route trodden underground by those who seeded our DNA so long ago which waits for us to awaken to the fact again. It brought us serious danger and saved us from it again in validation. It pointed the clear way forward, always.

And even before this time it was necessary to understand the mechanics of life and life beyond in order to see beyond the third and deep into the fourth and fifth when necessary. The path was so designed that no doubt was there; to know the difference between Thoth's curves and angles. So here we are friends and all. Within this journey it will seem as so much chaos and jumble as it once did for us. But as the pull to another frequency increases, the comfort will only be felt in awareness and a yielding to the order that will emerge to you also from the apparent chaos. All you need is to give yourself the thinking time for understanding to filter through. It must become the first person singular for you too, but tested through *your own* experience.

Fancy names in banner publishing lights are no more use than useless to the process. All those who pimp themselves from within their own perceptions will dissolve in their own right. If the seeker seeks, then the words or actions will appear to inspire a self-awakening. We hope through the fullness of our journey, we may assist this process.

As a planetary race we have a lineage that dates beyond antiquity. Our ancestors had a superior knowledge which we can rediscover. We are not the only sentient beings inhabiting the Cosmos. In modern times there is ample evidence to show the interaction that has been taking place at a most secret level for decades. Open public contact with beyond-earth visitors will not happen until we grasp how they can be there and what their interest is. There were times in our past when our connection to some of them was complete. Our connections to them are now covert. Their teaching legacy was left for us to unravel when the time was right. That time is now as the planet faces its biggest transformation for nearly 13,000 years. Some of that knowledge has already been deciphered and is being withheld for covert self-interest. The power and technology of our true ancestors must be revealed. Their elite finally misused their power and paid the price. We must learn this time.

I have tried my best to give an explanation of the way of things as they were revealed again to me. I continue within my own part of the story, and beyond all the explanations, my own dramas unfold. My Birth Plan is intrinsically linked with my Twin Flame Judith to a higher purpose. We have recently followed an intense pathway together, laid from out of body experiences and extraordinary adventures for some years in Egypt. These things and more in abundance point us to a final purpose. I have shared my pathway in part to offer the same new direction to others. However my pathway serves a larger purpose. It is simply impossible to grasp the enormity of the cosmic world beyond us without having a full appreciation of the workings of its structure. How could anyone understand the mind set of our ancient ancestors in a modern world where reality beyond physical has been forgotten? Constantine for the Romans ensured at Nicea that concepts such as continuation or reincarnation would henceforth be judged as heresy and lead to execution. Passionate modern Priests who decry reincarnation would do well to remember that their forbearers were forced to accept such nonsense under pain of death; when for all time previously its reality and much more, was a normal part of human experience. We all have to relearn what we have forgotten. My Birth

Plan requires me to pursue a goal in Egypt with my twin flame which may lead to the discovery of a cache of knowledge hidden by our ancestors. This task would be impossible without a living acceptance and appreciation of the techniques used by the ancients to conceal their stores. My pathway and Judith's has been the preparation for this. Since meeting with my twin flame and others who share our goal, we have followed an incredible set of adventures that we hope will end soon in success beneath the Giza Plateau. The early journey lays a foundation. The story of what happened next will follows. It is time to expose what we know because we are at the eleventh hour. The end is the beginning. The beginning is the end. There is no difference. We are One-Another.

Part 3: The Calling from the Kings Chamber

Our Journey of the Last Decade at Giza. 251
First Contact in Cairo..252
The Visitation in Jesus' Grotto 254
The Message at the Wailing Wall 256
Picking up the Story..258
The First USA Visit...261
A Meeting with the Wolf..262
The Exploding Bowl 264
Our First Return to The Sands 266
The Horse Cave...269
The Man with The Broken Leg 272
Time with the Blessed Father 275
Explosions in the Desert 277
The Coffer Vision..279
The Experiment in the Kings Chamber 281
The Intonement Recording 286
The Capstone Experiment...288
The Mysterious Bedouin..290
The Rock Dog..292
An Introduction to the Underground..294
A Handful of Sand 297
Lost to the Desert..298
The Strange Desert Petroglyph 301
Senior Connections & The Holy Family 303
Double Dealings and Betrayal...305
Entering the Village as Chickens 307
The Ancient Finds of the Village 311
The Ghosts of Abu Lifa. 317
The Mystery Temple of Sobek 322
Treasures on our Doorstep..324

The Connections Start to Appear 326
Getting Closer to the Source 331
Starting Back to the Future 332
Ticking Boxes at Other Sites 335
The Solar Cross 337
The Sun Temple of Abu Ghurab 339
The Underground Vortex and Stargate 341
Free Explorations on the Plateau. 343
Henutsen and The Temple of Isis 348
The Causeway Shafts and the Osiris Tomb 350
The Central Mastaba Field 353
Qar, Idu, Meresankh 111 and Seshemnefer 1V 355
Going Back 4500 years 358
The Magnetism of NC2 361
Reflections and a Final Revelation—for now! 372
Don't dare forget the Animals 375
School's Out 378

Plate 3: Featuring the Sphinx Harbour with the GP in the background 380
Plate 4: The corner of Nazlet el-Samaan Village. The Harbour is right of pic. 381
Plate 5: The Entrance to the Tomb of North Cliff 2 382
Plate 6: The Schematic of the known front levels of the NC2 Chamber 383
Plate 7: The Schematic of the Tunnel/Cavern system beyond the NC2 Tomb 384

Back Cover Featuring:

A montage featuring one sample picture from the NC2 System Walls filled with orbs and secret images. You can visit our website and download the original HD image for your own investigation. Also featured is a thumbnail image of an alien type figure from the main NC2 reception chamber.

http://www.richardgabriel.info

Part 3: The Calling from The Kings Chamber

Our Journey of the Last Decade at Giza

Special Note: *Many of the following stories are elaborated in their own right with extensive accompanying galleries of pictures on our website.* http://www.richardgabriel.info

By 2002 Judith and I had discovered the bond of our pathways. We also discovered that we shared a purpose which would lead to Egypt for a task which is still seeking its ultimate fulfilment. If the test of a correct pathway is in the extraordinary/supernormal experiences it delivers to move it forward, then the path we have followed over the last decade has produced more than sufficient validation. The following recollections are but a small sample of the intense experiences of Spirit which have occurred throughout. But in Egypt and in connection with our work, Judith and I enjoyed many more adventures than I will be able to record here. The ones I share will serve to show the major lessons, or stepping stones of our Birth Plan together. You will see as we did how sometimes apparently adverse events laid down amazing synchronicities which would take years to be realised.

If we are to share the key events of our journey with you, we are faced with one small problem. It is that nearly all the people we have interacted with are still alive and working. We cannot compromise them or our continued work with them. This means therefore that we can be truthful and accurate, but we must disguise two things. These are the identities of many of those involved and the very exact dates when things happened. However the events we are about to describe are in chronological order over the last decade. Many of the events are supported with feature stories and copious picture galleries on our two websites. These provisions will subtract nothing from the meat of what you will now read. But, whenever you see initials only for a name, or the hash sign, you will know we have deliberately omitted information for the reasons given above.

First Contact in Cairo

Before delving into the pathways of the last decade-plus years I need to mention two incidents which brought me a portent of things to come. During the strife years of my second relationship there was a particular family holiday trip I was a part of which had particular significance. My partner received an insurance windfall and arranged a trip for her and daughters to visit Cyprus. I would be a part of the group, but only if I could find sufficient funds from my cash—strapped business to pay my way. I agreed though in truth I was to be a mule. The trip provided supreme contrasts between the beauty of the surroundings and the underlying conflict of will between my partner and I. During the trip a special extra trip was discovered by ship to the Holy Land. This would stretch the finances further, but I was more interested in the fact that there would be a whistle—stop journey along the way from Port Said by coach to visit the Pyramids.

Our guide on the coach trip was an Israeli who quickly rendered us all deaf to his Nationalist monologue which he managed to sustain for much of the long tiring journey to Cairo. All other problems in my mind diminished in proportion to the excitement that built inside me as we closed on the Pyramids. Finally we were there and I prayed we would be able to enter the Great Pyramid. Entry to a Pyramid had been promised, and to the praise of our driver, our coach was the first of a long convoy from our ship and gave us first unfettered access at our destination. I was awestruck as we snaked up the road on the Plateau. I was a little disappointed as we passed the Great Pyramid—then Kephren and finally came to a stop outside Menkaure. The other coaches were not far behind us and our guide explained we would have only a very short time (in truth to be hustled like fast speeding cattle) up the steps to glance inside Menkaure before boarding again for the return trip.

He was not kidding and I was crestfallen. I had imagined time to explore and at least see all the Pyramids properly. The coach park then was a few hundred yards from the SW corner of Kephren and I proceeded to stir a big scene with my partner as I insisted at all cost I *had* to at least approach Kephren. I was dismissed out of hand but following several precious minutes of arguing I started running across the sand towards the Pyramid. I was told I had very short time and the driver would not wait for me if I failed to reappear on time. I had not reckoned on the heat. It was such a shock following the air—conditioning of the coach. I had not reckoned on the child-touts who zeroed in on me like flies. I had one focus in mind and it was to get to the Pyramid. I dismissed them roughly from my path. I had not reckoned on the cliff set back from the Western side of Kephren, tapering from the North to the South West corners. I arrived at the mid-section and cursed as I had to run back to the lowest point of the cliff in order to close the last distance.

Finally I was at the South West corner of the Pyramid. My chest was heaving from the exertion. I was draining with sweat in the heat. But, I looked up and was lost to the sight of the blocks towering above me to the capped summit. I outstretched my palms and reached forward to finally place myself, resting in contact with the corner block.

Immediately a strange thing happened. I felt as if I had suddenly been plunged into a deep-freeze box which was at sub-zero temperature. I felt the cold air over me draining the exhaustion of the heat and cooling me in moments. I felt the familiar wind of spirit over my entire body. In my mind, knowingness saturated my thoughts. The trials and tribulations of my life were irrelevant to the fact that some time in the future I would return here to do important work. Someday in the future I would be enabled to stand once again at this place but in wholly different circumstances. A tranquil calm replaced all the turmoil inside me. I stepped away from the rock, now quite content. I spread and quickened my steps to return to the coach and the angry ignorant reception which awaited me. It all flew over my head because I knew what I knew. It was indeed several years later when I recounted the story to Judith as we stood together again at that exact place.

The Visitation in Jesus' Grotto

This cruise trip was to provide another couple of surprises. Much of the return journey and then on to the Holy Land, was a bit of a blur. My mind was back at the pyramids. It was not hard however to be caught up in the dust and the crowded hustle at Bethlehem as thousands of tourists of all denominations vied for space to claim a part of the surroundings. I could not help noticing the similar tourist look on people's faces as the perpetual queues hustled along with a motion of their own. I wondered how many would consign the sights of their visit to just another visited trophy in their photo albums. I wondered how few would leave enriched from the swell of unmistakable higher spirit that oozed from the buildings and the ground.

We reached the Church of the Nativity in Bethlehem. There was the chance to join the crowds in a moving single file, then to descend the steps into the Grotto of Jesus built above his believed birth place. I wished so hard it would have been possible to visit there in tranquillity. It was not to be as we shuffled along in our place among the crowd. I tried hard to centre myself as it became my turn to climb down into the Grotto—which was more like a well-worn cave tomb. I looked behind me and was surprised to see I was not immediately followed. I wondered why, but grabbed the opportunity to stand quietly and go instantly to *higher* level. As I looked into the depth of the grotto I was surprised to see a patch of mistiness in the air, like a large very slow motion puff of cigarette smoke, bright and distinct. I stifled my excitement and tried to link to what I was seeing. It was certainly not smoke or mist! Every hair on my body stood on end and I felt overcome with emotion. I felt the closeness of a powerful Presence. In those few seconds a thought entered my mind that I wanted to take the moment with me. I had my camera in my hand even though photographs were discouraged at every turn; and certainly in the Grotto. Still no one had followed me and those in front had gone ahead. I was completely alone. I raised my camera and clicked for one shot. The misty region was still there. I continued to watch for a couple more minutes as the manifestation slowly faded back to nothing.

My camera was an old fashioned film—spool type. I clutched it and checked the holding strap was fixed and secure now around my wrist. I didn't care if I never took another photo on the trip. This would be my personal evidence. I had captured an image of what I had experienced. I left the Grotto as the clamour of the next visitors finally erupted again. I could not stifle my excitement as I joined with the others. I spilled my story, quite forgetting in the moment the half disbelieving patronage I had learned to expect. I was adamant. It did not matter, I had my proof.

We returned to the ship and from the loading ramp we had to climb a long carpeted flight of internal stairs to our deck level. It was one of those grand style stairways with an intermediate landing such as were shown in the later Titanic movie. I still clutched my camera in my right hand with the carrying strap secure around my wrist. There were some other passengers on the stairway, but not many. As we neared the top of the flight I felt what I can only describe as a blow or strike of some kind to my wrist area. There was no one beside me and I had struck nothing myself. I turned to see my camera struck from my grasp and broken from the security strap. In horror I saw it begin to bounce down the flight of stairs. My reaction was instinctive. I bounded after it trying to halt its tumble at gathering speed down the stairs. I saw that as it was rolling and bumping down the steps it was not broken and I had almost caught up to it at the bottom. Just out of my hand reach it bounced one more time to finally land on the bottom carpet. As it landed and flopped finally on to its face, the access catch released and the back cover sprung open, exposing the whole film inside.

Anything on the film was now lost forever, or so I thought. I look back and realise, if we are true to an important Birth Plan that we have chosen to fulfil, then validations will appear along the way, either as amazing synchronicities, or as seemingly supernormal happenings. Whichever; these are often of a design which renders them personal to you and no one else. They are validations which despite circumstances to the contrary, are meant to show you are on the right pathway of probability for the desired outcome. I captured what I saw. I know what I saw, but it was not in the plan or purpose for it to be shown to others. It was enough that its message satisfied the test of *my* experience. I had in fact lost nothing; but gained another validating lesson. By the way, there was one more incident prior to the camera experience I should share with you and which I accept with relevance.

The Message at the Wailing Wall

We had been taken to the Wailing Wall and it was optional for anyone to know they had actually walked over to the wall to offer a prayer. Devotees by the hundred milled backwards and forwards over the open square, to and from the wall for prayer. Women had their own section and men had to wear a cap of conformity which was freely offered to non-denomination visitors. I absolutely wished to visit the wall. To me it did not matter if I did not share the local doctrine. It did not matter that I held wider beliefs. I knew that a raised vibration of Spirit filled this place and it would be possible to make a powerful connection just as within the Grotto.

I walked alone across to the wall and stood in silent meditative prayer. I felt the rush of Spirit again. I felt the height of the vibration and was deeply moved by its power. I remember noticing left and right, men shoving their small folded prayer notes into cracks in the wall. I remember checking myself harshly for being judgemental as I imagined how less powerful their paper effigies were than the living message from their higher mind. I returned to my own hopes for the future and wished for the connections of higher understanding to always be my guide.

Reluctantly I turned from the wall and proceeded to walk back across the huge approach square. The square at that moment was quite open, with no other people appearing to cross the line of my walk. However off to the left I noticed a tall man full—suited as a person of orthodox Jewish faith, with hat and long side curls. I figured him to perhaps be one of the Church ministers at the site. The man was walking on a line which I realised would intercept me. It was not accidental, because at the point where one person would simply yield to the other, his eyes caught mine and I knew he was about to say something. He spoke to me briefly, but his encounter stays with me to this day. He spoke in perfect English and said as a question,

'*You are not a Jew are you?*

I replied, '*No, but this is a place of powerful Spirit, and I am a person of Spirit.*'

He replied, '*That is why I wished to speak to you.*' He continued, '*I see you will do important things for Spirit. Will you accept my Blessing?*'

I was moved, and accepted.

He gave his Blessing, embraced me and finally said, *Now go my son and do what you have to do,* and turned gently to leave.

I walked the last distance back to the entrance in a complete trance. The trip had given me this encounter and my experience at the pyramid plus the Grotto. How could anyone ignore these wonderful things?

Picking up the Story

By the time Judith and I met in this life, our obsession to understand the nature of things; the source of our origins; the direction of life on a grand scale and the mysteries of the Great Pyramid at the Giza Plateau—had surfaced separately in both of our lives. It did not matter that we lived, and continue to live, over 3500 miles apart across the ocean. We knew immediately that we had a twin-flame pathway of strongest probability that was going to steer us to a task in Egypt.

There was much more, because before I met Judith again, I had gone through a complete breakdown from my second long term relationship having been severely betrayed also in business. I had lost my home, my family, my business and everything that was a part of it for the second time in my life. All that remained was the shirt on my back and the tools of my trade; and miserable bewilderment. I could not fathom why it was I had my original *Event* of understanding and then was no longer able to figure the reasons behind the apparently disastrous tactical route I had taken since.

It is utterly impossible to convey to someone what it is like for the mind to approach the *abyss* unless they have also lived it and survived. I have been to that place twice. So for me when I say my big *Event* was a blessing and a curse, I still had not accepted that knowing the strategy of order in the way of things did not protect me from the lessons of bad tactical decisions in my own life. I was at rock-bottom, and my only refuge was to stay a long distance away at the home of my sister and family for a time. It was far from the territory of my former home for over 20 years.

Family members on my Sister's side tried to help but I went into an automatic—pilot frame of mind. I steered into trade work immediately. There was no problem there because even on my worst day I could do my job as well as anyone on a good day. There had been no grain of closure on what had happened. But I did receive a phone call at my lowest point following the break. It was a screwball story of financial help needed from within the step family I had lost. In my equally screwball state of mind I foolishly yielded up all the saved earnings of my first few weeks of work, and it bought more pain but still no closure. I was £2K lighter, penniless until my next wage and heading to that dark place for the third time. I remember sending out prayers for guidance until it hurt. My prayers were answered because out of the blue and on the recommendation of my sister, I was given the opportunity to make

Elderly Retirement Management work, my new vocation. I was no stranger to care work as I'd had considerable involvement in these areas through my previous relationships and their work. It was a turning synchronicity. In a female dominated working field, a male role had become available for me to fill.

At home and at work I was introduced to the computer properly for the first time. Privately that was back in the early days when forum chat on matters of spirit centred hugely on one particular Forum site. All the understanding of my event spilled out and I began to take part. But there was a second turning point. I had another mind-blowing out of body experience. In this I was shown the vision of an outcome of strongest probability for the future. This concerned a twin-flame I was to meet. It concerned Egypt, the GP and the underground of the Giza Plateau, and it concerned specifics about things which we would encounter. I was shown that the actualisation and outcome of this pathway would depend entirely on the awakening of my twin-flame to it also. I was shown things which tied to previous OBE's in connection with the Great Pyramid and the ancient underground. Suddenly, it was as if a second huge light of understanding had been switched on in my head. I understood now the *why* of my latter relationships, and in this there may be a lesson for others.

My second partner shared my birthday but some years apart. I had followed spiritual instincts/memory when the *like to like* vibrations brought us together for our contractual purpose. I thought at the start I had recognised her as my twin-flame partner. We were almost too alike, and there were clear instances of telepathy between us. My false reading of our purpose together led to too many years of pain, before being forced to face the fact that it was not so. But the pain of those years and the disastrous material and emotional outcome for me, were commensurate with the time it took for the lessons to be learned the hard way. We were on parallel tracks, but her distance along the tracks was not synchronised to mine. The deep scars will always remind me of the lesson. I hope that she too gained as much as I finally gained from our classroom together. I am grateful for the experience.

My OBE gave me the pieces which released me at last into tranquillity of mind and purpose. I finally had the freedom of knowing and being at peace with myself permanently, whatever happened next. They must have been smiling on another level, because it was next day on that chat Forum when I first encountered Judith again in this life. She was in her own desperate private situation of suffocation and pain. But for me there was an instant blinding light of recognition. I knew that I knew her. I knew she was a shining light who shone dimly in her situation. I saw the suppression of her true nature beneath the decades of pain which she had not learned to free herself from. I knew she was the person of my OBE. I had hardly spoken to her but I still knew these things.

It was crazy. I remember laughing and talking out loud to my Minders. I said they must be having a laugh. I had just emerged to take the first breath of fresh air in my life. I had just woken up for the first time for real. I expected to have been allowed a quiet period in my life with no more dramas for a while. Instead I was immediately being given the choice of change with another very long-distance partner for an arranged task in Egypt, and I had not even spoken to her properly yet. It really did seem crazy. However this time my mind was truly free. This time I knew my decisions were not being driven by conditioning. This time I knew I would be making a free choice. I began speaking with Judith and before long we both knew what choice we had already made for the future. It was also our Contract, and had been agreed as a choice option a very long time ago.

The First USA Visit

The first thing I learned when we met was of the decades of adversity Judith had endured. She had battled in her past through terribly serious personal and medical problems and survived, but with a legacy that would forever test her strength of character. I was introduced to her family and friends and had enough time to forge strong bonds with some. Along with her adult son we visited distant places of great wilderness and beauty. We reinforced the spiritual connection under inky black sky and tapestries of stars at the great lakes, and in the depths of the US forest regions with bears for company. These places gave us the same opportunity that we found years later in the Western Desert, to soak in the powerful energies of higher levels and strengthen all connections to the greater mind.

At home there were the crystals which Judith already worked with. For her there was none of the emerging mumbo—jumbo of pet names and pseudo crystal knowledge. She already instinctively understood the energies of the earth and worked directly with the special matrices and properties that each crystalline form offered. She used them as they were originally understood for things such as directed healing and enhancement of her own vibration when calling upon her higher mind. At home also there were the rescue animals in abundance. The cats include an amazing blind Egyptian rescue cat which can better see than if it had normal sight.

A Meeting with the Wolf

One special pet was a magnificent Wolf Dog. Judith was pack leader and always took the precaution of keeping it behind barriers when visitors were there. I don't know how many readers know of the wolf's traits, even when one is relatively tame in captivity. This one had been reared as a rescue almost from birth but still displayed usual characteristics. It was very big! It had thick bushy white fur. It had a mouth which swept in a curve at the sides of its jaw, of the kind which makes all wolves appear to be smiling. It never barked. It kept its head low and studied everything with an unnerving intelligence. I thought he was the most magnificent creature I had ever met and my hair stood on end the moment I saw it.

I used a sleeping bag and blanket on the floor in the Lounge, set against the settee. It may have been my second night there and the dog was behind its barrier in the kitchen. The weather had been warm and I lay on top of my sleeping bag, half dressed. It must have been in the hours approaching dawn when I was stirred from sleep. My awareness was instantly sharp as I realised I was not alone. I did not dare move a muscle until I knew what to expect. Somehow the barrier had opened and I realised the wolf dog was somewhere in the room with me. I did not know how it would react, and in any case if things went badly, I would have little chance of getting help in time from others in their bedrooms.

I was laying on my side, facing into the room and through my half opened eyes and peripheral vision I saw the dog standing a short distance away from my feet. It hunched down on to its forefeet and began to shuffle backwards. By now another chair obscured my limited view. Suddenly I heard a thud as the dog bounded with another couple of thuds, and with belly almost on the ground, it slid forward until its snout was almost touching my feet or legs. It took every ounce of my willpower to resist my natural instinct for flight! I continued to lie there absolutely still, but tense. It backed off again and repeated the performance. I continued to lie there absolutely still and tense. It stood upright and from my position on the ground it seemed huge. I began to speak for the first time in a quiet reassuring voice, saying,

'It's all right, it's all right my friend.'

The dog proceeded to trot towards the area of the floor near my head. It positioned itself facing me about six feet away as I continued to speak softly to it. Once again it went down on its forefeet and then leapt in a bound towards me, sliding the last distance until its snout was only inches from my face. I continued to lie there absolutely still and even tenser! It backed away in a crouch and did the same thing a second time. In any other circumstance I would have climbed half way up the nearest tree by now, but from my bed on the floor I had nowhere to go. Instinctively also I felt the stirring of a deep affinity with the animal.

The Wolf's behaviour shifted. He trotted to my feet and began sniffing, but it was more like a deep huffing sniff as if he was vacuuming and processing my smell. He continued up my body huffing and sniffing at every inch until he reached my face. He paused with his nose to mine literally smelling my breath and then my hair. In his final move, he trotted to my feet and lined himself with my direction. I want you to picture the sight that everyone must have seen when a dog finds an interesting smell on the ground for example. The dog goes down on its forelegs and twists its neck and then its body and torpedoes its back and side along the ground to give and take to the scent it has found. Well Wolf dog did the same thing with me twice. He pushed his body the full length of mine and the sleeping bag, and on the second time he flopped himself down, resting like a heavy furry sand—bag right against me. I had continued to speak with him and reached my hand to scratch at his neck. He simply sighed and let me continue and before long we must have drifted to sleep together.

Everyone was amazed when they emerged for the day. He had never displayed such behaviour to anyone. I loved him so much and was devastated when I heard a couple of years later that age and ill-health finally transported him to a higher place. My abiding memory will be that first encounter, and of all the encounters thereafter when I returned from an outing for example. Wolf dog always greeted me with such friendly excitement. I felt such privilege to have passed his test to be accepted by him as of his own on that first day of meeting. Such experiences of spirit are priceless.

The Exploding Bowl

Judith and I constantly seek out places and occasions where we find power of spirit. This reads as places and occasions when the higher vibrations are intensified. As explained in the first part of the book, it is possible at such times to elevate one's own vibration and feed from the substance of the prevailing vibrations; to rise with a higher affinity and insight one's self. On another visit we were all sharing a large Log cabin in the wilderness of the forest near to a lake. Snow had fallen heavily. In the night time we were visited by deer, skunk, bears and other animals. We built a large open fire close-by and swam with the river of flying embers as we roasted first one side of our body and then the other against the chill air. It was pure magic.

One evening we arranged to be alone to experiment with a crystal bowl from Judith's collection. This one was particularly large and was tuned to the note of C. I have told the story of what happened earlier in this book, but it is relevant now in context to reproduce it again here. We had the moment to ourselves within the large lakeside log cabin. On the table sat a beautiful 14inch, rock-quartz bowl. We were meditating to its sound; a perfect middle C.

Standing at the opposite side of the narrow table, Judith ran the rubber mallet around the bowl rim, intensifying the sound while meditating on its power herself. I held my hands either side of the bowl a couple of inches away, holding a rose quartz in one hand and a double point clear quartz in the other. With my eyes closed, it seemed like waves of blue light were passing backwards and forwards between my hands like the wave effect of wind over a cornfield. I began to intone my own matching frequency. I could feel the sound intensifying and the timbers of the building started to vibrate in harmony. I remember even feeling the floorboards moving. In my mind's eye, the wave motion of the light was becoming narrower in proportion to the intensity of the sound. It narrowed and narrowed until I saw it was almost like a pulsating blue laser light.

The feeling of Spirit-Presence was huge. Then the laser light brilliantly flashed just like lightening. At that instant there was a deafening loud sonic boom which resonated through the building. The bowl simultaneously exploded into a circle of powder and a million minute pieces thrown all around the cabin. These tiny sharp shards were everywhere and especially in places completely out of line from their source. But none had touched us! Most of the bowl had been turned to a fine powder which covered the table. We were both startled but intensely aware of the overwhelming spiritual energy in the building. The energy remained for days, and was noticed by unknowing visitors who detected the powerful effect but were unable to pinpoint its source. The vibrational energy from the bowl coupled with our input was more than the physical structure of the bowl could sustain. We hope to have a full set of crystal bowls again someday!

All my trips to the USA were filled with visits to places of high vibration, and constantly the discussion returned to topics of Spirit and Egypt. We both wanted to pursue our calling but had not yet arrived at any plan. The stage however was set when the plan simply fell into our laps.

Our First Return to The Sands

The emerging internet was already weaving magic as likeminded people came together. Judith and I were in discussion and early friendship with a number of people who all had a calling to Egypt, each with their own agenda. There was G. who had received psychic messages over a long period of his life and was obsessed with finding the location of the Arc of the Covenant. His messages had been reinforced by other intuitive friends who seemed to validate his own theories. He linked the disappearance of the object with the legends in the Western Desert of a King and his entourage who had been lost along with their Gold possessions and the Arc, never to be found.

There was H. together with his working partner J. who had published applauded books describing theories of the origins and use of the pyramids, linking them intrinsically to coded Biblical accounts. These seemed also to point to a specific region of the Western Desert where a hidden sacred temple may be found. They wished to visit the desert for field exploration and research as well as taking measurements from well-known sites near Cairo. H. is the Egyptology scholar and J. was the explorer and intuitive investigator. Another friend was P, a respected documentary film maker and deeply spiritual man who wished to be a part of any work in Egypt.

G. and I had spoken at great length and I found I was also drawn to the desert. I did hours and days of research and found in fact the Western desert was not so barren after all. There were oasis and countless ruins which showed how in a time long gone, many people lived in lusher version of what is there now. I had read that beyond the melt of from the last ice age, the sea levels would have settled at around 200 feet higher for a time, and indeed the evidence of what we eventually called the Horse Cave, seemed to bear this out. That early information led to our later extensive research in the Western Desert which proved human activity at around a former 200 feet/plus sea level. This coincided by the way with the sea once lapping at the base of the Great Pyramid.

In the desert I found evidence of many abandoned hermitage monk structures and I found the legend. I linked it possibly to the Biblical story of David, who travelled his granary estates with his wealth and entourage in convoy. That was a time when great desert depressions were likely fed from ancient canals and flooded to perfect depth for grain production and other food types. Beyond the Southern Lake Fayoum; where we were delighted on one trip to grab the opportunity for a swim—there is a Protectorate area. Escarpments funnel a long wide valley and a blind second valley to the great-beyond of the Western Desert. On the N.N.Western sides of the main entrance valley, there has been a Coptic Christian hermitage community for centuries. This was experiencing a trickle revival as new monks chose to move there and claim more living caves from the rocky side of the escarpment. We determined that if anyone would know more about the history of the area, they would. I decided to join with G. in a trip there to find out.

My concern however was that my motivation with Judith was to get to the Great Pyramid. We took the decision that Judith would join me in Cairo on a second week while the first week would be given to the more arduous desert search. I didn't realise until later trips alone with Judith to the Desert that she was perfectly capable of matching any efforts of rough travel and exploration that we encountered. At the time of first plans with G, a similar discussion with slightly different motivation was taking place with J. and H. They decided to visit the desert with us, and a final member of the trip would be P, who would record it all for a video documentary in the future. Ours then would be The Quest Project.

Upon arrival in Cairo there was confusion because our pre—arrangement for jeeps and guide had messed up! Our arranged guide was not available. However a hurried substitute in the name of JO. was hastily contacted and agreed to be our guide. We discovered later his zone of comfort was Cairo and he was less skilled in dealing with the logistics and controls for us to travel into the desert without major hassle. We eventually arrived at the valley of the Monks after sometimes angry encounters with officialdom, unnecessary stops and the tourist police. We had to accept one policemen breathing down our necks as an escort for much of the time. On later trips, Judith and I were able to access the desert freely and under protection, but I still remembered our original guide previously being flattened to the ground by a greedy policeman.

Our visit to the hermitage site was idyllic and generated first love for the desert and the Coptic Monks. They extended an open welcome to us and shared all they had. We brought far too many perishable items of food with us and were happy to share most of these to the Monks. It led to the most wonderful cauldron hotpot meal later that evening, which everyone was able to sample.

We were placed in a communal visitor's cave which was like a set from a James Bond movie. From the central passage, platforms had been hewn from the rock at waist level on either side. We slept comfortably on camel-hair mattresses on these ledges, with the roof almost at touching height above us. In the semi darkness small pieces of salt crystal within the rock sparkled like stars in the sky. On that first night the moon was high. P. and I stood outside into the early hours and looked down and across the valley to an amazing sight. The moonlight picked up the differing areas of sand for miles, making some of them fluoresce. It tricked the eyes because the valley now looked like it had vast areas of snow covering the surface. It was so surreal and beautiful.

We explored and integrated with the life of the Monks, especially visiting the brackish water spring out in the middle of the valley. This was where there would be battles of politics in subsequent years as the local authorities used violence and intimidation to try and force the Monks from their remote home. The oasis, or spring as preferred, was bounded by old woven palm panels to keep the sand away. A fairly large area within its protection was being sparsely cultivated to produce vegetables and desert palm trees dotted the perimeter. Water emanated from the water table just below the surface by its own pressure; and in one place, piping sunk into the ground allowed the water to spout out above head height. This had been turned into a screened bathing area. It was highly amusing when we saw the huge Victorian cast—iron bath positioned on the sand below the spout as a wash and bathing station. It also seemed so surreal but perfect in its resting place so far out into the desert. We were glad of the chance on many occasions to douche under the freezing ground water ourselves. The bathing enclosure was primitive and allowed me with the help of Judith and A. on a later visit to create a shaped concrete floor area for all to use in comfort. On that day we ran out of daylight. A. was paranoid at the possible danger from the abundant tree snakes, scorpions and spiders that emerged after dark. My uncovered arms during the work had been bitten to hell by the mosquitos but I was determined to complete the job. As the last light of the day faded, huge ants were invading the space we were working and quite a few were definitely immortalised as fossils in the final spread of concrete. Movement could be distinctly heard in the palm fronds above us. A. was literally dancing to get us out of there in case a snake dropped down. It was a great relief when we could abandon our tools and trek back to the caves. The job was worth it however as everyone made greater use of the more comfortable bathing station in the desert.

Our gang on the first visit expressed our interest in any ancient structures or caves in the area. There were mentions of caves a long way across the valley which Judith and I explored on later trips. The Monks told us of another intriguing cave only a few miles away. It was the Horse Cave that I mentioned earlier. This was a cave—complex high on an escarpment which once would have been at the shoreline of an ancient sea. Much of it was collapsed with damage that suggested earthquake. But within its depths there were horse and human skeletal remains.

The Horse Cave

Walking out into the desert is the deepest experience day or night. On this occasion even the prospect of a long walk under a scorching sun did not deter us and we grabbed the chance. We hiked for a few miles over the fairly flat top of the escarpment. This averaged circa 550 feet height above sea level and is littered with perfectly round stone balls and iron ore fragments. The balls range in size up to 12 inches or more in diameter. When they are cracked open they reveal just below the surface, a perfect iron shell, and with a solid stone centre. We were told that some contain crystal at the core, but we didn't have the tools to go hunting. They were as hard as concrete. Towards the N.NW side of the escarpment, the edge is split and fragmented. In many places along its almost 10 mile length it has eroded to produce gullies and valleys out to the lower ground. Large boulders and slabs have either fallen from the face of the cliff, or occasionally from sections of the lower strata.

Our destination was one small valley which cut out beyond the escarpment to the Northern Valley. The Horse cave is located half way up the side of the right hand escarpment just as it turns the corner out of the valley. There is a deep cave also on the left hand side escarpment that is as hard to get to. We found an ancient iron horseshoe there too. The climb to the horse cave is very difficult. Below the cave entrance there is a long dangerous drop to the boulders and huge slabs which have broken away. It is necessary therefore to climb to the right, up two levels of marl slope. This leads to the cliff. A lengthy traverse along the cliff has to be accomplished while clinging for dear life to the crumbling ledges. At the cave entrance the ground opens out to a flattish area for several feet. It is obvious to see from the precipitous edge and the jigsaw of boulders and slabs lying below, how they once fitted together to give a very substantial entrance area leading to the cave. To the right and left of the cliff from the cave, there is plenty of boulder spoil from the upper part of the cliff, but it seemed as if it was only at the cave area where the fallen debris matched the cave level perfectly. This was maybe significant as you will read presently.

Inside, the cave is extensive. The chambers follow a natural meandering fissure which reaches high up through the escarpment. Passage is severely restricted however because of more giant fallen slabs of stone. In places therefore it is possible to stand upright with plenty of space and look around, but elsewhere it is necessary to crawl on hands and knees to get to other chambers formed from the fallen stone. An instant impression is that at one time, the cave must have been roomy and substantial. We already knew that significant changes had occurred to escarpments over the centuries from earthquakes, and this cave had most likely suffered that fate. We noted another strange feature of the cave. We would have taken many more pictures at the site. However some of the pictures displayed strange lighting/energy effects. On a next visit to the cave Judith and I came prepared with fresh batteries for both our cameras and a fresh set in use. To our amazement as we each tried to take pictures, the batteries plus reserve batteries to both our cameras had discharged to zero! When we returned to camp, the cameras worked fine again with more batteries from the same batch. It was easy to stir up dust in the cave from the powder and spoil on the ground. The true floor level was obscured to a depth of several feet in places and powerful lighting would have been needed to explore it properly. There was the ever present danger of hidden deadly scorpions and spiders. We explored as best we could and saw how the cave could easily have had passageway access to the escarpment high above. We wanted to see if there was another way into the cave through the fissure but our lack of equipment and the fallen rock made a search impossible. From what we saw, it was also improbable. The cave thankfully is in a Protectorate area and several permissions are needed to travel within miles of it. However, those who live closest are also the most to be trusted. Since the cave was found, it has been little disturbed. Visits to it are conducted with the utmost respect for its archaeology. The cave holds an important secret. Within its chambers, on the ground surface and surely still buried in its sediment, there are human and small horse bone remains. At least one human skeleton has been found among the bones, but no extensive dig has been conducted to determine what else lies beneath the dust. Upon examination, it was found that one horse leg bone still had an iron clad horse shoe. This shoe is highly unusual however. It is made of two parts. There is a plate which fits around the hoof and is cleated to the base plate of the shoe. It fits the hoof almost like a horse shoe slipper, but firmly fitted. The base plate is solid, and where the rear of the hoof ends, the plate curls up into a flat swan-neck shape. The metal looks like thin strong beaten iron. An instant speculation was that this type of shoe would give an animal double purchase over desert sand and undoubtedly a lot of extra speed..

How had all of them met their deaths? Could it have been as a result of a violent earthquake? Were they put to death? Or could all of them have drowned in an ancient catastrophe. How did at least one human, and horses, get into the cave in the first place? It is situated half way up a 550 feet high cliff face that can only be accessed on hands and knees after doing some rock climbing. The remains must pre-date the cave collapse, because the horses could not have navigated the entrance; assuming no other completely hidden entrance. Horses can't rock—climb, so it can be assumed they gained entry when the level outside the cave was either the mean ground level, or when it formed the shoreline of an old sea. There does not appear to be evidence of the ground-level having continued along the cliff, so possibly the cave originated as a sea cave and was utilised as a way station when the water receded sufficiently. The shore line would have provided good access. It is also possible in more recent times that the inhabitants could have been victims of foul play, but if so, why kill valuable horses?

Many dating clues may be found through earthquake research and in particular through a proper archaeological examination of the cave. More information may be gained from the nature of the horse shoe cladding. The final speculation would be that the cave was used in an ancient time when sea levels were 200 feet higher. People sheltered there with their horses and lost their lives in a faraway time, and it will be a tragedy if the cave system and its evidence are not properly explored. Its height above present sea level by the way, mirrors finds we made at similar heights over tens of miles of desert. The Horse Cave became the trigger for more research that linked to a better understanding of the ancient history of the Giza Plateau and the secrets beneath *its* surface.

There was another event towards the end of that first week in the desert which profoundly affected me. It opened me for the first time to the way and the humble spirit of the poorest people in Egypt and the story deserves to be reproduced here from our site.

The Man with The Broken Leg

While we were wandering about, exploring the site of the Monks I noticed someone who was clearly from outside the community. He was a short spindly, wizened Egyptian man, maybe in his late 50's. He had the demeanour of someone like a farmer perhaps who had put on his Sunday suit to visit . . . the same one that had been taken from the closet perhaps a dozen times in as many years for such purpose. It was as if the worker—Presence reached beyond the tired crease in his city trousers and the faded 60's pattern of his nylon shirt. If his clothes and his persona seemed odd and out of place in this savage, beautiful wilderness, there was something else about him more obvious that caught my attention. He was limping badly with a splint; holding his left leg as stiff as a board as he walked about in obvious discomfort. He looked extraordinarily out of place!

I asked one of our Monk friends to tell me about him. He explained, the man lived in a community many miles from there. He apparently made visits a couple of times a year to the desert Monastery, always seeming to catch a lift to the nearest roadway, at least 2 to 3 miles across the desert. He always opted to walk the last distance alone as the start of a sort of Soul-cleansing exercise for himself. He always felt he had to give best respect to the Monks by dressing, wholly inappropriately for the desert, in his finest clothes. There was a difference this trip. The man had broken his leg in two places.

In Egypt . . . unless you have the means and wherewithal to afford the best medical treatment for anything serious, and if you are one of the sub—classes, you do the best you can under the circumstances. For this man, the best was a simple splint, and a mile of bandage binding his leg from top to bottom. He had actually managed to get across the desert, on foot, in his state, just to merge with the Holiness on offer there. I was utterly amazed. I thought I had seen everything, but the story was far from over.

A few days later we had completed our work and reluctantly it was time to leave. Our four-wheel drive vehicles were all loaded. Our Police escorts had taken their seats inside. We said our goodbye until the next time and off we set. I have to tell you that when you see those film shots of vehicles in desert terrain, moving at high speed, and performing like a bucking raw stallion, they are not faked at all. The rocks and sand are uncompromising. They threaten to suck the tyres off the vehicle in one section, rip them out in another, or catapult them and the vehicle into the air in the next few yards. Momentum is the key. You keep your foot down, grab tight, brace yourself and pray! If you are lucky, your head will not bang against the roof or windows on the way.

We had travelled less than half the distance to the road when we looked up ahead in astonishment. There was the man with the broken leg, hobbling impossibly along through the sand and blazing heat, still wearing his Sunday suit, and carrying nothing but a plastic supermarket bag. We stopped the vehicles to give him a lift and did an immediate reshuffle. The man would sit in the back seat with me. He had to feed his splinted broken leg to rest along the side foot-well, and was satisfied to perch half on the seat, wedged between it and the driver's backrest.

We drove on and managed only to drive about 30 yards over an enormous sand dune. We took off into the air and landed with a bump and a loud scream of pain from our new passenger. He was nearly unconscious from the shock. It took many minutes for him to recover any composure at all.

I suggested a solution which was adopted. I reached my arm across from the nearside back seat to the driver's backrest and this formed something of a cradle. I draped spare clothing on my arm for extra padding. The man sat fully on the back seat, elevating his splinted broken leg at about a 45 degree angle to then rest it on my arm. This acted as a shock absorber and we were able to get to the road with as little pain to him as possible. At the road there was going to be a delay while we waited for our new Police Escort to arrive. This was convenient because it took a while to help extract the man and settle him at the roadside. Everyone was a bit preoccupied to sort the paperwork etc. so I stayed with him. He had hobbled over to the roadside to rest and recover. I called our guide to translate for a moment. I was concerned because the man had no transport. He had neither water nor provisions with him. The police and locals clearly had no cares about it. The man intended to just sit there and wait for the very occasional passing vehicle, hoping to get a lift. My heart went out to him as I saw the agony he was in.

I spoke to him using gesture. I raided our own store for spare bottles of water to give to him. He showed embarrassing deep gratitude to me, and downed half a bottle immediately . . . I caught a glance in his eyes and realised he had seen the huddle of our group as they had been lighting cigarettes. I got the feeling he wanted one too, but had none. I only had a plenty supply of finger rolling tobacco, so I was able to give him a pouch along with rolling papers and a spare cigarette lighter. I rolled a first one for us both. I thought he was going to faint with excited and humble gratitude when he realised I meant him to have them and keep them.

For a moment I was actually embarrassed at his reaction and the fuss he was making. Our Guide came over again to see what was happening. He translated the obvious to me . . . The man was humbled and overwhelmed at the kindness he felt was being given. I instructed our Guide to translate back to the man, that it was I who had to thank him for the opportunity, because he had taught me a lesson in humility.

The man struggled to rise to his feet from the sand. I helped steady him and he was weeping. He had nothing of value on him whatsoever, and he probably lived in a state of poverty that I would never experience. But there was one thing I learned he did consider valuable. Around his neck there hung a battered tin badge showing the worn image of the late, Saintly Coptic Pope Kyrillos (of miracles) He balanced on his good leg, lifted the old string from his own neck, and placed this prize over mine. I wept too as I felt the crushing weight of his faith and the Power of his humble Spirit. I have the badge beside me now as I type this. It is never far away, and still mists my eyes as I remember. I swear the eyes of Pope Kyrillos are watching me from the badge. The Man was truly blessed. He came with nothing, but had everything. We came with everything, but without his faith, we had nothing. It is a lesson I will never forget and I knew I was leaving the Monks and the desert far richer than I had been when we arrived.

The first week of the trip was a wonderful experience but produced no tangible evidence to help my companions in their quests. For me the pressure was less as I looked forward to the following week with Judith at the Great Pyramid. I was therefore able to reflect more deeply on the surroundings. The analogy for life was perfect as it was possible to stare into the distance of the desert and see only unbroken sand, while in reality the vista was broken with hidden gullies valleys and caves filled with history and so many kinds of wildlife. The human interaction with the Monks taught lessons too. Their environment was filled with life-threatening snakes, scorpions, spiders, jackals and other things. They walked far in the complete darkness of night and often for miles alone anyway, but without fear. They lived in complete harmony with their surroundings and none had ever suffered injury or poisonous bite. Father M. explained to us that the Monks lived with God and offered no harm to any creature, and therefore the creatures never troubled them—and in any case, they were all too big to make a meal for a scorpion or a snake.

Judith and I later shared in night time explorations, joining in with their loud songs and happy excitement as we sometimes walked miles with them to reach a new area for investigation. Our original gang visited their simple rock Church and after the service there was an animated discussion as each of us gave our reasons for being there. I was allowed to take photographs within the separated altar area and when I returned home I found I had captured thick swirling energy in the air. My mind went back to the Temple Grotto in Bethlehem.

Time with the Blessed Father

One evening before dark I was invited to an audience in the cave of Father E. who was in charge of all the Monks and with many more responsibilities in Cairo. He is a man of such loving Spirit and warmth. We were told by another monk that it was a surprising privilege to be invited to his personal cave as this was not something that usually happened. We spoke together at great length, discussing matters of Spirit, our lives and the world. I expressed my wish to return to the desert in future with Judith. I knew there was an absolute rule that no women were allowed within the community. In fact we had been told that when the renowned camel explorer Arita Baajiens came through the area in recent times, she made camp in the desert nearby.

I felt we were especially privileged therefore when Father E told me that Judith and I had his blessing to be there and we would be welcomed in the future. He was true to his word and on subsequent visits Judith and I shared the wonderful hospitality of the Monks and used the same guest cave from our first visit. Father E spoke of the new cave church which was being constructed further along the escarpment. The existing small cave church where our pictures had captured the amazing energy streams was too small. The roof was about head height, and a team of monks had been excavating a new much larger cave. The new cave excavation had tunnelled into a large seam which was still only a little over head height, and there was disappointment that it could not be created spaciously like a normal church. The only thing we saw that distinguished the cliff at this stage was a varying seam of up to several inches of rock crystal cutting along the line of the layers of ancient sediment. The roof was supported over about 3000 square feet by rock pillars which had been left strategically in place. One evening the monks had all just finished work when there was a tremendous fall of rock within the whole excavation. When the dust settled, the men began to excavate the fallen rock. They were blessed at the miracle they found. When all the rock had been cleared, they found that a huge stable cavern had been formed with a high oval domed roof, even allowing for a separated altar area at one end. In their minds there was no doubt in the fact that it was providence as an act of God.

Presently we concluded for the night and I took his warmth and generosity of Spirit with me. This would show itself again the following year when Judith and I needed help and direction. When we were arranging the trip I telephoned and managed to speak again with Father E to ask for advice. He knew of someone close to him but not a Monk, who was an expert desert driver. He told us to contact A and all arrangements would fall into place. So it was that we were directed to A and his family; especially his father Z. Through A we were taken on long memorable jeep safaris into the deep desert and to the cave homes of the Monks again and again.

Explosions in the Desert

Between this and subsequent visits by Judith and I, we became recorders of another unfolding story I entitled *Explosions in the Desert*. It seemed that some miles away at the other side of the valley, over 200 men during a two year operation had been trying to dynamite and excavate their way into a particular area of vast escarpment. This would have remained a mystery but for the fact of A being approached by a government hydrologist, wishing to hire his skills for a deep desert reconnaissance. He revealed that sites of special interest were secretly targeted for initial investigation from government satellite before a more involved archaeological team took over. In his case, an underground aqueduct made of stone had been detected beneath the desert. It ran apparently from nowhere to nowhere, starting in a distant desert mountain range and travelling for tens of miles into the desert. From this information we speculated the reason for the escarpment work. Perhaps it was that they had found something below ground using satellite technology. That work was halted abruptly when the worker's illegal excavation activities became an increasing intrusion to the Monks and the Protectorate area generally. Complaints escalated internally to the leadership of the Church and into Government. A person right at the top of the Archaeological chain was alleged to have been deeply implicated in the clandestine work ( ) and that it had been financed from another country.( )

We visited and inspected the whole area and our website presentation shows copious photos with much more descriptive detail. At another time we interviewed someone who was in charge of a working party just before the work was halted. We were told that a deep fissure which was investigated from a shaft they dug down into it, yielded a partially collapsed tunnel entrance travelling into the plateau. A stone frame and lintel with strange symbols were described to us, but the men were so spooked by what they found and because of the danger of the site itself, they were unable to pursue their exploration before their work was halted. The shaft was filled from a sand dune cutting across the top of the escarpment, and possibly the shaft was spared with a blocking trap to board it below ground level. We were told of objects that were excavated nearby made of green granite. ( ) There has been no conclusion to this story, yet!

From that first week visit to the desert, and then to the Saqqara pyramids to take measurements I had thought all would go smoothly when Judith arrived. Some of our group had to return home early but we found our inexperience of the ways of Cairo coupled with our inability to function comfortably alone there, meant that it was still a tourist experience for us. We aspired to do so much more, but that would wait until we returned again and again and again. However there was the one important validation which we sought and got in the Great Pyramid. Due to the style and effort of one of our group, G, we managed to gain a private pass into the GP to secretly to conduct our Out of Body experiment.

The Coffer Vision

Prior to the experiment, Judith and I visited the Kings Chamber casually the previous day. We went with no expectation but it was impossible to ignore the surging feeling of Spirit wind as we ascended the gallery and finally stood inside the Kings Chamber. No words were necessary as we both centred ourselves to the ambience of the place. Judith intercepted and engaged a man who was intent on disrupting me as I was powerfully drawn to stand facing North and a few feet back from the Coffer. I intoned and went to alpha and found myself quickly visioning something.

With eyes closed I still felt almost blinded with light. I caught the shape of the light in my peripheral vision left and right and extending away at forty five degrees. By analogy imagine a row of fluorescent tubes next to each other rippling into the distance. Imagine them angling away from about waist level like delta wings, where the leading edge from each wing would converge to a point in the middle distance ahead of you. It was as if the tubes were lighting in sequence to confer movement. The movement of light got faster and I saw that the expanding convergence point was very dark and becoming darker.

My whole focus went to the dark hole and as I stared at it, it suddenly turned a deep cobalt blue and I saw shapes silhouetted around the inner diameter of the hole. It was like looking at a scene through a powerful fish-eye lens. The image cleared and I saw foliage that I interpreted in my mind as like trees. I recognised the fish-eye perspective and saw in the distance of the skyline there were pyramid shapes and instantly knew I was seeing Home Planet again. I had been here Out of Body and in Lucid Dreams on other occasions. For me it is a place in the system of the Pleiades and has many pyramid structures miles high with polarised sides. I had given it the pet name of Home Planet many years previously because each time I had a lucid vision of it; I was moved with emotion and the feeling of distant belonging.

In that moment of recognition my mind switched to see a chamber high in the GP above us. I saw also a (levitation) access shaft within the chamber that I knew went very deep into the earth below the GP to other working chambers. Judith and I have had simultaneous OOBs in those chambers and we both came away with a knowingness of their content and use. I saw constructions in the centre of the Containment chamber; (another pet name.) I was completely aware of myself and understood how all that I was seeing tied to things shown to us in the past.

My vision darkened to the hole again and it transformed into a shape like a dimly glowing hollow orb; or from a distance like a miniature sun. But it was not really burning. The shell seemed to have the consistency of dense tightly woven wool? There was a pinprick explosion of light on its surface and in just the same way that a crumpled ball of soft tissue paper will continue to burn away from its source if touched with a cigarette, the burn on the orb spread away across the surface from its source on the shell. Simultaneously the orb began to expand and the energy burn spread exponentially across its surface. The energy was gaining, not dissipating. It was as if I was now in space and the orb was sun size and growing. In my head I knew the orb was synonymous with planet earth and the GP was connected with it in some way.

I literally spoke to myself in the vision and said, *'My god this is a Star Gate'* and I had an instant awareness that it was not just to enable Out of Body escape—but its use would be detected across the cosmos and would herald Pleiadean arrivals through the same portal. The realization and Wow factor for me was huge. As always when I lose my calm on these occasions I drop my vibration and snap back out. I was so annoyed with myself to have lost control, but even now I can still see the content clearly.

The Experiment in the Kings Chamber

It was the second week and we were in Cairo. There was only one thing on my mind and Judith's mind. It was to conduct our experiment in the King's Chamber. My party-piece since childhood was no longer a joking matter. I could intone a sound which in certain places would cause a deafening resonance. *(Download from our website)* I always just knew the sound was linked in some way to altered body states. In this case I believed that if the resonance could be reproduced in the Kings Chamber, it would help induce a Conscious Out of Body experience. Furthermore, the knowingness told me the ancients had concealed their knowledge—store in a way that could only be discovered Out of Body. This is what happened:

We had secured special permission to visit the Great Pyramid privately, but only because ZH had not arrived back from a trip to the USA. In the morning our motley group had been playing follow the leader to a guide specially appointed to us from the Director's office. We knew the guide was with us more to discover our plans than to play nursemaid on the plateau. We were all very pushy however and stretched the hospitality. This led to free entrance into off limits tombs and into the Solar Boat exhibition at the side of the Great Pyramid. Even with our reluctant permissions we detected a growing nervousness in our guide and in the official people we met along the way. He had taken and made several phone calls and apparently ZH was due back early and everyone was scared.

ZH had the final word in everything that happened on the plateau. Woes betide anyone who did not receive his permission first. We timed our approach to the right people while he was away and won our limited freedom. We wanted our private time in the Kings Chamber. We were going to be allowed plenty of time from the midday closing time to tourists, but ZH's impending arrival and the worker's paranoia cut our chances considerably.

We had not got off to a good start because when we arrived to the GP entrance, we found a guard there who was not the one that had been arranged. To our dismay, this one was doing a bit of freelancing himself. For a bribe, he had allowed an American couple to go alone up to the King's Chamber. They would be the last tourists before closing time. We nervously waited for them to vacate while *our* guide argued with the entrance guard nearby. We knew time was against us and decided to head into the pyramid regardless. We met the couple slowly descending as we more rapidly ascended.

Finally in the Chamber again, Judith and I looked across to each other. Our arrangements had been so messed up and I was in the wrong frame of mind. I was angry and frustrated. We had wanted a whole night there to do what we had to do. We were also supposed to have spent a week in deep preparation but the circumstances were against us H had agreed to take guard position at the top of the Grand Gallery and G was supposed to take guard at the entrance the Chamber. Our now limited time plus the other hold-ups had wound my brain into the very state it did not need to be. It was as if everything was being thrown at us to disrupt the one event in our lives we had been waiting for. The final straw was when G promptly lay down on the ground within the entrance passage and began reciting some kind of personal invocation. I finally blew my top and reminded him that I had helped him in the purpose of his visit in the first week to the desert, so why the hell was he compounding the opportunity of a lifetime we had been waiting for. (I may have used different language, but he did stop!)

I looked to Judith and I could see behind the frustration in her eyes. She was saying, *'We're here now. We have to at least give it a try.'*

I overcame myself and said to her, *OK let's do it*. I quickly gripped the sides of the coffer and lowered myself into a reclining position. The air was cold and coffer seemed bigger than I imagined. In seconds the years of practice kicked-in and I stilled my Presence. Judith also knew what she must do. As my twin flame, she would be my physical and vibrational guardian. She would try and stop me from being disturbed, and if I went too deep, she would be the one to bring me back safely again.

In an induced Out of Body state, the functions of the physical body are shut down to the barest minimum. There are great dangers from any physical disturbances while in that state, plus there is great danger if the projected Presence does not follow natural principles. As Thoth advises in the Emerald Tablets, one must always travel in curves, and never in angles. I could handle things out of body, but if there was a disturbing danger in the Chamber, Judith knew to say particular words to me that would alert me to break-off and snap back safely. However in that first minute as we began, Judith could not resist to take a photo snap of me in the coffer. I was already deep. The camera flash was like an electric shock. I jumped as I saw my own skeletal bones through closed eyes. I resisted the sensation and concentrated again. I began to intone. Judith had focussed back to the script and assumed her position by the coffer in linked meditation with me.

I already knew from our previous visit with the tourists that my throat sound could set the chamber ringing. I had carried the weird party-piece with me all my life where the sound sometimes produced an harmonic resonance in other places. The volume would crazily increase without any effort. I felt the vibration fold back to me as the coffer and the whole Chamber began to vibrate like a tuning fork. As I reached the end of my breath to draw another one, the sound did not decay. I continued intoning, breath by breath. At each breath it increased the volume and I was aware the whole Chamber was booming louder than any sound I had ever heard.

My mind was telling me I should stop because the returning sound waves felt like they would burst my head. I could actually feel the pressure of the sound on my skin. I continued and I felt my body start through the stages to lift me out. It happened quickly, but this time it was very different. There is a meditation technique for OBE to withdraw from the body while reclining, by imagining you are in a tank being slowly filled with water. As the imaginary water slowly creeps up the body it acts like a total anaesthetic. In the coffer with no effort, it felt as if my body was slowly crystallising from the feet upwards. I could feel the cells in my body changing as the crystal wave swept slowly up through me. I felt the familiar floating sensation and I knew I was heading close to breakout. I was as deep as I had ever been and yielded completely to the process.

Unknown to me in that moment, the startling effect of the intonement made sure we were about to be interrupted. There was drama in the Grand Gallery as H had been unable to halt the armed police who were rushing towards the chamber.

At that point, my senses were disturbed by a voice that seemed a long, long way away. I fought the intrusion, but the voice intruded more. My concentration was disturbed as I heard my name and the words being called over and over. At some point the intrusion broke through. I snapped back and opened my eyes to the sight of Judith now quietly but firmly saying to me,

'Richard, Richard, you have to stop. They are coming with guns with guns'

The Chamber was still reverberating so loudly that we could hardly hear our own voices . . .

I could only have woken to Judith's voice because I was primed to it, but it had taken a long time for her to get a response. It was only when she reached to me and put her hand on my shoulder that I responded. She was helping me to my feet and out of the coffer as the first guard burst into the Chamber, then another, both brandishing automatic weapons in our direction.

I was becoming angry again. I was totally disorientated and my head was pounding. As the other guard arrived I saw their faces were ashen. They were clearly scared. The first guard was screaming at us and frantically motioned towards the entrance with the point of his gun barrel. I still had no idea what had happened and allowed myself to be bundled along in the hands of Judith; though she was also disorientated. Two more armed guards had caught up and were waiting in the gallery. Their faces matched the first two. They were also hyper agitated. Our other watchful colleagues in the Grand Gallery had followed their orders and were nearly at the bottom of the gallery waiting for us to catch up. Under the barking orders of our escorts we made our way down the walkway while the sound from the booming chamber slowly decayed behind us.

From H I picked up the story. The louder and louder resonance had carried down the gallery and out to the plateau. It had taken tourists and guards outside by surprise, and for the guards it turned to shock as they realised there was some kind of experiment taking place inside the Great Pyramid without top authority—and it might discovered. We had been foiled before completing the job. Clearly it was not our time, and now we knew there were other refinements to make. Below the main entrance, tourists were gathered to see what was happening and thankfully the guards seemed satisfied to see us just melt away amongst them.

It is difficult to be exact about the time we eventually spent in the Kings Chamber. Time itself seemed distorted there. It probably took longer to reach and return from the Chamber than the time of action. It was enough to provide a validation I had waited most of my life to receive. One function of the Chamber was indeed to assist the process of an induced Out of Body journey. But, we knew this was only part of the story, and an even smaller part of the solution.

We had plenty of time to think about what had happened as we recovered from the adventure. Judith and I had kept our full story from even our colleagues, because the journey to this point was so fantastic we were sure no one would ever believe us unless we produced astonishing proof from our task. Even before we ever set foot in the GP we were fully aware of undiscovered chambers in the pyramid. Off to the side beyond the walls of the Kings Chamber there is the passage that raises to higher levels, and of course the separate shaft that links deep down into the earth. This connects to chambers and passages below. I remembered them as they had been to me many times when we visited them out of body. As we visioned the shaft there was only one way to negotiate it naturally which involved a form of energetic elevation. Much later, from trusted sources in Nazlet, we would receive information that verified their existence; even without our sources knowing of my visits there.

We speculated how we should now proceed. We had no idea of the greater adventures that were waiting for us on the Giza plateau and in the deep desert. For now we would be taking stock and remembering the incredible synchronicities that brought us there and how we could complete the task. I will return in a moment to what happened next, but it is worth recalling some of the things that led to this adventure, and to the basic understandings behind it.

Judith and I have shared a private motivation which has been pivotal to our activities in Egypt. It has been there since our pathways came together in this life. It also has its roots in the supernormal experiences I have had since childhood; and especially in a culminating experience I had nearly three decades ago; my *Event*. During this profound experience I had the total recall of a lost memory that exposed the detailed workings of creation through quantum and beyond. It went much further to explain the workings of a living reality beyond physical life, and the role we play in it. The things I experienced such as manifestations, precognitions, incredible synchronicities, clairvoyance, journeys out of the body, automatic writing and more, were now to be understood.

My Birth Plan for Egypt along with Judith emerged from our lifetime of opportunities and choices . . . My probabilities therefore helped me form all my choices of association to fulfil its purpose. It certainly brought me together with my twin flame Judith, even though we live thousands of miles apart. The result is the story summarised briefly here. The first part of this book is the Mechanic's manual for anyone else to follow. It would allow others interested in the mystery aspects of life and the nature of the cosmos at all levels to hopefully bypass many other books and get right to the heart of the matter themselves as it did for me. The ancients lived the knowledge I had been privileged to recall, and I know now it would be impossible for anyone to perform the coffer task without an understanding that matched our predecessors.

The Intonement Recording

After returning home from our experiment trip I was naturally overcome to understand the detail of the outcome. I knew the attempt had served its purpose as a validation, despite the fact that we were prevented from completing the process. I meditated and prayed to my minders for new inspiration. So it was then that one night I woke from another lucid dream. In it I could see the intonement represented like vibrating particles in the air repeating in a circle. It revolved round and round in the air like a vortex, and then into a disc shape. In ancient times, subjects were assisted by trained helpers who were able to enhance the intonement frequencies artificially using musical instruments. I knew although our efforts proved a validation of the process, we would be more likely to succeed if I did not have to produce the sound myself. Ideally my senses should be totally undisturbed. The dream snapped me awake with the solution.

I turned to the telephone directory and found there was a recording studio not far from where I lived. I made arrangements. Before long the intonement sound had been captured, analysed, and laid down to CD disc in a loop. If I got the chance again, I would be able to play the intonement continuously from speakers, and with greater initial volume. I would be able to use my own intonement while being properly free for the experiment. At the studio we found the intonement was from a range of frequencies that hit the standing frequency of the Kings Chamber and the coffer. We were ready to return, but now we needed something small and powerful to play the CD in the chamber. We went hunting for a CD player and speakers thinking it would be such a difficult task to find the right equipment. The first store we visited was specialist to computers and electronics and we could find nothing portable and adequate, but just as we were about to leave I spotted one product which was perfect. It comprised two miniature speakers which packed together into a pouch. They were powerful and had their own volume controls and seemed ideal to take into the chamber. The CD player was no problem and would attract no attention. At home the setup worked perfectly. We were consumed with the urge to be back in Egypt. We thought the doors would be opened to us completely on the next visit. We could not wait to the following year. In the September of the same year we were once again in the chamber armed with our new equipment. However, I noticed a difference immediately. I tried as soon as we entered to intone and test the vibration. The chamber did not ring in the same way. I adjusted my frequency and got a better reaction.

I realised the frequency of the whole chamber had shifted slightly. I got my chance in the coffer but my intonement from the speakers failed to hit the exact frequency. We were very disappointed as we realised the rumours of ZH conducting secret tunnelling above and around the chamber must have been true—and his work had caused a shift in the resonance of the whole chamber!

    I asked myself the question: If it had suited our plan simply at this stage to get a validation of the possibilities from the chamber, then what on earth were we meant to do next? We seemed to be blocked. We need not have been worried because adventures since these visits have steered us full circle with a far greater perspective and understanding of what secrets are to be found in plain sight within the pyramid structure. We realised we were being taken on a curved route, and would return to where we began. Furthermore, our trip was to yield more surprise adventure lessons for the future!

The Capstone Experiment

So now it was our second visit. We had arrived to the company of our friend J and his wife who had also returned and would overlap the start of our visit by a few days. During those days we were in hot contact with a few friends who themselves had been involved with black ops. We were sometimes fed helpful information. In the first few days we were informed by R from the group about a particularly influential stellar triangulation relating to the GP. The prevailing energies would apparently be heightened at a specific time the next night. We were very interested and when we discovered we could reproduce the triangulation on the ground we decided upon an experiment. Ideally we needed to get to a coordinate which lay distant but still within the confines of the Giza Berlin Wall. Within the hours of the time we were targeting, our arrangements broke down so we had to compromise. Our corner hotel complex was in sight of the GP. We managed to gain access to the very high roof. Our idea was that Judith and I would assume positions apart from each other and try for a combined OOB experience focusing at the peak of the GP. A comparison of our experiences may then provide further cross validations for our journey. The experiment exceeded our expectations.

I will give my own recalled details but afterwards before we spoke together we had written notes to test the comparison. Our recollections were similar. I found a ledge at the edge of the roof in direct line to the GP. I lay down and at a synchronised time with Judith in her chosen spot, we commenced the process. I found myself standing on the platform of stones at the top of the GP. I was completely aware of the Presence of Judith there also. I could see there were solid square metal sections like iron girders triangulating from the corners of the pyramid and rising to an apex point above. As I adjusted to the vibration I saw they were not metal but more like solid dark smoked glass or crystal. The triangular side sections became dimmer and I realised I was looking from the inside through polarised sides just the same as the sides of the huge pyramid structures on our Pleiadean home planet. I became aware of a vibrational/spirit wind from beneath me. The rush grew stronger and I felt a river of energy gathering strength and rushing up through the GP. It was fearsome and would have ripped me from my position but for the fact that I seemed rooted to the rock. I looked up and the apex structure was replaced with the sight of the energy river transforming into rushing cloud stream high above me. It was like being in the fastest river possible and was awesome.

I saw how the energy in the form of boiling rushing clouds was spreading out in a swirling expanding donut shape filling the sky as far as the eye could see. In my mind I remembered it looked like a huge smoke ring, or like the rotating torus I had seen at my *Event*. The experience was mind-blowing but I did not feel threatened by the power of it.

At some point the flow of energy seemed to effortlessly change and reverse direction. Now the Torus was spewing energy back through its centre like a Pulsar down through me into the pyramid and the rock beneath it. It surged and rushed like a spiralling tornado. I looked down to see where it was flowing and felt myself being drawn into the flow. I could not resist this time and in a second I was inside the energy stream gushing down through the pyramid. In my mind I was completely aware of myself within the experience. I remember the excitement building inside me as I realised I was being carried to the energy source.

As always it is a flawed thing to allow excitement in one of these experiences. My energy began to ground and I knew in an instant what would happen even before it happened. My next awareness was of sitting bolt upright on the ledge, fully awake, gasping and cursing my lack of control. Eventually Judith and I spoke together and we were satisfied as expected at the similarities of our experience. For us it was just another personal validation and a reminder that we were still following our correct probability path together. However the wider meaning of the experience reached far deeper to help the awakening process of our ancient memories.

As I have indicated already, this trip was to hold many surprises. It was as if the universe had been saving it all up for us so that we would get the message for sure. When J and his wife returned home we were on a loose end. We were overwhelmed and wanted to know and experience more and more. However we reaffirmed together that our method was to pray and command for everything, but then to be satisfied with the synchronicities that would be faithfully arranged from a higher place to assist our journey. It would not be long before our trust would be rewarded once again.

The Mysterious Bedouin

On a following day we entered the Plateau from the North entrance near the Mena. We had nothing planned and no expectations beyond trust. We had not even reached the top of the road close to the GP. We noticed off to the right there was a very tall Bedouin in a brown full length galabeya. His arms were tucked into opposite sleeves. I wonder if readers know the experience when you just know when someone; a stranger—is going to speak or interact with you. This was one of those occasions. Just before we drew closer to him there was a pathway on the right, cutting towards the tombs of the Western Cemetery and leading to a large Mastaba. He was a few feet away and beckoned to us to come closer to him. By now we were hyper—wary of touts and sellers and would normally have just given him a brush off. But we both saw and felt he was different in some way. He beckoned and started walking up the path with us following. At the Tomb he indicated to the entrance. It did not seem to matter or impede us that there were other tourists milling about. At the entrance, he disappeared for a second around the corner and another older man in western clothes appeared' He greeted us warmly in heavily accented English and beckoned us to follow him now. The wow factor was building again. We looked to each other with a common feeling that we must go along with whatever was happening. The man proceeded to give us a normal but detailed tour of the building; elaborately explaining everything within it. Finally we were back at the entrance and I began to feel guilty and anxious. This man had given us an excellent information tour even if we had not asked for it. I thought I must reward him even though we had little spare money. I reached into my pocket and indicated I wanted to give him something for his efforts. He reacted very forcefully to stop us from doing so and we knew he would be offended if we persisted. We thanked him warmly as he indicated for us to continue on our way.

We had little time to think because as we stepped from the entrance the tall Bedouin was still standing off to the side on the high ground. He beckoned to us again to come to him. We obeyed and he led off away from the tourists and down alongside the Mastaba. We were within the first line of Tombs and Mastabas of the Western cemetery. He stopped and showed us forwards. I protested, *'No, no, the police will stop us.'*

We had learned how vigilant the camel and tourist police could be. Normally they would pounce on anyone who so much as stepped outside the pathways they designated for the tourists. The Bedouin finally spoke in good accented English. He told us to take our time; to enjoy our time there, and no one would disturb us.

We looked out over the ruins. There was not another soul in sight. We were nervous, but half the reason was excitement from the continuing wow factor. We looked back and the Bedouin was gone. Cautiously at first, we began to explore. We wandered freely among the constructions for the next few hours taking in everything we saw. At one stage we stopped for a meditation break. We could see through gaps in the line of tombs, to the tourists by the thousand on their assigned pathways. They were only a short distance from us but may as well have been on another planet. The place we finally rested blocked any tourist view but gave us a fantastic close view of the side of the GP. We took many photographs and we were only restricted from exploring the deep shafts by our lack of equipment. There was another exciting moment when we turned a corner and almost walked into two camel police who were also resting. Next to them a saddled camel squatted on the ground. It made loud grumbling noises when we appeared but the camel police were indifferent to our presence. One of them indicated that the camel had stomach ache and not to go near. They signalled for us to take whatever photographs we wanted and made no reaction when we continued on with our exploration. We also stumbled across a path between tombs where one tomb was being used as a horse stable. The stable boys were completely casual and friendly and happily introduced their horses. They posed for photos and made absolutely no effort to ask for reward. Eventually we were satisfied with the information and photographs we had gathered and made our way back towards the road. We realised what a privilege we had been given, as we immediately saw camel police preventing other tourists from stepping a few yards off the road towards the Mastabas. We were dazed by what had happened. We wandered completely off the road again close to the West of Kephren, still expecting the police to pounce on us at any time. We sat to rest and meditate again for a few minutes.

The Rock Dog

Judith and I agreed we seemed to under some kind of extraordinary influence that day, but we still debated if it was just our imagination. I sent out a thought to my Minder on another level for a sign to show it was true. I turned to Judith and over her shoulder I saw a rock close-by that had the uncanny profile of a jackal or dog. It could only be seen from one particular angle. I had to ask Judith to sit in my exact position before she saw it too. In itself this may not seem too remarkable but there was another part that linked to the story.

Previously while walking the Plateau beyond the other side of Kephren, way out in the open ground leading to Menkaure, we had spotted movement. We approached and found a tiny feral puppy. It was in beautiful condition and its sand coloured fur was as smooth as silk, but it was distressed. Judith comforted it as we debated how on earth it had arrived there to be completely alone and nowhere near other dogs or cover. It was very young and not yet capable of looking after itself. From afar, two local youths approached us. Their interest had been drawn to these two tourists whose attention was given to something they had found. We began to speak to the boys but they were pushy and aggressive. They saw the puppy and wanted us to give it up to them. We refused and they even tried to snatch it.

Some distance away I saw a tourist policeman and sidestepped the boys and loudly hailed him. The boys were mouthing—off in Arabic as the Policeman approached us. He spoke no English but it was not difficult with sign language to explain what was happening. He shouted angrily at the boys and sent them off with a harsh warning that was obvious for anyone to understand. He indicated *he* would take the puppy and it would be ok where he was taking it. We gave it up, but still with some misgivings. Now we can return to the story where we were having our rest-stop off-road by Kephren. We were amazed at the sign of the Rock Dog and took photographs. We recounted finding the puppy. However the story is even more fantastic if I explain that later as we rounded on the same side of Kephren near where the puppy incident took place, we stumbled on a boulder where the ground had been hollowed out underneath. It was a den, and a row of feral puppy heads appeared into the open to check us out. We gave up what food we had and improvised a cut bottle to leave water at the den.

This must have been where the lone puppy had originated, even if we still had no idea how it had travelled so far away from the den on its own. It was impossible to tell which one had been the lost puppy, but for sure the policeman knew about the den and returned the lost one to its home.

An Introduction to the Underground

We set off on our ramble again and saw an efficient camel policeman clearing tourists back to the road ahead of us. We were still off-road but he went past us with a nod and left us alone. We wandered along the path and made a detour behind Menkaure. It was late afternoon and there seemed to be few others about. From nowhere we were approached directly by another short Arab,(LM) He greeted us in a familiar friendly way just like the Bedouin earlier, and with accented halting English we began conversation . . . He said he knew us and had been expecting us! The Wow factor for us was now off the scale. We were truly baffled at the situation.

On our first visit to the Plateau earlier in the year we had been introduced and made friends with all the main Officials at the Administration House and Police Barracks not far from the GP roadway entrance. We had obtained our permission for the GP access at the time and many photographs were taken with the people we met. We had brought some of the photographs back with us for identification purposes. At the meeting behind Menkaure we were carrying some of them. LM was rabbiting on about a previous incident which we couldn't make sense of. He indicated across the Plateau in the direction of the Offices so then we remembered the photos and produced them.

There was one young man at the Administration Office we had struck a meaningful conversation with about matters of spirit and the ancients. He had told us he was one of the plain clothed police guards for ZH when he was on the Plateau. We had been drawn to him because despite his close link to ZH it was obvious he was a deeply spiritual person. Immediately, when LM saw the picture he validated the Policeman's name and told us he was the young man's father. We never discovered why LM had been expecting, or waiting for us. Everything that day happened so spontaneously and fast that we were bowled along. We had time much later to speculate the why's and wherefores' but by then it was too late to ask directly. At the time, LM was intent on showing us something and set off at a pace.

He took us on a tour of the restricted areas of the quarry and rock cut tombs to the South East of Menkaure and Khafre. We saw deep shafts and tunnels below ground. We saw the ones that linked to the complex below the GP and far beyond. As we trotted behind him from fantastic stop-to-stop, I engaged in conversation with him as Judith followed behind taking photographs. I had to keep asking her to calm down when I heard a big Wow each time we were shown something fantastic and new. We came to a large section of the cliff tombs where a substantial barbed wire barrier enclosed a large area. LM showed us a safe way through the barbed wire and immediately we saw it was also a Police control post. There were many policemen milling about inside the restricted area. I turned and said to Judith that we were likely going to be chased away for sure. It was not hard to recognise the Police Chief. We had previously seen him at the Police HQ next to the GP offices, and he is a big imposing man. LM walked over to him and we have no idea what was said but LM returned to us with the Chief. They exchanged a few more words and the big man reached out to shake our hands with a big smile and wished us a good stay. He then left us to get on with it!

LM took us down a columned side alley which could not be seen from above, nor from any tourist vantage point. He indicated and we followed. We went down into levels below ground sliding and climbing through the dust and darkness with little light to help. At one final point he stopped us abruptly. He had gathered a sheet of newspaper from somewhere and proceeded to set it on fire with his cigarette lighter. Directly in front of us from the light we could see we stood in front of a huge deep shaft. We were already at least three levels below ground and as LM dropped the burning newspaper down the shaft we wondered how deep it plunged. The newspaper and the flames disappeared deep into darkness before we could guess any idea of its depth. I felt like a child who had been given the cookie bag. We were not even surprised when we learned that Mark L. and his excavation team were elsewhere on just that day. Our guide moved some builder's planks in a tomb not far from where Mark had recently been excavating. From beneath the planks we were able to view directly down two deep square shafts to see clear squared intersection tunnels at an apparent pristine junction below ground. LM told us this was an underground intersection where the tunnels led out into the labyrinthine network under the plateau. He told us of shafts which descended from some places in these tunnels to much greater depths and that there were wonderful things there. This specific information was validated independently to us a couple of years later when we spoke with a new friend in the village who had worked with ZH and the teams for 30 years.

We were shown towards another entrance only a short distance from the Sphinx and the milling tourists where inflatables had been dragged through a sump to negotiate the underground lake everyone had heard about. It would mean a trek across the middle Plateau to get to the place and LM was intent to take us to the exact location The time by now was getting late and Judith shared my anxiety for another very important meeting we had arranged that day with a very senior Coptic Father and friend. We were in a terrible dilemma because to have inspected an actual entrance to the underground which had been explored would have been the cherry on the cake for us. We stopped to have a conversation with LM and explain how time was against us to continue and be able to fulfil our meeting on the other side of Cairo. He understood and said it was right that we keep our appointment; and it would be ok anyway because we would return—and we would meet with him again in the future!

We realise now, all these things were simply validations to increase our knowledge and understanding of the past in preparation for the future. We didn't realise these adventures were just the tip of experiences in Egypt that would overwhelm us over the next few years. Everybody we encountered who may have been a barrier had melted away before us. We photographed where we wished. Our first visit was just our introduction to the next ten years. The second trip drew us back to the desert and revealed the probability of a lost history waiting to be discovered. Then later we were steered into the deep of the Plateau where we experienced things that people do not get to see even after years of exploration. On the first week of the second trip we privately visited the Labyrinth at Hawara before the latest surveying was to be carried out. Then we were off on an almost mystical visit to the deep Western desert, guided by A and our Coptic friends. It is utterly impossible to adequately describe the sheer power and beauty of the desert beyond experiencing it first-hand. It took us by surprise every visit, even following previous visits. First there is the feeling of complete insignificance when faced with the vastness of it. Then there is the calm; when the vehicles have been left behind along with the road and the caves. Even when there is a group of you together, it is impossible to prevent a silence from descending. Chat slows, chat stops and it is as if you acquire super hearing for sounds never heard before. The wisps of wind; the unique sound of sand grains alive and shuffling across the surface; the cry of a distant hawk; the crack of a rock in the heat; the crunch of sand powder beneath the feet; the clink as a shard of space iron is kicked against another piece; the sound of your own breathing and heartbeat. The feeling of insignificance is replaced with a feeling of greatness as the atmosphere sucks you into its Presence. There is no environment we have known to compare, and we have been deeply affected to leave it each time of departure. The Monks live the daily blessing of this environment and share it willingly with all. I wrote about one brief occurrence in the wilderness which captures the feeling.

A Handful of Sand

Have you ever picked up a fistful of sand?
You know what I mean—like when you are on the beach, or in the garden or somewhere. A handful of sand; held just long enough to make a connection to it before you scat it back to the ground. We were deep in the Western Desert and I had a handful of sand.

The Sun reached over my shoulder and I noticed the sparkle here and there as specs of rock—quartz reflected the light back into my eyes. The texture was mixed and it was powder dry. I angled my hand slightly to study the piece of flat shell that was mixed in with it. I knew the shell was old; very old! We had just uncovered several inches of sand from a crystallised fossil. It was a big fish; a Coelacanth or something similar. Teffi said that maybe it was complete and, if we could dig it out we would see!

A Couple of scaled pieces had broken away like lumps of sandstone covered in fine crystal. Malai said, 'Yes, take some; there are many here,' as if it was the most natural thing in the world to say. 'We can dig, next time you come'. We had been taking a break, and now we returned to it and silence. I noticed how beautifully the colour of their Monk's robes contrasted the deep beige of the sand. I saw how Judith's boot made a scoop in the sand when she sat down—and as the grains of sand slipped back to surround it again I wondered if they would slip inside as a keepsake . . . In front of us and behind us the valley merged to the horizon. The illusion of monotony ironed out the dunes and hills into Flatness and Distance.

I went back to my handful of sand.
The absolute perfect stillness probably only lasted a few seconds before someone spoke again. But I noticed it. It was just for a few seconds that were timeless. It was as if in that moment the desert and the ancient fish had joined with us to give a collective sigh. I felt the force of God; the Source, move closer—and I grabbed the Moment. It still lives fresh with me now when I close my eyes and link to it. The ancient fossil didn't fix the precious moment for me. It was the vast desert in a simple a handful of sand.

Lost to the Desert

The Desert had a profound effect on us and was to consume us on the next visit. We were interested in the time long before traditional history. Our personal beliefs hold to an advanced civilization which was almost completely wiped out or buried following ancient catastrophe. Our added research in the meantime was sufficient to convince us we should be searching the desert at a height among the escarpments and mountains which reflected possible water levels after the last ice melt. We speculated these levels centring around 200 feet would yield clues or evidence. Our suppositions were rewarded with a visit to Abu Lifa in the vicinity of Fayoum which I describe later; and to the Horse Cave site near the Monk's home. Many other distant sites that we explored gave extra confirmations. We gathered fossilised bones that were wedged between boulders brought down from the entrance of one huge cave complex. We believe these are from a large extinct creature, but they await positive identification. We want to explore the whole system properly in a later trip, along with other very high cave systems where we would need specialist climbing equipment. We slept on the sand under the inky black sky with the stars so clear and close that we wanted to just reach out and grab them. Every morning the sand around us was decorated precisely with twin tracks from many visiting scarab beetles. We saw them rarely unless we searched the grass outbreaks. In the morning we were often woken by a desert fox within yards of our bivouac; attracted to the dates and figs we left out to attract them.

We helped with the digging of a new remote hermitage cave for a monk friend, and we explored all over the immediate surroundings. He had invited us to visit the location of his new home. It was a walk of several miles across the valley to a fresh place of solitude. Initially he had found a fissure more than half way up the side of a high escarpment. Access was via an erosion slope that would rival the biggest sand dune. It was a hellish climb to get up to the rock wall, but from the top we were surprised to find the slope levelled out to a fairly flat approach. The leading edge was marked by a huge group of rocks that had broken from the escarpment above us. They were easily visible from the valley floor but the fissure was well concealed in the background.

We stayed overnight with NF inside the fissure He had fashioned a door at its entrance and although inside, fallen sections made deep exploration impossible, NF had shaped a rock platform as a living and sleeping place. We had our sleeping bags and we would bed down on the squashed but levelled floor at the entrance. By the light of the fading day, NF worried us when he told of the snakes and rats he shared his home with. He reassured us that he saw them sometimes but they never caused him harm. We didn't know how much he was having fun with us and we were wary when we finally lay to sleep.

I was stirred in the night by the flicker of a candle from the platform where NF was sleeping. He was sorry he had disturbed me and whispered it was ok, but he had been woken by one of his friends nibbling his toe! To be honest I was so intoxicated by the ambience that I was not concerned. I knew I would not sleep more. My limbs were aching from the stone under our beds and I tiptoed outside without disturbing the others.

I walked over to the boulder peak and climbed nearly to the top and found a comfortable position to simply rest and meditate. That time was also magical for me but more so as we approached sunrise. The sky went through a whole spectrum of colour change even before the sun broke the horizon. But some while before this, my concentration was diverted when I heard the howl of a jackal, high on top of the escarpment. I listened keenly and heard another howl from further away. It was just like a plaintiff wolf call. The call and return continued for a while like a canine conversation and I couldn't resist the opportunity to try and imitate them. I cupped my hands and did my best to mimic their howl. The other calls stopped for a couple of minutes so I repeated my call. After a while, first from one location and then another, the calls were returned. I kept going until I heard no more calls and so returned to my moment with the sunrise.

It was a short while later when there were stirrings from the cave. Judith had missed me and came to look. NF followed and together they joined me to welcome the sunrise. I was eager to share my experience about the jackals and expressed I was surprised that they had suddenly vanished. However OS revealed something new. He explained he often spoke with them and there was a narrow path from the top of the plateau that led down to the level of the fissure. NF often left food out for them and he volunteered to show us. Only a short distance from where I had been sitting there were fresh dog track tracks in the sand. NF said the jackals had responded and came to have a look. We learned they would only let anyone see them when they became more familiar. It was enough to know we had at least made contact with them.

Further around the cliff face where it was even more inaccessible, NF had begun to hew a new cave from the rock. He had toiled on it for a very long time and so far there was a short tunnel entrance leading into a small chamber. Then from another face of the cliff around the corner he had been working on a second tunnel which would join to the chamber for air flow and light. The other tunnel was many yards long and must have taken incredible effort. There were only several inches to break through for it to join with the cavern and he was glad to let me wield the big iron spike he had used and help to make the breakthrough. I worked at it for a couple of hours and marvelled not only for how tough the rock was, but at the amount of effort it had all taken. Eventually exhausted I managed to get the first breakthrough and the refreshing air began to flood through. We were guests of NF in following years and by then he had turned the small cave into living quarters with a substantial chapel burrowed away through another tunnel link inside. There were two additional air tunnels from the cliff face and all together the site was now a masterpiece which the other Monks sometimes visited to bring needy items and to meditate in prayer. Years later inside the NC2 system we were particularly reminded of the desert when we saw strange markings on one wall. They had similarities to something we found on the high escarpment on the side of the wide valley not far from the cave home of NF . . .

The Strange Desert Petroglyph

This high escarpment is vast; stretching 10 miles x 5 miles. Less than a mile from where it noses to one end, it appears almost as if the cliffs have been pinched together from both sides to form a narrowed section about half a mile wide. It is as though a giant hand has raked a 75 feet deep Saddle across this narrowest point. The escarpment was clearly the victim of ancient water power. The limestone ground surface of the saddle is deeply striated and even in the semi-darkness when we first visited, it was clear this anomaly was formed from the rush of water and not from sand and wind erosion.

A foot trodden pathway meanders down from the higher escarpment either side of the saddle and is lost as it crosses the hard striated limestone. However, a little way before the path drops down to the saddle on one side, there is a large petroglyph on the ground which appears to have been deliberately created on a prepared platform. It appears to be a gathering of strange symbols. Arguably it could be natural, but straight logic told us the circumstances of its creation must have been extraordinary. Its position is remote but we returned there in daylight and found it to be even more astonishing. It seemed as if it had once been larger. Around its edges its shape was eroded. We played the *'what if?'* game.

If it was writing in pictorial relief, what could be its purpose? The saddle and the sea washed cliff caves on its steepest approach had been created by the rush of water for sure. The sea level we propose would have been at the right height at the time of the ice age melt when Giza was an island, and must have been subject to big tidal swings. Furthermore, if there was a sea level at this height, the narrow nose of the escarpment would have offered an amazing sight. On one side it would have commanded the entrance to the narrow blind valley and on the other side would have looked out over an inland sea stretching several miles. It is now a wide flat, sea level valley. The blind valley would have been perfect as a harbour, with the escarpment nose as a perfect lookout position.

We had this in mind with our research and we uncovered other intriguing signs to support the idea. So much waits for deeper investigation. At the innermost part of the blind valley on our escarpment side we discovered faint satellite traces of anomalous squared shapes on the ground like building outlines. This is the general area also where the secret explosive diggings were conducted. It is the general area of the Horse Cave, the unexplored giant cave complex mentioned before, and a few other additional possibilities.

We visioned the scene in ancient times for someone standing on the final nosed part of the escarpment. It would not be barren as now. There would have been lush vegetation. The escarpment would have been much enlarged prior to natural erosion over the millennia. From a lookout position, the larger tides would have filled the sides of the escarpment up to the saddle, sloshing against the cliff from the greater sea side to create the obvious sea caves we explored. At that point below the saddle the topography of the desert is curious because there seems to be a huge hollowed bowl which would fit with a whirlpool or eddy effect from water gushing almost like a gigantic waterfall across and down from the saddle. On the saddle itself the raked limestone is consistent with tidal water surging across it from the main sea to the blind valley sea. It would have presented a magnificent spectacle. The area of the petroglyph is a platform cut above the saddle by a few yards and possibly would have been above the average tide race beneath it. A pictorial sign or message would have been very useful to instruct the best times to cross safely from the nose to the main body of the escarpment. Such speculation places the whole anomaly back beyond 10,500 years. As said, the escarpment is miles in area, with fissures, caves and other anomalies on its surface. It has never been systematically explored especially with these possibilities in mind. Recently at home I had the idea to apply the analysis techniques I developed with the NC2 photographs to the batch of photographs we have of the petroglyph. As with all photographs we have taken everywhere, we followed the natural instinct to identify a central subject for the photograph, even as in the case of NC2 where these were just general pictures of the tunnel and cave system. People do not normally range their camera to take pictures of apparently bland surfaces of ground, walls, or ceilings. I can reveal: We believe we have captured animal images imprinted to the limestone surface on the rock surrounding the petroglyph just as we did inside NC2. These must now be validated with the capturing of properly targeted pictures of the anomaly and its surroundings. We await our chance to return there.

Senior Connections & The Holy Family

Back in Cairo we were introduced to an extraordinary man, the father of our desert guide. He had been aide to a former loved President of Egypt, and still commanded great respect in high circles. In his earlier years he had privately conducted a substantial study of the Holy Family journey in Egypt. He was especially interested in our involvement with the Coptic community and our connection to the ancient knowledge. He told us of the Osiris Chapter of the Rosicrucian's, disbanded officially in Cairo, but with highly influential members still active behind the scenes. In fact we were able to trade much useful information on this source because of the similar details that emerged during our journey—which tied to deeply held Rosicrucian understandings. We had a standing invitation to meet and become involved with them too but our limited material circumstances prevented us from moving forward at the time. M could make a single telephone call and immediate arrangements were arranged for us to see someone important to our research, or to visit with them. It happened many times. He still had many friends in the highest places of government and civil life. On one occasion he spoke with Zahi for example, and a couple of hours later along with M, we held a private meeting together where we received freedom passes for the Plateau plus a lot of informational items to take with us.

By arrangement we received other special passes. One time we were scheduled to have a private audience with the Coptic Pope to discuss proposals concerning promotion of the Holy Family Route. From the office of M there was an exchange of fax's with the office of the Pope and shortly before our proposed meeting we received personal word that the influenza which afflicted the great man currently, meant he would have to postpone our meeting. We were particularly disappointed because we were almost at the end of our stay and had no time left to pursue the matter before our departure.

M arranged yet another important visit where we spent a highly productive session with the editor of an important Cairo and international newspaper. All these meetings and more were arranged on the turn of a phone call from M in our presence. His power of Presence and generosity of spirit are very great, and in the lost time since we were last in contact with him, we pray his health held through and that he remains well. Life steered us in new directions but when we met with M on the last occasion we were deeply honoured when he gave us his detailed Holy Family in Egypt research notes. Along with the notes came his blessing for us to use them when the time was right, to promote and inform as many as possible so they may be persuaded to visit the Holy Lands of Egypt also. We were humbled by his trust and the responsibility he passed to us. We have often thought since that maybe he already knew we were about to be steered into consuming new pathways of discovery. However we have promised on our website there will be a substantial section of pages which will elaborate on the Holy Family in Egypt. The intention from this was always to travel the route ourselves in preparation to commence an unusual Holy Family Route safari trip for the public. It is what M always dreamed to do. He always referred to the wonders and miracles of this route as the forgotten Holy Land of Egypt. If there is to be a future that everyone will enjoy in peace, then Insha'Allah we will fulfil the task of the Holy Family Route in honour of M.

Double Dealings and Betrayal

We were home again. An agonising year had passed and all we wanted to do was to return to all we had begun in Egypt. In the meantime all of us who formed the Quest gang kept in contact through information sharing and research objectives. Unknown to us, G made a private extra trip to Egypt arranged through L where he continued his personal quest. However as we were to discover later, L was sorely aggrieved because as he alleged to us, G had betrayed him. It was in a matter of payment to his personal contacts which he had yielded to G to help him. The story was that G had miscalculated his coordinates for research when we had travelled as a part of the Quest Project, but with L's help he had since returned to explore widely North of Cairo into the desert again. The whole truth came out when we shared our contradictory Email communications from G with L. These proved double dealing between G, to us and L. We learned a hard first lesson with regard to subterfuge in Egypt! We also learned that often behind the lesson, another surprise synchronicity had been arranged to steer us forward.

L was well known on the circuit and has a coloured past in his exploration and dealings in Cairo, especially with high officials. However he was an unknown quantity to us and a potential source for information sharing at the time. I had previously tried to make contact with him but only now began to communicate with him in earnest. L also had an interest for the implications of an ancient time where sea levels and habitation were much higher than now. We traded material and ideas. L also shared details with us about his believed rediscovery of a unique feature of the GP. He had applied himself to the physics of the shape of the Pyramid. We all know that each side was in fact formed from two facets which converged at the perpendicular centre of each face. L showed firstly that there were other unnoticed smaller facets. By experiment he found that all these facets effectively turned the sides of the GP into quasi parabolic reflectors. The sun at various stages in its path created a moving reflective focal point a little over 7 miles away. Thereby a phenomenal focus of the Sun's energy could be harvested at the strongest arc of that focal point. L has patented this work and it is very clever; but its significance to us would not come full circle until many years later as you will read about in due course.

There was no denying the contributory work and huge experience of L; and in the space of a very short time before we had arranged a return to Cairo, he made us an offer we could not refuse. We felt honoured as he was prepared to place us with local family friends of his in the village next to the pyramids. It would cost us nothing, except to do right by the family, as they were poorer than poor. He would be happy, simply to share the detail of our experience when we returned, and quite possibly thereby we would be trusted into the *quiet* world of the sustenance diggings carried out by the villagers for artefacts beneath their homes. L now found it difficult to operate in Cairo due to past demeanours. Within a couple of weeks our trip was booked and we were set to not only learn some of the hardest lessons of our lives, but also to be redirected for the next few years on our strongest pathway in a wholly new direction. It is worth mentioning that the option was always there to return to A and his family. We were persuaded that for the first week of that visit we would take the offer from L because we felt it would bring us closer to the real life of ordinary villagers and their activities. We felt we may learn more. We did not tell our usual guide A of our first week plan because we knew for sure he would have been severely against the idea on the grounds of safety; and naturally he would have preferred that all our time in Cairo and the desert would be spent with him.

Entering the Village as Chickens

Just prior to the trip, L suggested that although the trip itself would cost nothing, it would be a good gesture if we wired some advance money to the host family so they could prepare for our visit. This seemed reasonable and we sent them a reasonable sum of money. We also took a very expensive practical gift with us to give to them. We were met at the airport and were whisked straight into the slums of the village. We thought we had prepared ourselves for the poor conditions we would meet but we were very shocked at what we found. An enduring sight was the little girl openly toileting into the gulley on the floor as we arrived.

I noted as we walked towards the pathway ramp which would take us to our home, that we passed the front door of a neighbour's house. It was marked Number 13, which holds significance for me. The number or combination of 13 has always followed me, even with Judith, as I was recorded born 13thMinute 13thHour of Friday 13thOctober—so you can imagine my interest was roused by the adjoining house number. (Note this as Site A *(SA)* for future reference.) We had no idea in the following year several men would meet with heinous deaths beneath house 13 amid official subterfuge and cover-up. We had no idea either of the importance of a tunnel being driven from beneath our host's house towards the future death site. Even to this day, that tunnel has never been officially acknowledged. We suspect it was used following the deaths as a secret back door tunnel for the authorities to continue work in the death chambers and beyond, after the act had taken place. We know for example the house where we stayed was used during that time as a rest base for the police and men working on the death site.

Our tiny host house *(SB)* appeared like a squat which had been devoid of care and attention through years of abuse. We were shown into a tiny upper bedroom which seemed to match the age of the GP looming large a short distance away. From our stone balcony entrance it felt as if we could reach out and touch the pyramid sides. The order of the day as late as it was, was to eat. There was nothing prepared, or rather, nothing available unless we bought some food. We provided money to satisfy the hospitable insistence that we should rest and food could be brought. However when we opted for Kentucky, the whole family accompanied us to the shop, situated across from Gouda's place, and waited to pick up the escort again for the few minutes back to the house when we had done. The biggest bucket of chicken with accessories that we have ever bought lasted a few minutes on the floor as ravenous hands claimed the offering like the last earthly meal. Our hunger immediately diminished and we retired amid mixed feelings for what may be to come.

Next day we learned that tourists who stray into the hospitality of some villagers are regarded as chickens. We wanted to know what this meant. Apparently such visitors are there to be plucked clean—and we heard copious exact details of previous visitors who had suffered the same fate that was unfolding for us. Our saving grace was that our knowledge of the Plateau and its hidden secrets had been lost in the translation when arrangements had been made for us to be there. They eventually stood-off from us to a large degree because they realised we had information which they did not have and which would be valuable to them. You have to understand that the mentality of entrepreneurs in the village was confined to anything that would help them recover goods from the ground which could be converted into big cash. The superior value of any wider implication from finds, just did not register at all. We realised our benefit from the visit would be confined to whatever may relate to ancient knowledge, either in the architecture around us, or from secret diggings that we may learn about. We realised very quickly the trade-off to this would be a battle of will and character as our hosts used every trick of brilliance to separate us from our money and possessions. The poor-me drama was successfully used as a weapon to a captive audience—which was us. There was only one occasion we managed to sneak away briefly from our hosts. It lasted about 20 minutes before we were reeled-in by a gang of family members who came chasing after us when we were found missing. We were very inexperienced and very naïve at the time and we swallowed the lie that we must be with them all the times for our own safety.

As the days passed, our holiday cash diminished as we were persuaded to help them with many things. For example, the house did have a toilet but it was broken! L had fitted one into a blocked-off corridor when *he* had been there previously. *I* could have managed from a stand-up position, but I could not allow Judith to face the prospect of squatting into an exposed gulley. I paid for the parts that were needed and as no-one could be brought with any plumbing skills; I ended up taking a day in the operation of refitting a new one myself.

We paid their advance mortgage payments on threat that they, and us, were about to be thrown on to the street by heavies. The whole story was delivered so convincingly at the time that we were swept up in the practiced drama of it. Damn, they were good at-it! In another example there was a build up as apparent arrangements were being made to take us to see something mind-blowing. We would need to wait at the house and be summoned by telephone. The one belonging to our host was broken so we would lose the chance. However we were again persuaded that as the phones were not expensive, perhaps if we got a new one for them, they would be able to freely make the best arrangements and keep us safe for the rest of our time there. Needless to say, the rest of that day was taken with an escorted village shop tour to finally purchase and set up an expensive mobile phone. Meanwhile the time and opportunity conveniently evaporated for us to rendezvous with those who were going to show us something that would blow our minds. Our minds were rapidly becoming blown anyway!

Looking back, we are ashamed and embarrassed that we were so gullible, but fresh tourist chickens just like us by the thousand, pass daily and are ripe for similar plucking. On a successive day we were caught once again. There was to be an evening feast ceremony of some kind. Many of the houses around us were filled with relatives of our host. Another Oscar performance of sadness and melodrama unfolded as our hosts bewailed the fact that they would not be able to attend. It was brilliant and despite all that had already happened we were sucked into the drama. The pitch was that each family brought a food contribution sufficient for their family. It would be mixed into a grand feast where everyone would share the bounty. We were determined if we gave-in to the pressure and helped; it would be a last time. All they needed was a sign that we had given-in and a food purchase gathering was mobilised. It amounted to another small fortune but there was a second sting when we attended the neighbouring event. We realised the food we provided was sufficient to feed half the neighbourhood and that is what practically happened! Again we lost our appetite.

The final most serious threat to us was at the hands of X who was a Taxi driver member of the same family. He was arranged to take us to places and coincidentally to people who aggressively tried to rip us off at remote sites. That is a story on its own. On our final trip with X, he ripped us off again only because of the hand-pistol he menacingly flashed at us from his glove compartment. We only escaped from the whole deal when we finally made a phone call to A for help. We know that the powerful status of A's father and the connections that A also had, ensured we would never be unprotected again; and that certain people would be dealt with without the need for direct police involvement; although that always remained an option. To this day, evidence and statements are on file which would be used if there were ever any future problems concerning us from any of those involved. From what we know now, and with local powerful people who are our real friends, we know that anyone in future would come to far greater harm than anything they dished to us. The fact remains however, by the end of that first week we were many thousands of American dollars lighter and we had acquired the Presence of kidnap fugitives; but we were so much wiser.

As a balance, we must state that from many subsequent visits to the village of Nazlet el Samaan and deep interactions with other villagers—we found there are many more good generous, genuine villagers who would give their lives to protect a complete stranger.

Our first visit gave us an insight to the worst part of poor life in the village. We know also however, this was encouraged by our worldly clever contact L, whose shocking game was to send unsuspecting chickens to be plucked, in return for all the information he needed about clandestine activities; which he was currently unable to participate directly in. A book could be written on aspects we have not shared, but every last detail is held in official files.

So the question must be asked: What was it we got from the trip that helped steer the direction of our future journey for many years?

The Ancient Finds of the Village

Part of the softening process for tourist chickens was the carrot and the stick. Our hosts and their arranged friends would go so far as was necessary to feed us the information we sought, in order to get what they wanted. It became clear to us, especially when we met at the start with a group of young friends of our host that they were taken aback by our deeper knowledge. In a nutshell we played with information they wanted, just as they held back with information for us. We realised early we were being fed with partial truth based on real situations they were involved in. Their skills did not stretch to complete story inventions, and we were able to verify this through later discoveries. The result was that we were taken along with them on a number of occasions and we recorded information which would eventually dovetail to our future activities.

One excursion was to be a simple walk around the village and started as a perimeter walk along the village side of the Berlin wall of Giza. Parts of the wall were pointed out to us where the village touts illegally breached the wall to get on to the plateau and harass tourists with souvenirs. We waded in sections through knee deep layers of garbage to an open area where we veered down a side road as if to go back into the village. However there was a dirty open stable and we were urged to follow our leader to the back of the stable and climb the end wall. We had to negotiate under barbed wire so we could drop to the derelict yard on the other side. We were all dirtied with horse dung but were intrigued to see what would come next. The ground had disappeared under garbage within this fairly large and isolated place in the midst of occupied slum houses. Buildings were all around us but we were off-sighted and it was possible to pass unnoticed into a very old abandoned low building.

It was below mean ground level. An access hole had been smashed through to another room. There was ground-spoil everywhere from digging. The walls were constructed from a mixture of materials including mud brick, natural rock and sandstone; and there were pieces of red granite lying around. The centre of the room was clear and revealed a hole broken through the concrete floor. With our flashlights we were able to see the floor was built above another stone floor a few inches lower. In the lower floor there was a deliberate square hatch opening and beneath that there was an earth floor at about a six to eight feet drop from the hatchway. We wanted to go down but were refused. We were told we needed equipment. They told us the hole led to a tunnel which traversed the pathway and went under the Berlin wall of Giza into excavations on the other side. From the room we were shown some scattered remains of what had been brought out. These were clearly the cast-offs but still evidentially interesting. There was no doubt the excavators had tapped into very old levels of history.

Reluctantly we had to leave, but we will code this as Site C *(SC)* for later reference. We retraced our steps and walked further into the village. With great hush-hush drama we went to a house belonging to one of the group. In the bedroom we were told this was the site of a major dig where they had found really spectacular things. They used a ploy that we came to recognise easily in future. They claim another conveniently missing person has final authority to allow outsiders to see the work. By the way, every time something is shown, the visitor is obliged to make another insufferable baksheesh payment. This is standard BS practice everywhere in Egypt, at every level. We guessed the mysterious missing person of authority would suddenly be made to appear if we produced a big enough backhand payment up front.

At this stage we were already weary of being robbed and we played hardball with them. We played them at their own game by talking as if we knew all about the dig and what it represented. They compromised and showed us a very interesting section of granite lintel which they said they had broken from a much longer piece still buried beneath us. It was covered in hieroglyph markings. We paid a small amount and took photographs. They described the dig site but said we would have to wait to negotiate another day to get to see it.

Under the carpet of the room we were shown fresh concrete. We were told this was formerly an entrance to the dig we were there to see. Also by the way, every local knows not to refer to clandestine excavations as digs. Ironically they are named *safaris*! We noticed something else in the room. A large section of the lower wall of the room was much bigger, wider and odd shaped as if naturally used as a foundation wall. We were able to confirm it was the main adjoining wall to the next house and that the wider part was from an original construction. Both Judith and I had a very strong intuitive feeling there was a dig/safari entrance located just the other side of the wall—Site B *(SD.)* Remember all these items are photo featured on our website.

We proceeded for the rest of the day to walk around the village taking photographs accompanied by our host. However our host was unaware of what really interested us. These were not sight-seeing photos. They were photos to record differences in possible ancient architecture and building materials. Many of the pieces we saw had come from below ground and were now abandoned or used as house door stops etc. We had cleverly mentioned in a laid back way, almost as if the subject was taken for granted, the interesting old stone archway which L had told us about. It was guarding a large abandoned derelict plot of land between the houses. The archway had a mysterious carving which looked like a classic alien man. We visited and captured a whole bunch of pictures. We returned to this site a number of times over the years and recorded the stages before its destruction, or removal! On another occasion even though we were chaperoned by a respected don of the village, we were harassed by a rapidly assembled gang of foreign looking heavies. On that visit we captured that the alien had been defaced with plaster. Finally on a more recent visit we recorded the archway had been removed completely and an expensive house was being constructed on the waste ground behind. The other relevant fact is, that this is part of the area which Zahi Hawass and Mark Lehner had published as their estimated location underground for the lost palace or tomb complex of Khufu. *(SE)*

We were frustrated back at our village house also because L had categorically given us details of a safari project that he and our host were involved in closer to home. We asked S about it, citing the descriptions of L as if we knew a lot more about it. S elaborated further, describing mummies and other things they had found deep underground. We formed the conclusion that the house where we were living, was in fact not in full use, but was used as an occasional chicken home for others like ourselves; and that it did conceal a major safari! The house was filthy and some soil from digging was stored around the side of the main living room. S was not going to yield the safari to us though, certainly not unless we produced mega-bucks! But he talked about it, trying to disguise his story as if he was referring to another location. However he was unaware that just before the trip, L had dangled a carrot by giving more detail of a safari which had to be the same one that S was flowingly describing. L had described an underground corridor step and slab. Efforts had not been successful to breach the stone before L had previously returned home. Copious water had been used to assist the drilling process and this was heard to slosh down apparent steps on the other side of the barrier slab. We determined there was a hidden room in our holiday home which separated us from the adjoining the pathway and the Berlin wall of Giza. At the bottom of the entrance ramp to the house there was a door which was always locked. We were told it was another room belonging to the house but was the property of another relative! For sure this was where the activity was taking place. Well beyond the time of the deaths we met with S again. This time we were calling the shots and we got confirmation the mysterious tunnel did in fact emanate from the secret room and reached under almost the whole distance underground of the entrance ramp. To us it was inconceivable that this tunnel did not eventually join with the underground death chambers.

As the week progressed we were becoming more and more stressed and more bold. We became more agitated with our hosts especially as we were feeling suffocated and we wanted them to stop faffing about and show us something new. If not, we would not share any more with them! We learned about another dig where a deep shaft in another open part of the village had yielded a small Ruby monkey icon. This could have been untrue; but, the story was described to us in spontaneous detail. All present joined in to elaborate the difficult circumstance of getting to the dig site undetected, including full details of the dig itself. We filed it away as just another story, but much later we discovered the location was another hot spot which tied to the Fibonacci geometries of the Plateau perfectly. The difficulty of the site was that although it is accessed across cultivated ground there are surrounding houses in a better part of the village overlooking from all sides. This means that a quiet visit to its location can only be achieved in darkness. We have more details but we want to gain access ourselves before commenting further.

It was nearing the end of the week and there was another arranged meeting which included a few other friends of S. A couple of nasty things happened when I produced documentation pictures and maps to refer to, and which they were desperate to get their hands on. They were now convinced we possessed deep information that would be very valuable to them. At one stage I had to literally wrestle the documents back when one of the men tried to snatch the paperwork from me. We extracted ourselves from the meeting on the promise that although we needed the paperwork for our research activities on the following week, we would let them have them all before we returned home. We would do a deal with them for much more but only if they would finally produce something for us. Miraculously a trip was arranged that evening to see something *interesting*. It would be beyond the village. We were told they had procrastinated because the local authorities were taking too hot an interest in their activities and they wanted to lay low for a while. We didn't believe it at all, but the chance to get away from the village to possibly see something else was too great an opportunity to miss.

We had no idea that we were travelling to the old part of Cairo. The new city ring-road was incomplete so the journey seemed to take forever. We travelled two cars in convoy and parked close to a well-known market square we recognised from a previous visit with A. Our destination was down a side street and we were being taken up a wide alley raised from the road by steps. We were heading for one of the houses bordering the alley but we were told the safari was so significant that the excavators insisted we did not see the actual house location. This meant blindfolds! We were apprehensive but went along with the arrangement. At least that part was genuine because inside the house when we could look around, it was clear the ground floor had been given over to a full digging crew. The householder's wife and children were in another part of the house.

Presently a wardrobe was swung away from the wall to reveal a curtain hiding a doorway. Inside was sight to behold. Earth and stones had been piled up from the floor level to above waist height against the walls. In the centre was a huge gaping hole through the concrete floor and a wide rough-cut winding shaft that disappeared into the ground for a depth out of sight beyond 20 feet. It was huge undertaking which we were assured had been in progress for around two years. They had broken into ancient chambers below the Mosque adjacent to the building we were in. We learned little of what they had found so far, but even from our vantage point, and from the photos we got from below ground, we know they had accessed something very old and very important. They told us they had just broken through to catacomb chambers and were still trying to structure a better underground entrance. The pictures showed this along with an abandoned side tunnel from earlier in the dig. We were told by those involved if we could help them with a donation we would be able to return at a later date and see more again. We were already financially burnt-out from the activities back at Giza so I had to think quickly. Like before, I spun that we were in touch with very important people who had money and we would approach them for serious funding. We convinced them, and apart from some small baksheesh for the photographing we were allowed to leave peacefully. Somehow the blindfold procedure was forgotten on the way out and we were glad to take a fix on our location as best we could.

Back at the house we should have been happily making arrangements for our departure. We secured our gear and despite vigilance I found later that expensive items had been stolen from us. We dreaded the fact that the taxi driver friend was to be the one to drop us close to A's location so we could enjoy our second week. They tried every way to find out who we were visiting next. We had consistently concealed A's identity. We continued to resist and it became clear as the deadline for our pickup and departure came and went time and time again, that they were deliberately trying to obstruct us from leaving at all—or at least until they plucked us a little more. Incredibly S made it clear he wanted us to send him a weekly family allowance! He pleaded their poverty and helplessness and how they would provide so much information for us just like to L. We were numb to the BS by now, and it was in any case well into the early hours of the morning. We had been trying to get away for so long and finally I telephoned A and asked for a rescue. I only had to explain briefly. *His* subsequent conversation with S led to S miraculously now being able to contact our Ahole driver. The mood was soon angry and dangerous when we bundled finally into his taxi and got the hell out of there.

Our friend A greeted us like prodigals returning but he was steaming that we had taken such a risk without letting him know in advance. He had a few very angry words with our driver even before he heard our story; but from whatever he said, our Ahole taxi driver disappeared in double quick time with his tail between his legs. When we were settled into the house and explained everything, A's father (M) had to restrain A from calling upon his own followers to go immediately and deal with those involved, Egyptian style. We believe he would have done so and would have retrieved all our money. We were emotionally wrecked as M made a couple of phone calls to *his* contacts. He told us he was dealing with the situation another quiet way through his best Police contacts to ensure we would be always be protected in future. However like A he said that upon our request he could also have the matter dealt with immediately and severely because he knew such things happened to some visitors, and we were his guests. He was incensed at the bad reputation from a few which affected everyone. Judith and I discussed the situation and agreed we had been caught by our own naivety; and we already had a familiar knowingness of some other significance to our experience. We accepted some blame for what happened and we did not want the blood of several people on our conscience if we agreed to the brutal option. Our wishes were accepted, but we were told those involved with the chicken-run would still have to pay for their dishonour. Things always have a habit of coming full circle and these events certainly did, about a year later!

For our second week we needed to get back to the sanctuary of the desert, and with the time left to us, it would be only be a short trip. After our previous visit with A to Abu Lifa, I had researched the site extensively on the internet. More detail will follow in a moment, but just to say that this Coptic fort is constructed into the high sides of another desert escarpment nose. My research and satellite pictures showed the site must be much more extensive than we thought from our first exploration there. We were eager to return and test the theory.

The Ghosts of Abu Lifa

The escarpment hides its secret well. It is tricky to find and harder to reach. It is situated within sight of the Qarun Lake at Fayoum and is even closer to the Qasr el Sagha Temple. The Qatrani mountain range tries to reach it with its shadow, but the darker shadows are reserved for the collapsed caves and tunnels throughout the whole high end of this unique escarpment. From above, the damage of an ancient earthquake is evident in the huge crazy paved sections of either fossilised reef or basalt rock which have fractured and collapsed around its edge. The complex reaches back to an unknown time, but its history can be traced in modern times to when Coptic monks hid here in a fortress community as the Romans commanded the country below.

It requires all the skills of an experienced 4x4 desert driver to negotiate the various levels of strata around the mountain to the right of the Temple at Qasr el Sagha on its lower approaches. On our first visit we confined ourselves to just getting up into the caves and enjoying the incredible view out across to the distant Qarun lake, which in the distant past, lapped to the foot of the mountain range. It would have seemed like a huge inland sea. On our first trip we learned only that it was an old Coptic fortress Monastery, long abandoned and now in ruin. The main caves are intact and have ceilings and walls covered in fragments of old Coptic writing. Slightly deeper, there are other caves in stages of construction which had been hacked from the basalt rock seam. In the main cave, a deep shaft reaches down into the mountain, as do other less accessible shafts in the complex. The deep shaft could have held water, grain or could be a route to deeper underground passages and caves. The caves are also heavily obstructed by blown sand. On the first trip we did not have the equipment to explore further.

Now we were heading off for another visit using the old military road roughly parallel to the Fayoum desert off-road from Cairo. The sand we crossed was particularly tricky. The tyres sank 2 inches wherever we drove, and the horizon was featureless. In this landscape there are many hidden gullies that blend to the surface. Without skill and care, the jeep can buck high in the air and dump itself terminally into one of them. We were glad to reach the asphalt road used in recent times as a military road. However the asphalt came from quarries we passed in the distance, first to create one of the earliest and longest roads of its kind—leading to the distant receding lakeside, and eventually to transport the material into boats for their onward journey. We detoured at the end of the road towards the quarry near Kom Awshim by the lake. This is where we would eventually make our exit to continue our journey to the deep desert. However our route now led us back again at last to the Qatrani mountain range. It is necessary to bypass the Roman fort of Qasr el Sagha to get to Abu Lifa and you will also read of it soon. We followed the contours of the escarpment with difficulty and were filled with familiar excitement when the site came into view with the tell-tale cave entrances high above us. I had arranged for us to have ropes with us this time to explore properly. You can imagine what was said when we arrived this second time to find that A had accidentally left the climbing gear behind. We were not happy. There were only a few tying ropes to use and we had to make the best of it! There would be no exploration of the deep shafts, or of a particular high observation cave which was inaccessible without climbing gear. We were wary enough of possible spiders, scorpions and vipers, and it would have been foolish to have entered the shafts unprepared.

I learned later, that the site of Deir Abu Lifa was attributed to Saint Abu Banukhm/Panoukhius and probably dated close to the time of Christ. Some of the inscriptions in the main cave had been dated to between 686 and 858AD. Translations showed some by the hand of Steven saying,

'Christ remember me; Do penance for me; Pray that God will give me patience.'

More recently, French archaeologist Henri Munier had published a study on the site in 1937, but for us it was like a first time discovery. At the approach to the site, any vehicle must be left behind in a small gulch. The escarpment towers a few hundred feet above, with the cave entrances off-sighted from view to the open valley. Access is via a tiring climb to half the height of the escarpment up the huge scree slope along its sides. This is peppered with broken pottery sherds. Finally it is then possible to do a rock climb to the main entrance about 25 feet from the top of the escarpment. This is still tricky and at the mouth of the main entrance there is an outcrop of rock which shows signs that it has been extensively used in the past to tether climbing or safety ropes. The main entrance cave has a wonderful view and has a wonderful energy about it. Plaster survives on the roof with old Coptic writings and symbols. From this it is only possible to negotiate into other parts of the system by squeezing past and crawling under vast slabs which have fallen to block the tunnels that once would have allowed free passage throughout. Undoubtedly, earthquakes shook the life out of the formation and caused its collapse. In the deeper recesses of the system a seam of Basalt is obvious. In fact it looks as if some of the peripheral caves were works in progress where the Basalt was being hacked out. Off to the left of the main cave, there are other caves made poorly accessible from a substantial fill of sand and the obvious huge collapsed slabs.

I had crawled a little way between these the previous time but this time I was determined to discover the extent of the system by negotiating the debris as far as I could get . . . The satellite images showed it must travel around the escarpment nose. It was possible to get through the first small section from a crouched position while scraping between the fallen slabs. The crack opened out a little. Thereafter it was necessary to crawl completely flat with my back scraping the underside of the slab above. It was a tight squeeze, but then I found the sand seemed to hollow out substantially just in front of me. I was in a sand bowl beneath a fallen section of the escarpment that must weigh hundreds of tons. The light was dull and it took a moment to adjust my eyes. I could not contain my excitement when I realised I was in a filled chamber that had once been a large domed cell with elaborate painted plaster on the walls. For me it was the first time of naked discovery. I was laying almost at ceiling level, looking at the remains of the most glorious plaster paintings. I could see the Saints with their halos and other decoration. The hairs stood up on my neck as I felt the sudden contact with all that must have happened in this Holy place and I felt the wind of spirit. I grabbed for my camera and took many pictures.

I managed with difficulty to squeeze through another low gap on the other side and was able to stand up at the start of a pathway ledge which looked down the sheer drop of the cliff. At last up ahead on the ledge path it widened out and I could see the strange structure in front of me that we had puzzled over from the ground. It was a square lookout position less than six feet square and built from modern materials. It must have been a wartime lookout position and commanded perfect views over tens of miles of open desert landscape. I was right on the edge of the cliff and as I went to step forward I noticed movement and froze. A huge spider had appeared suddenly over the nap of the cliff and stopped as it crossed my path only about 3 feet away. It was a Camel spider, as big as a tarantula, but hairless and the colour of amber. I could see where they get their ferocious reputation from. Immediately I recognised its oversized pincers and recalled the stories of it grabbing like a vice and causing terrible poisonous injuries. In a second it scurried as fast as a mouse and disappeared under another section of rock not too far away. I shuddered because I was going to have to crawl close to where it had disappeared when I retraced my steps.

There was more of the cave system along the ledge ahead of me and I wanted to call Judith and A to come take a look. It was obvious there were even more workings around the corner. I called at the top of my voice and got no reply; so reluctantly and cursing, I headed back while keeping a razor sharp eye out for the movement of the durned spider! I got back to the fissure and there was still no reply to my calls. Judith was below in the gulch with the jeep at the time pointing up to me with the camera, and A was somewhere up on top of the escarpment. I used the sides of the fissure like a chimney to climb to the top, scraping my knees and elbows in the process. I saw A in the distance, exploring the top of the escarpment and I called him to come and see something. Judith had also realised there was reason for some excitement. I called again to A to come immediately as I had found something incredible. He was reluctant because of the danger down below. I urged him, saying there really was something amazing he had to come and see. I was already scraping down to the bottom of the fissure again before he arrived.

When he finally joined me he was just as excited at the sight of the hidden paintings. We moved to the next section but not before I scared the bejabers out of him with the camel spider story. He was nervous anyway and was happy to risk the ledge if only to put distance between him and the spider's location. We continued past the lookout post and between the slab fissures for the whole nose of the escarpment. We found there were even more caves on the other side mostly filled with sand and mostly inaccessible under the rock slabs. It was entirely possible the whole place was linked with underground tunnels joining to the ones at the main entrance. It was obvious the site deserved proper archaeological attention because the painted plaster was deteriorating and there must surely be a wealth of other finds awaiting discovery. Much later we learned the authorities gave the site little priority as all resources were allocated to better known sites. We felt so privileged to have seen so much despite the lack of ropes. We could do no more and still keeping an eye out for the spider, we made our way back. At the cell hollow we went through a proper performance as A was reluctant to risk the spider's reappearance. I told him it would be worse if he waited and the light failed because he could not stay perched on the ledge forever. He finally followed.

Another version of this account was published as a newspaper article in Cairo in April 2008. The version was delivered by A, who for reasons we do not understand, chose to describe that he made a solo re-discovery of the complex when in fact he was with us. Each to their own motivation, but be assured I have described it exactly as it happened. We guessed it was simply the Egyptian way to use our photographs with his own creative recollections for promotional purposes; but we were disappointed with his actions.

In general, the position of the fortress gave the widest possible view of the whole valley stretching to Lake Qarun over 8 miles away. Speculatively in very ancient times the complex would have been a perfect community lookout home when the sea lapped to the foot of the mountain range. The view is spectacular and the caves ooze with tranquillity—though in its earliest days there must have been much tension as the Coptic brothers concealed themselves from the occupying Roman soldiers. In the wide desert leading away from the mountain range and especially in the vicinity of Qasr el Sagha, the footprint of very substantial ruins can be seen beneath the sand of the desert. We would definitely wish to return to this valuable site in the future to see if it remained preserved, and to see what other gems of history it concealed.

The Mystery Temple of Sobek

I mentioned earlier that we had to bypass another mysterious site on the approaches to Abu Lifa. In fact we also visited this site each time we were in the area. All around it in the lower desert the foundations of ancient buildings can be traced. The Qasr el—Sagha Temple is thought to have been dedicated to Sobek the Crocodile God and is situated circa 3 miles North of Lake Qarun near Fayoum on a lower outcrop of Mount Qatrani. It is 180 feet plus above the shoreline that once came to its feet and which is now over 3 miles distant. At one time the marshy shore lines of the Fayoum lakes must have been teeming with crocodiles. The Temples of the crocodile God Sobek flourished around Al Fayoum. Some still remain. In fact the town Arsinoe was known to the Greeks as Crocodiliopolis. At some Temples, sacred crocodiles were tended with prime meat and became quite tame. Their carcases were mummified and buried in special animal cemeteries. Sobek also came to symbolise the produce and fertility of the Nile and so his status became more ambiguous. The crocodile's ferocity, power and strength made it a perfect patron for the Army. Others regarded Sobek as a repairer of evil, rather than a power for good; and therefore more likely to go to the Duat to restore damage done to the dead. He was also said to call upon other Gods and Goddesses to protect people in particular situations, effectively having a more distant role nudging things along, rather than taking an active part. In this way he was seen more as a primal God, eventually becoming regarded as an avatar of the God Amun who at the time was considered the chief God. When his identity finally merged, Amun himself had become merged with Ra to become Amun-Ra; so Sobek, as an avatar of Amun-Ra was known as Sobek-Ra. Source: http://en.wikipedia.org/wiki/Sobek With all these connotations and especially with the status of Sobek being acceptable as an Army icon it is easy to imagine this fort being conceived at a time of original inundation, and then adapted through time for continuous use. No one is certain and the truth may only be discovered if very extensive excavations ever take place nearby.

We were heading towards it again, bucking and bumping up the rising dirt track. We levelled over the top of the Butte and were confronted with the familiar sight of the imposing Temple. This unfinished building is awesome for many reasons. It is huge and is formed from sometimes massive sandy limestone blocks with a best modern date tying with the time of the Basalt quarries during the Late Old/ Middle Kingdom 2125-1570 BC. No one is sure. There are several compartments inside including a completely enclosed cell. It is thought the place was a mortuary Temple containing iconic Statues of Gods. The building is also unusual in that it uses huge blocks intricately hewn with interlocking faces much the same as seen in ancient Peruvian constructions with no mortar—but able to withstand great structural disturbances such as from earthquakes. The whole building is shaped oblong and has no roof. We were able to examine all over the structure and note the massive lintels and lack of corner joints. Instead, the builders had used corner blocks which negotiated the corners and interlocked to the side elevations. Pivot holes were evident at the entrance and at the openings to internal alcove stations, and these could have been designed for door pivots. I missed Judith at one stage and eventually spotted her a long distance away towards the rising mountain. She had been drawn to surrounding ruins which are prehistoric.

To the right of the entrance there is a curious smaller entrance, or opening, leading into a corridor between the two skins of stone which make up the walls. We think this was a deliberate connection with the main door arrangement at least. Apertures showing through to the main doorway suggest that doors could have been braced from the wall corridor. However the entrance to this wall corridor is contradictory as it is accessed from outside of the building. The main doorway has a threshold rebate at the bottom, and top pivot holes which were evident elsewhere. We marvelled at the internal highly polished blocks, showing incredible graining patterns like best marble.

Those who believe the Temple is a Roman epitaph believe also that there must be a substantial undiscovered cemetery in the area. We know for sure the area sustained many nationalities with their families and may have accommodated ancestors tens of thousands of earlier. Indeed the main mountain range rising nearby has not been fully explored, and as with so many other sites, Qasr el-Sagha provides more questions than answers. We felt great tranquillity there but we also had the feeling that the whole area was once filled with many people in the distant past.

Treasures on our Doorstep

When we returned from the desert to A's home we learned that other family members of our hosts were about to make an unannounced stop-over. The space was needed and as was right, we had to be moved to a hastily arranged cheap hotel. It was unfortunately several miles away and we would have arranged it differently for our last couple of days with a little more notice. The place was all that was available and was a complete dive in the back end of nowhere. We were damaged from the first week and longed to be back in the desert again. We had no idea there were nearer places of good vibration. At first we did the best we could, and left to our own devices we went on a couple of long walks. We felt very insecure and self-conscious but nevertheless discovered a market. Yet again, its location became a place-marker for future reference when we were much more familiar with the city and its ways.

The final days were not lost entirely when A collected us and took us to see the Monastery of Saint Macarius at Wadi Natrun. That was a wonderful experience, not only for the great preserved monastic history of the place but especially for when we visited the preserved hermit cave of Saint Magar. Originally he had lived there as a hermit for over forty years and was inspired to build a Church which was the forerunner of the existing Monastery. He died and was buried in his hermit home in 390AD. Later, the Church was raised from destruction by Pope Shanudah. We felt such a high presence of spirit at the shrine and we received a surprise from the photographs we took through the protective grilles of the cave. In one picture there is an extra figure showing in a reflection from within the cave. We felt blessed.

We had time to visit the Hanging Church in Old Cairo which was so named for the fact that it was built over the foundations of the old Bastion in the 7th century. The Bastion dates back probably to the 3rd century. It became the official residence of the Coptic patriarchs of Alexandria and has a grand sense of history inside. Not far from the Hanging Church we also visited the 5th century Church of Saint Sergio. This was where the Holy Family were said to have finally rested at the end of their three year journey in Egypt to escape Herod. The location is at the centre of what was the ancient Roman fort of Babylon. We visited the Church late in the day and delayed near the entrance to say hello to a small dog which was just sitting there quietly watching passers-by. The dog was so friendly and had the most human eyes. Right beside it we noticed a wall panel had been displayed showing all the differing materials and techniques of stonework that had been used in the various stages of construction on the site. It was a double photo-call.

At the door of the Church they were closing for the day. Whatever we said or did I am not sure, but the priest unlocked the door again and took us inside alone. He conducted us on our own tour. Inside was spectacular and filled with positive spirit. We were overcome and took time to meditate from the pews. Afterwards we were led to a lower section. Doors were unlocked. We removed our shoes and were allowed our own time alone in the crypt of the Holy Family. The experience was magical and the air so charged that every hair stood on end. We lit candles on the way out and took the feeling of higher spirit with us.

On the same day we had also visited the Coptic Museum and were astonished at the ancient artefacts on display. It had been established in 1910, and solid community support had produced many thousands of fine exhibits from the whole of Coptic history. We were even able to view the Nag Hammadi codices exhibit. The Museum easily rivals the Egyptian Museum in its own way and the ancient Coptic art took us back to the concealed paintings of the forgotten monastery of Abu Lifa.

We thought we had rounded the trip quite nicely despite the early traumas but there was one impromptu treat left to enjoy. A had some business with a friend who owned a motor launch on the Nile. We went along and were happy to savour the flavour of Cairo from the river as we motored up and downstream for a few miles. Out in the river the smells and sounds are so different. In the city the incessant noise of car horns and general hubbub are in your face the whole time. On the river it was like a movie in the background with the sound turned down. Along the river shore there are the launches tethered and filled with partygoers. We had visited one of these previously with J and his wife, and would have been happy to have remembered our pleasant meal with them on the river. On the smaller boat speeding with the current, we realised the shore launches were just an illusion in place of the real thing. How much more real it must be to work from the river on a small local boat.

Our time in the village and later with A marked a turning point in our journey. All that had happened up to that point was a precursor to a shift in direction which would gather up so many events and produce major synchronicities in our future. I was back to desk research and on another trip to America to plan our next phase. Events however were unfolding in the background.

The Connections Start to Appear

The year rolled on and due to the astute brokerage of Paul Bader of HOA group site http://groups.yahoo.com/group/Halls-of-Atlantis/ we were introduced to Bill Brown.

The synchronicities in our work and experiences were amazing. Despite our dubious placement in the village, we had been staying in the house which was slap bang on the Hot-Spot target area for the speculated Khufu Temple complex, and where Bill and Lucyna Brown had also identified a complex of tunnels and voids validated by GPR. Bill had been working for years with Star geometries and how they might apply to ground architecture. Deep intuitions and hard work paid off as a clear chronology appeared to him showing how important archaeological sites especially on the Giza plateau, not only tied in to Star geometries, but to a chronological time clock which stretched back through previous Precessional periods.

Bill had made multiple research visits to the Plateau and had worked on ground penetrating radar (GPR) surveys with top Egyptians and the Wroclaw University. On his trips he had met his wife to be, Lucina. She had been acclaimed with pinpointing the sites for major archaeological finds following psychic messages gained under hypnosis. Bill was at the stage where from his research he had produced his Geomatrix Blueprint. This was derived from a unified theory tying the constellations through time to a ground map for important ground/below ground constructions especially on the Giza Plateau. On the blueprint, the pattern identified specific hot spots which could be verified as sites of particular significance or historical importance.

Some of these fell to the hidden chambers which the GPR surveys showed along the Kephren causeway and alongside the corner of the village where we had stayed. The most sensitive results from this official survey material were completely hushed-up by the authorities despite the fact for example that Zahi Hawass and Mark Lehner had published work to speculate the likely location of the lost tomb/palace of Khufu under the same area of the village. Bill wished to spend much more time investigating the, difficult to get to Hot Spot locations. We were able to tell him we could save the trouble with a whole list of locations we had visited and inspected already. They included the site we went underground near the rock quarries at Menkaure and all the sites marked earlier in our story with coded initials. These included the area of the house we stayed in the village and in particular house 13 next door to where we stayed: The site at the causeway stable where the tunnel disappeared under the Great Wall of Giza; The excavation in line with the extended Khufu causeway which we failed to see fully: The general site of the alien archway, and the site of the Ruby monkey. (This turned out to be centred within the Fibonacci spiral geometries which connected from the Solar Cross.) . . .and a bunch of other locations.

Unknown also to us at the time, Bill had taken his research a few steps further. A few wealthy villagers had their own GPR equipment which was used officially and unofficially to conduct their own research. Bill had obtained GPR scans of the wider Hot Spot area around where we had stayed in the village. From such scans it was possible for a less trained person to deduce anomalies. However it required experts to do a full analysis from the data. Bill sent the scans to the equipment manufacturing experts in the USA for them to make an evaluation. In the meantime he wished to help his adopted Foundation to find local business premises. By pure coincidence he discovered another old building used as a dilapidated stable close by. It was conveniently only a spit away from the Hot Spot location of our village visit and from house 13, and was a free prospect for purchase. Our website details the exact sequence of events thereafter but a chain of connection was unfolding which came under the heading of; *You couldn't make it up!*

We had determined already there were powerful interests who wielded great influence in archaeology matters close to and inside the village. There was a lot at stake! We were aware of the feelings Zahi had for the villagers. His views are on film, on public record. He wanted the villagers all swept away! He had published his views of the great prize waiting to be found deep under the village; and the terrible villagers were a constant tease to his authority with their secret digging. He could do little about it—and the misery of the living conditions for the villagers had the opposite effect of spurring them on to find even more items beneath their houses which could help them escape their conditions. Their activity was often highly organised either through the village mafia or as a result of wealthy backers from outside. Later for example, Bill was able with senior local help to inspect and verify the big dig we came so close to seeing ourselves on the other side of the bedroom we visited in the village. It should be for Bill in his work to share this exactly with you, but we do know the dig leads to significant very ancient archaeology—and it leads to an area of altered vibration powerful enough to cause a physiological reaction.

At every turn it seemed as if more and more dark secrets were seeing the light of day. The more that surfaced, the easier it became to pull the threads of a long dark saga together. We had been introduced to our neighbours at house 13 when we were there. We heard of one son from the following house who was being held quietly in a police cell and had been receiving on-going readjustment treatment! His mother was distraught and pleaded with us if we had any influence to help her get him back alive. We know much more about this case than we can share at this moment; and it is worth injecting here that for all the information we hold about so many dirty aspects of powerful behaviour on the Plateau, we have taken steps that will ensure its whistleblowing release should the need ever arise. We are not so naive now and know that it is always vital to have an insurance policy!

The actual house 13 boarded a number of men, including members of the group we interacted with on our first visit. The sub-plot in all of this had no limits it seemed! By way of another example, powerful and wealthy people had taken an interest in Bill's early Geomatrix work—since a suitcase containing many of his papers was singled out and stolen from amongst a briefly unprotected gathering of suitcases at his guest house. We learned that the unofficially recognised tunnel from within the building we stayed headed South beneath the entrance ramp, which was also alongside house 13.

News reached us of the second bigger excavation which had been started from within an adjoining room of house 13. This was a much grander affair. Some of the men we met had been recruited to the operation which ultimately led to their ignominious deaths. It took no effort to realise the new operation was a hasty but highly financed secret excavation. The pieces began to fit together when we visited to meet with Bill for the first time in Giza.

The second illegal excavation had produced a shaft and tunnels of some yards and depth which broke into chambers. Some are under house 13 and others veer towards the Great Wall. The previous official GPR survey work that Bill had helped with, had identified deep tunnel voids on the Plateau side of the Giza Wall close by, and the new excavation chambers seemed to have a connection. Bill met us with the news that a couple of weeks before our arrival, several men had met their deaths in heinous circumstances at the dig site. We visited and we were able to gain first hand evidence, with photographs, before the authorities stepped up security. Coincidentally, Bill received his communication from the USA from the GPR experts at about the same time. He read the report and handed it to us to read. It was mind blowing. It identified a pure gold target area underground and it described another small chamber with an anomalous object in it like a case, which was issuing high energy of some kind. The scans had defined the chamber clearly because the interior edges of the room had been delineated by the energy emissions.

We had grown in knowledge and confidence since our first village visit and we therefore made bold contact with people we knew there. We were able to gather a comprehensive snap-shot of what had happened from their point of view. As evidence, it was of course hearsay, but nevertheless very compelling. We were told of how the dig was very secret even from villagers and that big money from outside had financed it. The same name kept cropping up behind the cash supply and for the name of a main organiser. We were told the operation was known about at a very high official level, but it was not openly rumbled by the police until a couple of the gang were arrested elsewhere trying to sell on-the-side, gold objects they found there.

Villagers first reported noises in the night which some later claimed as detonations down the entry shaft to collapse it while the men were underground. It was claimed that high value objects were removed by the authorities along with an alien looking sarcophagus which shed some ceramic-looking tiles in the operation. Coincidentally, we recovered samples from the ground which fitted the photo film and the descriptions. We were told that although the (rescue) excavator standing-by would have taken less than an hour to dig down to the men, the authorities procrastinated for 4 days until the men were all dead before opening a supposed rescue shaft. It was said later that the unstable ground forced the authorities to take time and effort to construct a safe (rescue) shaft, but as another villager commented to us—in the time they took, they could have excavated a hole the size of a house. It was also said before the men were dead for sure, the site was visited by an Antiquity Senior who was able to communicate and angrily argue with the men below ground before leaving them to their fate. You can make your own mind up about the motivation for these actions if true; but we were also told it was wrapped up in the fact that the brother of a *very* significant village controller was one of those below ground. It was alleged that the Antiquity Senior knew of the possibility for desirable underground Ancient technology at the spot and believed that it was what the men were seeking; plus there was a score to settle with the family of the brother.

Alleged eyewitness villagers described how the precious objects were brought out first and were taken away disguised inside an ambulance before the bloodied bodies of the men were removed. A goat sacrifice of appeasement was made into the shaft, but yet again it was claimed this was to disguise the bloodied clothes of the victims and the blood soaked soil in the chamber. We recorded such blood and clothing ourselves, mixed in with the spoil from below ground. Many more details of the whole affair are on our website, but for sure, there was never any closure to the stoty. It was essentially hushed-up and the idiot well-known establishment detractors spouted bucketsful of bullshine on the internet to add to the mix; as if they knew a damned thing about it.

The fact was that many men had possibly been murdered in the most heinous circumstances, even though their activities were illegal. The operation had unquestionably been well organised and highly paid-for. Two cell phone movies emerged purporting to show the dig and precious objects found underground. These had clearly been prepared before the deaths and from our own knowledge contained some fakery. We believe the films may have been in preparation for the sales pitch that would have been delivered at the end of a successful operation to elicit the most money from potential buyers. The whole issue begged fundamental questions. What was so important about this location that several men would die for it? What would attract the money needed from powerful sources to conduct the operation in the first place? Perhaps we need to return to the evidence I described earlier. Perhaps underground in this place there is still a *real* prize waiting to be unearthed and the men were rumbled because it was thought they not only knew about it, but that they may have reached it already? Either way if true, the men could not possibly be the allowed to surface with it or with any knowledge of it!

Not far along the Great Wall on the Plateau side, despite the stranglehold placed on new excavations funded from outside Egypt, the Russians have been working on deep cliff tomb excavations for years under official licence. It is ironic therefore as Bill was about to seal a deal for his working property not far away, the deal was suddenly usurped and he was intimidated by several swarthy men with Russian type accents. We were accosted by similar men ourselves on one visit to the death site around the same time. It is heading towards three years since the men met their deaths. They and their families, and the villagers, deserve better, but we know the story has yet to come full circle—as undoubtedly it will, eventually. A new regime is in place despite the dark grip still there from the old school. New clean-up excavations have taken place on the Plateau side of the wall and although you will not have read about them officially, they are a small step in the direction for when the whole truth and secret of the vast underground network is finally revealed to Egypt and the world.

Getting Closer to the Source

Yet another major story was unfolding in the background. The lost underground chamber and tunnel network of North Cliff2 (NC2) had been pinpointed and visited by Andrew Collins and his friends. We were especially interested because when we heard about it, we discussed with Bill the fact that the location matched another Hot Spot identified on his Geomatrix Blueprint. We were due soon to revisit Giza but despite previous unfruitful contact between Bill and AC we agreed it may be beneficial for us to pool our research with him and see where it may lead.

AC was due to present a seminar on his NC2 work in conjunction with the publication of his book on the subject. There had been much public aggravation between ZH and AC where ZH denied the existence of the system, so it was a safe bet at least that AC would fill some gaps in the story. Judith was due to visit from the USA and we would therefore travel together to the seminar and sound-out AC with a view to collaboration. I obtained tickets for the two of us but arrangements went astray leaving me with the choice of going to the presentation alone. I literally decided to go ahead alone at the very last minute. However we had agreed it would be wise for me not to simply divulge the work that was central to us until we saw how AC would react to my contact. At the end of the presentation I tried to speak with AC. That in itself was not easy, but eventually I was able to form the clear impression he was only interested to pump me with questions to learn of work that we were involved in—and especially for me to share Bill's latest findings with him. The presentation itself added nothing new to the material that had already been hyped and when I realised any attempt at mutual cooperation was going to be out of the question I wished I had not wasted my time on the long journey to attend. We were sorely aggrieved much later when AC tried to demean us publically by alleging the reason for our eventual first visit to the NC2 complex was as a result of what I gleaned from his presentation. Yet again, much more detail is to be read on our website, but it is enough to say the notion was ludicrous.

Starting Back to the Future

Judith finally joined me and we returned to Giza for another visit. We were fortunate now in that through Bill we were able to stay privately at another village location whenever we visited in future. This was at the hands of Bill's good friend there. He and his family are very wonderful people and we have been under his powerful protection ever since; even to the point of him possibly saving my life when things went badly wrong during a later adventure.(I will explain later.) On this visit we journeyed to new sites which were to provide a completely new set of synchronicities at a later date.

But first I wish to jump to the last day of this visit. We had gone about our agenda for two weeks and we had one last day before the overnight return flight. The trip had been as memorable as all others and we decided to go on one last relaxing soiree to the Plateau. We were east of the GP, and NC2 came into the conversation. I remembered the map position of its entrance maybe some way off and on the blind side of the cliffs beyond the highest ground where tourists never stray. Judith simply suggested in an off the cuff way;
'Come on, let's try and find it.'
I protested that we did not have enough time, but she persisted and we headed over the rough ground in the direction we thought it to be. We walked the general route out to the West of Kephren near the Harvard site where no tourists go, expecting any minute to be stopped by guards; but about ten minutes later we were standing inside the entrance of NC2 being dive-bombed by the bats as they flew at us from the deep cave system. Initially it was comical as well as unnerving. The myth was blown that bats are so good with their sonar that they would not hit anything in flight. I reversed into the tunnel entrance in a stoop with bats slamming into my back. The inside floor level was slightly lower and I looked back to Judith. She was calling, *'Where are you?'*

She had her jacket up over her head as a shield and didn't know which way she was facing hehe! We had stepped into a huge first chamber and immediately began snapping away to gather the first of hundreds of photographs of the whole system. Many of these would later be offered free for the public to download from our website. Just being in the first chamber seemed a world away from the world outside. The feeling was intense. From the light of our torches we noted major features. The chamber orientates north/south like the main tomb corridor and from its southern wall behind a big fallen slab; a tunnel entrance leads away into darkness. At the opposite side where the roof is lower, another cavernous entrance leads to a second chamber which we have called the sub-reception chamber. In the several feet from the entrance to the opposite side the ground falls away by a few feet to a lower level; and just before the split in the centre there is a massive flat slab of rock elevated from the floor by natural rock trestles.

We were not armed with proper lighting and our torch lights were just sucked into the blackness. The tunnel proceeded with slight changes in direction as caverns were encountered. The route was extremely hazardous as we clambered over large unstable boulders and pitfalls. Deeper into the system the air became more foul with the smell of ammonia from the bat droppings. We were blissfully unaware of the poisonous spiders and possible live snakes. Along the way it was possible to discern many mummified animal and bird remains along with other human objects. All the rock surfaces screamed with age. They were covered in lime scale, dust and bat guano. At greater depth the change in vibration was palatable but not uncomfortable, but at almost 350 feet the smell and heat was almost unbearable. It took many minutes of carefully edging forward before the apparent end was reached. At least the end of the easy part of the tunnel system was reached. A wall blocked the way—but a tunnel had been hewn into it, disappearing out of sight. This Tube Tunnel is about 4 feet wide and could have been hewn from an original water fissure. It had been obvious to see evidence along the way that the system had been subject to massive water erosion. Such water flow has to go somewhere and there was no logic to suppose there would have been an original blocked ending at the start of the Tube Tunnel. Our lights were so bad we knew we would have to rely on what the camera would capture by its flash. I made sure to take dozens of flash photographs every step of the way. The entrance to the Tube Tunnel was the point where AC had said they heard animal sounds coming from its depths. The only sound we could hear was the sound of silence and our hearts beating. We retraced our steps to the tomb entrance and made our way back to base, resolving to return soon armed with better lights and camera equipment. We were not to know that the furore was about to escalate between AC and ZH and the system was about to be prematurely barred with an iron gate!

We returned from the visit having explored the cave/cavern system to its current depth of penetration at around 350 feet, with a bag full of pictures, observations and profound impressions.

Nothing much had been said or published about the extensive hewn chambers under the main entrance tomb and we paid particular attention to gather first evidence from there. These are accessed from narrow winding stone steps from alcoves either side of the main entrance of the main tomb, and we had descended into these as a final exploration before leaving. On the left there are only two huge chambers, one branching almost immediately from the first, but both were severely obstructed for half their depth by sand bars. It was amazing to us that wind-blown sand had accumulated like desert dunes so far underground.

The steps on the left/western side led to a more interesting sight. There was plenty of sand barring the way again, but it was possible to negotiate a long corridor which gave access to a total of six known chambers. The two on the left of the corridor seemed as if they must stretch under the corridor of the main tomb above, and the one furthest at the end was particularly large. On the right, it was possible to discern an oddity in the second one as it seemed as if there was a large object of some kind at its depth, behind a sub-chamber wall section that had been demolished to expose it. We were becoming nervous of the time we had been inside and wanted to return at a later date for sure with proper equipment to record everything properly. We expected that a quickly organised return trip would allow us the same easy access. We were sadly mistaken! The AC/ZH story and its repercussions caught up to us. However we were also not to know that we had captured dynamite information in our photographs. These would provide a vital directional pointer for the successive stages of our journey.

Ticking Boxes at Other Sites

Prior to the last day NC2 visit we had visited several other locations and had gathered a lot of new data from the Plateau itself. The excavations were underway to scalp the thousands of tons of silt and sand which had buried the original constructions from the sphinx to the cemetery. They were to include the installation of up 16 water pumping stations which would draw-down the water-table at the most favourable times of the year. Back then under the rule of ZH we were not sure of the work schedule, but since then we learned that the USAID excavation contract was due to run its initial course by the end of 2011. The USAID and the Russian Excavation contracts were the only two which ZH had allowed to run on the plateau. The world was begging at the feet of ZH to support new archaeology projects but he still had a bloody nose from previous finds made by damned foreigners. That would not do!

By the time the main work tailed off, the full harbour excavations under the remaining days of ZH were scalping very close to the light-show staging area. Our worker contacts told us they were under instructions if they started to uncover anything, to carry on and completely expose whatever they were on to. Directly over the deeply buried sphinx harbour basin, a large section of mud-brick wall was uncovered. This has since been attributed to King Thuthmose IV 3390-3400 BP. Its discovery although notable would seem by all logic to pale against the significance of the red Aswan granite lined ancient harbour basin beneath it. Extraordinarily, artificial walls were speedily constructed to shore up the exposed south end of the mud brick wall, and the whole area around it was back-filled with hundreds of tons of recently excavated sand! No one has ever addressed with importance, the mere fact that under such a huge depth of sand and silt there are still enormous constructions in sandstone and granite, and that directly nearby, previous official GPR investigations revealed significant tunnels and voids. One thing is certain, we know in the space between the harbour and the corner of the Great Wall/village death site, the tourist road runs over a previously exposed temple, and at least three new well pumps have been installed in close proximity. It was also during the installation of one of these pumps we were unable to discover why a bowser was injecting thousands of gallons of some kind of liquid substance *into* the drill hole? The contractors went to very great lengths with strategically placed shutters to prevent the line of sight for anyone to take photographs of the operation. It did not stop us and a few of these have already appeared on our website. Finally to say; the vast depth of silt alone is not easily explainable by shifts in the Nile River and would be clearly a major dating clue as to the age of the first constructions of the Plateau. Always we found more questions than answers, and as usual there was a stone cold lack of information being released by the authorities.

Everyone gets bogged down with the construction of the pyramids, but what about the gigantic exquisite constructions tens of yards beneath the ground, hidden in plain sight but never addressed properly for explanation? The authorities conduct a little excavation, find mud-brick and stop. Then sometimes years pass in procrastinating measurement and investigation of the mud brick dates and layout, while the real archaeology waits indefinitely to be uncovered far beneath the mud bricks. We recorded so much evidence for the greater constructions appearing under the later mud brick, but seemingly untouchable by the archaeologists. Why is this so?

We learned more of the tunnel and shaft network under the plateau. Many times we found ourselves in conversation with important people who had been involved for decades on the Plateau and they all gave the same validations. Shafts lead to tunnels which themselves have deep shafts to even lower levels. These have led to accidental deaths in the past, and key shaft entrances were sealed and forgotten as a result. There is a very old aerial photograph which shows a huge open-hole excavation not far from the cemetery. We understand this led to a very deep system, but because of the expense and difficulty of proceeding, the shaft was capped for the time being and can only be located now under tons of excavation spoil. Why is this so? The old photograph is in the public domain and is shown again on our website, and others can search the aerial photo of Brigadier General PRC Groves to take a similar view.

On a previous visit to the South of Menkaure our way was barred because of earth-moving excavations taking place. The guards were overly hyper about us or anyone even having a line of sight to the work that was proceeding. This came home to roost on a later trip when we struck a friendship with someone who had been one of the inner circles of workers at Giza and Hawara for over forty years. He explained how during the removal of ground-fill from near Menkaure to use on the new roadway infrastructure, they had uncovered polished red granite temple blocks which had hieroglyphics giving details about the sphinx. We were allowed to see photographs taken during the earth moving. In the emerging Harbour area beneath the sphinx, similar blocks were uncovered. These select blocks were all apparently transported quietly to a secret location. Why is this so?

The Solar Cross

The Solar Cross had been a location we wanted to visit ever since reading the Flower of Life books of Drunvalo Melchizedek. Locals had much to say about these shafts and tunnels where they explored as children. Drunvalo speaks of the energy of Fibonacci rising while the locals speak of strange effects and scary moments underground. We spoke with one very wizened Arabic guardian who spoke of the tunnels and much more. He had a habit of aggressively chasing people away from his isolated lookout post. We eventually managed to befriend him and spoke at length through an interpreter. At one point when my questions became much more elaborate, he stopped the interpreter and told him in Arabic there was no more need to translate what I was saying as he understood. I still needed his answers translated back to English but he continued to take my questions directly. Our local Police translator's jaw was on the ground because he knew the man well and he knew he could speak no English. Our friend explained to us of how the tunnel system connected out of the Plateau, through the deep Solar Cross complex and on to places far away. We were aware he had held his lookout position over many years but also learned that no one would accept to replace him. This was because of the supernatural things that seemed to happen in his area which they were scared of. We tentatively asked him about rumours of people of some kind, permanently living in deep underground homes. He laughed and affirmed them in a casual, offhand way as his friends. He gave two descriptions of men who were taller and had very light sandy hair, and other much smaller almost dwarf sized individuals, but all friendly and benign.

His account reminded me of one of the lucid/OOB experiences I had in the NC2 system. I was with Judith in the deepest chamber recently found, at about 250–300 feet. We heard sounds from deeper in the system towards the tube tunnel. We both crawled up on to a ledge to conceal ourselves. A tall sandy haired man came in followed by smaller people. The smaller ones were searching about and then stopped as the tall man addressed me by name and told me he knew we were there. He told us we were not in danger and to come and join him. The smaller people led ahead and he asked us to follow. Just before the tube tunnel, the passageway branches off to a dead end after several feet. This time the end was open with a rock doorway of some kind. I passed through it into a clean tunnel with downward steps ahead with more excitement welling in me than I could contain. Typically as with every involuntary

OBE, my awareness of myself within the experience coupled with uncontrolled expectation dropped my vibration and I was instantly snapped back and wide awake. I went through my usual curses for losing control again. That would have been the end of it—consigned to a maybe of whatever; but something immense I discovered recently still waits to be tested. We have hundreds of photographs we captured from within the system. I have spent hundreds of hours studying a fraction of them so far. There is one photograph in particular of that blind passageway. From the image I believe I may have identified evidence of some kind of metallic protuberances which would be dead-ringers for hinge positions at the side of the blank rock wall. We will see . . .For our wizened watchman it was,

'Yes he knew of them,'

And occasionally he met them sometimes above or below ground. We inspected above the shafts of the Solar Cross a number of times. They are endlessly deep. The most Southerly slopes backing on to the Solar Cross site has entrances that can be negotiated with difficulty. These lead down to intermediate levels which intercept some of the deep shafts. We were only able to crawl with difficulty through these as they are filled almost to the roof with wind-blown sand, even to deeper levels. They are very extensive. However it was plain to see where these had been a magnet for local artefact hunters. The remains of their activities are strewn everywhere. It was clear also why the deeper connecting system has been preserved. As with the deeper shafts of the main Plateau they needed the use of specialist safety equipment to explore them. Our host told of when they were children they used to explore parts of the system and knew there were extensive parts underground which had not been reached. He told us of one time with a small group were underground exploring when all of the power in their torch batteries discharged together completely, just as it had happened for us in the desert Horse cave. He said they had only travelled a short distance but it took them forever to find their way out. It scared the hell out of all of them. He recounted how friends were known to have paid with their lives when they got lost in the same way. If anyone is familiar with the Flower of Life books of Drunvaldo Melchizedek you will know how he expertly describes the emanation of earth/Fibonacci energies from the Cross, and further proposes the Solar Cross as the energy datum point for the whole Plateau, so clearly there is a lot to be still to be discovered in this almost overlooked area of the Plateau.

The Sun Temple of Abu Ghurab

We had been drawn to visit this site for a long time and eventually made a few visits including a night time meditation visit. Situated at Abu Sir and less than half an hour drive from Giza, the site is not easy for tourists to visit. We were lucky with our connections again. The contrast as we walked up through the avenue cutting through the nearby grove of trees is stunning. Suddenly the apparent desert bursts forth, but this is misleading. In fact the sand dunes and mound before us concealed the stonework of the destroyed pyramid and its extensive enclosure behind. We immediately felt the much heightened energy of the place. The whole site gives the impression that it has been completely ravaged by vandals. Blocks of polished rock crystal, granite and alabaster are strewn everywhere and the ground looks as if a mechanical digger has rampaged throughout in a mad treasure hunt. However, the eye soon begins to find an order. We saw how the whole complex is surrounded by the remains of an extensive stone enclosure. There are huge stone bowls that have been gathered up in lines, and in the centre of the compound beneath the pyramid we saw the alabaster platform with unique arrowed forms indicating the four cardinal points. Historians say it once supported an obelisk and that parts of the needle are strewn around. We concentrated as always on our intuitive impressions first, and in any case we had not yet conducted any deep research about the site. From the top of the pyramid it was possible to clearly see the three pyramids of Abu Sir. I captured a 360 degree movie of the surroundings from the top which I will share on our website in due course. Between us we agreed several deep feelings. One was for the presence of a tunnel or large void of some kind beneath the complex, and another strangely was for the presence of exotic animals, but not in a sacrificial way. We had heard the alabaster bowls were thought by some to be for sacrificial purposes, but we felt they had been used for a completely different unknown purpose. We also felt that the bowls and other feature blocks were all displaced, as if like a jig-saw puzzle that had been jumbled up. We felt the site was charged with incredible energy and was very important in the scheme of understanding for Egypt's past. We needed more quiet time there to test it further.

We noticed how Egyptian bees have taken up abundant residence at the rear of the pyramid, and lizards darted about everywhere. As we wandered about in the stark silence, it was impossible to ignore the absolute tranquillity of the site. Judith spent some time on the centre of the alabaster base and described how light-headed she felt when we had to move on. We resolved to return in the future to try and gain a deeper insight. As an anecdote, when we returned home I turned to the internet to do some serious research on Abu Ghurab and was amazed at the observations and findings of William Henry. He was able to draw a link to our familiar stellar system of the Pleiades, and to several other indicators. These included the separation of gold through the use of flowing water and the electrical qualities of the mica that was evidenced on the ground at Abu Ghurab; along with the alabaster bowls for separation of the harvested gold. If a back door route is taken to get to the site it is impossible to ignore another stark contrast between the sheer beauty of the Temple and the sight of the canal bordering the agricultural road which yields access to it. The canal is as filthy and septic as the worst descriptions of old London before the fire. It is a marvel that local people live, work and eat only yards from its poisons. We are sad every time we see it, and even more sad for the animal carcasses casually dumped occasionally along its banks. For your own research on Abu Ghurab, read the William Henry report on:

http://www.bibliotecapleyades.net/stargate/stargate10.htm

The Underground Vortex and Stargate

Back at home-base we had been introduced to energies of a similar kind which related to the Solar Cross and the underground water table. We had been invited to visit the home elsewhere of another very important and respected keeper of the village. It was a visit we had long wished for and looked forward to. We found we had a powerful affinity with our new friend. Upon stepping through his front door to the ample hallway we saw there was a large rug decorating the stone floor. We took a few steps forward together in response to his welcome and were hit with the most powerful, tangible energy we have ever experienced. We were both dropped to our knees completely overcome with the power of an energy vortex which seemed to be rising irresistibly from beneath the floor. It was impossible to withstand it and we grabbed for each other as we fell to our knees and then right down on to the carpet. I called to Judith to just go with it, and everything else around us seemed irrelevant. I was as emotionally overcome by its power as Judith was. Impressions began to form clearly in my mind. I could see a rock dome beneath me with stone steps which wound down in a spiral under it. Some way below, these stopped at the edge of a strange water pool, and at the other side I could see a tunnel going straight off in the direction of the Plateau where we were absolutely aware of another important temple awaiting rediscovery.

As I looked down into the water I realised it was swirling like a huge whirlpool in a larger flow. Above its surface there was a fine energetic mist which was hypnotic and beautiful. I felt drawn to it and quite unable to resist its power. I let go and felt myself falling forward as if in slow motion. As the surface came towards me I had a complete awareness again of myself in the experience and I remember anticipating that I was about to hit the water with no sense of danger at all. But at the point where I should have splashed down, the feeling changed instantly and now I was falling through it. In a second I found myself in deep space just floating against a backdrop of stars and planets. No words can describe how beautiful it was. My Presence was overwhelmed and I could not stop my emotions rising to grab me. I tried to pull back, but couldn't stop my vibration condensing. In an instant I was fully cognitive, sitting on the carpet and reaching for Judith who was in a similarly overcome state. She had risen also with the energy rush. We got to our feet and began to gush with apologies to our host while our emotions spilled out. We tried to explain ourselves, but he was so calm. He took us to the inner room and asked us to sit with a drink and then we could talk. He asked me to sit in a particular place.

I told him we could only tell the truth to explain the experience. He then shocked us by naming three VIP spiritual men from over the years who had visited him and had felt something similar—and had all given their account from the same seat he had asked me to use. We were profoundly affected by what happened and in truth I had only felt a stronger and more enduring effect on the night of my *event* so many years ago. He told us that especially following this event he was going to finally investigate properly beneath his home.

We learned later he had gone only so far as to have a GPR survey done of his land. It showed a rock cap with stone stairway leading to moving water, and a tunnel stretching away from it. To our shock and sadness, our friend passed to spirit before he did any actual excavation. The time was evidently not right for the underground secret to be exposed. The site is still there today, undisturbed. However we know of yet another site not far from it where a shaft has located a further tomb complex. Initial items recovered have positively identified it as reaching back many thousands of years.

Free Explorations on the Plateau

Back on the Plateau there were many other places we wished to visit, but the time and the circumstances always had to be right. We knew better than to simply go as tourists and see some things under the strict control of the police or a guide tout. These only give limited access and cost a king's ransom. We have visited Giza many times and we know we must only put out a higher desire to see or experience something new, then like magic, the circumstances open for us.

It was on one early occasion we set off to walk along the outside wall of the cemetery. We had previously been taken as members of the mud-brick excavating team in the area bounded by the sphinx harbour and the cemetery. I guess we had been mistaken as data recorders or something close, but a member of the archaeology team on the site came to chaperone us carefully around the excavations to take whatever notes we wished, along with unlimited photographs. We evidenced the mud-brick built directly on top of the much earlier massive hewn stones and turned our attention to the harbour excavation in front of the Sphinx. It is configured thus:

A wide level pavement exists across the whole width of the front of the Temple and drops down to a second level. This continues out for an equal distance before sloping away gradually to the edge of the buried harbour basin. From the first stone pavement (like a quay) there are two narrow stone bridges (like jetties) which reach out on the same level until they drop away also to meet with the harbour edge. Just beyond where these bridge/jetties leave the initial pavement, a stone underpass has been formed beneath them. Hence their bridge description. At the lowest point of the underpass a slab had been removed to reveal a water filled shaft. The conversation revealed to us that this and another had been traced via tunnel and sumps back to the Nile, but we still seek corroborations . . . Our speculation is that they would have been perfect to regulate the water supply to/from the harbour when everywhere else was at the mercy of the Nile flood levels.

Back at the cemetery wall, we were approached by N, a stranger then, but a good friend now. He is not Egyptian but is a man of big stature and bigger Spirit. Once again he reacted to us in a friendly way and with a desire to help us. He asked us what we wanted to see. Our wish was to explore the cemetery inside and out. It was no problem and he simply led us forward. We walked the perimeter, taking a good look at the Wall of the Crow and noting along the way where a huge flood catchment sump had been excavated in the sand just west of the cemetery. Between the sump and the harbour there was word on the grapevine of an excavation that was undermining the wall of the cemetery. We had a good look and N explained there had been an undercutting excavation which was now shored up with blue sand-bags along the line of the cemetery perimeter path. However, he understood when it was opened; objects from elsewhere were brought to the site to embellish a photo/film call for public consumption. He said it was the reason was why there was such crazy security at the location for a while.

Eventually we were led into the cemetery. At each encounter with officials, N spoke a few words and we were able to continue. Inside the cemetery we were led to the famous Well for the first time. So much has been speculated about this Well and we were very excited to be there. We noted several things about it like for example the deep round shaft is not quite plumb. The brickwork of the shaft goes down until it meets with a thin rock shelf through which it continues into water. The foot-holds inside of the shaft seemed very precarious and slippery, but it must be easier to retrieve lost ropes and buckets by climbing down than trying to hook them out. It was possible to discern a swell in the water, indicating up-current or an active water flow, and the water itself was refreshing and delicious. We encountered others there. Questions drew answers that in the past the Well had been examined. We were told this produced evidence of a North/South and East/West tunnel traversing beneath the Well at different depths. We knew the Well dated back to a time long before the cemetery developed as it is now, and we also knew of its strategic importance for several geometric alignments on the Plateau. I am sorry it would be extremely detrimental to our current activities to share these openly yet, but they involve several important monuments. We have a huge, detailed plan-view photograph of the Plateau covering most of one wall at home. It is easy on this to check alignments. It was, and still is, a shock to see the precision of so many key geometries linking the most important features above and below ground. We were to visit in and around the Cemetery again in the future and gather much more information.

We had earlier recorded much work taking place beyond the workers village south of the Wall of the Crow at a position where the ground begins to rise to the highest point overlooking the lower Plateau. This is Gebl Gibli. On the ground however it was fascinating to see how workers had been recently manufacturing mud-bricks. These were lined up in hundreds. Row after row waited to dry before the pickup trailers came to fetch them. We understood these were being used for repairs to existing mud-brick constructions elsewhere on the Plateau.

From below Gebl Gibli we explored the caverns at its base adjoining the cemetery. A lot of excavation has taken place there which has all the appearance of being modern exploitive work. This was where we had observed the local dog pack often coming to rest in the day time, but the position was at the boundary of other dog packs which clashed from the western side of the mount or from the Crow area. We had no idea how useful our observations of the activities of the dogs would be to our later involvement with the animals of Giza; but it has always been fascinating to observe their interactions and their skill to escape unfriendly exchanges from other dogs and locals. Beneath the cliff of the mount we noticed an unusual feature not seen before in that when we examined photographs later, we saw a terrific simulacrum of a head formed by the main large rock formation—which seems precariously perched at the top of Gebl Gibli. We will be featuring this on site along with a 360 degree movie we took of the whole area from the summit. The narrow pass between the cemetery and Gebl Gibli is where dozens of workers with camels and horses take a short cut to the Plateau each day for work, and some can often be seen camped for a rest on the south side where the Wall of the Crow cuts into the Cemetery.

We paid another visit around 11.11.11 where there were no restrictive guards or police and we were able to explore at ease over the entire area. It was good to conduct first hand examinations of the Wall of the Crow and match them with the photographs and detail of Mark Lehner's work. In fact when we examined from topside of the wall we were surprised how untidy it looked. From the ground or from a distance the line of the wall looks quite level and orderly. On that visit we freely navigated Gebl Gibli itself and were able to gain great perspectives on other Plateau locations and their relationship to each other. It is popularly speculated that the geometric alignments from the datum point of Gebl Gibli, signify it as from where the pyramid fields were laid out. We looked down on a funeral taking place in the cemetery and we felt drawn to it from our vantage point. Our close friend had been laid to rest nearby, so it was even more poignant to know the funeral entourage were mourning where we had been earlier to pay our respects. We departed through the Wall entrance and through the well-worn break in the concrete tunnel-funnel which shepherds visitors into and out of the cemetery from the main Giza village road.

I mentioned earlier the special date 11.11.11. For us it was special because we went to the Plateau as it opened, just to see if any of the hugely speculated shenanigans would kick-off and to have another good day of exploration ourselves regardless of any other distractions.

We were buzzing as we woke to the day. We had been there almost two weeks and according to the fear-mongers we were facing the prospect of protest and mayhem at the gates to the

Plateau. However we already knew from our local contacts, the real outcome would be quite different. The pundits were sending messages around the internet that the plateau was to be blockaded by soldiers. The world was being told that access to the Plateau would be denied to everyone. Little did we know how bountiful the day would be.

The background to 11.11.11 and the political subterfuge weaving its tangled web of deceit and misdirection has been a wonder to unpick. The day was important, so it is worth taking a moment to examine the background events in a little more detail. At the heart of it, a planned and SCA approved proposed ceremony of *energetic spiritual invocation* was to have taken place within and around the Great Pyramid. The ceremony was organised through the auspices of a group called Project Cheops.

Those who search and visit their site will note that all description and photographs for the proposed ceremony are long gone. They were followed at the time with a simple message to bemoan the cancellation of their GP ceremony. The ceremony was to involve a private morning session of invocation in the GP to include the Manager of the group with the incumbent spiritual Medium of the organisation, plus a couple of other select participants. The self-proclaimed group of four were there in their capacity as *Human Angels* for the *chosen* people of Poland! Use was to be made in the coffer of a specially prepared crystal, which was shown in their promotion material. The crystal was formed loosely in the shape of a squashed tetrahedron; but as noted by another victim of the fiasco; its design followed the dimensions of the GP more than it followed a regular star tetrahedron. By other accounts it could have easily been described as a 3d actualisation for the Star of David. Accompanying the crystal tetrahedron, two rods of gold were to be used. These had been instructed to be inscribed with words from the Bible: *Man does not live by bread alone.* Incredibly, one rod inscription was to be in Polish and the other to be in Hebrew. We only had the word of the Medium at the heart of the Cheops group as to why they had to be prepared in this way, but it had been noted that the Hebrew version potentially exalted its Jewish origins.

Many people had been attracted to visit Giza to attend the second ceremony. This was to be, *hands around the Great Pyramid* by the required minimum of 1200—1500 people. We understand that while the encircled people directed their energies towards the group leader, a simultaneous second ceremony would be held in private in the King's Chamber. This was all to take place much later in the evening. Previous visitors will know how unprecedented it would have been anyway for the Plateau to be opened late in the evening for any public ceremony at all involving the Great Pyramid.

Right up to the day as we can vouch first-hand, people were arriving to Giza for the event. In the background, conflict was developing where the former and then the current director of the SCA publically announced their opposition to any ceremony, which in their view possibly sought to continue the 30 year effort by the Jewish nation in their claim upon Egypt's heritage as pyramid builders. An allegation was even made that Jewish people had been recruited to form the human ring of hands around the GP!

The whole issue became very loud and public. People were openly discussing it; and it was just before the event that the organisers took-down the event description from their website and replaced it with a message, effectively implying that arrangements were on hold only subject to security concerns being sorted out. Finally there was a summary cancellation of the event. Tickets had been bought and even the group leaders who organised the event flew in for the day only to be confined to meetings and discussions from their hotel base. It was to no avail and speculation was rife that there would be a whole lot of bovver on the plateau on 11.11.11. However we knew different. We knew that ordinary people had been turning up from mixed countries and with mixed beliefs. Those we spoke to were united in one aim and that was to generate a positive spiritual vibration on the day. Wild speculations were rife. From more than one source it was suggested that the deposed ZH had reached out in bitterness and had spiked the event to embarrass specific high officials who had helped in his downfall. We were told with far more certainty however by good friends in the village there would be a police and army presence there for sure; but only as a security precaution because of the whole whoohaa!

So it was. On the day we wanted to go up on to the Plateau for other reasons. We arrived at opening time and went through as normal. At the gate and inside, the Army and Police were there as a predictable show of force. Initially it was a bit surreal to be met with the sight of tactical army vehicles sporting machine guns and a number of police decked in riot gear. But they did not resist us taking photographs, and even posed. Within the plateau it was absolutely fine. It was still a local festival day. The police and watchmen continued to play a hands-off role. This was fantastic for all as it enabled free access to areas which would not be allowed any other time. Locals climbed all over even the most sensitive monuments unopposed, including the sphinx. As you will read, we took full advantage of the freedom ourselves.

Henutsen and The Temple of Isis

We made our way to the head of the Plateau by the GP and probably should have waited until a few more people were there. We climbed the southernmost of its three pyramids; thought to have been the tomb of Queen Henutsen. There was an enthusiastic and unfriendly tout/guard at the base who tried to shoo us away, but very soon afterwards there were scores of locals all over it. We managed to get fine panoramic photos over the lower plateau. We descended and turned our attention to the Temple of Isis (G1C) at the foot of the Henutsen pyramid. We had always wanted to get a closer look at this temple. In the past we found this area crawling with tourists and touts so it was refreshing to explore and photograph in peace. The temple is intriguing because of the dispute to correctly attribute it. James Henry Breasted, 1906, attributed it to the 4th dynasty, and this seemed to stick; aided by Sitchin in 1976. The dispute arose from the interpretation of a Steele found nearby which was later dismissed as fake by Egyptologists. The Steele inscription was given weight by the fact of the word Henut from it being translated as mistress, and therefore the temple was assumed as correctly dedicated to Isis, The Mistress of the pyramid. However as a contradiction in terms, the name, Mistress of the Pyramids does not appear until circa 2700BP long after the supposed birth of the Great Pyramid. Certainly the physical evidence on our visit supports the later date because it can be seen that the adjacent Mastaba has been damaged to facilitate the temple construction. Neighbouring mastabas were normally built for family members and in this case for Kephren, son of Khufu. The argument therefore is that Khufu, having built the mastaba for his son, is unlikely to have ripped into it to enable an extension of the Isis temple.

On site, it is clear to see how the temple extends across the quasi road/pathway between the satellite pyramids and the Mastaba field, and continues on with an avenue through the adjacent mastaba. There are many hieroglyphic characters preserved on the extended temple blocks and plenty of evidence for more elaborate (missing) sections; and there are also several clear examples of machine tooling on the rocks. Just as the avenue extends into the mastaba field there is a podium at the side, a little more than waist height. It holds a stone bowl atop which a guide previously speculated to us was for hand washing or purification before entering the main temple. For many people when they visit here it must seem like a simple opportunity for a photo shoot against the backdrop of a few preserved pillars and stonework with the GP in the background. It would be so much better for the visitor experience if they knew the background story to the site. We agreed it was yet another missed opportunity for the Egyptian authorities to position simple information boards for tourists. Whatever the truth, we felt a tremendous amount of energy there.

The Causeway Shafts and the Osiris Tomb

It was still early morning and we decided to walk along Kephren's causeway. Walking east down the causeway there are several very deep shafts on the left, which we had tried repeatedly to get close to in the past. Excavations here are on-going and guards are over enthusiastic! On one occasion we simply took photographs in the direction of the shafts and were warned off sternly by plain clothed police and were followed for the rest of that day on the plateau. This time there were no restrictions and no guards. It was such a pleasure to go from shaft to shaft gaining valuable observations and taking close photographs. I was also able to take useful laser depth measurements. Judith and Bruce waited on the causeway while I got on with the inspection. Seven shafts so far are dotted close to the causeway, ending with the so called Campbell's tomb. At this, as the lowest and most easterly grand causeway shaft, I was able to go down into the trench surrounding the central shaft. This is filling fast with blown sand but it was interesting to get a feel for its speculated purpose. One could easily imagine it being part of a ramped inner access to the shaft and its underground, with a stone temple superstructure which has long since been robbed from its position above the shaft.

Some of the shafts have deep rebated grooves in their sides, and most reach to a depth of around 100 feet, commensurate with the Osiris tomb. Just like in the Osiris, water could be observed at their deep base and in many cases there are side tunnels leading off into the plateau. I was able to tie these observations with those from the Osiris tomb but I will talk more on that shortly. The rebated grooves in two opposite sides of so many shafts suggest a hydraulic rise-and-fall use of some kind? At the higher end of the causeway, the latest two shafts to be worked on are rigged with professional winching equipment. Alongside there is a mountain of spoil removed from below ground. These are the ones most sensitive to the authorities. At least now everyone will have the chance to judge from themselves when we publish photos and descriptions from all of them on our website. Even simple examination of the shafts seems to confirm their connection with the Osiris shaft and with the (Swiss cheese) network of deep plateau tunnels. The published work of Hamilton M Wright in collaboration with Dr Selim Hassan in 1935, extensively described a fabulous underground tunnel, shaft and chamber complex which was lately rediscovered and explored. Ever since then, the whole topic of possibility has been blocked solid by the establishment. Hmm!

We have been blessed to descend the Osiris Shaft a number of times including the visit a few days previously thanks to the arrangements of our colleague Bill Brown. I was concerned for Judith when she made her first descent because the ladder drops into darkness after the first level. The second strenuous climb is like descending a fire escape from a three storey building wearing a blindfold. I need not have worried as she followed with no hesitation. The second level at about 80 feet below ground contains the seven niche tombs with what is left of basalt sarcophagi. We have studied the convoluted records regarding the Osiris shaft and it is frustrating to know there may be another entrance or shaft on this level which was deliberately concealed by the authorities. We did not have the time or the equipment to search greatly, but the profile of the excavation suggests many positions where there may be concealment. We continued down to the magical final water-table chamber.

You can smell the water before you finally step down to the rock platform at 100feet. The chamber is filled with crystal clear water and only floating scum obscures its depth. So clear to see, the four broken pillars of the Osiris tomb strain to rise above the water surface, while the sarcophagus beckons through the surface from a couple of feet below. A wooden staging has been constructed from the chamber entry point and across to the other side alongside the west wall of the chamber. To negotiate this it is necessary to crawl low to the ground with back scraping the roof, until the space opens out to give a few feet more height. Immediately on the other side of the walkway we were confronted with the big hole cut into the side of the chamber. This is the entrance to the mud tunnel, so called because first exploration by ZH it was found it to be blocked by mud slurry. I climbed into it and made my way inside its tight fit for several yards as far as I could reach safely. Nevertheless I noted how the tunnel rose at about 40 degrees and just beyond my position, split into two tunnels, both probably travelling to shafts not too far away which were identifiable from the surface. By the way, I paid the price of not wearing appropriate clothing as I found when on the surface again. I was covered with the wet mud/clay still evident on the bottom of the tunnel! The purpose of the mud tunnel has not been officially determined, but it is assumed to have had a hydraulic function. The authorities as ever give no public explanation; and in fact under ZH they have been positively devious and untruthful in their reference to the *known* facts about the Osiris shaft. When we studied the water chamber we noticed on the lower east side, the rock overhangs and crooks, as if hiding a fault entrance. We would love to have been able to get into the water and explore for ourselves.

However we do know from record when the water/tomb chamber was investigated under the disputed licence of Boris Said, in February 1997, his colleague Dr Thomas Dobecki determined the lid of the large sarcophagus to be about 30 inches thick. More importantly he determined a domed ceiling tunnel over 6 feet beneath the sarcophagus. The tunnel, itself is over six feet wide and runs at a 25 degree angle towards the sphinx. Furthermore, in 1996, Dr Dobecki's radar equipment detected another likely tunnel anomaly of the same description, emerging about 9 feet below ground from the rear of the sphinx heading towards the tunnel from beneath the Osiris shaft sarcophagus. No one can be surprised to find a complete official denial of this evidence and a complete absence of motivation to investigate it fully—at least as far as the public are concerned! The same can be said for the shafts of matching depth on the other side of the causeway and not too far away which all have features in common with the Osiris shaft. You don't have to be a Brain Surgeon to work out that the authorities are motivated to prevent anyone beneath them from knowing about the World Heritage prize below ground of the whole Plateau and Village areas.

On each visit we have wanted to spend much more time there with better photographic equipment. No one ever pays much attention to the raw surface of the walls, but as you will read later, this fact is central to our journey coming full circle again back to the Kings Chamber of the GP. We have many photographs from the Osiris shaft which need to be investigated deeply to see what they may reveal.

The Central Mastaba Field

However, back now to our excursion of 11.11.11.
I completed my tour of the causeway shafts and joined again with Judith and Bruce. Many more locals were now appearing on the plateau and we decided we would continue walking down towards the sphinx harbour. Just as we started on our way a solitary watchman greeted us in passing. We walked on as if to ignore him but a gut feeling told me not to pass him by. I turned back, greeted him, and held out my hand to give him a small cash handshake. He seemed reluctant but embraced me and indicated for us all to follow him. He was unlike the usual jabbering frantic touts and instead seemed almost humble or meek and spoke only using gently gesture. Only on one occasion he raised his voice to chastise some local children close to a deep shaft.

Judith and I have been in and around the central Mastaba field East of Kephren many times. There are constructs of huge importance there. However our surprise guide took us to see a host of places we had not seen before, and gave us a number of validations for things we have been working on. It was ironic actually because on a previous normal visit, Judith had strayed into the central field until we lost sight of her. I went to find her as Bill scanned from the causeway. I searched everywhere and became alarmed until she reappeared some time later. She had clambered almost as far as the 4th dynasty Queen Khenkaus pyramid tomb. I was sure the guards who were in abundance at the time would home-in on us. It didn't happen, but now we were being systematically guided throughout the whole central field where before we had been hopping like gazelles on the structures and walls above the pathways we were now exploring. With our guide we were able to fully explore Khenkaus tomb site. We had been there before also when we were let inside to descend the sloping ramp and explore the large chamber below. At the time we were informed that ZH had plans to commence a fresh major excavation, but this was never validated. On this trip it was a joy to examine its outer surface properly and the recently uncovered mud-brick house foundations nearby. We continued to explore outside and inside tomb after tomb along the way as we headed back towards the causeway.

Soon we knew we would need to return to base but we noted the time was fast approaching 11.00am of 11.11.11. For whatever importance the time and date may or may not have held, it seemed spontaneously important for us to just halt in silence. Our guide initiated the moment and we all felt a distinct rush of spirit as our tiny group stood there lost to the rest of the world amid the shafts, tunnels and Mastabas of Kephren. It was a golden moment. Then Judith and I had to move on to another appointment while Bruce opted to continue productively with our guide. We walked the shortcut at the southern end of the sphinx harbour where it is possible to cut parallel to the cemetery wall and join up with the back road out to the main sphinx road. In this way we were able to record the latest progress with the extended harbour excavations. These have revealed many later mud-brick building constructions. As we walked amongst the exposed wall stumps we longed for the day when these would be recorded and scalped down to the real ancient treasure constructions many feet further below. Along this back route we photographed more new pumping wells appearing here also like an ugly rash. We hoped we would be able to make sense of the gauge dial results later when we studied the photographs.

Qar, Idu, Meresankh 111 and Seshemnefer 1V

During this stay there were four other locations which were drawn into our path and had a powerful influence on us. On a previous visit I had mentioned to our host there was a mastaba entrance which intrigued us. It was centre east of the GP and off the beaten track for tourists. We had been investigating the shafts of the eastern cemetery and their layout and saw steep stone steps leading down to a huge mastaba entrance well below ground level. We noted the solid padlocked metal doors and the substantial electrical cables leading into the mastaba. We felt it must be a really important location, but it was not until the following year when the subject cropped up again.

We had been with Bill and joined with a group of friends who were on a paid tour of special sites. Access permissions had been acquired and we were lucky to have been accepted as late additions to the group. We were only asked to make a token contribution and we felt very privileged as we made our way to the Tombs of Qar and Idu. We had heard of these tombs and knew their interiors were very beautiful and covered with depictions and reliefs. We were not disappointed. The tombs are south of the GP causeway not far from the pyramid. Qar was overseer of the towns of Khufu and Menkaure and was married to Gefi. She was known as the Prophetess of Hathor. Inside the tomb the wall decoration is spellbinding, but there was another attraction which brought me a bit of trouble. In one of the anterooms I had the strange vibrational feeling that I experienced in the Kings Chamber and just had to try the intonement sound. Immediately the whole chamber rose in a booming resonance just as in the GP. It was exhilarating, but in the main chamber the guide was trying to give a lecture tour to the main group and he was completely drowned out. There was consternation until someone homed in on me as the culprit. I was oblivious, and was just building it more and more as I drifted to another place! Oops as I had to stop and allow the resonance to slowly decay. Later before we headed for the exit I could not help giving it one more burst, just to feel the way the stone responded and the magical feeling as the resonance returned to the body.

Right next door is the tomb of Idu and he is argued to be the son or even the father of Qar. Idu's tomb is smaller but no less fascinating with its well preserved wall depictions. Idu also held many titles and like Qar was tenant of the Pyramid of Pepu1. He was an overseer of the Scribes and was Inspector of the Khufu and Kephren pyramid priests. Visiting these tombs in such well-preserved condition shaved centuries of time from them. It made us feel so much closer to the life of their users; and of course added weight to the idea that their resonant quality was not accidental.

There was still time for another tomb visit. When Bill, Judith and I joined with the group we knew the group was on a visiting tour but had only thought it was to the Osiris Shaft. Bill had pulled strings with close friends who were organising the outing. The Qar and Ida tombs were therefore a beautiful bonus we had not expected. When we learned there were a couple more locations to see, we were overjoyed. We had no idea where we were being taken and tagged along at the back. We cut through the mastabas of the Eastern cemetery, parallel to the Great Pyramid and I realised we were walking in a direction that would intercept the intriguing locked mastaba entrance I mentioned earlier. I could hardly believe the synchronicity as we climbed down the steps to go inside; and of course as we know now, it is the double mastaba of Queen Merasankh111. The tomb is absolutely beautiful inside. Meresankh111 was the wife of her half-brother Khafre. She was also the daughter of Kaweb who was born of Khufu and Hetepheres11. The interior walls have reliefs and colourful depictions of daily life. Carvers and sculptors are shown in progress with depictions of the subjects; and surface after surface is filled with other aspects of their lives. On one wall, gold smelters can even be viewed making a palanquin. A rickety staircase winds nearly twenty feet down the shaft off the main chamber to where the Queen's black granite sarcophagus was excavated by Reisner, before it was then removed to the Egyptian museum.

When we emerged to the sunlight there was a big phew from all of us. Everyone was very impressed. All that would have been enough, but there was one more delight to the day. Once again we tagged along as the group was led with purpose up on to the road south east of the G.P. Just at the top of the road there is an iconic pillared Mastaba set back from the road. It is often the subject of souvenir photo shoots and in recent times was substantially cleaned and restored. Previously during more sensitive times, this was another location that Judith and I had tried hard to visit. Back then it was sealed tight and well-guarded. We just couldn't get near it! Now it was open and inviting, and we were striding up the walkway to enter it. It is actually the tomb of Seshemnefer IV who was clearly a very important person in his day. In DynastyV1 his titles included Guardian of the King's Secrets, and Overseer of The Two Seats of the House of Life. There are spacious halls inside with statues and side offering chambers, all showing daily Old Kingdom scenes. From the far end we were quick to grab a chance to descend the sloping shaft to the impressive burial chamber. Here it was possible to squeeze around the sarcophagus and climb up to peek inside where the lid had been displaced. We captured many photographs there which had much more significance than we could ever realise. This aspect would reveal itself much later following further explorations into the NC2 system. In fact it was out of a major discovery from NC2 that several of the major places we visited would be given an exciting common denominator. This will become clear later.

Going Back 4500 years

We had other plans afoot and left the plateau early. Now it was much later and we were in the pitch dark of night. In a whisper we were ushered forward through the bare minimum of an opening past the heavy louvre door of a building. We had been warned to be silent, and I could feel Judith clutching behind me at my jacket for balance. The door was closed very quietly and our guide allowed a peep—hole of light to escape to the ground from his flashlight. There was a heavy musty smell of soil and dust in the air. We gingerly followed the light, hardly daring to breathe. A second door was banked up either side with the debris of cast—aside clothes and personal items. It was opened with even less sound to more darkness and silence. We tiptoed forward, following the shadow in front of us. From the tiny light we could see dirty grey sand piled up to our right, leaving a small track where the passage had been. Our guide whispered,

'*Stay quiet and be careful when we go through the doorway.*'

The next door had been removed leaving just the frame to grab hold of. Finally the voice said,

'*Ok it is safe now but talk only in whisper;*' and then speaking into the room he added

'*Make some light.*'

We immediately realised there were others there as the sound of a light switch brought illumination to the room from a dim light bulb. It was like one of those I have seen in old gangster movies where the small bulb swings from a high-strung electrical flex. But even in the dim light, what a sight greeted us! We had been given a privilege for sure this time even though blindly led to the site of the excavation. There were a few other men present. They squatted in silence around the perimeter of the room on a continuous pile of soil which framed a raised wooden shaft at the centre. They had been warned of our arrival and reached in turn to greet us warmly with a smile or a nod and a handshake. These were clearly not reckless youngsters but sensible seasoned men. We learned that between them they would have had enough archaeological and engineering skill to have done justice to the escape committee in a prisoner of war camp. We knew at least from how we were taken to the place that we were at ground level, but the shaft, about six feet square, reached down perhaps 18 feet to water. We were allowed to go closer to the edge for better inspection. In more whispers it was explained to us that a very old and important tomb site had been pinpointed. We were already aware these men were not traditional ground robbers. They were of the same order as others we had encountered along the way who were pursuing their ancient heritage. I was surprised by an invitation to climb down and readily agreed even though it was going to be barefoot and without the agility of youth on my side. Judith nodded in affirmation and I climbed over the edge. At the bottom there was a spindly Egyptian. We learned he was a highly experienced shaft builder/tunneller and was directing operations. At the bottom the water and silt covered to my ankles. Side by side, we had little room for manoeuvre. He spoke freely with me to make sense of the confused sides of the lowest exposed section of the shaft. There was about 18 inches of the unsupported side walls to examine. He had me kneel beside him in the water and pointed to where one wall was hollowed out to a depth of almost two feet. He used the water to splash either side which revealed coloured handmade bricks tiered with thin, shaped granite slabs. They formed the side walls to an opening or channel of some kind. He indicated the opening would lead to a tomb entrance. I asked how he knew so much and he began to grope amongst the fluid silt beside him. He produced a dome shaped, smooth round carved rock about 12 inches across where an arrow indicator had been carved on its top surface. It had been found pointing in the direction of the entrance that they would continue excavating. This was a recognised indicator. Again he reached behind us and pulled another carved rock from where it had been temporarily embedded to the wall. It was a fantastic stone carving of a raised cobra. It was missing its head. There was another carved rock the same up top which was being shown to Judith. We were told the missing uraeus snake heads had probably been deliberately broken off and sealed inside the tomb to protect it. The sculptures had been discovered either side at the start of the bricked entrance way. He explained they would be working carefully and it would take a long time to make further progress as they were level with the water table, and sections of the tomb continued to lower levels. They were sure they would find other offerings around the entrance. Apparently this site was linked to a larger even more obscure site a long way off by a deep underground connecting tunnel which had already been detected. I was awestruck by all we were being exposed to but the experience was not over. There was a haulage basked alongside us and my companion wanted to fill it and send it to the surface before we climbed out. He asked me to help him scoop more watery silt into it so it could be cleared away. I joined him to do so but after a couple of scoops I felt him grab my arm firmly. He said, *Richard look at this!*

From the silt beneath us he swished his other hand in the water and lifted it to reveal an exquisite bifacial chert knife several inches long. It was phenomenal. He had just found it and handed it to me to examine. Its edges were worked with master precision and it was immensely beautiful. He said, *This is good. It will give us a date.*

It would place the site to at least 4500 years old. The blade was very high quality and was shaped from imported chert. I later confirmed its distinct profile was of the 1st to 4th Dynastic period. We wished we were a part of the on-going work but we were just on a privileged visit and soon had to leave. I climbed reluctantly to the top of the shaft to let Judith and the others see the knife close-up. We were led home by the same careful and obscure method used to bring us to the site. Even now we get occasional updates which tell us how considerable engineering skill has had to be applied because of the fluctuating water table at the level of the tomb complex. We met the attitude often that if the authorities continue to keep the really ancient finds to themselves, then work will continue in abundance privately to uncover a true understanding of our ancient past. One recent development was a find in the same shaft below the water. The first of four known slabs were found. These thick slabs were placed as coverings to deeper existing shafts. At least the first shaft had stone steps leading down into the murky depths of the compacted silt slurry. Upon more careful examination, the first slab was seen to also have a twin hollowed basin on one side. This suggests its dual purpose as a funerary offering table. We hope may learn the outcome of further work at the site.

The Magnetism of NC2

Although all of these experiences were fantastic and generated an ever greater respect for the sophisticated society behind them, our minds never strayed from a desire to explore the underground. We have never wavered from the expectation of finding preserved and conclusive evidence there which would overturn the established time blockage to a final understanding of our true roots. We wanted to follow in the footsteps of such as Henry Salt and Giovanni Caviglia. Since our first visit inside the NC2 complex we had visited its barred entrance a number of times just make the connection again. We were now interested in it to the point of obsession, from day research to night time dreams and OBE's underground. Originally our combined experience drew us towards the Kings Chamber of the GP or to the GP itself. We struggled to understand why an equal pull had developed for NC2. Each time we visited we picked up more hearsay about the place. The strongest was from police friends who told us it had been used temporarily by ZH to store sensitive items before their permanent removal from the plateau. We have no idea if this was true, but we knew from a new exploration into the sub-tombs of NC2 that significant items *were* removed and *had* disappeared with no mention or trace. Furthermore, everyone who had anything to do with the western area of the plateau seemed scared or paranoid if NC2 was mentioned.

Following the public debacle and slanging match between ZH and the modern re-discoverers of the system, Andrew Collins and his colleagues, its entrance had been barred by a solid Iron Gate and grille. Officially this was placed to keep out any *pyramididiots* as ZH termed anyone outside the establishment. It was also justified to preserve the contents of the tomb and its underground cave system until an official archaeological investigation could take place. I can at no point give details of our unusual and charmed method to enter the tomb each time, suffice to say it could never implicate any innocent Official, Police Officer or civilian. Just ask yourself if it seems logical that any vast system of such huge importance would have a single front door in the back of a tucked-away tomb!

We knew that the official attitude was to whitewash anything to do with NC2 and keep all information from it completely secret. Our follow-up visit told a completely different story, but not before I was saved from a severe beating at best on a preceding official attempt to re-enter the system. Perhaps it would be best to elaborate a little of what happened.

Dr Hawass had featured the cavern system in the meantime in his television series Chasing Mummies. In a Blairwitch style camera expedition, an excitable Dr Hawass led a troupe of pseudo investigative film crew witnesses tramping like blind elephants throughout. Between his screams of complaint at the bats and the caves, he declared that from this (professional) evaluation, the caves contained nothing and led nowhere! It can easily be proved, even from the dissection of stills from the episode, that the whole thing was an unforgivable deception which flew in the face of any serious archaeological evaluation. The video episode had undoubtedly been stitched into the series in response to the public furore whipped up again by the DVD offered by AC to the public. It did not matter that the DVD basically presented only what had already been delivered ad hoc to the public. For ZH, the subject was now a matter of saving official face!

We had been drawn into the public debate in dispute with AC. Initially we presented our copious evidence very quietly but it became impossible to be divorced from the deceptions that were being woven about NC2. Our first visit photographs had shown simulacrum, carvings, mummified remains, painted images on the walls and a crocodile sculpted sarcophagus in one of the lower tomb chambers. We thought there may even have been another sarcophagus obscured behind the first. Eventually we offered almost 100 HD original photographs from within the caves and caverns to be downloaded free for the public for them to investigate themselves; but not before offering all of our findings and evidence privately to the Egyptian authorities. There had been no response and indeed to date there has been not a shred of serious investigative feedback from any of the numerous people who have downloaded our pictures.

Time was passing and I made enquiries to see if it may be possible to gain official access. A generous free donation would be offered in exchange, to be used for the general work of the plateau. Via intermediaries the negotiations were looking optimistic. On the day, I was actually in the car at a remote Giza gate, about to be taken for a final official meeting before I would be allowed very limited visiting time at NC2. However, unknown to me, a very senior person at the head of this chain had mistakenly identified me as AC. I learned later that the person had drawn a wrong conclusion when my enquiries had reached his level. He had a particular interest because following the Collins/Hawass public conflict, many senior people including him had suffered wrath from the fallout as new security was hastily put in place—deployed as a reaction to the public loss of face suffered by Dr Hawass.

By synchronicity, my host who had been with me a short time earlier to drop me off for my connection had left with an uneasy feeling. He felt compelled to call a favour from a very trusted friend at the location I was to be taken to. He stopped and managed to reach him on the phone. The friend tipped my host that all was not well with the arrangement. He knew my identity had been mistaken and my intended patron would not be there to greet me when I arrived. Instead, I was to be met by a *reception* committee. They were going to take me somewhere to *re-educate me* and set an example. I did not learn how severe the lesson was going to be.

The synchronicity was completed when my host returned across the desert at high speed to retrieve me from my link car. I had been delayed by just enough minutes as my driver chatted to a colleague. It was like a spoof from Indiana Jones with great clouds of dust as my host screeched into the compound. He explained the whole plot to me when we were some distance away in safety. There was a de-brief with official friends next day which confirmed the whole story. I swear these facts to be true. Such is the intensity and base feeling when it comes to the power playing and control of affairs of the plateau. One would think there was much more at stake than a few old ruins under the sand!

So following the shameful official investigation visit by Dr Hawass into NC2, we were faced with the questions we hoped the public would also be asking themselves. Everyone can imagine how excruciatingly long it takes to complete even a simply excavation! Most will also realise how painstaking and careful the work must be in order to measure and record everything. This was one good reason why we never disturbed anything within the NC2 system though it would have been so easy to have removed a host of valuable items while they were still there. The Zahi Hawass, Chasing Mummies visit could not even hold a candle to these same basic standards. Here was a vast, complex underground system which potentially stretched miles, and equally may be stuffed full of items of heritage reaching well beyond the established time frame of establishment archaeology. So, clearly there may be years of skilled archaeological work to be carried out at NC2. The entrance was barred, but feverish activity nevertheless subsequently took place. It seemed that an official handpicked gang of workers were there digging inside for a few weeks. When we visited the system again we were able to make a direct comparison with the state we had found it in originally. This indicated the lack of care and expertise that had been employed during the few frantic weeks of official archaeological excavation. Read on to see what we found and be your own judge.

We were shocked immediately to find that the whole system had been raped of any items of obvious significance. There was no pretence. A full scale clear-out operation had taken place. Even layman's logic would have expected a legitimate archaeological clean-up operation to have concentrated on the hundreds of tons of windblown sand blocking the main tomb sub-chambers. Some sand had been cleared, but the sub-chambers are substantially still choked with sand. In the tunnel system there were plenty of smaller or more obscure items remaining, but anything large or meaningful was gone. Significantly in one of the lower tomb chambers where there had been at least one large sarcophagus, and maybe another one; now only debris remained. We have published the pictures from before and afterwards to prove it but nothing compares to the stark reality of witnessing this in person.

The world had been told that the barred entrance was to stop robbers from gaining entry to the system. Now we knew it was to stop the public from learning that the system had been raped of its initial archaeology treasures by official thieves; and therefore also the knowledge that went with them.

We were astonished that those in charge were blatantly stealing the truth from their own people and the world. Yet again we agreed that the contents of this officially dismissed tomb system must be a thousand times more important than the lies given to the public.

We examined the sub-chambers more carefully. There was one area that had previously caught our attention. It linked two chambers in the form of two apparent small tunnel entrances high at the ceiling levels where they joined the walls on their south west corners. Both entrances would be difficult to access and in any case were obstructed by large loose boulders. However it was clear to see these were entrances to another natural tunnel system which had all the hallmarks of being linked to a further part of NC2. From what I could remember of our previous visit I realised the boulders in these new tunnels had been disturbed since then. It was sufficient to make the effort to investigate further. The height was not great in real terms, perhaps 8 to 10 feet, but in the semi-darkness on a smooth wall and with no climbing equipment it was difficult. Inside the entrance to chamber G as I have marked it on our schematic drawing, I was able to confirm that person/s had been there recently trying to clear a passage. The tunnel is awkward, small, and branched north, presumably to join with the similar cave entrance from chamber H. The main tunnel direction continued in an upward elevation south/south east, which would put it on a connection course with the huge sub-reception chamber inside the actual NC2 tunnel system. Whoever had been there recently had failed to clear rocks which prevented deeper exploration. If this additional tunnel network had started life as a natural water course, there were clear signs it had been enlarged in the distant past for a purpose yet to be determined. Later we discovered absolute evidence to validate this theory.

Out of the tomb sub-chambers, we turned our attention to the cave system itself. Through the opening at the end of the ground level tomb corridor, we entered the remodelled natural system. The same evidence of recent disturbance met us in its enormous reception chamber and in the previously mentioned sub-reception chamber. No effort had been made to systematically examine the archaeology. The rock strewn floors had been completely rummaged and items we had first photographed were mostly gone. Much deeper into the plateau where we had previously identified plugged openings near to the Tube Tunnel; these had been opened and pillaged of whatever had been inside them. It was the same story throughout. The official working party had been a snatch and grab raiding party. It seems our hundreds of photographs and our testimonies are the only substantial independent record of what was in the system before this recent official activity!

I held back and stood in the deep inky blackness; and at one stage I turned off my light and stood quietly for a time to try and feel the powerful vibrations we felt there before. It was hopeless. This part of the system had been so badly violated. My emotions were overcome and spilled out. I am consolidated by the fact that whoever was in there missed other very significant things which we are keeping quiet about at the moment lest the same official thieves return again for what they may have missed!

At well over 250 feet into the system the journey falters amid the stench of ammonia from the bat droppings and urine; though the bat colony is much reduced from disturbance. The next section is via the Tube Tunnel barely big enough for a person to crawl through in any comfort. I was familiar with it sufficiently to still have a fairly accurate picture in my mind of what I would find. Alongside on the ground there was a discarded ammonia protection mask plus other items junked by the mystery working crew who had been in there. Upon arrival at the Tube Tunnel my fears were justified even by the vandalism done to the plugged openings I had seen before in the adjacent chamber. These had been broken open and were clean as a whistle of whatever they had contained. I peered into the Tube Tunnel and I saw there was now a blockage. I saw that the stone tablets which previously appeared to be plugging a small shaft in the floor of the tunnel, along with several objects some distance further into the tube by the left hand wall, were also gone.

I was properly suited-up and had my mask & gloves and I crawled into the Tube. At about 2x body lengths into it I noticed a number of things. First there were small openings from the tunnel right side into extensive narrow tunnel niches. I could barely move and tried to take pictures of these. Some worked and we have published these. In the darkness by flashlight, the camera struggled to find focus. Ahead of me the Tube was blocked by a mass of fairly fine multi-coloured spoil. It gradually sloped away from me over perhaps 6 to 8 feet, rising until it nearly blocked to the top of the Tube Tunnel. The spoil did not seem to completely match the colour of the walls of the tube, and there was no way it was all naturally in place. More caught my eye. I saw at the bottom of this slope of sandy debris, slightly larger stones of a couple of inches had rolled off and gathered in front of me. It was the glint that caught my flashlight, because there amongst the spoil was aluminium foil of the kind that workers use from the shop to wrap food. I had crawled more than 12 feet into the Tube Tunnel which contained no blockage on the first visit. It was now blocked with alien material for at least another 12 visible feet by material that had been introduced deliberately and by hand. The elevation angle of the gradual slope coupled with the rolled off stones and the worker's debris under it, spelled out a clear message. The early explorers, Salt and Caviglia described how they gained access to the belly of the Plateau through a forced tunnel, *The Tube Tunnel*. We could have followed their trail on our first visit, but now the Tube Tunnel had been blocked from the other end! That meant only one thing.

Others had gained an alternate access to the NC2 system deeper underground, and had heaped spoil into the Tube Tunnel to block it from the deeper system end. Their blockage spoil tapered in my direction just as our photographic evidence proves. I was shocked to be faced with this affirmation of the secret underground system, and to realise the supreme effort of powerful persons to conceal its existence and purpose, from the world.

The visit was traumatic because we felt the violation that had been carried out. It almost seemed personal, and it was not long before we were planning more visits. Now we needed to take measurement so that a first schematic drawing could be developed. This was needed to make sense of the orientation of the chambers and their relationship to each other. A schematic would also help to speculate hidden connections within the system. This time I needed to visit alone to make use of the quiet freedom to work. Neither of us had any aversion to potential hazards in the system and in fact I can say the feeling to us was welcoming and even comfortable. That is not to say there were no dangers. The tunnels and caverns contained poisonous insects as our photographs showed, and the rocks themselves posed a severe hazard. I would need to be properly suited, with other safety equipment ready for use.

So it was on a following occasion, but this time I had a better camera, a new Laser measure and better lights. It was still hard work to carry out a measurement survey of the whole interior. There was little problem with the ground level tomb, but the variances and the accumulated tons of sand in the sub chambers made the job extremely difficult. In the natural tunnel system it was very clear that far more specialised survey equipment would be needed to produce a really accurate schematic diagram. Those who had been there officially had strung a mains electrical supply to halogen lamp units in scattered locations, but unfortunately the supply was no longer connected. Time ran out on me and it was on a further visit alone that I was able to take more definitive pictures of specific areas of interest. By the second time alone in the system, I had had time to study some of the early pictures and produce our schematic drawing of the system as we knew it so far. We had been able to make first educated deductions from this. The tomb sub-chambers are accessed from the tomb entrance, set back and down steps either side to corridors. The left hand east side had a short corridor which simply joined the openings to two chambers. The corridor to the right hand west side of the entrance was much longer and the chambers held more obvious promise. There are four to the right of the corridor and two to the left. The last one on the left lies directly under the floor of a higher chamber which branches from the end of the main tomb corridor, and opposite the opening into the natural cave system. The upper chamber is still full with sand and perhaps there is hidden access between them.

The right hand corridor curves a little to the west and ends in a stepped niche. No special significance could be noted about this until we completed and studied the schematic. The main reception chamber of the natural system is directly above it, and the corridor lines up directly with the continuing tunnel into the deeper natural system. This is not all! Up in the big chamber it had been clear to us the big elevated slab in the centre was very significant. Closer examination showed there was a deliberate hewn channel below it which emerged at the lower level of the reception chamber like a throne. We were able to estimate that the sub-chamber right hand corridor came to a stop, crossing directly beneath the feet of the slab/throne feature in the reception chamber. These features and the chamber must conceal more, and it was certainly not constructed in this way by accident. I can tell you in fact that we discovered one specific secret held by the chambers which has yet to be properly deciphered. I will reveal this shortly; but first to say, there were two other locations that got my attention. Firstly I obtained validating evidence to my own complete satisfaction that the sub-chambers conceal a route into even lower voids, tunnels or chambers. Secondly within the natural tunnel system there is also a confirmed way to lower voids, tunnels or chambers. I am not going to share their details exactly here, but in the moment we get the opportunity to share all of our work officially, I will be happy to direct anyone official and under legitimate open terms to these very specific places.

Being alone deep in the natural tunnel system for hours has been a wonderful experience. Judith and I had already felt the change in vibrational atmosphere there, but when I turned off my flashlight it was something quite new. Here I was in the depths of the underground which had obsessed my mind since I knew of them. I had woken from dreams of the place so many times; and on one of a few lucid dreams, or Involuntary Out of Body experiences I adventured beyond the Tube Tunnel blockage to explore the deeper tunnel network. I sat there long, listening to the silence until the noise crept in. I don't know if others know what I mean by describing the noise of silence, where the mind becomes centred beyond the physical senses and a euphoric feeling creeps in. The mind reaches to another place and in this case I sensed the huge ancient importance of my surroundings. I sensed lush smells and the sounds of purpose and orderly bustle. I did not feel alone at any time, and in fact waves of invisible wind constantly pricked up the hairs on my body. There was no feeling of discomfort but quite the opposite feeling of familiarity and of long lost knowledge. At least I had the privilege of embracing these feelings, but a deep sadness filled me also for the violation of ignorance which was still abusing and avoiding the message that was still hidden here and waiting to be reclaimed.

Just before the point of the Tube Tunnel at the current deepest accessible point, the tunnel corridor comes to a halt. The passage continues into the rock and then just stops. In order to negotiate to the offset Tube Tunnel chamber, it is necessary several feet back from this to veer left. The Tube Tunnel chamber was the grotto with additional blocked entrances that we recorded on our first visit. Its floor and rock shelf had been stuffed with goods of all kinds. After the establishment pirates had been there we found the additional small entrances had been breached and everything stripped clean.

I mentioned previously in this work about a Lucid/I.OBE where we passed through a concealed rock doorway with others who were awaiting us. The doorway seemed to be where I encountered the right hand blocked tunnel. We wish to examine this area again if ever possible, because it is where the photographs seem to show metal anomalies that I missed when I was alone inside the system. Otherwise my greatest regret by far was that I did not have a long-handled agricultural adze with me. If so I would have definitely tried to drag a path through the blockage in the Tube Tunnel for a chance to explore deeper into the underground system in the footsteps of Salt and Caviglia.

The greatest surprise or shock was to happen later at home. We now had hundreds of photographs which we had used ad hoc to display on our website, including first obvious examples of loose items in the system—and in particular, some of the obvious images captured from the walls. When we were there in person it was very hard with our light to distinguish any wall images at all. The simulacrum and carvings are obvious but it was not until we began to look more closely at the flash-photographs that we realised we had found something very significant.

Imagine if you will, fairly soft cave walls painted with complex scenes which are then left to the ravages of aging and the disturbance of periodic use over multiple thousands of years. Imagine further to account for the deterioration from bat guano, dust, calcification, and cultural vandalism; and from this could you easily believe that the evidence of the original paintings would remain only as shadow traces of pigment in the deeper levels of the stone surfaces? It is exactly what we found. I was looking at one wall picture in particular and just had an instinct that there was something I was missing. I had just bought the latest Elements Photo Editing software and I began to play around with the colour filters, focus, saturation, contrast and light quality etc. The picture was of reasonably high density and I took it to its maximum focus without losing clarity. By now I had zoomed into a fairly small section of wall and as I made one more adjustment I was absolutely astonished to see the figure of a cloaked man looking back at me from the pigments in the wall surface! I turned to the obvious images we published on our website and sure enough, with great care and application, new images leapt out from the wall surfaces. It took so much time to work on each one but it was worth it every time. I tried it on completely uninspiring wall sections and got the same result. I experimented for weeks and the excitement grew. Judith and I passed the images back and forth for extra validation, but the best of them could not be denied. During the process we had picked up that in many places there was more than one layer of imaging. It was as if later images had been applied like graffiti over the originals. We noticed also that on the apparent oldest level of imaging, the larger images were usually formed by smaller fractal images. The smallest ones were sometimes tiny.

I decided to take a step back and search our photo collection for interesting whole wall surfaces to examine. When photographs were taken into the dark of the system, we least of all considered they should be ideally framed pictures of just blank walls. Nevertheless I did find a few interesting candidates. I printed one high resolution picture after I had completed adjustments to it. I decided that in order to see the greater detail of what it had to offer, I would use a fine pen to delineate every tiny change in tone or colour across the whole print. I decided also to work on the task with the print upside down so that I would be unable to influence any recognisable shapes as they were appearing. Finally the result was equally astonishing. I found I had a complex picture which showed a lush jungle mural with trees and animals long extinct from the area. It also had pyramid structures emerging from the jungle and strange poles with energy bursts coming from the top of them.

There were structures and symbols and much more. The operation had painstakingly taken me dozens of hours to complete but I moved to do the same with a second frame. I got another jungle scene equally elaborate. Since then I have examined more pictures, using the same analysis technique. The full delineation process would take weeks of time on more pictures and to date as I juggle with the responsibility of my mundane job I have not had sufficient time to do this. But the walls have already spoken to us with complex scenes involving animals, people, ceremonies and processions. It is very clear that highly specialist photography equipment must be used in the caves system, perhaps even using infra-red or other techniques to greater effect. Ideally an official examination would capture properly staged pictures of the walls themselves.

Judith and I discussed the issue at length and we came up with the notion that we should test other surfaces beyond the depths of NC2. Sure enough, first from the walls of the main tomb, we found images again. In fact even on the exterior frontage walls to the tomb entrance there are clear images recorded in the surface layer of rock. They can barely be seen with the naked eye and have to be subjected to invasive photographic analysis which delves beneath the surface reflection. If this was not enough, another revelation was waiting for us. Our attention was shared to other sites of involvement and interest on the plateau. We had been gathering information for Bill from another area close to Kephren. I was searching our photographs and had stopped to look at a particularly good photo of a deep shaft. The sun illuminated down into it quite strongly and I had one of those moments again. I could see discrepancies in the surface of the shaft walls which I would not have given a moment's thought to at any time before. Now with the whole business of the image finds, I saw there may be more to the stone surface than it was obviously showing. I applied the special analysis and again nearly fell from my chair. A few feet down the shaft, it now revealed a band of relief carvings. On the walls above, hieroglyphic writing had emerged.

There is strangeness about the images because when the filters are used to examine them, they appear as layers upon layers, with the deepest as fractal compositions of great depth and extent. Larger images of animals dominate, but these are most often formed from tiny fractal images of humanoid, ape or reptilian heads. However we believe we have also picked up depictions of buildings, apparatus, and pageants. It is possible to draw out the deepest layering with extreme manipulation of the filtration, but this causes the images to fluoresce in 3D. The discovery of this finalised our initial conclusions. The images could not have been created in this way by any ordinary artist's technique that we have yet discovered. It was as if they had been imprinted deep into the wall surfaces by some kind of holographic energy transference—as crazy as it sounds! The deepest images showed huge mural scenes involving animals long extinct from the land amid lush jungle scenes, with pyramids and other structures. If these were a reflection of the time, then the time had to be of a very great distance into antiquity; and the artists were reflecting a level of technology and sophistication beyond ours today. We asked ourselves: Could it really be that the so called ancient records had been hidden in plain sight all this time? Could it be that holographic methods unknown to us now were used to record life as it was then, into the ancient wall surfaces below and across the Plateau? Could the real roots of our fabled past under the guidance of star visitors be validated by this perfect method of preservation; and for the right people to decipher when the time was right? We couldn't help feeling that for decades while everyone has been fixated to discover physical records hidden for thousands of years (which would likely still exist,) but that maybe an accompanying record of history is there in plain sight, captured on wall surfaces.

I knew I had to test the technique elsewhere for greater validation. I asked myself which surfaces I should look at. The answer was of course to look at the disputed oldest surfaces on the plateau. I scoured our photo collections and found a candidate. It was a photograph of the apex stones above the original entrance to the GP. I was ecstatic because from one of the huge elevated western gable slabs the technique seemed to have revealed a Technicolor version of a huge panel filled with tables of hieroglyphic writing. My joy was short lived however because I researched this and found it was created in modern time.

Karl Richard Lepsius, under the patronage of Friedrich Wilhelm 1V, mounted a Prussian expedition between 1842/45. Lepsius wished to thank his patron on the occasion of his birthday and had the panel created for him. You can read the full story here :

http://uday-interesting.blogspot.co.uk/2010/04/theories-and-facts-of-pyramids.html

The result did not matter because the panel can barely be seen close-up with the naked eye—and the analysis technique had found it and clearly illuminated it. There was one more glorious twist to the story which I will tell you about in a moment. It turned the wheel of our journey full circle at last to where we began.

Reflections and a Final Revelation—for now!

For more than a decade since Judith and I came together again we had visited the plateau multiple times. We had followed our higher instincts and allowed ourselves to be directed where we must be. On every visit we had been privileged to learn new aspects pointing to our ancient past, and all from situations and places not normally ever encountered by other visitors. All were extraordinary on their own, but even more extraordinary was how these events and understandings synchronistically knitted together over time. For myself, the journey in Egypt had been an inevitable conclusion to a lifetime of supernormal experiences, all driving me finally to Egypt; all pushing me forward with an irresistible force to uncover the truth of our ancient past; all connected with probabilities for the world right now, and activated in my mind over 30 years ago.

Just like my journey, Judith's life path had been a preparation. We believe this as fact from our own tested experience. We believe it from the understanding released from my *Event* so long ago and the subject of the first part of this book. We believe therefore, from following our driven instincts with all the doors opening for us along the way, that we have followed our pathways of strongest Probability to fulfil the contract of our Birth Plan. As the early book explains, this Plan was one we agreed upon before we ever began this life journey. It is one thing to have a belief in our alternate past, it is quite another thing to carry an understanding of our vibrational universe and how it functions from higher levels. Without this it would have been impossible for us to go boldly without fear on our journey. The early book offers the same explanations to you so that you may have the opportunity to arrive at the same freedom of understanding. An observer may say, so what? And we would say: Test our conclusions. Look at life and the world and test our assertions against your personal experience; but be careful what you wish for, as there is no harder test than to look yourself and the world in the eye with stark honesty and understanding.

We believe in the cosmic vibrational transition we have entered which will transform our race. We believe it is within us to follow the expansion of our DNA with the expansion of our minds and higher selves. Then to be free from the collapsing control structures in the world that were birthed when *we* were birthed as a race over 10,000 years ago. We believe in our roots beyond the control establishment view, to a time when creatures of evolution were boosted by intelligent interference from afar to create us. We believe we were of them, and we are of them now, incarnated and driven by the same impulses we left behind at the end of the last cycle. We believe it was we who left the advanced knowledge and understanding behind us. It can help us all make the transition into beings of higher Presence, freed from the entire system of mortal control and suffrage that our world has been based upon.

We believe there *are* ancient records of such knowledge. We believe the centuries of secrecy, slaughter, and subterfuge were designed specifically to prevent us in our emerging re-awareness from discovering the full truth that will free us to a higher level where their control will be useless. Theirs *is* a system of control and fear. Our system is one of collective freedom born out of individual understanding, truth and empowerment. There are undoubtedly still physical items of advanced science to be found from a former time, but we now contend there are other records of such proof in the images still retained in the surfaces of stone. We recently heard of someone who years ago found many hidden images within the Queens Chamber and it was alleged he was muzzled from making an announcement. Apparently evidence was discovered to show they reached back beyond the magic 10,000 years. We know much more about the story but we have not been authorised to reveal all about it yet.

I therefore turned to pictures I had taken of apparently blank wall surfaces within the Great Pyramid! If you feel we may be right, it should come as no surprise to you that I discovered more jungle animals and scenes from the polished surfaces of the Great Pyramid chambers and passages. Some we tested are from obscure places, but just as within NC2, they are all in plain sight. Yet again we speculated with wonder at how this would be such a perfect way to record history for posterity. We speculated also how much more would be revealed when sophisticated equipment can be used to test our findings. In every case in the GP and elsewhere, the jungle animals appear like a date stamp for a time beyond 10,000 years. The jungle scenes plus heads with a Mayan/Native American profile appear again and again. Can we possible afford *not* to investigate this further?

We stood again as ordinary visitors in the Kings Chamber where it all began. We looked at the coffer where we would have succeeded with an induced Out of Body experience. We have looked to wall surfaces with different eyes, knowing their blank reflection conceals deeper knowledge. We have looked beyond the walls to the secret shaft and the Containment Chamber high above. We know each aspect has reached out to touch us with an awakening to our past for the sake of our future. Who can tell what ceremonies and aspects of civilization are also represented in the depths of NC2 or in the stone carvings; or even by the configuration of the chambers and tunnels, and within those which still have to be discovered. Who can tell for example of the ceremonies carried out in the NC2 reception chamber around the giant slab and throne shaped channel. Oh and by the way, we found distinct depictions of snakes and other creatures around the edge of the Altar slab and throne stones too!

Who can tell what history and knowledge is still locked within the wall surfaces of the Great Pyramid and other monuments? From one ancient site we had visited at home in England I proceeded with casual enthusiasm to examine a few pictures we captured there. We were utterly amazed again to discover new images that had been lost to casual inspection. If our methods and discoveries can be validated through an official investigation it will open the floodgates to a new potential source of hidden knowledge anywhere, provided those in power do not bury it again from public awareness or consumption. The search for the records must be wrenched back from the illegal control of those who wish to suppress it. We hope and pray we will continue to be a part of the process. For now we have our plans for more exploration and we continue to work on our pictures. We still seek the financial means to allow full time working on the task. We can assure you of one thing: Whatever we uncover, we will share it all with you!

Don't dare forget the Animals

Our story has been carried on the back of some major adventures but we have had to leave so many other stories out for lack of type space. We urge you to visit our websites where all the stories here and many more are deeply elaborated along with copious photograph galleries. Details are at the base of the page.

It would not be fitting to end this work without devoting a mention to one other equally important aspect of our work. It was inevitable that wherever we went in Egypt on the trail of ancient archaeological evidence, we would encounter animals. Judith and I have a life passion for animals anyway and home is a menagerie of rescues. We deeply believe that an empathy with animals can only come from an elevated spirit, regardless if the animal is wild or domesticated. The poverty in major parts of Cairo is mirrored in the lowly lives and expectation of the locals. It is also mirrored in the degraded view of animals as objects that are there to produce the next meal, and to have their overburdened life beaten out of them if they are not quick enough to comply. Children copy the attitude of their elders and practice this schooling amid laughs and whips when they get their frequent chance to beat on animals that are almost dead from abuse anyway. We witnessed this and intervened more times than we could count. It brought *us* abuse sometimes, even when we challenged them on the teachings of the Holy Quran, which preaches the opposite attitude.

Smaller animals fare no better. We encountered a crowd of young boys one day, mobbing the one who was roughly possessing a small kitten. We expressed concern to adults nearby and were told it was their pet and all would be ok. You can imagine how we felt as we walked from the alley from our village house next morning and saw the tiny lifeless kitten half buried in the sand. Its limbs were twisted as if it had been trying to corkscrew beneath the ground to escape its torture. All around us life continued and everyone was as completely blind to its body as they had been to its terrified form when it was alive.

We pursue the ancient archaeology, but we also pursue humanity wherever we meet with animal cruelty. It was a regular occurrence. Only sometimes a local would intervene with compassion and scathingly berate the perpetrator, quoting all manner of holy words to shame the person and assist the animal. For now, addressing the problem there is like trying to hold back the waters of the sea. The collapse of tourism has severed the lifeblood which sustains the poorest people. Many thousands exist on an average of a couple of dollars a day. There is little understanding when there is little money to feed the family—that food should be shared equally to tend the animals serving the tourists and bring more cash. The animals are rationed and some forgotten. They become weaker and weaker and as we witnessed one day, a skin and bone horse returning from the plateau was being unsaddled. It was too exhausted to move, even though a little food was nearby. It was whipped and dropped dead on the spot. In the aftermath we went to talk to the horse owner and the stable owner. We heard the same response, which is a confusion of anger and circumstance that needs its own forum, and a separate book to unravel the problems.

We seek some of the answers in the work of The Giza Foundation and on occasions where we meet the daily reality we can only add to our evidence to be used later in the right places for change. The task is daunting, but as we began to gain reputation locally for our attitude and stance to the animals, wariness developed in the neighbourhood. We were becoming better known, and a few locals were less free with their cruelty. We realised that however small to begin with, it *was* possible to open the minds of others to a better way; the way of the ancestors. The Foundation website *is* a forum where these issues are spelled out and are being addressed. Having analysed the situation from personal experience, we are trying to turn a whole raft of initiatives into a reality. Please go to the site and examine these along with the stories and photographs from so many of our animal encounters and interventions.

We have limited resources of our own and have conducted all of our work throughout on a shoestring. We longed for the means to be a greater part of the educational change in attitudes toward animals. Something happened which forced us to step forward with a new initiative. Out of the blue we received a charitable offer of $10,000 from an American corporation to support our initiatives. We liaised with them and it was a legitimate offer. However we were just ordinary people with no organised company status. We could offer no proof of charitable incorporation. This was to be an official company charitable offer and required the recipient to prove their company status. As we had none, we were unable to receive the donation. It was utterly crushing. We had struggled financially for so long, and we knew how very far we would have been able to put that money to work in ways to improve things locally. It was the moment we decided we could never allow such an opportunity to be lost again. Immediately we incorporated **The Giza Foundation** as a not-for-profit company which would pursue honourable aims to address all of the issues we felt so passionate about. For a large part of the last year we were forced to liaise heavily with our friends in Cairo from the UK via the internet. This has been because of a bout of illness and the months needed to become fit again. However, time at the computer has not been wasted because aside of our regular direct contact with our Cairo colleagues, Judith has been helping me intensively to plan our next moves and also to finalise this book. The aims of The Giza Foundation address three issues: The Animal Welfare, Higher Understandings and The Roots of our Origins. This book concentrates on the two latter aspects but a book dedicated to the Animals of Cairo and their issues will be forthcoming.

Since the incorporation of the Foundation in hard economic times, there have in truth been only modest responses of cash aid despite high visitor numbers to the site. But those few good souls who have given help, cannot realise how valuable their assistance has been to our progress. We thank them deeply. Now our struggle continues in the battle to fulfil all the aims of the Foundation. We realise how hard it is to generate enthusiasm for giving during a recession, but we swear, if you had seen what we have seen in the land of our common roots, you would not falter to give even a tiny amount to help us make a difference at last. None will be wasted, least of all any earnings from the sale of this book.

As a balance to the terrible lives of the animals in Cairo and the avenues of their discarded carcasses expressing death on the way out of the city, the pristine contrast of the deep desert beckons us always. It is there our memories are refreshed, waking to the company of foxes; tracking the desert deer; seeking the ancient camel trails; spotting the scorpions, spiders and snakes. They are all beautifully free and natural, expressing life. As passionately as we will continue to pursue the message of our ancient roots, so we will also continue to pursue a new educated humanity so that the city animals can once again enjoy the symbiotic expression of life that was enjoyed by our common ancestors.

The Foundation seeks to fund a mobile veterinary ambulance to be staffed by out of hours Veterinaries from the village. We are liaising with other organisations such as the well-known Brooke hospital for horses, and with other privately funded organisations. We will become heavily involved with school and public re-education which will teach the benefit of the old ways with animal care. We will continue to survey and gather comprehensive data from Giza that will assist all groups with the better humane management of all the animals. We will seek to influence the decision makers so that no more illegal practices are used by officials to poison stray animals on the streets. We will seek also to ensure that the topic of animal welfare in regard to tourists as a part of the future Plateau reorganisation plans, is not consigned to self-serving cash benefit for a few. These are our main objectives. They are achievable but only with cash help from the tourists and public. Wherever we are, we are to be judged by our concern or indifference to animal cruelty and suffering wherever it may be. For this reason we hope you will read through the content of The Giza Foundation website and help in whatever way you can.

http://www.thegizafoundation.org

School's Out

So it is at the end of each day we can say, *'School is out,'* to be ready for the next day. From today's lesson we will make our choices in tomorrow's classroom again. Isn't it just so for the cycles of our whole life; and by *our* belief and understanding, isn't it also just so for the cycles reaching beyond our physical life to tangible higher dimensions?

Choices beget choices, and the outcome is the personal responsibility of all of us. Our early mundane life was a choice to enable our rough karmic edges to be knocked into shape. Our later life is a choice to place an understanding of it all within context of ourselves. In culmination there is the opportunity to fulfil a progressive act of balance which will help bring order to our whole environment.

Judith and I had much to learn. Our early years provided much pain until we recognised it was just a lesson to understand ourselves. We returned to life within a cosmic cycle which would offer the choice of transformation in our lifetime to all who could or would awaken to the fact. We came as one of many across the world who would awaken to ancient memories and lessons; this time to fulfil acts of balance beyond ourselves with a greater willingness. For us it was to be a part of the movement seeking to uncover the ancient lessons and knowledge that others with a darker choice wished to keep to themselves once again.

This time there will be a difference, because the cosmic influences bring a higher vibration which will enable the choices of light to prevail. Our pathway therefore is lit and signed for us by others on higher levels seeking even greater balance. My *event* over thirty years ago was *my* turning point when the early lessons were delivered in a package of returned memory. It took many years and more pain before I accepted the lesson and grasped its full meaning.

The impetus which drives us to the Plateau and its concealed knowledge is a knowing of the truth, confirmed constantly through the incredible synchronicities which charm our pathway. We were directed with our understandings to the Great Pyramid and via the tunnel system of NC2 back to the Great Pyramid. We believe our trust and yielding to whom and what we are in the scheme of things delivered the truth. Ancient technology worthy of our advanced true ancestors awaits the bold and the ready beneath the Giza Plateau and elsewhere in the world. The recorded knowledge of that time is encoded to the surfaces of the ancient rock faces of the Giza Plateau, hidden for millennia in plain sight, but especially below ground. We will continue to be true to whom we are, and to face whatever futile obstacles may be placed before us. We are carried by the mantra that those who fear, are really only afraid of . . . themselves.

Finally we once again thank all of our families, friends, colleagues, acquaintances, higher helpers, and then even our adversaries, for helping to provide *our* lessons in this life. We hope all will be blessed with second sight and make a choice to escape the box which has been *their* illusionary prison also, in this life.

Asking for A LifeLine

Our continuing work involves much that is current. We will share it all in due course. Our travel; our research; our exploration, and help with the animals, has been funded entirely hitherto from our meagre personal savings. We live simply, based on needs alone.

We are drawing very close to the ancient Sources through many of our hot investigation leads. We know we are so close to opening a new pathway, not only to the understanding of where we came from, but also to discover the greatest prize of all.

Personally we believe our ancient ancestors knew how to determine the Probabilities for their future; and our future. We believe it is no accident that we are on the point of proving this in 2012. Impending cosmic changes are unfolding which will challenge us all and they knew it, and wanted to help us. We believe within their advanced hidden knowledge we will find the means to help guide us through the difficulties we all face.

We hope as you complete this book that you will choose to help us with a donation so we can begin to pursue our research with complete freedom at last. No help will be wasted, and everything we do will be on *your* behalf.

Our work will continue also to assist with the catastrophic animal situation in Cairo and Egypt. Visit our websites please and you will find donation buttons there. Blessings to all who join us for the journey,

Richard and Judith.

At Home and Door always Open

http://www.richardgabriel.info

http://www.thegizafoundation.org

Plate 3: Featuring the Sphinx Harbour with the GP in the background

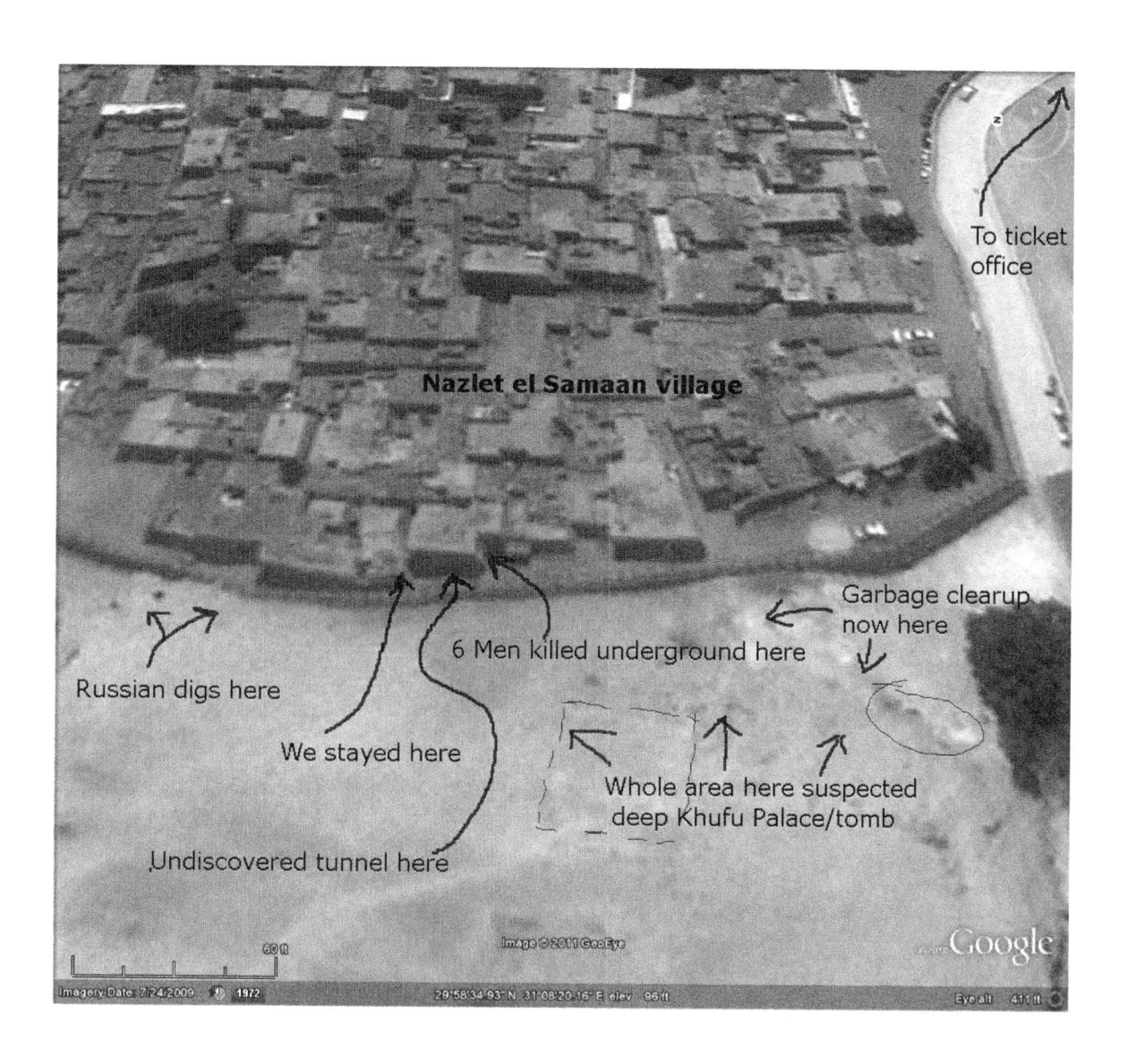

Plate 4: The corner of Nazlet el-Samaan Village. The Harbour is right of pic.

Plate 5: The Entrance to the Tomb of North Cliff 2

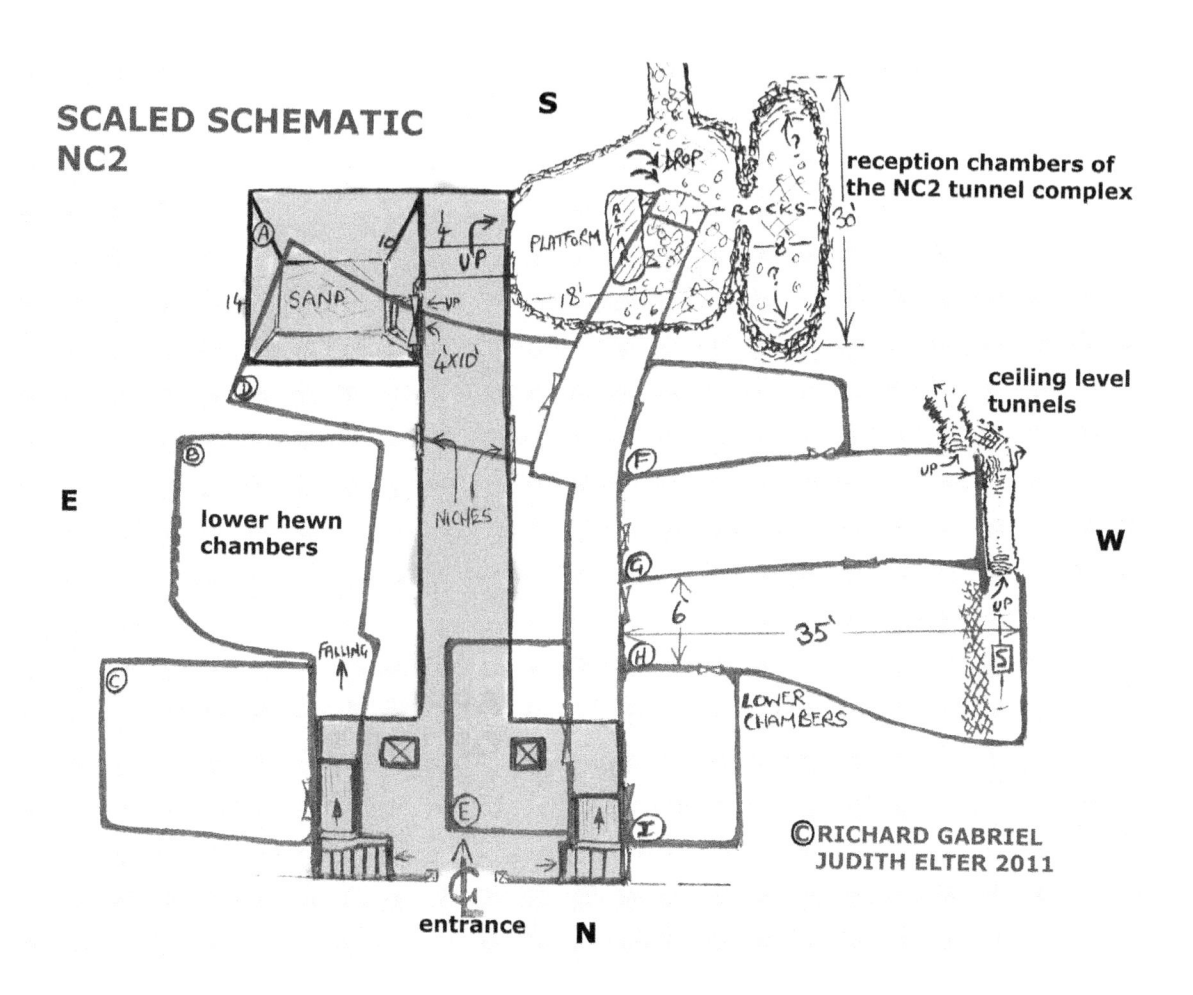

Plate 6: The Schematic of the known front levels of the NC2 Chamber

TUBE TUNNEL AT 20' (BLOCKED)

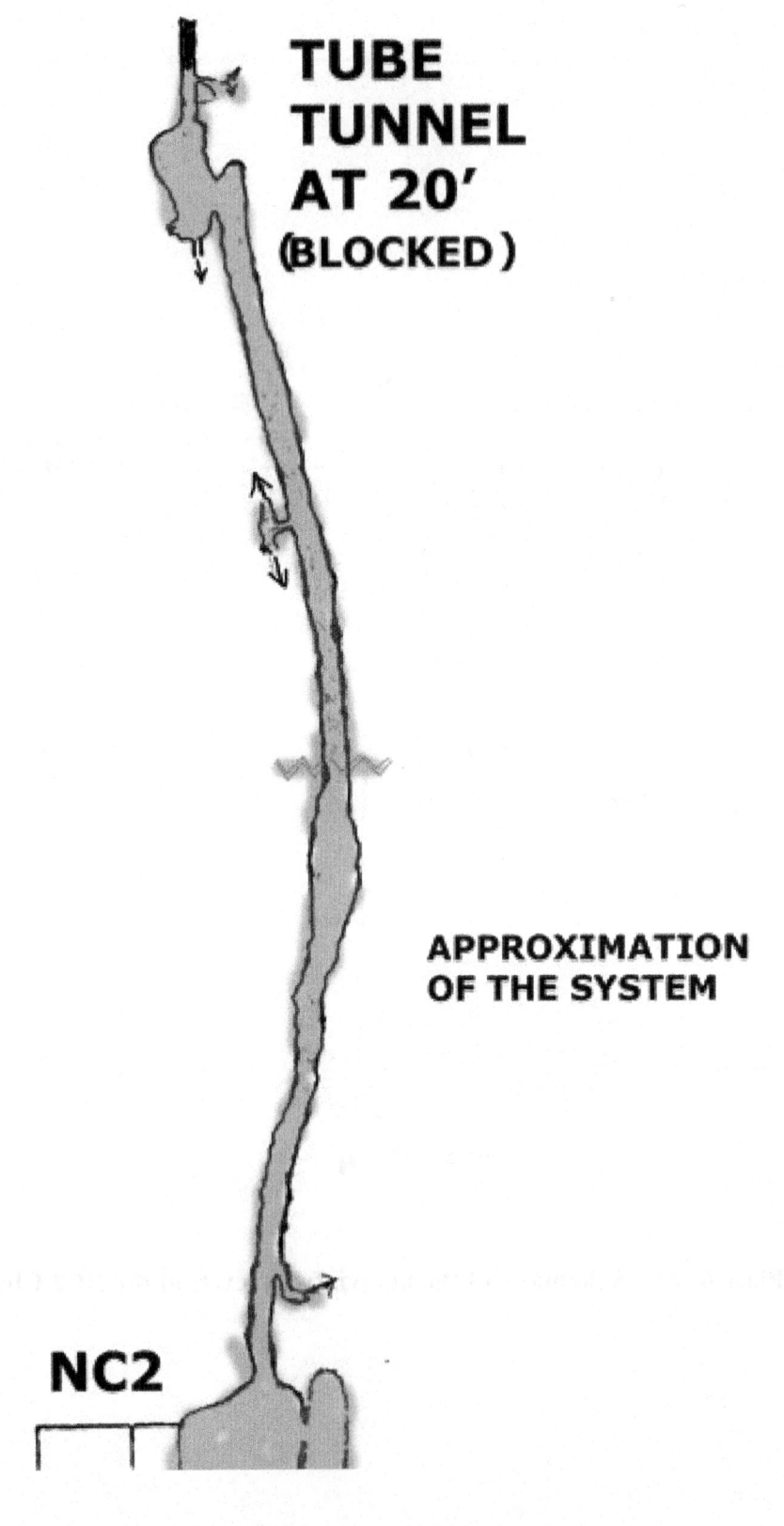

APPROXIMATION OF THE SYSTEM

NC2

Plate 7: The Schematic of the Tunnel/Cavern system beyond the NC2 Tomb